# HEALTH ANXIETY

The Wiley Series in

# CLINICAL PSYCHOLOGY

Titles published under the series editorship of:

**J. Mark G. Williams**   *School of Psychology, University of Wales, Bangor, UK*

*A list of earlier titles in the series follows the index.*

# HEALTH ANXIETY

## Clinical and Research Perspectives on Hypochondriasis and Related Conditions

*Edited by*

Gordon J.G. Asmundson
*Regina Health District, Saskatchewan, Canada*

Steven Taylor
*University of British Columbia, Canada*

Brian J. Cox
*University of Manitoba, Canada*

JOHN WILEY & SONS, LTD

Chichester · New York · Weinheim · Brisbane · Singapore · Toronto

*Other Wiley Editorial Offices*

John Wiley & Sons, Inc., 605 Third Avenue,
New York, NY 10158-0012, USA

WILEY-VCH GmbH, Pappelallee 3,
D-69469 Weinheim, Germany

John Wiley & Sons Australia, Ltd, 33 Park Road, Milton,
Queensland 4064, Australia

John Wiley & Sons (Asia) Pte Ltd, 2 Clementi Loop #02-01,
Jin Xing Distripark, Singapore 129809

John Wiley & Sons (Canada) Ltd, 22 Worcester Road,
Rexdale, Ontario M9W 1L1, Canada

*Library of Congress Cataloging-in-Publication Data*

Health anxiety : clinical and research perspectives on hypochondriasis and related conditions / edited by Gordon J.G. Asmundson, Steven Taylor, Brian J. Cox.
    p.  cm.—(Wiley series in clinical psychology)
    Includes bibliographical references and indexes.
    ISBN 0-471-99992-X (cased)—ISBN 0-471-49104-7 (pbk.)
    1. Hypochondria.  I. Asmundson, Gordon J.G.  II. Taylor, Steven, 1960–  III. Cox, Brian J.  IV. Series.
    RC552.H8 H43 2001
    616.85'25—dc21

                                           2001026199

*British Library Cataloguing in Publication Data*

A catalogue record for this book is available from the British Library

ISBN 0-471-99992-X (cloth)
ISBN 0-471-49104-7 (paper)

Typeset in 10/12 pt Palatino by Best-set Typesetter Ltd., Hong Kong
Printed and bound by Antony Rowe Ltd, Eastbourne
This book is printed on acid-free paper responsibly manufactured from sustainable forestry, in which at least trees are planted for each one used for paper production.

To Kimberley and Aleiia.   G.J.G.A.

To Amy S. Janeck.   S.T.

To mentors Ron Norton, Richard Swinson, and Norman Endler.   B.J.C.

# CONTENTS

# ABOUT THE EDITORS

*Gordon J.G. Asmundson*, Ph.D., is Director of Clinical Research and Development at the Regina Health District and holds positions as Adjunct Professor in the Department of Psychiatry at the University of Saskatchewan and the Departments of Psychology and Kinesiology at the University of Regina. He completed his doctorate in psychology at the University of Manitoba in 1991. He has published over 85 journal articles and book chapters as well as several books. Dr. Asmundson's research efforts have been recognized through early career and fellow awards received from the Anxiety Disorders Association of America (1998), the Canadian chapter of the International Association for the Study of Pain (1999), and the Canadian Psychological Association (2000). He is co-Editor-in-Chief of Cognitive Behaviour Therapy, sits on several editorial boards, and is a regular guest reviewer for 17 journals. He recently served the American Psychiatric Association's DSM-IV Text Revision Work Group for the Anxiety Disorders. His research interests are in the anxiety disorders (particularly panic disorder, posttraumatic stress disorder, and social phobia), chronic pain, health anxiety, and the association of these with disability and behavior changes.

*Steven Taylor*, Ph.D., trained as a clinical psychologist at the University of Melbourne, Australia (M.Sc., 1987) and at the University of British Columbia, Canada (Ph.D., 1991). He is Professor in the Department of Psychiatry at the University of British Columbia and for 10 years was Associate Editor of *Behaviour Research and Therapy*. He has published over 100 journal articles and book chapters. He has also published three books, *Anxiety Sensitivity* (1999, Mahwah, NJ: Erlbaum), *Understanding and Treating Panic Disorder* (2000, Chichester: Wiley), and the co-authored Abnormal Psychology (2001, Toronto, Prentice-Hall). Dr. Taylor received early career awards from the Canadian Psychological Association, the Association for Advancement of Behavior Therapy, and the Anxiety Disorders Association of America. He is actively involved in clinical teaching and supervision, and maintains a private practice in Vancouver, Canada. His research interests include cognitive and cognitive-behavioral treatments and mechanisms of anxiety disorders, particularly panic disorder, post-traumatic stress disorder, and obsessive-compulsive disorder.

*Brian J. Cox*, Ph.D., is an Associate Professor in the Department of Psychiatry and Adjunct Professor in the Department of Psychology, both at the University of Manitoba. He completed his doctorate in clinical psychology at York University in 1993. He has published more than 100 journal articles as well as several book chapters. He has received early career awards from the Anxiety Disorders Association of America, Association for Advancement of Behavior Therapy, and the Canadian Psychological Association. Research interests are primarily in psychosocial mechanisms in anxiety disorders and depression. His work is currently funded by a grant from the Social Sciences and Humanities Research Council of Canada.

# LIST OF CONTRIBUTORS

Lesley A. Allen, Ph.D.  *Department of Psychiatry, University of Medicine and Dentistry of New Jersey–Robert Wood Johnson Medical School, Piscataway, New Jersey 08854-5635, USA.*

Gordon J.G. Asmundson, Ph.D.  *Clinical Research and Development Program, Regina Health District, Regina, Saskatchewan S4S OA5, Canada.*

Brian J. Cox, Ph.D.  *Department of Psychiatry, University of Manitoba, Winnipeg, Manitoba RE3 3NE, Canada.*

Georg H. Eifert, Ph.D.  *Department of Psychology, University of Hawaii, 3950 Kalai Waa St., #T101, Hawaii 96753, USA.*

Murray W. Enns, M.D.  *Department of Psychiatry, University of Manitoba, Winnipeg, Manitoba RE3 3NE, Canada.*

Javier I. Escobar, M.D.  *Department of Psychiatry, University of Medicine and Dentistry of New Jersey–Robert Wood Johnson Medical School, Piscataway, New Jersey 08854-5635, USA.*

Mark H. Freeston, Ph.D.  *Newcastle Centre for Cognitive and Behaviour Therapies, Newcastle upon Tyne, UK.*

Patricia Furer, Ph.D.  *Anxiety Disorders Program, St. Boniface General Hospital, Winnipeg, Manitoba R2H 2A6, Canada.*

Michael Gara, Ph.D.  *Department of Psychiatry, University of Medicine and Dentistry of New Jersey–Robert Wood Johnson Medical School, Piscataway, New Jersey 08854-5635, USA.*

Heather D. Hadjistavropoulos, Ph.D.  *Department of Psychology, University of Regina, Regina, Saskatchewan S4S OA5, Canada.*

Thomas Hadjistavropoulos, Ph.D.  *Department of Psychology, University of Regina, Regina, Saskatchewan S4S OA2, Canada.*

Constanza Hoyos Nervi, Psy.D.  *Department of Psychiatry, University of Medicine and Dentistry of New Jersey–Robert Wood Johnson Medical School, Piscataway, New Jersey 08854-5635, USA.*

Robert J. Kastenbaum, Ph.D.   *Department of Communications, Arizona State University, Tempe, Arizona 85287, USA.*

Kevin Kjernisted, M.D.   *Department of Psychiatry, University of Manitoba, Winnipeg, Manitoba RE3 3NE, Canada.*

David G. Kingdon, M.D.   *Mental Health Care Delivery, University of Southampton, Royal South Hants Hospital, Brintons Terrace, Southampton SO14 0YG, United Kingdom.*

Mark Lander, M.D.   *Department of Psychiatry, University of Manitoba, Winnipeg, Manitoba RE3 3NE, Canada.*

Carl W. Lejuez, Ph.D.   *Department of Psychology, University of Maryland, College Park, Maryland 20742, USA.*

Katherine Lemos, M.S.   *Department of Psychology, University of Iowa, Iowa City, Iowa 52242-1407, USA.*

Howard Leventhal, Ph.D.   *Institute for Health, Health Care Policy, and Aging Research, Rutgers University, New Brunswick, New Jersey 08903, USA.*

Scott O. Lilienfeld, Ph.D.   *Department of Psychology, Emory University, Atlanta, Georgia 30322, USA.*

René Martin, Ph.D.   *Department of Psychology, University of Iowa, Iowa City, Iowa 52242-1407, USA.*

Erin B. McClure, Ph.D.   *Department of Psychology, Emory University, Atlanta, Georgia 30322, USA.*

Russell Noyes, Jr., M.D.   *Department of Psychiatry, University of Iowa College of Medicine, Iowa City, Iowa 52242-1000, USA.*

Katherine M.B. Owens, B.A.   *Department of Psychology, University of Regina, Regina, Saskatchewan S4S 0A2, Canada.*

Shanaya Rathod, MRCPsych   *Royal South Hants Hospital, Brintons Terrace, Southampton SO14 0YG, United Kingdom.*

Paul M. Salkovskis, M.D.   *Department of Psychology, Institute of Psychiatry, University of London, De Crespigny Park, London, SE5 8AF, United Kingdom.*

Serperi Sevgur, B.Sc.   *Department of Psychology, University of Regina, Regina, Saskatchewan S4S 0A2, Canada.*

Allison G. Snyder, Ph.D.   *OB/GYN Associates, Katy-West Houston, Katy, Texas 77494, USA.*

Melinda A. Stanley, Ph.D.   *Department of Psychiatry and Behavioral Sciences, University of Texas, Houston Health Science Center, Houston, Texas 77030-3497, USA.*

Sherry H. Stewart, Ph.D.  *Department of Psychology, Dalhousie University, Halifax, Nova Scotia B3H 4JI, Canada.*

Steven Taylor, Ph.D.  *Department of Psychiatry, University of British Columbia, Vancouver, British Columbia VT6 2A1, Canada.*

Douglas Turkington, FRCPsych  *Department of Psychiatry, Royal Victoria Infirmary, Newcastle upon Tyne, NE1 4LP, United Kingdom.*

John R. Walker, Ph.D.  *Anxiety Disorders Program, St. Boniface General Hospital, Winnipeg, Manitoba R2H 2A6, Canada.*

Hillary M.C. Warwick, M.D.  *Department of Psychiatry, St. George's Hospital Medical School, Cranmer Terrace, London SW17 0RE, United Kingdom.*

Margo C. Watt, Ph.D.  *Department of Psychology, Saint Francis Xavier University, Antigonish, Nova Scotia B2G 2W5, Canada.*

Kristi D. Wright, B.A.  *Department of Psychology, University of Regina, Regina, Saskatchewan S4S OA2, Canada.*

Michael J. Zvolensky, M.A.  *Department of Psychology, University of Vermont, Burlington, VT 65405, USA.*

# FOREWORD

The highest scores on self-report measures of state anxiety have been recorded from people awaiting the results of medical tests. Will the biopsy reveal that the growth is malignant? Will the X-rays/scores reveal a tumor? Am I positive for HIV? Do I carry the gene for Huntington's chorea? Small wonder that waiting for such results arouses intense anxiety.

We all experience health problems at one time or another and, in some instances, we also experience anxiety about the significance and possible outcome of the problem. The occurrence of health anxiety can be appropriate and is sometimes of direct survival value. An absence of anxiety when there is a significant threat to one's health can be damaging. In common with other forms of anxiety, health anxiety is normative, appropriate, universal, and functional—but like these other forms, excessive or inappropriate anxiety about one's health can be unadaptive and distressing.

People also experience considerable anxiety about the health of relatives and friends. In an evaluation of the effects of psychological preparation of children for impending tonsillectomy, Rachman and Parkinson (1981) incidentally collected information from the mothers of the children. The mothers reported the highest state anxiety scores we had ever recorded, and their anxiety rose to a high peak immediately prior to and during their child's operation. Similarly, their unwanted, frightening intrusive thoughts increased steeply as the time for the operation on the child approached. Fortunately, and adaptively, the mother's anxiety and intrusive thoughts rapidly returned to low normal levels as soon as they were reunited with their children after the operation.

It is curious that even though it is universally experienced, intrusive, and usually adaptive, health anxiety was seldom considered until the mid-1980s. The closest that doctors and psychologists came to the phenomena was evident in the concept of hypochondriasis. This concept incorporated the phenomenon of health anxiety but usually in a negative and even pejorative sense. It implied that health anxiety is often psychopathological, and worse, that it is an exaggeration, bordering on faking; it was frequently negative in its implication that hypochondriasis is a sign of weakness; and it was too often a disapproving, dismissive, and demeaning diagnostic concept.

The introduction of cognitive analyses and concepts into clinical psychology has been a major advance, and this is particularly evident in the increasing replacement of the diagnosis of hypochondriasis by the concept of health anxiety—most effectively accomplished by Paul Salkovskis and his colleagues. The 1986 paper by Salkovskis and Warwick was a landmark contribution and has led to a variety of fresh, constructive, and therapeutic ideas. Most of all, it placed the concept of health anxiety on a solid foundation that enables clinicians and researchers to think, and act, more clearly than was possible before the Salkovskis analysis.

Many of these fresh and constructive ideas, and important examples of the rapidly expanding body of knowledge about health anxiety, are evident in this highly informative, welcome collection. Important advances have taken place and many, many more will follow. The ultimate goal is to develop a comprehensive, incisive, and practical *cognitive clinical psychology*. In this wider scheme of things to come the concept of health anxiety will occupy a central position. This timely volume will advance these developments.

Professor S. Rachman
*Vancouver, July 2000*

Rachman, S. (Ed.) (1981) Unwanted intrusive thoughts. *Advances in Behaviour Research and Therapy*, **3**, 89–123.

Salkovskis, P., & Warwick, H. (1986). Morbid preoccupations, health anxiety and reassurance: A cognitive approach to hypochondriasis. *Behaviour Research and Therapy*, **24**, 597–602.

# PREFACE

Health anxiety refers to health-related fears and beliefs that arise from misinterpretations of bodily signs and symptoms (e.g., pain, gastro-intestinal distress, cardiorespiratory complaints) as being indicative of a serious illness. Everybody experiences health anxiety to some degree; however, there are people for whom this anxiety becomes an extreme, debilitating, and chronic condition. Many severe cases of health anxiety meet DSM-IV and ICD-10 diagnostic criteria for hypochondriasis. This condition, occurring in approximately 5% of the general population, is among the most prevalent of the mental disorders.

In recent years there has been an increased interest in advancing our understanding of severe health anxiety. This interest has focused pri-marily, but not exclusively, on hypochondriasis. Based on theoretical refinement, considerable strides have been made in methods for assess-ing and treating severe health anxiety. Cognitive-behavioral treatment regimens have shown promise in mental health settings. In-roads have also been made in the application of enhanced medical care and phar-macological treatment. These advances are encouraging; nonetheless, the complexity of severe health anxiety has made progress a slow and challenging task.

While there have been a number of excellent books and book chapters that have focused on various aspects of hypochondriasis, no single book has provided comprehensive coverage of important issues and develop-ments in research and treatment from the broader perspective of health anxiety per se. The purpose of this book is to fill that gap by providing a comprehensive and critical analysis of the health anxiety literature. Theoretical positions are delineated, assessment and treatment issues are outlined with an emphasis on empirically validated approaches, related conditions scrutinized, and emerging areas of investigation summarized and accompanied by suggested future research directions. Throughout the book, clinical vignettes are used to help to illustrate important con-cepts and clinical points.

The book is organized into four parts. In Part I, you are introduced to the clinical features and current theoretical positions on health anxiety. Part

II provides comprehensive coverage of assessment issues and approaches to treatment. Regardless of your clinical background or practice setting, you will find valuable information that can be applied in dealing with people who present with hypochondriacal concerns. Part III highlights clinical features and empirical issues of conditions that present with hypochondriacal features. Finally, Part IV provides a summary of the current state-of-the-art and highlights future challenges and directions for research.

The book is intended for a wide audience of mental health and medical professionals, including psychologists, psychiatrists, medical specialists, general practitioners, counselors, and students in mental health and medical professions (e.g., psychology graduate students, general medicine interns, psychiatry residents). We hope the book will not only serve as a reference source on assessment and treatment, but also provide theoretical and empirical foundation and direction.

*August, 2000*

Gordon J.G. Asmundson
Steven Taylor
Brian J. Cox

# ACKNOWLEDGMENTS

We are indebted to Linda Picot, Jennifer A. Boisvert and Kristi Wright for their editorial assistance and to our families and close friends for their inspiration, encouragement, and support.

Part I

# CLINICAL FEATURES AND THEORETICAL PERSPECTIVES

Chapter 1

# HEALTH ANXIETY: CLASSIFICATION AND CLINICAL FEATURES

*Gordon J.G. Asmundson\*, Steven Taylor†, Serperi Sevgur‡ and Brian J. Cox§*

## INTRODUCTION

I've always been a worrier. When my older sister developed breast cancer all my worries began to focus on my health and my chances of getting cancer. I've tried to tell myself that since I'm only 27, I'm too young to get cancer. But that doesn't seem to help. Barely a day goes by without me worrying that I might have breast cancer. I also worry about skin cancer because I had a lot of bad sunburns as a kid. What frightens me the most is the prospect of a long and painful death. I used to see my doctor all the time for checkups. He showed me how to do a breast examination. He also did a few tests and told me that I was okay. I used to phone him a lot whenever I noticed a lump or a blemish on my body. I guess he got mad at me for calling so much, because he stopped returning my calls. Since then I have been too embarrassed to see him, and so I haven't had a checkup for nearly two years. I'm too frightened to check myself because I am really scared about what I might find. Yesterday I started to worry so much that I started to panic. I felt shaky, nauseous, and lightheaded and was certain that I was going to die. I've panicked a few times in the past couple of months. I have been unable to talk with my sister, even on the phone, and I have been missing work more and more because

\* Regina Health District and Universities of Regina and Saskatchewan, Canada; † University of British Columbia, Canada; ‡ University of Regina, Canada; § University of Manitoba, Canada

*Health Anxiety*
Edited by G.J.G. Asmundson, S. Taylor & B.J. Cox
© 2001 John Wiley & Sons Ltd.

one of my coworkers is always talking about our boss, who is being treated for bowel cancer. I even had to stop watching one of my favorite soap operas because I discovered that one of the actors was being treated for cancer. Just thinking about it makes me very nervous.

Health anxiety is a ubiquitous experience. It is common for people to experience at least mild forms of this anxiety. Severe forms, as in the case of Abby described above, are less common, but nonetheless afflict a significant proportion of people. With regard to its milder forms, most of us, at some time, have become anxious upon noticing a bodily sign or symptom that might indicate a potentially serious disease. You may experience a gastrointestinal upset and worry that it might be due to a peptic ulcer. Or, on feeling a sharp pain in your chest, you may be afraid that something is wrong with your heart. In most cases like these, the anxiety abates as the symptoms diminish or, in cases where a medical opinion is sought, upon reassurance from a doctor that there is nothing wrong. And, in cases where the signs and symptoms are found to be associated with a serious illness, the initial anxiety may have actually played an adaptive role in facilitating early identification (e.g., by prompting a visit to the family doctor). However, for some people, like Abby, the anxiety over signs and symptoms, and belief that they indicate a serious illness or disease, remains intense and persists despite reassurance that nothing is physically wrong.

In this introductory chapter we will (a) define health anxiety, (b) discuss the diagnostic systems for classifying severe health anxiety (i.e., hypochondriasis), (c) review definitions of related concepts (e.g., illness behavior), (d) describe the phenomenology and other features of severe health anxiety, and (e) highlight important research trends and clinical issues. Discussion of these issues will set the stage for the chapters that follow.

## HEALTH ANXIETY

Health anxiety refers to health-related fears and beliefs, based on interpretations, or, perhaps more often, *misinterpretations*, of bodily signs and symptoms as being indicative of a serious illness (Lucock & Morley, 1996; Warwick, 1989). Such signs and symptoms include normal and aberrant somatic variations, which may extend from the vague and generalized to the specific, and most often include pain, gastrointestinal distress, and cardiorespiratory complaints (Barsky & Klerman, 1983). Chapter 2 describes the cognitive, affective, and contextual influences on symptom perception, interpretation, and behaviors. Understanding these influences provides a basis for understanding symptom perception and (mis)interpretation.

The experience of health anxiety can vary considerably from one person to another and, as such, it has been conceptualized on a continuum ranging from mild to severe (e.g., Barsky, Wyshak, & Klerman, 1986; Salkovskis & Warwick, 1986). Severe or clinically significant health anxiety, most often considered under the rubric of the somatoform disorder known as *hypochondriasis*, can be distinguished from nonclinical presentations by the degree of fear and conviction about having a serious illness, distress, and interference in functioning (e.g., work performance, leisure activities, interpersonal relationships; Barsky, Fama, Bailey, & Ahern, 1998; Lucock & Morley, 1996; Noyes et al., 1993; Robbins & Kirmayer, 1996). Several theories, described in Chapter 3, have been proposed to explain why some people are more susceptible than others to severe health anxiety. The relationship between health anxiety and personality is described in Chapter 4.

Hypochondriasis is not the only disorder characterized by severe health-related anxiety. As discussed in more detail below, severe health anxiety frequently co-occurs with other clinical conditions, such as anxiety disorders (e.g., illness phobia, panic disorder) and mood disorders. These disorders are discussed to some extent in this volume; however, hypochondriasis is the disorder of primary focus.

## Hypochondriasis

In a landmark volume, Ladee (1966) provided a stimulating, detailed review of the historical origins of the concept of hypochondriasis. The term *hypochondria* dates back to approximately 350 BC. It appears that Forbes Winslow, in his 1863 edition of *Obscure Diseases of the Brain and Mind*, provided what is perhaps the first contemporary description of the condition:

> That psychosomatic disease termed hypochondriasis, which manifests itself principally in a morbid anxiety as to health, and is in its primitive nature essentially a diseased concentration of physical sensibility, resulting from slight bodily ailments, which eventually assume to the distempered and deluded imagination a grave significant character. (Cited in Ladee, 1966, p. 13)

It was, nonetheless, another two decades before psychopathologists began describing hypochondriasis as a distinct clinical syndrome, and another half century or more before diagnostic definitions were formalized.

Formal diagnostic definitions first appeared in the publication of the DSM-II (American Psychiatric Association, 1968), where *hypochondriacal neurosis* was defined as a condition 'dominated by preoccupation with the body and with fear of presumed diseases of various organs ... [that] persist despite reassurance ... [and for which] there are no actual losses or distortions of function' (p. 41). Here the focus was on bodily preoccupation and fear of having a disease. This definition was refined in subsequent editions of the DSM.

### DSM-III

As shown in Table 1.1, DSM-III (American Psychiatric Association, 1980) clarified that hypochondriacal neurosis (i.e., bodily preoccupation and fear of having a disease) was characterized by unrealistic interpretations of physical signs or sensations and, importantly, was not due to any other mental disorder. So, in this context, the diagnosis would not be made if the preoccupation and fear could be better accounted for by another diagnostic entity, such as schizophrenia or major depression. The severe health anxiety experienced by Abby would have met DSM-III diagnostic criteria for hypochondriasis.

### DSM-III-R

The DSM-III-R (American Psychiatric Association, 1987) included further revisions to allow for (a) the belief, or conviction, that one has a serious disease (in addition to preoccupation with the fear of having a serious disease), (b) the diagnosis in the presence of other disorders, provided that symptoms are not solely those of another disorder, and (c) a minimum duration of at least 6 months. The clinical features in the case of Abby meet all three criteria; she had long-standing fear and conviction about having a disease that was, in some instances, associated with, but independent of, her episodes of panic.

### DSM-IV and DSM-IV-TR

The DSM-IV (American Psychiatric Association, 1994) shifted to some degree the definition of hypochondriasis. The requirement that preoccupation with fear of having, or the belief that one has, a serious disease be based on a misinterpretation of physical signs and sensations was retained as was the exclusion of conditions in which the individual has no insight that their concerns are excessive or unreasonable. Boundaries with other disorders (e.g., body dysmorphic disorder, obsessive-compulsive disorder, panic disorder) were clarified through the addition of specific exclusionary criteria (see Table 1.1). Finally, a requirement for

**Table 1.1** *Diagnostic and Statistical Manual of Mental Disorders* (DSM) criteria for hypochondriasis

| DSM-III criteria | DSM-III-R criteria | DSM-IV and DSM-IV-TR criteria |
|---|---|---|
| (A) The predominant disturbance is an unrealistic interpretation of physical signs or sensations as abnormal, leading to preoccupation with the fear or belief of having a serious disease. | (A) Preoccupation with the fear of having, or the belief that one has, a serious disease, based on the person's interpretation of physical signs or sensations as evidence of physical illness. | (A) A preoccupation with fears of having, or the idea that one has, a serious disease based on the person's misinterpretation of bodily symptoms. |
| (B) Thorough physical evaluation does not support the diagnosis of any physical disorder that can account for the physical signs or sensations or for the individual's unrealistic interpretation of them. | (B) Appropriate physical evaluation does not support the diagnosis of any physical disorder that can account for the physical signs or sensations or the person's unwarranted interpretation of them, *and* the symptoms in (A) are not just symptoms of panic attacks. | (B) The preoccupation persists despite appropriate medical evaluation and reassurance. |
| (C) The unrealistic fear or belief of having a disease persists despite medical reassurance and causes impairment in social or occupational functioning. | (C) The fear of having, or belief that one has, a disease persists despite medical reassurance. | (C) The belief in Criterion (A) is not of delusional intensity (as in Delusional Disorder, Somatic Type) and is not restricted to a circumscribed concern about appearance (as in Body Dysmorphic Disorder). |

*continued overleaf*

**Table 1.1** (*continued*)

| DSM-III criteria | DSM-III-R criteria | DSM-IV and DSM-IV-TR criteria |
|---|---|---|
| (D) Not due to any other mental disorder such as Schizophrenia, Affective Disorder, or Somatization Disorder. | (D) Duration of the disturbance is at least 6 months. | (D) The preoccupation causes clinically significant distress or impairment in social, occupational, or other important areas of functioning. |
| | (E) The belief in A is not of delusional intensity, as in Delusional Disorder, Somatic Type (i.e., the person can acknowledge the possibility that his or her fear of having, or belief that he or she has, a serious disease is unfounded). | (E) The duration of the disturbance is at least 6 months. |
| | | (F) The preoccupation is not better accounted for by Generalized Anxiety Disorder, Obsessive-Compulsive Disorder, Panic Disorder, a Major Depressive episode, Separation Anxiety, or another Somatoform Disorder. |

significant distress or functional impairment was clearly delineated. The DSM-IV Text Revision (DSM-IV-TR: American Psychiatric Association, 2000) includes some minor changes to the descriptive text, but no changes to diagnostic criteria. In Abby's case, the panic episodes were restricted to periods of rumination about having cancer and, as such, panic would be diagnosed as an associated feature of hypochondriasis, rather than indicating a separate diagnosis of panic disorder.

### ICD-10

While the DSM is the most common diagnostic system used by clinicians and researchers in North America, the International and Statistical Classification of Diseases and Related Health Problems (ICD: World Health Organization, 1993) is widely used in Europe. The ICD-10 includes diagnostic criteria for hypochondriasis (termed therein as *hypochondriacal disorder*) that differ from the DSM-IV in several important ways. First, ICD-10 criteria stipulate that there must be persistent belief that one has no more than two serious physical ailments, and the person must specifically name at least one of these. When the person has a fear or conviction of having more than two ailments, or where the person cannot identify the ailment, a diagnosis is not made under ICD-10 (but would remain with DSM-IV). Second, unlike the DSM-IV, ICD-10 criteria allow for a diagnosis of hypochondriacal disorder when the persistent belief is of a body dysmorphic nature (i.e., a belief that one has a physical abnormality such as a misshapen nose). In DSM-IV, hypochondriasis and body dysmorphic disorder are regarded as different entities. Both DSM-IV and ICD-10 exclude a diagnosis of hypochondriasis when the requisite symptoms occur only in the context of psychotic disorders or mood disorders.

## Related Concepts

In addition to hypochondriasis and hypochondriacal disorder, there are several concepts that are frequently mentioned in the literature on severe health anxiety. Such concepts include cardiac neurosis, illness behavior, illness phobia, illness worry, reassurance seeking, and somatization. Of these, somatization, illness behavior, and illness phobia are most widely used.

### Somatization

Somatization refers to 'the tendency to experience and communicate somatic distress and symptoms unaccounted for by pathological findings, to attribute them to physical illness, and to seek medical help for them' (Lipowski, 1988, p. 1359). It encompasses a range of presentations which may or may not be pathological in nature. Pathological forms include unexplained somatic symptoms that lead to excessive health care utilization. Milder forms include complaints of physical symptoms in response to emotional distress. In short, somatization can be conceptualized as the somatic expression of health anxiety.

*Illness Behavior*

Illness behavior refers to the 'ways in which given symptoms may be differently perceived, evaluated, or acted (or not acted) upon by different kinds of persons' (Mechanic, 1962, p. 189). Implicit in this definition is reference to individual differences in cognitive processes and behaviors in response to somatic sensations. Illness behavior can be understood within the context of psychological and social processes (Mechanic, 1962). Extending this concept, Pilowsky (1969, 1990) coined the term *abnormal illness behavior* to describe clinically significant health-related behaviors, such as the denial of illness, exaggeration of illness, and illness-related avoidance. These are sometimes the behavioral expressions of severe health anxiety, although abnormal illness behavior can arise for other reasons (see Pilowsky, 1997).

The concept of abnormal illness behavior has been criticized for necessitating comparison against norms in an area where there are few established standards against which to judge whether the behavior is abnormal (Kirmayer & Robbins, 1991; Mayou, 1989). This criticism is not limited to abnormal illness behavior; indeed, it applies to almost all psychiatric concepts including the mental disorders described in DSM-IV and ICD-10, where the distinction between normal and abnormal is typically based on arbitrary criteria.

*Illness Phobia*

Illness or disease phobia refers to a specific fear of contracting an illness. This phobia is characterized by distress, apprehension, and avoidance of situations that may, in the mind of the individual, lead to contracting the feared illness. The primary distinction between illness phobia and hypochondriasis is that the former involves fear of *contracting* an ailment whereas the latter is based on preoccupation with fear of *having*, or the idea that one has, a serious illness. While this distinction can be drawn, and is adhered to throughout the chapters that follow, it is noteworthy that some writers have viewed illness phobia as a dimension or subtype of hypochondriasis (Marks, 1987; Pilowsky, 1967). Boundaries between illness phobia and hypochondriasis are discussed in more detail in Chapter 6.

## PHENOMENOLOGY AND OTHER FEATURES OF SEVERE HEALTH ANXIETY

### Epidemiology

Epidemiological data are important in understanding the natural course and developmental progression of clinical conditions, in detailing the impact they have on society, and in planning service delivery and prevention initiatives. Below we define some important epidemiological terms that appear here and in other chapters, and provide an overview of the epidemiology of severe health anxiety.

A *case* is an individual who meets criteria for a given disorder. Because definitions of disorders change over time (as in the case of the DSM), the number of cases diagnosed with the disorder can also change. This underscores the importance of considering the definition used for identifying cases. *Incidence* refers to the number of new cases of a disorder that arise in a defined population during a particular period of time. Typically, incidence is expressed as the number of cases per 100 or 1,000 people. *Prevalence* refers to the proportion of a defined population affected by a disorder at a given time. Some of the most commonly used indices of prevalence include the proportion of cases at the time of study (i.e., point prevalence), the proportion of cases in a specified period of time (e.g., 6-month prevalence, 12-month prevalence), and the proportion of cases at any time (i.e., lifetime prevalence).

There is little information on the incidence of hypochondriasis. Grasbeck, Hagnell, Otterbeck, and Rorsman (1993) reviewed the case notes of 118 individuals from the 1947 Lundby cohort diagnosed with anxiety. Based on DSM-III-R criteria, the incidence of hypochondriasis was 3.4%. Schmidt, van Roosmalen, van der Beek, and Lousberg (1993) evaluated 155 new ENT referrals using interview, questionnaire responses, and specialist opinion and, on this basis, reported the incidence of hypochondriasis to be 13.5%. Unfortunately, these two investigations were conducted on selected samples and, in the latter case, it appears that the reported figures may more accurately reflect point prevalence as opposed to incidence. As a consequence, it is difficult to extrapolate the findings to infer the incidence of hypochondriasis in the general population.

Prevalence estimates of hypochondriasis in primary care and general medical settings vary considerably, ranging from as low as 0.8% (based on weighted 12-month estimates and ICD-10 criteria: Gureje, Ustun, & Simon, 1997) to as high as 8.5% (based on point estimates and DSM-III-R criteria: Noyes et al., 1993). Prevalence estimates in specialty settings are also variable but, for the most part, tend to be lower than estimates from primary care and general medical settings. For example, based on DSM-III-R criteria, Aydemir and colleagues (1997) reported a point prevalence of 1.2% in cardiology out-patients with permanent pacemakers. Altamura, Carta, Tacchini, Musazz, and Pioli (1998), using DSM-III-R and ICD-10 criteria, reported a lifetime prevalence of 1% in psychiatric inpatients and outpatients. Similar lifetime prevalence rates have been reported in patients presenting with chronic pain (e.g., Gatchel, Polatin, Mayer, & Garcey, 1994; Polatin, Kinney, Gatchel, Lillo, & Mayer, 1993; also see Chapter 12). In the community, prevalence estimates range from 1.5% (based on point estimates and unspecified criteria: Saz, Copeland, de la Camara, Lobo, & Dewey, 1995) to 4.5% (based on 12-month estimates and DSM-III-R criteria: Faravelli et al., 1997).

Prevalence estimates tend to be highest under two conditions. The first condition is when hypochondriasis is assessed in individuals presenting to medical outpatient clinics with medically unexplained symptoms. To illustrate, Speckens, van Hermert, Spinhoven, and Bolk (1996) observed, using DSM-III-R criteria, a point prevalence of 19% in these patients. The second condition is when criteria other than DSM diagnostic definitions are used (e.g., abridged/sub-threshold definitions, symptom cut-off scores). For example, when Noyes et al. (1993) based their point prevalence estimate on cut-off scores on modified versions of the Whitely Index (Pilowsky, 1967) and Somatic Symptom Inventory (Barsky et al., 1992), the estimate was considerably higher than when based on DSM-III-R criteria (13.8% versus 8.5%). Likewise, Kirmayer and Robbins (1991), using cut-off score on the Illness Behaviour Questionnaire (Pilowsky & Spence, 1983), and Barsky, Frank, Cleary, Wyshak and Klerman (1991), using cut-off scores on the Whitely Index and Somatic Symptom Inventory, reported prevalence estimates that were considerably higher (7.7% and 9.4%, respectively) than most estimates obtained using DSM diagnostic criteria.

In summary, the available data suggest that although hypochondriasis is not highly prevalent, it is as common as many of the other major mental disorders (e.g., schizophrenia, bipolar disorder, panic disorder; American Psychiatric Association, 2000).

## Onset and Course

According to the DSM-IV, hypochondriasis can begin at any age, with the most common age at onset thought to be in the early adulthood. Little is known about its course. Health anxiety often occurs transiently in normal populations (Kellner, 1987). Typically, it arises when the person is under stress, seriously ill or recovering from a serious illness, or when the person suffers the loss of a family member (Barsky & Klerman, 1983). Health anxiety also can occur when the person is exposed to illness-related media information. When health anxiety arises as a consequence of some other psychiatric disorder, treatment of the latter can reduce health anxiety (Kenyon, 1976).

Some people are frequently worried and preoccupied with their health for many years, without meeting diagnostic criteria for hypochondriasis (Barsky, Cleary, Sarnie, & Klerman, 1993). These cases can be regarded as chronic, sub-syndromal hypochondriasis. For people meeting full criteria for hypochondriasis, the disorder persists over periods of up to five years in 50–66% of cases (Barsky, Wyshak, Klerman, & Latham, 1990; Barsky et al., 1998; Noyes et al., 1996; Robbins & Kirmayer, 1996). The strength and duration of hypochondriacal beliefs, presence of comorbid psychiatric disorders, and degree of sensitivity to bodily sensations at initial assessment predict the persistence of hypochondriacal symptoms (Barsky et al., 1993; Noyes et al., 1994).

By definition, patients with hypochondriasis are reluctant to regard their problems in terms other than physical (Warwick & Salkovskis, 1989). As a result, they frequently visit their doctor and many undergo many different medical and surgical treatments (Barsky & Klerman, 1983). Although these treatments rarely help and often produce complications, side effects, or new signs and symptoms, the patient consistently returns for further medical consultation and treatment (Barsky & Klerman, 1983). In addition to numerous doctor visits, the patient may, as in the case of Abby, ask for repeated explanation of the same or similar signs and symptoms. When a physical or organically based diagnosis is not forthcoming, many patients will go 'doctor shopping'. That is, they may visit several different doctors in effort to find a physical explanation for their symptoms that is, to them, satisfactory.

Whether people become more or less health anxious as they age is a question that remains to be answered by longitudinal investigation. The cross-sectional studies on this issue are contradictory. Altamura et al. (1998) reported a tendency towards higher rates of hypochondriasis among older adults (45 years and older) compared to younger adults (under 45). Gureje et al. (1997) reported that patients with abridged (sub-threshold) hypochondriasis were significantly older than those without. However, Barsky et al. (1991) found no significant differences in the symptomatology or prevalence of DSM defined hypochondriasis in older (≥65 years) versus younger (<65 years) patients. While further investigation of the issue is warranted, it is conceivable that the elderly are more prone to reporting hypochondriacal symptoms because they are socially isolated, have more psychiatric disorders that have symptoms of hypochondriasis as secondary features, and have declining physical health (Barsky, 1993). This issue is explored in greater detail in Chapter 10.

## Functional Impairment

Health anxiety can interfere with interpersonal relationships, work performance, and leisure activities. In an early study of women with somatoform disorders, Cloninger, Sigvardsson, von Knorring, and Bohman (1984) reported that somatizers (described in terms similar to patients with hypochondriasis) had high frequency of sick leave, more pregnancy complications per child, higher divorce rates, and lower occupational status compared to non-somatizing women. In more recent studies, it has been reported that most patients with hypochondriasis have serious and chronic limitations in social and work functioning and in activities of daily living (Barsky et al., 1990; Noyes et al., 1993, Robbins & Kirmayer, 1996). Compared to people without hypochondriasis, they are less likely to be employed outside the home (Noyes et al., 1993; Barsky et al., 1990), have more days of bedrest (Barsky et al., 1998; Noyes et al., 1993), have greater physical limitations (Escobar et al., 1998; Noyes et al., 1993), and are more likely to receive disability compensation. Some of these features are evident in Abby's case. Compared to patients without hypochondriasis, and controlling for medical morbidity, functioning of patients with hypochondriasis has been observed to decline with age (Barsky et al., 1991).

## Gender and Cultural Differences

Some investigators (Faravelli et al., 1997; Gumbiner & Flowers, 1997), but not all (Hernandez & Kellner, 1992), have found that women report more health anxiety than men. However, the majority of studies suggest that the diagnosis of hypochondriasis is no more common in women than in men (Altamura et al., 1998; El-Rufaie & Absood, 1993; Escobar et al., 1998; Garcia-Campayo, Lobo, Perez-Echeverria, & Campos, 1998; Gureje et al., 1997; Kirmayer & Robbins, 1991). Cross-cultural differences in prevalence of hypochondriasis have also been observed by some investigators (Barsky et al., 1990) but not others (Escobar et al., 1998; Gureje et al., 1997). Cross-cultural features of hypochondriasis are considered in more detail in Chapter 9.

## Family History

Only a handful of studies have investigated the family history of hypochondriasis. In a study of 14 monozygotic and 21 dizygotic twins, Torgersen (1986) found that no proband with hypochondriasis had a hypochondriacal co-twin. Other studies have similarly reported that the prevalence of hypochondriasis is not elevated in the families of hypochondriacal probands (Noyes, Holt, Happel, Kathol, & Yagla, 1997; Noyes et al., 1999). Together, these studies provide preliminary evidence that hypochondriasis is not familial in origin.

## Comorbidity

There are a number of conditions that are related to health anxiety and, in the clinical setting, to hypochondriasis. These conditions may present comorbidly, or may be variants around the central issues of fear of having a serious illness. Mood and anxiety disorders frequently coexist with hypochondriasis (Noyes et al., 1994) as does somatization disorder (Barsky, Barnett, & Cleary, 1994b). As well, hypochondriasis is a common comorbid diagnosis in people with other psychiatric disorders. For example, Barsky et al. (1994b) have reported that 25% of patients with panic disorder have current hypochondriasis. In another study, 50% of the people diagnosed with a DSM-III-R anxiety disorder exhibited features of hypochondriasis (Bach, Nutzinger, & Hartl, 1996). Issues of comorbidity are discussed in more detail in Chapter 6.

In addition to comorbid conditions, there are several conditions with close association to health anxiety based on variants of symptoms revolving around the focus of illness fears and convictions. These conditions, discussed in detail in Chapters 11 through 14, include, heart-focused anxiety, acute and chronic pain, psychotic disorders with hypochondriacal features, and death anxiety.

## CURRENT DIRECTIONS IN RESEARCH

It seems that health anxiety and related issues are receiving increased attention. This, indeed, was a major impetus in stimulating this volume. But the question remains as to whether there has been an actual increase in empirical activity in this area and, if so, whether different areas of focus have been differentially affected? To explore this issue we conducted an analysis of research trends using an archival database search strategy developed by Norton and colleagues (Norton, Cox, Asmundson, & Maser,

1995). This strategy involves calculation of the absolute number of published manuscripts in a given field of inquiry (e.g., health anxiety) abstracted each year in a specified database. As well, the proportion of total published manuscripts devoted to a given field of inquiry abstracted in a specified database can be calculated. Together, the indices yielded by the calculations allow for an examination of trends and patterns in the quantity and focus of published research.

We searched specific keywords on the PsychLit and MEDLINE databases between the years 1990 and 1999. PsychLit, a psychological database published by the American Psychological Association, references on an annual basis approximately 55,000 articles published in 1,300 journals. MEDLINE, a medical database published by the United States National Library of Medicine, annually references about 400,000 articles published in over 3,600 journals. There is some overlap in the articles and journals referenced on each of these databases. Keywords searched for the purpose of this chapter included terms with close association to health anxiety (i.e., 'hypochondriasis', 'hypochondriacal', 'hypochondria', 'health anxiety', 'illness worry', 'worried well', 'cardiac neurosis', and 'reassurance seeking').

The results of our keyword search indicated corresponding trends within the PsychLit and MEDLINE databases. The absolute number of relevant articles abstracted in both databases remained relatively stable between 1990 and 1999 (see Table 1.2). However, when examined as a percentage of the total abstracted articles, trends differed slightly between databases (see Table 1.2 and Figure 1.1). First, relative to MEDLINE, a greater percentage of PsychLit manuscripts were devoted to health anxiety and related issues. Second, PsychLit exhibited a gradual decrease in the percentage of the total abstracted manuscripts abstracted from 1990 to 1994, a slight rebound from 1994 to 1996, and stability from 1996 to 1998. MEDLINE, on the other hand, evidenced stability from 1990 to 1999. Finally, PsychLit had a slight jump in the percentage of abstracts devoted to health anxiety and related issues between 1998 and 1999 whereas MEDLINE did not.

When particular areas of research focus (e.g., epidemiology, theory, assessment, treatment) were examined, trends differed only slightly between databases. In PsychLit, the percentage of articles dealing with theory and treatment remained relatively stable from 1990 to 1999, whereas the percentage dealing with epidemiological issues evidenced a slight increase. In MEDLINE, the percentage of articles on epidemiology and theory remained relatively stable, while those devoted to treatment issues declined slightly. In both databases, the percentage of articles on assessment began high in the early 1990s, declined, and has recently rebounded,

**Table 1.2**  Number and percentage of abstracts related to health anxiety referenced on during the 1990s

| Year | Number | | % of total abstracts | |
| --- | --- | --- | --- | --- |
| | MED | PSY | MED | PSY |
| 1990 | 136 | 169 | 0.036 | 0.297 |
| 1991 | 144 | 155 | 0.038 | 0.271 |
| 1992 | 149 | 149 | 0.039 | 0.253 |
| 1993 | 137 | 136 | 0.036 | 0.218 |
| 1994 | 126 | 123 | 0.032 | 0.206 |
| 1995 | 128 | 129 | 0.032 | 0.223 |
| 1996 | 136 | 146 | 0.034 | 0.250 |
| 1997 | 132 | 146 | 0.032 | 0.251 |
| 1998 | 106 | 126 | 0.026 | 0.243 |
| 1999 | 108 | 145 | 0.028 | 0.285 |

*Note*:  PSY = PsychLit; MED = MEDLINE.

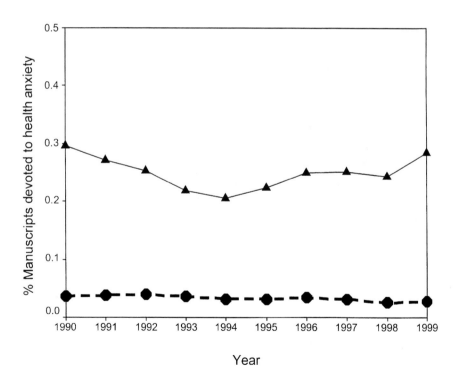

**Figure 1.1**  Percentage of MEDLINE ( ● ) and PsychLit (▲) manuscripts devoted to health anxiety and related issues.

and the percentage of articles focused on cognitive and biological mechanisms has been on the rise in the past few years.

Overall, then, it appears that there is stability and, perhaps, a slight increase, in the empirical attention being received by issues of health anxiety. The specific focus of this attention appears to have remained relatively unchanged, with many investigators focusing on descriptive, assessment, and treatment issues. It is not surprising that many important questions remain to be answered. What factors contribute to somatization and illness behavior? How is severe health anxiety related to personality? Is hypochondriasis a primary or secondary clinical state? What assessment tools provide the most reliable and valid symptom information and how can treatment outcome best be measured? What treatment methods are most effective? These questions, related empirical data, and numerous other emerging research issues are discussed in detail in the chapters that follow.

## CONCLUSION

Health anxiety is experienced to some degree by most people. Extreme health anxiety, such as that of Abby's case, involving intense fear, disease conviction, and functional disability often meets diagnostic criteria for hypochondriasis. This disorder occurs in about 5% of the general population and it is about as common as other major psychiatric disorders. Hypochondriasis is equally common in men and women, and has been observed in a variety of different cultures.

Much remains to be learned about the nature of severe and milder forms of health anxiety. Research over the past decade has focused largely on descriptive studies and on the development of methods of assessment and basic treatment. Further research on mechanisms—cognitive and biological—should lead to new insights into the treatment and prevention of excessive health anxiety. The remaining chapters of this volume delve into issues pertinent to a state-of-the-art understanding of health anxiety. This information should be useful to clinicians treating people with excessive health anxiety, and to researchers wishing to expand their understanding of mild and severe forms of this phenomenon.

## REFERENCES

Altamura, A., Carta, M.G., Tacchini, G., Musazzi, A., & Pioli, M.R. (1998). Prevalence of somatoform disorders in a psychiatric population: An Italian nationwide survey. *European Archives of Psychiatry and Clinical Neuroscience*, **248**, 267–271.

American Psychiatric Association (1968). *Diagnostic and statistical manual of mental disorders* (2nd edn.). Washington, DC: Author.

American Psychiatric Association (1980). *Diagnostic and statistical manual of mental disorders* (3rd edn.). Washington, DC: Author.

American Psychiatric Association. (1987). *Diagnostic and statistical manual of mental disorders* (3rd edn., rev.). Washington, DC: Author.

American Psychiatric Association (1994). *Diagnostic and statistical manual of mental disorders* (4th edn.). Washington, DC: Author.

American Psychiatric Association (2000). *Diagnostic and statistical manual of mental disorders* (4th edn., text rev.). Washington, DC: Author.

Aydemir, O., Ozmen, E., Kuey, L., Kultur, S., Yesil, M., Postaci, N., & Bayata, S. (1997). Psychiatric morbidity and depressive symptomatology in patients with permanent pacemakers. *Pacing and Clinical Electrophysiology*, **20**, 1628–1632.

Bach, M., Nutzinger, D.O., & Hartl, L. (1996). Comorbidity of anxiety disorders and hypochondriasis considering different diagnostic systems. *Comprehensive Psychiatry*, **37**, 62–67.

Barsky, A.J. (1993). The diagnosis and management of hypochondriacal concerns in the elderly. *Journal of Geriatric Psychiatry*, **26**, 129–141.

Barsky, A.J., Barnett, M.C., & Cleary, P.D. (1994). Hypochondriasis and panic disorder: Boundary and overlap. *Archives of General Psychiatry*, **51**, 918–925.

Barsky, A.J., Cleary, P.D., Sarnie, M.K., & Klerman, G.L. (1993). The course of transient hypochondriasis. *American Journal of Psychiatry*, **150**, 484–488.

Barsky, A.J., Cleary, P.D., Wyshak, G., Spitzer, R.L., Williams, J.B.W., & Klerman, G.L. (1992). A structured diagnostic interview for hypochondriasis. *Journal of Nervous and Mental Disease*, **180**, 20–27.

Barsky, A.J., Fama, J.M., Bailey, E.D., & Ahern, D.K. (1998). A prospective 4- to 5-year study of DSM-III-R hypochondriasis. *Archives of General Psychiatry*, **55**, 737–744.

Barsky, A.J., Frank, C.B., Cleary, P.D., Wyshak, G., & Klerman, G.L. (1991). The relation between hypochondriasis and age. *American Journal of Psychiatry*, **148**, 923–928.

Barsky, A.J., & Klerman, G.L. (1983). Overview: Hypochondriasis, bodily complaints, and somatic styles. *American Journal of Psychiatry*, **140**, 273–283.

Barsky, A.J., Wyshak, G., & Klerman, G.L. (1986). Hypochondriasis: An evaluation of the DSM-III-R criteria in medical outpatients. *Archives of General Psychiatry*, **43**, 493–500.

Barsky, A.J., Wyshak, G., Klerman, G.L., & Latham, K.S. (1990). The prevalence of hypochondriasis in medical outpatients. *Social Psychiatry and Psychiatric Epidemiology*, **25**, 89–94.

Cloninger, C.R., Sigvardsson, S., von Knorring, A., & Bohman, M. (1984). An adoption study of somatoform disorders. *Archives of General Psychiatry*, **41**, 863–871.

El-Rufaie, O.E.F., & Absood, G.H. (1993). Minor psychiatric morbidity in primary health care: Prevalence, nature and severity. *International Journal of Social Psychiatry*, **39**, 159–166.

Escobar, J.I., Gara, M., Waitzkin, H., Silver, R.C., Holman, A., & Compton, W. (1998). DSM-IV hypochondriasis in primary care. *General Hospital Psychiatry*, **20**, 155–159.

Faravelli, C., Salvatori, S., Galassi, F., Aiazzi, L., Drei, C., & Cabras, P. (1997). Epidemiology of somatoform disorders: A community survey in Florence. *Social Psychiatry and Psychiatric Epidemiology*, **32**, 24–29.

Garcia-Campayo, J., Lobo, A., Perez-Echeverria, M.J., & Campos, R. (1998). Three forms of somatization presenting in primary care settings in Spain. *Journal of Nervous and Mental Disease*, **186**, 554–560.

Gatchel, R.J., Polatin, P.B., Mayer, T.G., & Garcy, P.D. (1994). Psychopathology and the rehabilitation of patients with chronic low back pain disability. *Archives of Physical Medicine and Rehabilitation*, **75**, 666–670.

Grasbeck, A., Hagnell, O., Otterbeck, L., & Rorsman, B. (1993). Anxiety in the Lundby Study: Re-evaluation according to DSM-III-R, incidence and risk. *Biological Psychiatry*, **27**, 1–8.

Gumbiner, J., & Flowers, J. (1997). Sex differences on the MMPI-1 and MMPI-2. *Psychological Reports*, **81**, 479–482.

Gureje, O., Ustun, T.B., & Simon, G.E. (1997). The syndrome of hypochondriasis: A cross-national study in primary care. *Psychological Medicine*, **27**, 1001–1010.

Hernandez, J., & Kellner, R. (1992). Hypochondriacal concerns and attitudes toward illness in males and females. *International Journal of Psychiatry in Medicine*, **22**, 251–263.

Kellner, R. (1987). Hypochondriasis and somatization. *Journal of the American Medical Association*, **258**, 2718–2722.

Kenyon, F.E. (1976). Hypochondriacal states. *British Journal of Psychiatry*, **129**, 1–14.

Kirmayer, L.J., & Robbins, J.M. (1991). Three forms of somatization in primary care: Prevalence, co-occurrence and sociodemographic characteristics. *Journal of Nervous and Mental Disease*, **179**, 647–655.

Ladee, G.A. (1966). *Hypochondriacal syndromes*. Amsterdam: Elsevier.

Lipowski, Z.J. (1988). Somatization: The concept and its application. *American Journal of Psychiatry*, **145**, 1358–1368.

Lucock, M.P., & Morley, S. (1996). The health anxiety questionnaire. *British Journal of Health Psychology*, **1**, 137–150.

Marks, I.M. (1987). *Fears, phobias, and rituals*. New York: Oxford University Press.

Mayou, R. (1989). Atypical chest pain. *Journal of Psychosomatic Research*, **33**, 393–406.

Mechanic, D. (1962). The concept of illness behavior. *Journal of Chronic Diseases*, **15**, 189–194.

Norton, G.R., Cox, B.J., Asmundson, G.J.G., & Maser, J.D. (1995). The growth of research on anxiety disorders during the 1980s. *Journal of Anxiety Disorders*, **9**, 73–85.

Noyes, R. Jr., Happel, R.L., & Yagla, S.J. (1999). Correlates of hypochondriasis in a nonclinical population. *Psychosomatics*, **40**, 461–499.

Noyes, R. Jr., Holt, C.S., Happel, R., Kathol, R.G., & Yagla, S.J. (1997). A family study of hypochondriasis. *Journal of Nervous and Mental Disease*, **185**, 223–232.

Noyes, R. Jr., Kathol, R.G., Fisher, M.M., Phillips, B.M., Suelzer, M.T., & Holt, C.S. (1993). The validity of DSM-III-R hypochondriasis. *Archives of General Psychiatry*, **50**, 961–970.

Noyes, R. Jr., Kathol, R.G., Fisher, M.M., Phillips, B.M., Suelzer, M., & Woodman, C.L. (1994). Psychiatric comorbidity among patients with hypochondriasis. *General Hospital Psychiatry*, **16**, 78–87.

Noyes, R. Jr., Kathol, R.G., Fisher, M.M., Phillips, B.M., Suelzer, M., & Woodman, C.L. (1996). One-year follow-up of medical outpatients with hypochondriasis. *Psychosomatics*, **35**, 533–545.

Pilowsky, I. (1967). Dimensions of hypochondriasis. *British Journal of Psychiatry*, **113**, 89–93.

Pilowsky, I. (1969). Abnormal illness behavior. *British Journal of Medical Psychology*, **42**, 347–351

Pilowsky, I. (1990). The concept of abnormal illness behavior. *Psychosomatics*, **31**, 207–213.

Pilowsky, I. (1997). *Abnormal illness behaviour.* New York: Wiley.

Pilowsky, I., & Spence, N.D. (1983). *Manual for the Illness Behaviour Questionnaire (IBQ)* (2nd edn.). Adelaide, South Australia, Department of Psychiatry, University of Adeleide.

Polatin, P.B., Kinney, R.K., Gatchel, R.J., Lillo, E., & Mayer, T.G. (1993). Psychiatric illness and chronic low-back pain: The mind and the spine—Which goes first? *Spine,* **18,** 66–71.

Robbins, J.M., & Kirmayer, L.J. (1996). Transient and persistent hypochondriacal worry in primary care. *Psychological Medicine,* **26,** 575–589.

Salkovskis, P.M., & Warwick, H.M.C. (1986). Morbid preoccupations, health anxiety and reassurance: A cognitive-behavioural approach to hypochondriasis. *Behaviour Research and Therapy,* **24,** 597–602.

Saz, P., Copeland, J.R.M., de la Camara, C., Lobo, A., & Dewey, M.E. (1995). Cross-national comparison of prevalence of symptoms of neurotic disorders in older people in two community samples. *Acta Psychiatrica Scandinavica,* **91,** 18–22.

Schmidt, A.J.M., van Roosmalen, R., van der Beek, J.M.H., & Lousberg, R. (1993). Hypochondriasis in ENT practice. *Clinical Otolaryngology,* **18,** 508–511.

Speckens, A.E.M., van Hemert, A.M., Spinhoven, P., & Bolk, J.H. (1996). The diagnostic and prognostic significance of the Whitely Index, the Illness Attitude Scales, and the Somatosensory Amplification Scale. *Psychological Medicine,* **26,** 1085–1090.

Torgersen, S. (1986). Genetics of somatoform disorders. *Archives of General Psychiatry,* **43,** 502–505.

Warwick, H.M.C. (1989). A cognitive-behavioural approach to hypochondriasis and health anxiety. *Journal of Psychosomatic Research,* **33,** 705–711.

Warwick, H.M.C., & Salkovskis, P.M. (1989). Cognitive and behavioural characteristics of primary hypochondriasis. *Scandinavian Journal of Behaviour Therapy,* **18,** 85–92.

World Health Organization (1993). *The ICD-10 classification of mental and behavioral disorders: Diagnostic criteria for research.* Geneva, Switzerland: Author.

Chapter 2

# THE PSYCHOLOGY OF PHYSICAL SYMPTOMS AND ILLNESS BEHAVIOR

*René Martin\*, Katherine Lemos\*, and Howard Leventhal*[†]

## INTRODUCTION

When questioned, most laypeople can accurately identify common symptoms of a heart attack (myocardial infarction or MI), such as chest pain (Goff et al., 1998). This abstract knowledge does not appear to translate into action, however. After the onset of cardiac-related symptoms, almost half of all MI victims delay longer than two hours before seeking medical intervention (e.g., Rustige et al., 1997). Delay in the context of an acute MI is of concern for both victims and health care providers because serious complications and mortality are more prevalent among patients who are slow to enter the health care delivery system (e.g., FTT Collaborative Group, 1994). It is notable that transportation to the hospital accounts for only a small proportion of total delay time. Instead, MI delay primarily appears to be a function of the victim's activities and decisions after symptom onset (Dracup & Moser, 1997; Sharkey et al., 1989). The propensity to minimize or neglect serious symptoms is not limited to heart attack victims. For example, screening studies reveal that many symptoms that would have benefited from medical intervention go untreated (e.g., Clark, 1959; Ingham & Miller, 1979).

In contrast, many health care visits appear to be unnecessary. Practitioners frequently are unable to identify any objective source for patients' symptoms (Backett, Heady, & Evans, 1954; Barsky, 1981). In addition,

\*University of Iowa, USA; [†]Institute for Health, Health Care Policy, and Aging Research Rutgers University, USA

*Health Anxiety*
Edited by G.J.G. Asmundson, S. Taylor & B.J. Cox
© 2001 John Wiley & Sons Ltd.

physicians' records indicate that minor symptoms which could have been safely self-managed (e.g., the common cold) prompt most medical visits (National Center for Health Statistics, 1980). These unfounded contacts strain medical resources, escalate costs, and expose ostensibly healthy patients to the iatrogenic risks that often accompany medical treatment (Peters, Stanley, Rose, & Salmon, 1998).

Thus, health care providers are confronted with two very different, but equally problematic scenarios: (a) the sufferer who delays or even fails to seek medical intervention for overt pathology, and (b) the apparently healthy individual who utilizes health care resources inappropriately. These scenarios suggest that the associations among physical symptoms and illness behaviors are complex. The purpose of this chapter is to provide an overview of cognitive, affective, and contextual variables that influence symptom perception and related behaviors, thus providing a foundation for this volume's focus on health anxiety and hypochondriasis.

## SYMPTOMS INVOLVE MORE THAN MERE SENSORY PERCEPTION

Before delving into the psychological processes that influence symptom perception, it is necessary first to explore the symptom construct itself. To laypeople and health care providers alike, it seems self-evident that symptoms involve unpleasant or unexpected somatic sensations such as nausea, headache, or a scratchy throat. However, the perception of physical symptoms involves more than mere sensory feedback.

### Defining Symptoms

It is important for our purposes to distinguish between signs and symptoms. Whereas signs are easily observed, symptoms are accessible only through self-report. Specifically, a sign is an objective marker of overt pathology or injury (e.g., inflammation, hemorrhage). In contrast, a symptom is present when an individual perceives somatosensory information as either physically or psychologically aversive and the disruption is assumed to be the consequence of injury or disease. These definitions suggest a critical dichotomy. Health care providers are experts in the recognition and interpretation of signs (e.g., detection of an abnormality in liver function through a routine blood examination). However, symptoms are fundamentally private in nature (e.g., pain, fatigue) and often cannot be objectively quantified. Consequently, only the individual sufferer can be an expert regarding his or her own symptoms (Marchant-Haycox & Salmon, 1997; Shorter, 1992).

Laypeople and health care providers alike care about symptoms because they disrupt daily activities (Cameron, Leventhal, & Leventhal, 1993). This characteristic distinguishes symptoms from mundane somatic sensations. For example, as you read this chapter, you probably can feel your feet against the floor and your fingertips on the pages. These sensations do not represent symptoms, however, because they are not perceived to be troublesome. The disruption provoked by symptoms can be either direct or indirect. A tender knee directly impairs the ability to climb stairs. In contrast, a breast lump exerts no direct effects on function or activity. However, awareness of the lump may elicit anxiety that disrupts sleep and the ability to concentrate.

A second critical aspect of the symptom construct is the idea that symptoms imply disease or malfunction. In other words, disruptive somatic sensations generally are taken to mean that there is some underlying problem, damage, or disease. Symptoms figure prominently in lay conceptualizations of both illness and health. A layperson is likely to describe the presence of symptoms when asked to define what it means to be ill, whereas lay definitions of health usually incorporate the absence of symptoms (Borawski, Kinney, & Kahana, 1996; Lau, 1997).

The bottom-up process of receiving sensory information from the periphery of the body provides the raw data of symptom perception (Brownlee, Leventhal, & Leventhal, in press). We experience symptoms, at least in part, because a component of the body feels amiss. However, although symptoms reflect some sort of somatosensory reality, symptoms are not necessarily indicative of pathology. Top-down processes also contribute to symptom perception, although their effects may be less obvious to the casual observer. Consequently, this chapter will include an in-depth discussion of the effects of higher-order processes on symptom perception.

## Behavioral Implications of Symptom Perception

Individuals who appear to be healthy nonetheless report a wide variety of physical symptoms (Bishop, 1984; Leventhal & Diefenbach, 1991; Pennebaker, 1982; Safer, Tharps, Jackson, & Leventhal, 1979). However, the perception of symptoms does not necessarily prompt health-care-seeking behavior. Instead, many symptoms are managed at home without input from health care providers (e.g., Cameron et al., 1993). Estimates in the literature suggest that less than half of symptomatic persons actually seek medical consultation (Scambler & Scambler, 1985).

Nonetheless, symptoms are an important determinant of medical self-referral behavior. The vast majority of individuals seeking health care report one or more symptoms (Cameron et al., 1993; Costa & McCrae, 1980; Leventhal, Hansell, Diefenbach, Leventhal, & Glass, 1996; Stoller, 1997). Medical visits usually begin with an inquiry regarding symptoms because health care providers typically presume that the patient would not be present unless symptoms had been experienced. Thus, symptom reports provide an important means and focal point of communication between patient and health care provider, as well as a direction for treatment (Leventhal et al., 1996).

Safer et al. (1979) described the complex interplay between symptoms and behavior in three stages: appraisal, illness, and utilization. During the *appraisal stage*, a somatic sensation has been noticed and the individual attempts to determine the meaning of that sensation. At this point, some sensations are dismissed as trivial and non-disruptive. Others are judged to be symptoms; that is, they are troublesome and thought to be indicative of illness. During the *illness phase*, the sufferer explores avenues of symptom management. As many symptoms can be safely and economically addressed without professional assistance, the illness phase is characterized by self-care activities. Of course, some symptoms mark conditions that require medical attention. A key question during the illness phase is whether seeking medical care is an appropriate response. The *utilization stage* occurs only if the sufferer decides to seek medical care. During this stage, arrangements are made for entry into the health care delivery system (e.g., scheduling an appointment, traveling to the hospital). Ideally, serious symptoms are identified and quickly treated, whereas minor symptoms are managed at home. However, as illustrated by our opening examples, this is not always the case.

## Symptom Perception as an Exercise in Signal Detection

The associations among symptom perception, self-care, and medical self-referral lend themselves to an analogy with signal detection theory. Psychophysicists have investigated individual differences in how humans detect and report stimuli in noisy, distracting environments (Green & Swets, 1974). To summarize, four outcomes are possible for any signal detection task. Ideally, the subject accurately identifies the presence (a 'hit') or absence (a 'correct rejection') of the stimulus. Errors occur when a stimulus goes unreported (a 'miss') or when a stimulus is reported when in fact none was present (a 'false alarm'). Situational characteristics influence the prevalence of misses and false alarms. In addition, some people are typically quite cautious during the signal detection task (leading to frequent misses, but few false alarms), whereas others are more willing to take risks (generating frequent false alarms, but few undetected stimuli).

To extend this analogy to the domain of symptom perception, hits and correct rejections represent desirable conditions. A hit occurs when an MI victim promptly calls emergency services or when a doctor's advice is sought for a lingering cough. Correct rejections occur when minor symptoms are self-managed (e.g., a heating pad for sore muscles). In the physical health domain, hits and correct rejections reflect the judicious use of medical resources. Misses occur when serious symptoms are neglected (e.g., the MI victim who delays, or someone who ignores rectal bleeding). False alarms occur when medical intervention is sought for minor symptoms (e.g., the sniffles) or psychogenic symptoms, which are produced by the mind in response to stress (e.g., nausea that occurs only in anxiety-provoking settings). False alarms are of particular interest for the present volume, with its emphasis on health anxiety and hypochondriasis. We will return to the subject of false alarms in our discussion of psychological variables that influence symptom perception.

To summarize, symptoms occur when somatosensory information is perceived by the individual to be both disruptive in nature and the result of injury or disease. Symptoms are common and prompt both self-care activities and health-care-seeking behavior. Because symptom perception fundamentally is an intrapersonal or private process, occasional disagreements between sufferers and health care providers are inevitable (the false alarms and misses in our signal detection analogy). As we begin our review of psychological factors that shape the symptom perception process, it is important to recognize that the individual's perceptions of suffering and causation are more important than veridical reality in directing behavior. In other words, symptoms are equally 'real', whether psychogenic in nature or the consequence of objective pathology.

## THE COMMON-SENSE MODEL OF HEALTH AND ILLNESS BEHAVIOR

We will be guided by H. Leventhal's common-sense model of health and illness behavior (H. Leventhal, 1970; H. Leventhal & Diefenbach, 1991) in our exploration of symptom perception and behavior. The common-sense model of health and illness behavior is rooted in Heider's (1958) tradition of naïve epistemology. Heider noticed that laypeople use patterns of covariation when explaining events. He compared lay reasoning to the formal analyses undertaken by scientists. If we extend Heider's perspective to the health domain, it suggests that the lay response to physical symptoms is similar to the diagnostic procedures executed by highly trained physicians. When confronted with a patient's symptom complaints, the physician collects data (e.g., regarding symptom onset, quality, and temporal changes). The data are used to formulate a tentative medical diagnosis, which guides further diagnostic efforts and interventions. Often overlooked is the fact that the patient has gone through a similar process him or herself before ever entering the health care delivery system. Like their medical counterparts, laypeople suffering physical symptoms evaluate the nature of the symptoms and develop intuitive diagnoses, perhaps in consultation with family members or friends.

H. Leventhal's common-sense model of health and illness behavior places the process of symptom perception in the context of self-regulatory behavior. Symptoms often elicit fear and anxiety, leading the sufferer to engage in ameliorative behaviors. Simultaneously, the layperson evaluates the set of symptoms and develops a naïve theory (or common-sense model) of what the symptoms mean and how best to respond. In other words, symptoms serve as affective and cognitive warning signals, and coping behaviors emerge as the sufferer attempts to adapt. The common-sense model of health and illness behavior emphasizes that affect and cognition both are powerful and often independent determinants of behaviors. The common-sense model of health and illness behavior additionally recognizes that the context in which symptoms occur can influence behavior by moderating symptom-related affect and cognition. Thus, our discussion will address the independent and interactive roles of affect, cognition, and context.

## Implications of Negative Emotions for Symptom Perception and Illness Behaviors

Some of the earliest research on emotion and symptom perception focused on the fear-drive model and the effects of fear communications. The fear-drive model incorporated elements of both classical and instrumental conditioning (Dollard & Miller, 1950; Miller, 1951). First, the model recognized that fear can become classically conditioned to cues in the environment. For example, because dental visits often involve discomfort, many people come to feel anxious or fearful simply upon entering the dentist's waiting room. Second, the fear-drive model proposed that behaviors that reduce or eliminate fear are reinforced through the process of instrumental conditioning. In response to dental anxiety, one might learn to minimize the fear associated with dentists through use of distraction (e.g., bringing a book to the waiting room) or avoidance (e.g., never scheduling the appointment at all). The fact that avoidance can reduce emotional distress, at least temporarily, means that symptom-related fear can contribute to 'misses' in our signal detection analogy. A sufferer might elect to leave a potentially important symptom untreated because the concomitant fear and anxiety are too aversive to be tolerated. Consistent with this reasoning, researchers found that messages that simply provoked fear were unsuccessful in motivating health and illness behaviors. Instead, fear-inducing messages only were effective in motivating health-related behaviors when accompanied by an action plan for minimizing threat (Leventhal, Singer, & Jones, 1965; Leventhal, Watts, & Pagano, 1967).

Interestingly, behaviors that ameliorate emotional distress sometimes prove to be maladaptive over time. Levine et al. (1987) tracked denial in cardiac patients over the course of one year. Denial appeared to be an effective short-term coping strategy. Specifically, patients who denied the seriousness of their conditions tended to require fewer days in intensive care and manifested fewer signs of cardiac dysfunction. However, over the follow-up period, denial predicted non-compliance and rehospitalization. These findings highlight the interplay between affect and cognition. In the early days following a cardiac event, fear and anxiety place additional strain on the cardiovascular system and inhibit initial rehabilitation efforts. However, patients who persisted in denying their conditions were less likely to adopt medication and behavioral recommendations that ultimately facilitate recovery and survival. Levine et al.'s findings were consistent with a meta-analysis conducted by Suls and Fletcher (1985), who found that avoidant coping strategies were associated with positive short-term, but negative long-term outcomes. Thus, the sufferer is faced with two challenging and incompatible tasks. Distressing affect must be regulated. At the same time, the sufferer must come to comprehend the symptoms and their likely consequences. These examples illustrate why the common-sense model of health and illness behavior treats affect and cognition as independent pathways in determining illness behavior.

## COGNITION AND NAIVE THEORIES OF ILLNESS

At this point, we will turn our attention to illness cognition and its implications for symptom perception and illness behavior. A basic premise of the common-sense model of health and illness behavior is that people think about health and illness in much the same way that they process information in any other domain. Therefore, in understanding illness cognition, it is important to bear in mind that we sometimes lack the attentional or cognitive resources necessary to undertake truly well-informed symptom judgments. In addition, we tend to be strategic in the application of our cognitive resources, investing energy only when the issue is consistent with salient goals (Fiske & Taylor, 1991). This means that many of the processes that characterize cognition in general (e.g., heuristics) have been observed in the symptom perception domain.

## Illness Representations

*Content*

Cognitive representations or naïve theories of illness consistently incorporate several types of information regarding the personal manifestation and meaning of symptoms (Bauman, Cameron, Zimmerman, & Leventhal, 1989; Lau, 1997; Meyer, Leventhal, & Gutmann, 1985; Skelton & Croyle, 1991). First, naïve theories of illness include symptom labels. For example, a throbbing sensation in the right temple might be labeled as a 'headache'. Empirical evidence suggests that the process of labeling a symptom often involves comparing somatic sensations to beliefs or prototypes about the typical manifestations of various disorders (Bishop, 1991; Bishop, Briede, Cavazos, Grotzinger, & McMahon, 1987; Bishop & Converse, 1986). Symptom labels further incorporate both experiential and abstract dimensions. The throbbing right temple is a concrete experience, whereas the label 'headache' is a symbolic representation used to communicate information about the symptom.

Once a symptom label has been formulated (either by the self or perhaps conveyed by a health care provider), the sufferer often searches for additional label-consistent symptoms. For example, if our headache sufferer has labeled the symptom as a migraine, he or she now may attend very closely to sensations of nausea or light sensitivity. Bauman et al. (1989) demonstrated the symmetry between symptoms and labels in the laboratory. Participants provided with (bogus) elevated blood pressure readings subsequently noticed new sensations such as headache and flushing, symptoms believed by many laypeople to be indicative of hypertension. Thus, a reciprocal association exists between symptoms and labels. Symptoms generate labeling behavior and symptom labels can elicit additional symptom reports.

Illness representations also incorporate expectations regarding symptom duration and temporal fluctuations. For example, our migraine sufferer may expect transient episodes of discomfort to occur indefinitely. Temporal beliefs have several implications for the decision to seek medical care. First, symptoms that linger longer than expected may provoke a visit to the physician, even if those lay expectations are unrealistic. Second, rapid changes in symptoms suggest avenues of action. A symptom that resolves quickly is unlikely to be judged as requiring medical attention, whereas a symptom that becomes progressively more uncomfortable over the space of a few hours will seem to demand the ministrations of a health care provider. Finally, people often delay or completely avoid seeking medical care when symptoms develop in a slow, gradual fashion (Leventhal et al., 1997). This may occur because it is fairly easy to adapt to the symptoms when so little difference is encountered from day to day. Alternatively, the individual suffering the gradual onset of symptoms may simply assume (perhaps in error) that anything serious surely would be more intense or dramatic over time.

Naïve theories of illness further incorporate beliefs about symptom causation. For example, a throbbing head will prompt very different behaviors if the discomfort is attributed to a possible brain tumor, rather than to a migraine. Blaxter (1983) found that belief in a specific cause (e.g., 'I think I have shingles') often led to care seeking. Consistent with this idea, Cameron, Leventhal, and Leventhal (1995) found that self-referral was more common for unambiguous symptoms that had clear disease implications. Interestingly, E. Leventhal and Crouch (1997) also observed that care seeking sometimes occurred when the layperson failed to formulate a symptom label and attribution on his or her own. In this case, the intent of self-referral was to seek clarity (e.g., 'What are these odd, tender spots on my skin and where did they come from?').

Finally, perceived consequences and expectations regarding symptom control or cure represent the last two characteristics of illness representations. Both dimensions have important implications for illness behaviors. Contrast the perspectives of two menopausal women. One focuses on the risks of heart disease and osteoporosis that accompany menopause. The other views menopause as a completely natural transition. Given their differing beliefs about the consequences of menopause, the two women may adopt different strategies of menopause management. The first woman is likely to opt for hormone replacement therapy. The second probably will prefer soy isoflavones (a dietary supplement) over prescription medications.

*Implications for Health-Care-Seeking Behavior*

Health psychologists are concerned with illness representations because of their behavioral implications. Among matched pairs of community-residing adults, Cameron et al. (1993) compared illness representations between subjects who sought medical attention for symptoms and controls who were symptomatic, but who opted for self-management. The naïve theories of illness held by care seekers were rich in detail and tended to incorporate a disease attribution (e.g., 'I think I have Lyme's Disease'). Care seekers perceived their symptoms to be serious and disruptive. Further, they feared that their symptoms would lead to harmful consequences. Finally, care seekers reported that they had actively tried to relieve symptoms, although these coping behaviors were perceived to be ineffective. In contrast, the representations of self-managers were less detailed and they perceived their symptoms to be less serious, less disruptive, and less likely to be due to disease or injury. Other researchers have reported similar findings. Janz and Becker (1984) also found that care seeking was likely to ensue when sufferers perceived symptoms to be serious. E. Leventhal and Crouch (1997) observed that the decision to seek medical care tended to be triggered by the perception that self-care activities were ineffective.

*Intuitive Hypothesis Testing*

Anderson's (1987, 1993) 'if–then' rules provide an effective characterization of the link between illness representations and coping responses. In this approach, the illness representation reflects the 'if' dimension, whereas behavioral responses comprise the 'then' component. In other words, illness representations incorporate an implicit hypothesis, which is tested via coping behaviors. For example, *if* I have a cold, *then* I will drink fluids and rest. *If* I suddenly develop a high fever and greenish sputum, *then* I will reconsider the situation. *If* re-evaluation leads me to conclude that I might have pneumonia, *then* I will see my physician as soon as possible. The 'if–then' approach captures important distinctions among responses that might be missed by broad coping taxonomies (e.g., emotion- vs. problem-focused coping; see Carver, Scheier, & Weintraub, 1989; Lazarus & Folkman, 1984). To return to an earlier example, hormone replacement therapy and soy isoflavones both represent problem-focused responses to menopause. However, as we have seen, the lay psychologies and expectations underlying each behavior are very different.

## Shortcuts in Illness Cognition

Ideally, each and every symptom would be subjected to a thorough lay analysis before a behavioral decision is made. Unfortunately, symptom evaluation does not always occur under ideal conditions. In proceeding through the evaluation process, the nature of unpleasant symptoms themselves (e.g., pain, shortness of breath) and the concomitant emotional response (e.g., fear, anxiety) can be powerful distracters. Occupational or household responsibilities also may compete for attention. Thus, it often is necessary to evaluate symptoms as quickly and as efficiently as possible. Under these conditions, we rely on decision rules (or heuristics) in symptom evaluation.

The effects of several symptom-related decision rules have been documented. For example, E. Leventhal and colleagues (Leventhal & Crouch, 1997; Leventhal, Leventhal, Schaefer, & Easterling, 1993) observed that older people often view their physical and cognitive energies as limited resources. Therefore, when symptoms intrude, they tend to seek medical care quickly. This strategy allows the sufferer to delegate responsibility for effortful symptom evaluation and decision making to the health care provider, thus conserving precious energy (the 'conservation rule'). Information about age and prevalence also influence the lay understanding of symptoms. Mild symptoms that develop gradually are often attributed to normal aging, rather than to illness (the 'age–illness rule'; Prohaska, Keller, Leventhal, & Leventhal, 1987). Rare conditions usually are assumed to be serious, whereas more common disorders are perceived as less threatening (the 'prevalence rule'; Ditto & Jemmott, 1989). Finally, information about stress also influences the interpretation of physical symptoms. If new symptoms develop in the context of a challenging event, laypeople tend to assume that stress, rather than illness is the causal factor (the 'stress–illness rule'; Cameron et al., 1995).

## Judgment Errors in the Interpretation of Symptoms

*The Over-Application of Heuristics*

The decision rules described above often prove to be adaptive; that is, they generally lead to accurate, fast, and efficient symptom judgments. However, because heuristics are executed rapidly without careful analyses, they may lead to errors and serious consequences in certain circumstances. To draw on our signal-detection analogy, the conservation rule risks false alarms. In other words, the individual who routinely delegates sole responsibility for symptom evaluation to health care professionals inevitably will seek care unnecessarily on some occasions. In contrast, the prevalence rule can encourage misses. Clark (1959) observed that threatening symptoms often went untreated among Mexican-American migrant workers, in part because the sheer frequency of these symptoms in the migrant setting diminished perceptions of symptom seriousness. The age–illness rule also may generate misses in symptom evaluation. Older people frequently (and erroneously) are assumed to be hypochondriacal (Costa & McCrae, 1985). Thus, the age–illness rule may lead elderly sufferers and their support providers to misattribute potentially serious symptoms to mere aging.

*Somatization Stereotypes and Gender*

The stress–illness rule potentially is problematic because serious illness can, of course, occur in the context of stressors. Notably, recent evidence suggests that the stress–illness rule may not be applied equably to male and female victims. Martin, Gordon, and Lounsbury (1998) found that both laypeople and physicians consistently attributed symptoms of chest pain and shortness of breath to cardiac causes when the victim was a man. However, when the victim was a woman, a cardiac attribution was unlikely to be formulated if the female target reported concurrent life stressors. In other words, stress-related symptom discounting only occurred for female victims. The symptoms of male victims were perceived as serious, regardless of environmental stressors. Subsequent research found that this effect generalized to symptoms of diabetes (Martin & Lemos, 2000), suggesting that lay symptom attribution may be guided by a stereotypic expectation that women, but not men, tend to somatize in response to stress. The fact that women are more responsive to most potential health threats than men may provide a basis for this stereotype (Shumaker & Smith, 1994; Wingard, Cohn, Cirillo, Cohen, & Kaplan, 1992). In addition, a large literature indicates that healthy women of all ages report more physical symptoms than do healthy men (e.g., Corney, 1990; Hibbard & Pope, 1983; Pennebaker, 1982; Verbrugge, 1989). However, it should be noted that this gender difference disappears among ill populations (Davis, 1981; Gijsbers van Wijk & Kolk, 1997; Macintyre, 1993; Marshall & Funch, 1986). In other words, although healthy women describe more somatic sensations than their male counterparts, women are no more likely than men to complain when symptoms are the consequence of pathology. Thus, the stress–illness rule may lead to misses in symptom evaluation, especially for women.

*The Tendency to Equate Symptoms with Disease*

Our definition of symptoms emphasized a causal attribution to disease or disorder. To briefly review, somatic sensations that are not perceived as a manifestation of illness are dismissed and generally never evaluated by health care providers. It seems likely that the assumption of disease causality functions as a sort of heuristic in symptom evaluation, which could be called the *pathology rule*. In other words, 'If I feel bad, it must be because I am sick'. This approach is adaptive at least in some situations because experience teaches us that many symptoms are warning signals that require remedial action (e.g., rest, self-medication, health-care seeking). However, the heuristic assumption that any or all untoward somatic sensations are caused by disease opens the door for misjudgment in at least two ways. First, asymptomatic pathology poses difficulties for both diagnosis and treatment. Second, some symptoms are psychogenic, without organic basis. Although very different in their manifestations, asymptomatic disorders and unfounded physical symptoms both lead to a mismatch in the individual's perspective and that held by health care providers.

### Asymptomatic Conditions

Laypeople appear to have difficulty comprehending a disease that exists without symptoms. For example, high blood pressure (hypertension) is an asymptomatic condition. However, H. Leventhal and colleagues (Bauman & Leventhal, 1985; Meyer, Leventhal, & Gutmann, 1985) found that most hypertensive patients (incorrectly) believe that they experience physical symptoms which allow them to track fluctuations in blood pressure. This misperception has important implications for behavior, in that adherence to prescribed medications may fluctuate with the perception of hypertensive symptoms. For example, an acquaintance of one of the authors doubles her antihypertensive medication whenever she notices that her palms are flushed. Because such unprescribed medication changes may lead to untoward side effects (e.g., hypotension, toxicity), it probably is extremely tempting for our acquaintance's health care provider to correct her spurious notion that flushed palms predict blood pressure. However, this well-intentioned practitioner's strategy potentially may back-fire. Meyer et al. (1985) found that hypertensive patients were most likely to adhere to their medication regimes when they believed that the medication was effective in controlling unpleasant symptoms (which of course had no veridical relation to blood pressure). This surprising finding makes more sense when viewed from the patient's perspective. The hypertensive individual probably is more inclined to tolerate the expense, inconvenience, and side effects associated with the treatment, if he or she believes, however erroneously, that the treatment yields some tangible daily benefit. This lay approach can be summarized with the old chestnut, 'If it ain't broke, don't fix it' (or 'If I have no symptoms there's nothing to treat').

### Psychogenic Symptoms

Finally, the presumption that symptoms reflect pathology is potentially problematic because some symptoms are psychogenic in nature. As previously described, psychogenic symptoms are produced by the mind rather than the body, usually in response to stress (Shorter, 1992). A detailed discussion of somatoform disorders and their origins is beyond the scope of this particular chapter. However, it is useful for our purposes to distinguish between primary and secondary psychosomatic disorders (Helman, 1985). In the case of primary psychosomatic symptoms, objective pathology is exacerbated by psychological factors. For example, an asthmatic individual might experience more frequent bouts of wheezing during periods of stress. However, we primarily are interested in secondary psychosomatic disorders, in which no overt physical pathology can be identified. Secondary psychosomatic disorders generally are thought to represent false alarms in our signal detection analogy. Caution is warranted on this point, however. In some instances, the care provider may identify no pathology and view the visit as unnecessary when, in fact, subtle dysfunction goes overlooked. Thus, the sufferer faces a difficult task: 'Is it me? Am I crazy?' versus 'Is it them and their poor diagnostic skills?' Blaxter (1983) found that patients who felt their physician had provided an unsatisfactory explanation for troublesome symptoms tended to ruminate and often engaged in *doctor shopping* (i.e., seeking care from several providers for the same symptoms). Shorter (1992) further notes that patients often resist psychogenic symptom attributions because of the accompanying stigma. Patients often learn, usually from health care providers, that psychosomatic disorders are a consequence of personality or individual weaknesses (Helman, 1985). This suggests that the individual who habitually uses the *pathology rule* (i.e., automatically assumes that any and all symptoms are a consequence of disease) risks facing uncomfortable false alarm situations and psychogenic diagnoses. Thus, to summarize, not all diseases are accompanied by symptoms and not all symptoms represent disease. However, the heuristic linking symptoms and disease-related pathology may contribute to judgment errors.

## MODERATING VARIABLES IN SYMPTOM PERCEPTION AND ILLNESS BEHAVIOR

The common-sense model of health and illness behavior focuses on cognitive and affective determinants of health and illness behavior, which are likely to be stable across most situations. However, the model also recognizes that the environment has important implications for symptom perception and illness behaviors. The common-sense model of health and illness behavior views contextual variables, such as personality, the setting, and culture as moderating variables. In other words, context influences symptom perception and health and illness behaviors by enhancing or inhibiting the salience of various illness-related affects and cognitions.

## Personality: Negative Affect and Symptoms

Research on the association between personality and disease has identified several personality dimensions that influence symptom reports (Feldman, Cohen, Doyle, Skoner, & Gwaltney, 1999; also see Chapter 4). However, the association between trait negative affectivity (NA) or neuroticism and symptom reports has received the greatest attention. Specifically, individuals who score high on measures of NA also tend to complain of frequent physical symptoms, with correlations ranging from 0.20 to 0.50 (Costa & McCrae, 1980, 1985, 1987; Pennebaker, 1982; Watson & Pennebaker, 1989). Intuitively, it might seem that pathology should underlie these symptom complaints. However, NA often fails to predict objective indices of health, such as physician visits and disease incidence (Costa & McCrae, 1987; Watson & Pennebaker, 1989). It has been argued that this bias in symptom reporting is a consequence of increased attention and vigilance to somatic sensations (Feldman et al., 1999; Watson & Pennebaker, 1989, 1991).

The positive correlation between NA and symptom complaints has led many health psychologists to treat neuroticism as a nuisance variable when measuring self-reports of symptoms and illness (Davison & Pennebaker, 1996; Watson & Pennebaker, 1991). However, recent evidence indicates that the relations among NA, symptoms, and illness behaviors may be more complex than originally thought—perhaps even playing a causal role (Diefenbach, Leventhal, Leventhal, & Patrick-Miller, 1996; Leventhal et al., 1996). Diefenbach et al. (1996) measured both signs and symptoms among adults who had received a variety of inoculations. NA did not predict signs (swelling and redness at the injection site) or complaints of vague, flu-like symptoms in either cross-sectional or longitudinal analyses. Instead, participants' complaints were more strongly related to objective changes at the injection site than to NA. Similar findings have been reported by Smith, Wallston, and Dwyer (1995), who found that objective disease severity was a stronger predictor of pain and impairment among arthritis sufferers than was NA.

Most researchers linking NA and symptom complaints have used cross-sectional designs. A different pattern of findings seems to emerge in longitudinal studies. In two large samples of elderly adults, trait NA was not a strong predictor of longitudinal symptom complaints; however, current negative mood predicted new symptom complaints at 6-month follow-up (Leventhal et al., 1996). NA also has been found to predict sneezing and nasal congestion prospectively (Cohen et al., 1995). Components of NA, such as anxiety and depression, also have been linked to disease (Aneshensel, Frerichs, & Huba, 1984; Kubzansky, Kawachi, Weiss, & Sparrow, 1998). It has been suggested that negative mood state might inhibit immune function, increasing disease vulnerability and ultimately generating symptom complaints (Leventhal et al., 1996).

Thus, it appears that the positive correlation between trait NA and symptom complaints is most likely to emerge for the measurement of vague symptoms in cross-sectional designs (Diefenbach et al., 1996; Leventhal et al., 1996). Recent data makes it seem unlikely that negatively affective individuals simply complain indiscriminately about somatic sensations. Diefenbach et al. (1996) suggested that the cross-sectional association between NA and symptoms might occur because negatively affective individuals tend to remember unpleasant events, such as symptoms, quite well. Finally, it also is possible that trait NA is linked to the intensity, rather than the frequency, of symptom complaints (Diefenbach et al., 1996).

## Attention and Symptoms: The Competition-of-Cues Model

In the laboratory, people are especially likely to notice physical symptoms if instructed to focus on their bodily sensations—symptom reports decline when attention is directed away from the self (Fillingim & Fine, 1986; Padgett & Hill, 1989; Pennebaker & Lightner, 1980; Watson & Pennebaker, 1991). Similarly, symptom reports increase when occupational or residential settings are uninteresting or routine (Moos & Van Dort, 1977; National Center for Health Statistics, 1980; Wan, 1976). A recent finding by Feldman et al. (1999) suggested that the personality dimension of Openness to Experience, which incorporates a tendency to attend closely to feelings and sensations, may be positively related to symptom reports among individuals who are ill. The attentional perspective is summarized by Pennebaker's competition-of-cues model (1982), which posits that the situation competes for limited attentional resources. When the environment is demanding or engaging, sensory information that might otherwise have been labeled as a symptom goes unnoticed.

## Social Influence in Symptom Perception

Laypeople often discuss symptoms with family members and friends. These social interactions appear to influence symptom perception in at least three ways. First, many lay consultations occur in attempt to clarify and understand the meaning of a particular symptom (Cameron et al., 1993). Second, exposure to others who are ill can induce self-monitoring for similar symptoms. Family history similarly sensitizes people to the appearance and meaning of certain symptoms (Turk, Litt, Salovey, & Walker, 1985). Finally, the phenomenon of mass psychogenic illness illustrates how others can influence symptom perception, even in the absence of pathology (Colligan, Pennebaker, & Murphy, 1982). Kerckhoff and Back (1968) described an episode in which a factory was forced to close because large numbers of employees attributed nausea to an infestation of mysterious bugs. The Center for Disease Control failed to identify any objective source for the workers' complaints and instead concluded that the stressful factory environment and exposure to others with similar complaints led to hysterical contagion. In other words, ambiguous symptoms took on new meaning as a function of the social environment.

Lay support networks further influence illness behaviors. Lay networks sometimes sanction close others who appear to need medical attention (Cameron et al., 1993). Disruption of family or work responsibilities often encourages self-referral (Apple, 1960; Zola, 1973). However, the lay network sometimes discourages care seeking, especially if members dislike or fear the health care system (Suls & Goodkin, 1994). Surprisingly, strong social networks have been found to impede self-referral (Berkanovic, Telesky, & Reeder 1981), perhaps because members are encouraged to remain active and involved, despite symptoms.

## Naïve Theories of Illness as a Function of Culture

Most women in the United States characterize menopause as a disorder warranting medical intervention (Leiblum & Swartzman, 1986). However, Rajput, Thai, and Mayan women tend to perceive menopause as a positive transition that frees them from the burdens of childbearing and other social restrictions (Beyene, 1986; Chirawitkul & Manderson, 1994; Flint & Samil, 1990). Interestingly, women from these cultural groups report far fewer menopausal symptoms than their Western counterparts. This example demonstrates the effects of culture on symptom perception, illness representation, and health behaviors.

Empirical evidence from medical anthropologists indicates that all illness representations are structured (Helman, 1985). That is, laypeople develop detailed naïve theories of illness regardless of locale or ethnicity. What differs across cultures is the particular content or type of information that becomes incorporated into illness representations. For example, in North America, where treatment expectations tend to approximate the biomedical model (Peters et al., 1998), a feverish toddler is likely to receive acetaminophen. In contrast, a feverish child in Southeast Asia may be treated by rubbing oiled skin with the edge of a coin (Pachter, 1994). Fever is labeled as a symptom in both environments; however, beliefs regarding control and cure differ.

## The Media as Sources of 'Expert' Medical Advice

In Western nations, the media has emerged as a powerful source of influence effecting the perception of both organic and psychogenic symptoms (Shorter, 1992, 1995). Exposure to mass media health presentations has shifted the power balance between patients and health care providers. Where practitioners once were viewed as the sole purveyors of expert medical information, television and the internet now allow patients to enter a physician's office equipped with sophisticated and potentially demanding expectations (Shorter, 1992, 1995). For example, the press coverage that accompanied the publication of a *New England Journal of Medicine* paper regarding findings that chronic heartburn predicted esophageal cancer (Lagergren, Bergström, Lindgren, & Nyrén, 1999) prompted thousands of heartburn sufferers to seek medical attention (Brody, 1999). Most care seekers had suffered heartburn for some time and previously had been treated by gastroenterologists for the condition (Brody, 1999). This suggests that self-referral was not a consequence of changes in symptomology per se, but by media-induced changes in sufferers' cognitive and emotional responses to heartburn episodes.

## Culture and Psychogenic Symptoms

Freud postulated that repressed childhood traumas often were at the root of psychogenic symptoms (Freud, 1933; Shorter, 1992). This perspective persists in modern psychoanalysis, with the view that somatization occurs when our usual coping strategies are inadequate (McDougall, 1989). However, the hysterical paralysis so common among Freud's clientele has become rare. Instead, fatigue and pain top the list of modern psychogenic complaints (Shorter, 1992, 1995). This shift reflects the influence of culture on symptom presentations. A wide variety of symptoms can be provoked through psychogenic processes (e.g., sensations, motor changes, pain; Shorter, 1992). Which psychogenic symptoms predominate in any given setting is a function of culture. Somatization appears to be more common in non-industrialized settings (Angel & Guarnaccia, 1989; Katon, Kleinman, & Rosen, 1982; Kirmayer, 1984). Within Western cultures, somatization is negatively correlated with income and education (Kleinman & Kleinman, 1985; Leff, 1977; Mezzich & Raab, 1980). The tendency for psychogenic symptoms to change in prevalence and configuration appears to have been overlooked in the DSM-IV, which includes specific symptom sets in its diagnostic criteria for the somatoform disorders (Fink, 1996).

## CONCLUSION

We opened this chapter with the observation that some people delay seeking medical attention for life-threatening conditions, whereas others oversubscribe to health services for minor or psychogenic maladies. We have discussed a wide range of variables—affective, cognitive, and contextual—which may account for these two divergent patterns of health care utilization. The dynamic effects of these variables can be observed in a final example, which contrasts two individuals both suffering chest pain. The first, a woman, loses valuable time experimenting with home remedies and fails to realize she is suffering an evolving MI until several precious hours have passed. If fortunate enough to survive, she may very well report that it had never occurred to her that, as a woman, she might succumb to heart disease. The second chest pain sufferer, a man, immediately assumes that his midsternal heaviness must be an impending heart attack. His alarmed wife concurs and rushes him to the hospital. An invasive, inpatient work-up ultimately reveals that the discomfort was simply due to indigestion. An antacid would have resolved the discomfort safely. These disparate responses are difficult to reconcile without attention to the findings considered in the present chapter—cognitive, affective, and contextual variables allow us to make sense of both behavioral responses. Thus, naïve theories of illness have the potential to elucidate otherwise mysterious misses and false alarms. Finally, the cognitive, affective, and contextual variables that shape naïve theories of illness provide an underlying framework for this volume's discussions of health anxiety and hypochondriasis.

**Authors' Note:** Direct correspondence to René Martin, Department of Psychology, 11 Seashore Hall E, University of Iowa, Iowa City, IA 52242. Electronic mail: rene-martin@uiowa.edu. Preparation of this chapter was supported, in part, by the American Heart Association/Iowa Affiliate Beginning Grant-in-Aid, 98-06373X.

## REFERENCES

Anderson, J.R. (1987). *The architecture of cognition*. Cambridge, MA: Harvard University Press.

Anderson, J.R. (1993). *The adaptive character of thought*. Hillsdale, NJ: Erlbaum.

Aneshensel, C.S., Frerichs, R.R., & Huba, G.J. (1984). Depression and physical illness: A multiwave, nonrecursive causal model. *Journal of Health and Social Behavior*, **13**, 219–228.

Angel, R., & Guarnaccia, P.J. (1989). Mind, body, and culture: Somatization among Hispanics. *Social Science and Medicine*, **28**, 1229–1238.

Apple, D. (1960). How laymen define illness. *Journal of Health and Social Behavior*, **13**, 219–228.

Backett, E.M., Heady, J.A., & Evans, J.C. (1954). Studies of a general practice: II The doctor's job in an urban area. *British Medical Journal*, **1**, 109–123.

Barsky, A. (1981). Hidden reasons some patients visit doctors. *Annals of Internal Medicine*, **94**, 492–497.

Bauman, L.J., Cameron, L.D., Zimmerman, R.S., & Leventhal, H. (1989). Illness representations and matching labels with symptoms. *Health Psychology*, **8**, 449–469.

Bauman, L.J., & Leventhal, H. (1985). I can tell when my blood pressure is up, can't I? *Health Psychology*, **4**, 203–218.

Berkanovic, E., Telesky, C., & Reeder, S. (1981). Structural and social psychological factors in the decision to seek medical care for symptoms. *Medical Care*, **19**, 693–709.

Beyene, Y. (1986). Cultural significance and physiological manifestations of menopause: A biocultural analysis. *Culture, Medicine, and Psychiatry*, **10**, 47–71.

Bishop, G.D. (1984). Gender, role, and illness behavior in a military population. *Health Psychology*, **3**, 519–534.

Bishop, G.D. (1991). Understanding the understanding of illness: Lay disease representations. In J.A. Skelton & R.T. Croyle (Eds.), *Mental representations in health and illness* (pp. 32–59). New York: Springer-Verlag.

Bishop, G.D., Briede, C., Cavazos, L., Grotzinger, R., & McMahon, S. (1987). Processing illness information: The role of disease prototypes. *Basic and Applied Social Psychology*, **8**, 21–43.

Bishop, G.D., & Converse, S.A. (1986). Illness representations: A prototype approach. *Health Psychology*, **5**, 95–114.

Blaxter, M. (1983). The cause of disease: Women talking. *Social Science and Medicine*, **17**, 59–69.

Borawski, E., Kinney, J., & Kahana, E. (1996). The meaning of older adults health appraisals: Congruence with health status and determinant of mortality. *Journal of Gerontology: Social Sciences*, **51B**, S157–170.

Brody, J.E. (1999, April 27). Chronic heartburn, an ominous warning. *The New York Times*, p. D6.

Brownlee, S., Leventhal, E.A., & Leventhal, H. (in press). Regulation, self-regulation, and regulation of the self in maintaining physical health. In M. Boekartz, P.R. Pintrich, & M. Zeidner (Eds.), *Handbook of self-regulation*. San Diego, CA: Academic Press.

Cameron, L., Leventhal, E.A., & Leventhal, H. (1993). Symptom representation and affect as determinants of care seeking in a community-dwelling, adult sample population. *Health Psychology*, **12**, 171–179.

Cameron, L., Leventhal, E.A., & Leventhal, H. (1995). Seeking medical care in response to symptoms and life stress. *Psychosomatic Medicine*, **57**, 37–47.

Carver, C.S., Scheier, M.F., & Weintraub, J.K. (1989). Assessing coping strategies: A theoretically based approach. *Journal of Personality and Social Psychology*, **56**, 267–283.

Chirawitkul, T., & Manderson, L. (1994). Perception of menopause in Northeast Thailand: Contested meaning and practice. *Social Science and Medicine*, **39**, 1545–1554.

Clark, M. (1959). *Health in the Mexican-American culture*. Berkley, CA: University of California Press.

Cohen, S., Doyle, W.J., Skoner, D.P., Fireman, P., Gwaltney Jr., J.M., & Newsom, J.T. (1995). State and trait negative affect as predictors of objective and subjective symptoms of respiratory viral infections. *Journal of Personality and Social Psychology*, **68**, 159–169.

Colligan, M., Pennebaker, J.W., & Murphy, L. (Eds.) (1982). *Mass psychogenic illness: A social psychological perspective*. Hillsdale, NJ: Erlbaum.

Corney, R.H. (1990). Sex differences in general practice attendance and help seeking for minor illness. *Journal of Psychosomatic Research*, **34**, 525–534.

Costa, P.T., & McCrae, R.R. (1980). Somatic complaints in males as a function of age and neuroticism: A longitudinal analysis. *Journal of Behavioral Medicine*, **3**, 245–257.

Costa, P.T., & McCrae, R.R. (1985). Hypochondriasis, neuroticism and aging: When are somatic complaints unfounded? *American Psychologist*, **40**, 19–28.

Costa, P.T., & McCrae, R.R. (1987). Neuroticism, somatic complaints and disease: Is the bark worse than the bite? *Journal of Personality*, **55**, 299–306.

Davis, M.A. (1981). Sex differences in reporting osteoarthritic symptoms: A socio-medical approach. *Journal of Health and Social Behavior*, **22**, 298–310.

Davison, K.P., & Pennebaker, J.W. (1996). Social psychosomatics. In E.T. Higgins & A.W. Kruglanski (Eds.), *Social psychology: Handbook of basic principles* (pp. 102–130). New York: Guilford.

Diefenbach, M.A., Leventhal, E.A., Leventhal, H., & Patrick-Miller, L. (1996). Negative affect relates to cross-sectional but not longitudinal symptom reporting: Data from elderly adults. *Health Psychology*, **15**, 282–288.

Ditto, P.H., & Jemmott, J.B., III. (1989). From rarity to evaluative extremity: Effects of prevalence information on evaluations of positive and negative characteristics. *Journal of Personality and Social Psychology*, **57**, 16–26.

Dollard, J., & Miller, N.E. (1950). *Personality and psychotherapy*. New York: McGraw-Hill.

Dracup, K., & Moser, D.K. (1997). Beyond sociodemographics: Factors influencing the decision to seek treatment for symptoms of acute myocardial infarction. *Heart and Lung*, **26**, 253–262.

Feldman, P.J., Cohen, S., Doyle, W.J., Skoner, D.P., & Gwaltney, J.M. (1999). The impact of personality on the reporting of unfounded symptoms and illness. *Journal of Personality and Social Psychology*, **77**, 370–378.

Fillingim, R.B., & Fine, M.A. (1986). The effects of internal versus external information processing on symptom perception in an exercise setting. *Health Psychology*, **5**, 115–123.

Fink, P. (1996). Somatization—beyond symptom count. *Journal of Psychosomatic Research*, **40**, 7–10.

Fiske, S.T., & Taylor, S.E. (1991). *Social cognition* (2nd edn.). New York: McGraw-Hill, Inc.

Flint, M., & Samil, R.S. (1990). Cultural and subcultural meanings of the menopause. *Annals of New York Academy of Sciences*, **592**, 134–148.

Freud, S. (1933). *New introductory lectures on psychoanalysis* (J. Strachey, Trans.). New York: Norton.

FTT Collaborative Group (1994). Indications for fibrinolytic therapy in suspected acute myocardial infarction: Collaborative overview of early mortality and major morbidity results from all randomized trials of more than 1000 patients. *Lancet*, **8893**, 311–322.

Gijsbers van Wijk, C.M.T., & Kolk, A.M. (1997). Sex differences in physical symptoms: The contribution of symptom perception theory. *Social Science and Medicine*, **46**, 231–246.

Goff, D.C., Sellers, D.E., McGovern, P.G., Meischke, H., Goldberg, R.J., Bittner, V., Hedges, J.R., Allender, P.S., & Nichaman, M.Z. (1998). Knowledge of heart attack symptoms in a population survey in the United States. *Archives of Internal Medicine*, **158**, 2329–2338.

Green, D.M., & Swets, J.A. (1974). *Signal detection theory and psychophysics*. New York: Krieger.

Heider, F. (1958). *The psychology of interpersonal relations*. New York: Wiley.

Helman, C.G. (1985). Psyche, soma and society: The social construction of psychosomatic disorders. *Culture and Medicine in Psychiatry*, **9**, 1–26.

Hibbard J.J., & Pope, C.R. (1983). Gender roles, illness orientation, and use of medical services. *Social Science and Medicine*, **17**, 129–137.

Ingham, I., & Miller, P. (1979). Symptom prevalence and severity in a general practice. *Journal of Epidemiology and Community Health*, **33**, 191–198.

Janz, N., & Becker, M. (1984). The health belief model: A decade later. *Health Education Quarterly*, **2**, 1–47.

Katon, W., Kleinman, A., & Rosen, G. (1982). Depression and somatization: A review, Part I. *American Journal of Medicine*, **72**, 127–135.

Kerckhoff, A.C., & Back, K.W. (1968) *The June Bug: A story of hysterical contagion*. New York: Appleton-Century-Crofts.

Kirmayer, L.J. (1984). Culture, affect and somatization, Part I. *Transcultural Psychiatric Research Review*, **21**, 159–188.

Kleinman, A., & Kleinman, J. (1985). Somatization: The interconnections in Chinese society among culture, depressive experiences, and the meanings of pain. In A. Kleinman & B. Good (Eds.), *Culture and depression: Studies in the anthropology and cross cultural psychiatry of affect and disorder* (pp. 420–290). Berkeley, CA: University of California Press.

Kubzansky, L.D., Kawachi, I., Weiss, S.T., & Sparrow, D. (1998). Anxiety and coronary heart disease: A synthesis of epidemiological, psychological, and experimental evidence. *Annals of Behavioral Medicine*, **20**, 47–58.

Lagergren, J., Bergström, R., Lindgren, A., & Nyrén, O. (1999). Symptomatic gastroesophageal reflux as a risk factor for esophageal adenocarcinoma. *New England Journal of Medicine*, **340**, 825–831.

Lau, R.R. (1997). Cognitive representations of health and illness. In D.S. Gochman (Ed.), *Handbook of health behavior research I: Personal and social determinants* (pp. 51–69). New York: Plenum.

Lazarus, R.S., & Folkman, S. (1984). *Stress, appraisal and coping*. New York: Springer.

Leff, J. (1977). The cross-cultural study of emotions. *Culture, Medicine and Psychiatry*, **1**, 317–350.

Leiblum, S.R., & Swartzman, L.C. (1986). Women's attitudes toward the menopause: An update. *Maturitas*, **8**, 47–56.

Leventhal, E.A., & Crouch, M. (1997). Are there differences in perceptions of illness across the lifespan? In K.J. Petrie & J.A. Weinman (Eds.), *Perceptions of health and illness: Current research and applications* (pp. 77–102). London: Harwood Academic Press.

Leventhal, E.A., Hansell, S., Diefenbach, M., Leventhal, H., & Glass, D.C. (1996). Negative affect and self-report of physical symptoms: Two longitudinal studies of older adults. *Health Psychology*, **15**, 193–199.

Leventhal, E.A., Leventhal, H., Schaefer, P., & Easterling, D. (1993). Conservation of energy, uncertainty reduction and swift utilization of medical care among the elderly. *Journal of Gerontology: Psychological Sciences*, **48**, 78–86.

Leventhal, H. (1970). Findings and theory in the study of fear communications. In L. Berkowitz (Ed.), *Advances in experimental social psychology* (Vol. 5, pp. 119–186). San Diego, CA: Academic Press.

Leventhal, H., Benyamini, Y., Brownlee, S., Diefenbach, M., Leventhal, E.A., Patrick-Miller, L., & Robitaille, C. (1997). Illness representations: Theoretical foundations. In K.J. Petrie & J.A. Weinman (Eds.), *Perceptions of health and illness* (pp. 19–45). Australia: Harwood Academic.

Leventhal, H., & Diefenbach, M. (1991). The active side of illness cognition. In J.A.

Skelton & R.T. Croyle (Eds.), *Mental representation in health and illness* (pp. 247–272). New York: Springer-Verlag.

Leventhal, H., Singer, R., & Jones, S. (1965). Effects of fear and specificity of recommendations upon attitudes and behavior. *Journal of Personality and Social Psychology*, **2**, 20–29.

Leventhal, H., Watts, J.C., & Pagano, F. (1967). Effects of fear and instructions on how to cope with danger. *Journal of Personality and Social Psychology*, **6**, 313–321.

Levine, J., Warrenburg, S., Kerns, R., Schwartz, G., Delaney, R., Fontana, A., Gradman, A., Smith, S., Allen, S., & Cascione, R. (1987). The role of denial in recovery from coronary heart disease. *Psychosomatic Medicine*, **49**, 109–117.

Macintyre, S. (1993). Gender differences in the perceptions of common cold symptoms. *Social Science and Medicine*, **36**, 15–20.

Marchant-Haycox, S., & Salmon, P. (1997). Patients' and doctors' strategies in consultations with unexplained symptoms: Interactions of gynecologists with women presenting menstrual problems. *Psychosomatics*, **38**, 440–450.

Marshall, J.R., & Funch, D.P. (1986). Gender and illness behavior among colorectal cancer patients. *Women and Health*, **11**, 67–82.

Martin, R., Gordon, E.E.I., & Lounsbury, P. (1998). Gender disparities in the attribution of cardiac-related symptoms: Contribution of common sense models of illness. *Health Psychology*, **17**, 346–357.

Martin, R., & Lemos, K. (2000). Effects of stereotypes on symptom perception and illness behavior. A. Rothman (Chair), Understanding the impact of stereotypes, discrimination, and prejudice on mental and physical health. *Midwestern Psychological Association*, May 4 2000, Chicago, IL.

McDougall, J. (1989). *Theatres of the body: A psychoanalytic approach to psychosomatic illness*. New York: W.W. Norton & Company.

Meyer, D., Leventhal, H., & Gutmann, M. (1985). Common-sense models of illness: The example of hypertension. *Health Psychology*, **4**, 115–135.

Mezzich, J., & Raab, E. (1980). Depressive symptomology across the Americas. *Archives of General Psychiatry*, **37**, 818–823.

Miller, N.E. (1951). Learnable drives and rewards. In S.S. Stevens (Ed.), *Handbook of experimental psychology* (pp. 435–472). New York: Wiley.

Moos, R., & Van Dort, B. (1977). Physical and emotional symptoms and campus health center utilization. *Social Psychiatry*, **12**, 107–115.

National Center for Health Statistics (1980). *Geographic patterns in the risk of dying and associated factors ages 35–74 years* (Vol. 18). Washington, DC: U.S. Government Printing Office.

Pachter, L.M. (1994). Culture and clinical care: Folk illness beliefs and behaviors and their implications for health care delivery. *Journal of the American Medical Association*, **271**, 690–694.

Padgett, V.R., & Hill, A.K. (1989). Maximizing athletic performance in endurance events: A comparison of coping strategies. *Journal of Applied Social Psychology*, **19**, 331–340.

Pennebaker, J.W. (1982). *The psychology of physical symptoms*. New York: Springer Verlag.

Pennebaker, J.W., & Lightner, J.M. (1980). Competition of internal and external information in an exercise setting. *Journal of Personality and Social Psychology*, **51**, 468–496.

Peters, S., Stanley, I., Rose, M., & Salmon, P. (1998). Patients with medically unexplained symptoms: Sources of patients' authority and implications for demands on medical care. *Social Science and Medicine*, **46**, 559–565.

Prohaska, T.R., Keller, M.L., Leventhal, E.A., & Leventhal, H. (1987). Impact of symptoms and aging attribution on emotions and coping. *Health Psychology*, **6**, 495–514.

Rustige, J., Schiele, R., Burczyk, U., Koch, A., Gottwik, M., Neuhaus, K.L., Tebbe, U., Uebis, R., & Senges, J. (1997). The 60 minutes myocardial infarction project: Treatment and clinical outcome of patients with acute myocardial infarction in Germany. *European Heart Journal*, **18**, 1438–1446.

Safer, M., Tharps, D., Jackson, T., & Leventhal, H. (1979). Determinants of three stages of delay in seeking care at a medical center. *Medical Care*, **17**, 11–29.

Scambler, G., & Scambler, A. (1985). The illness iceberg and aspects of consulting behavior. In R. Fitzpatrick & J. Hinton (Eds.), *The experience of illness* (pp. 32–50). London: Tavistock.

Sharkey, S.W., Brunette, D.D., Ruiz, E., Hession, W.T., Wysham, D.G., & Goldenberg, I.F. (1989). An analysis of time delays preceding thrombolysis for acute myocardial infarction. *Journal of American Medical Association*, **262**, 3171–3174.

Shorter, E. (1992). *From paralysis to fatigue: A history of psychosomatic illness*. New York: Free Press.

Shorter, E. (1995). Sucker-punched again! Physicians meet the disease-of-the-month syndrome. *Journal of Psychosomatic Research*, **39**, 115–118.

Shumaker, S.A., & Smith, T.R. (1994). The politics of women's health. *Journal of Social Issues*, **50**, 189–202.

Skelton, J.A., & Croyle, R.T. (1991). Mental representations, health, and illness: An introduction. In J.A. Skelton & R.T. Croyle (Eds.), *Mental representations in health and illness* (pp. 1–9). New York: Springer-Verlag.

Smith, C.A., Wallston, K.A., & Dwyer, K.A. (1995). On babies and bathwater: Disease impact and negative affectivity in the self-reports of persons with rheumatoid arthritis. *Health Psychology*, **14**, 64–73.

Stoller, E.P. (1997). Medical self-care: Lay management of symptoms by elderly people. In M.G. Ory & G. De Fries (Eds.), *Self-care in later life: Research, program, and policy issues* (pp. 24–61). New York: Springer.

Suls, J., & Fletcher, B. (1985). The relative efficacy of avoidant and nonavoidant coping strategies: A meta-analysis. *Health Psychology*, **4**, 249–288.

Suls, J., & Goodkin, F. (1994). Medical gossip and rumor: Their role in the lay referral system. In R.F. Goodman & A. Ben-Zeev (Eds.), *Good gossip* (pp. 169–179). Lawrence, KS: University Press of Kansas.

Turk, D.C., Litt, M.D., Salovey, P., & Walker, J. (1985). Seeking urgent pediatric treatment: Factors contributing to frequency, delay, and appropriateness. *Health Psychology*, **4**, 43–59.

Verbrugge, L.M. (1989). The twain meet: Empirical explanations of sex differences in health and mortality. *Journal of Health and Social Behavior*, **30**, 282–304.

Wan, T. (1976). Predicting self-assessed health status: A multivariate approach. *Health Services Research*, **11**, 464–477.

Watson, D., & Pennebaker, J.W. (1989). Health complaints, stress, and distress: Exploring the central role of negative affectivity. *Psychological Review*, **96**, 234–254.

Watson, D., & Pennebaker, J.W. (1991). Situational, dispositional and genetic bases of symptom reporting. In J.A. Skelton & R.T. Croyle (Eds.), *Mental representations in health and illness* (pp. 60–84). New York: Springer Verlag.

Wingard, D.L., Cohn, B.A., Cirillo, P.M., Cohen, R.D., & Kaplan, G.A. (1992). Gender differences in self-reported heart disease morbidity: Are intervention opportunities missed for women? *Journal of Women's Health*, **1**, 201–208.

Zola, I. (1973). Pathways to the doctor: From person to patient. *Social Science and Medicine*, **7**, 577–689.

Chapter 3

# MAKING SENSE OF HYPOCHONDRIASIS: A COGNITIVE MODEL OF HEALTH ANXIETY

*Paul M. Salkovskis\* and Hilary M.C. Warwick†*

## INTRODUCTION

It is now widely accepted that anxiety is best understood as a reaction to perceived threat (Beck, 1976; Beck, Emery, & Greenberg, 1985). The more important and imminent the threat, the greater the anxiety likely to be experienced. Thus, those issues which people perceive as being most important to their welfare will be particularly likely to form the focus of anxiety problems and disorders. Threats to physical health are, of course, regarded by most people to be especially important. It is therefore not surprising that anxiety focused upon health is an almost universal phenomenon, and that persistent anxiety about health is common both in the community and in the clinic (Barsky & Klerman, 1983; Barsky, Wyshak, Klerman, & Latham, 1990). Hypochondriasis as a diagnosis can be readily conceptualized as the most extreme manifestation of severe and persistent anxiety focused upon health threat (Salkovskis & Rimes, 1997).

\*Institute of Psychiatry, University of London, London, SE5 8AF; †Department of Psychiatry, St George's Hospital Medical School, London, SW17 0RE

*Health Anxiety*
Edited by G.J.G. Asmundson, S. Taylor & B.J. Cox
© 2001 John Wiley & Sons Ltd.

## THE BASIS OF PERSISTENT HEALTH ANXIETY IN COGNITIVE PHENOMENA

The cognitive-behavioral hypothesis of hypochondriasis proposes that the central mechanism in people suffering from persistent health anxiety and hypochondriasis is a relatively enduring tendency to misinterpret bodily symptoms, bodily variations, and other information regarded as relevant to health as evidence of serious physical illness (Salkovskis, 1989, 1996a; Salkovskis & Clark, 1993; Salkovskis & Warwick, 1986; Warwick & Salkovskis, 1990). The impact of misinterpretations varies according to the degree of threat perceived, which is, in turn, a function of at least four factors. The most obvious of these factors is the perceived likelihood of illness, which interacts with the perceived awfulness of that illness. This factor can not only include factors such as the pain and suffering of being ill, but the more general consequences such as loss of role, upset, and disturbance to loved ones.

The other modulating factors are the extent to which the person perceives him- or herself as likely to be able to prevent the illness from worsening and the extent to which he or she is able to affect its course (i.e., having effective means of coping with the perceived threat and the possibility of external factors intervening to help). In health anxiety, this latter aspect often focuses on the likely effectiveness of medical help. In the worst case, some patients perceive 'rescue factors' as having a negative value—for example, believing that treatment of a cancer would be worse than the cancer itself.

Taken together, the interaction between these different aspects of appraisal can be represented as:

$$\text{Anxiety} = \frac{\begin{bmatrix}\text{Perceived likelihood} \\ \text{of illness}\end{bmatrix} \times \begin{bmatrix}\text{Perceived cost, awfulness} \\ \text{and burden of the illness}\end{bmatrix}}{\begin{bmatrix}\text{Perceived ability} \\ \text{to cope with the} \\ \text{illness}\end{bmatrix} \times \begin{bmatrix}\text{Perception of the extent} \\ \text{to which external factors} \\ \text{will help (rescue factors)}\end{bmatrix}}$$

Elevations in the patient's perceived likelihood of being ill thus *interacts* with the perceived awfulness of their feared illness, which in itself will often be inflated. An important implication of this analysis is that it is possible to be highly anxious about health despite relatively low perceived likelihood of illness, given a relatively high perception of the awfulness of being ill (e.g., people who believe that having cancer would result in being crippled by pain, disabled, becoming physically repulsive, being rejected and abandoned by those they love, and generally being

dehumanized). Furthermore, if such awfulness beliefs are not only prominent but also coupled with a *high* perceived likelihood of illness, very
extreme levels of anxiety are to be expected. Anxiety would be further
increased if the health anxious patient perceives him- or herself as unable
to prevent the illness, and unable to affect its course (i.e., as having no
effective means of coping with the perceived threat).

All four of these factors often need to be taken into account both in the
formulation and in any treatment interventions. It is also important to
note that the factors identified here as important to health anxiety are
those involved not only in other anxiety disorders, but also in normal
anxiety (Beck et al., 1985).

## THE ORIGINS AND MAINTENANCE OF
## MISINTERPRETATIONS

The cognitive model suggests that the *origins and development* of the tendency to misinterpret health-relevant information can most commonly be
understood in terms of the way in which knowledge and past experiences
of illness (in self or others) leads to the formation of assumptions about
symptoms, disease, health behaviors, the medical profession, and so on.
These assumptions predispose the person to develop health anxiety
when critical incidents mesh with the assumptions to generate specific
misinterpretations. Less frequently, relatively severe critical incidents may
directly trigger severe and prolonged episodes of health anxiety. Such
events can have the effect of invalidating previously held positive
attitudes about health. For example, a woman in whom a smear test and
subsequent investigations revealed that she had developed cancer moved
from the belief that 'your health looks after itself' to the idea that 'you can
be struck down by serious or even fatal illnesses at any time and without
warning'. It should always be remembered that actually being ill is a
particularly potent vulnerability factor for anxiety becoming focused on
health, especially when the illness is of a serious nature.

Figure 3.1 illustrates the cognitive model of the development of health
anxiety. General health-related assumptions can arise from a wide variety
of sources, including early health- and illness-related experience, later
events such as unexpected or unpleasant illness in the person's social
circle, and information in the mass media. Many of the assumptions
learned are likely to be universal or shared by many others of similar cultural backgrounds. Socialized beliefs concerning possible sources of misinterpretation make the understanding of health anxiety relatively easier.
The type of assumptions considered to be likely to lead to more severe
and persistent health anxiety are those which are relatively rigid and

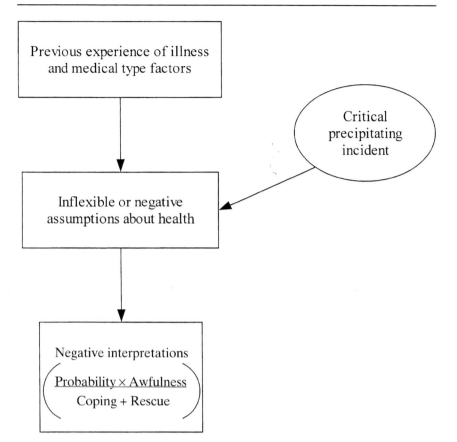

**Figure 3.1**  Cognitive model of the development of health anxiety.

extreme. For example, most people will share the assumption that 'persistent and intense physical discomfort of an unusual and unexplained type could be a sign of ill health'. The person prone to health anxiety, by contrast, will tend to believe that 'any unexplained change in my body is always going to be a sign of serious illness'. The former assumption is likely to be helpful in that it may lead to an acceptable level of consultation motivated by health concern. The latter assumption, on the other hand, is more likely to lead to constant self-monitoring of bodily variations and both frequent medical consultation and extreme fear reactions motivated by overly negative interpretations of benign situations and stimuli.

Previous experience of physical ill-health in patients and their families and previous experience of unsatisfactory medical management may also be important in generating problematic assumptions about risks to health. Examples of the type of potentially problematic assumptions which can lead to misinterpretations are 'bodily changes are usually a sign of serious disease, because every symptom has to have an identifiable physical cause' and 'if you don't go to the doctor as soon as you notice anything unusual then it will be too late'. Other beliefs relate to specific personal weaknesses and particular illnesses; for example, 'there's heart trouble in the family' and 'I've had weak lungs since I was a baby'. Such beliefs may be a constant source of anxiety and may be activated in vulnerable individuals by critical incidents.

## MISINTERPRETATIONS AND FACTORS INVOLVED IN THE MAINTENANCE OF HEALTH ANXIETY

Assumptions can also lead the patient to selectively attend to information that appears to confirm the idea of having an illness, and to selectively ignore or discount evidence indicating good health. A self-maintaining *confirmatory bias* can therefore occur once a critical incident has activated health-related assumptions and resulted in the misinterpretation of bodily variations or health information as indications of serious illness (Hitchcock & Mathews, 1992). Situations that constitute critical incidents and activate previously dormant assumptions include unfamiliar bodily sensations, hearing details of illness in a friend of a similar age, or new information about illness. Further bodily sensations may then be noticed as a consequence of increased vigilance arising from anxiety. In patients who become particularly anxious about their health, such situations are associated with thoughts that represent personally catastrophic interpretations of the bodily sensations or signs. These misinterpretations drive and motivate a number of reactions which can not only have the effect of maintaining the misinterpretations themselves, but also of generating further stimuli which act as further sources of misinterpretation.

Figure 3.2 shows how a cognitive model accounts for the way in which assumptions, critical incidents, and misinterpretations interact with some of the factors involved in intensifying and maintaining the perceived threat (and, therefore, anxiety) in people suffering from severe and persistent health anxiety. When patients become particularly anxious about their health, their preoccupation with such negative interpretations (experienced as personally catastrophic thoughts and images) will focus on bodily variations and other information that is appraised as relevant to their (ill) health. Catastrophic interpretations can, in turn, lead to one of two patterns of anxiety (or some combination thereof). If the sensations or signs are *not* primarily those that increase as a direct result of the

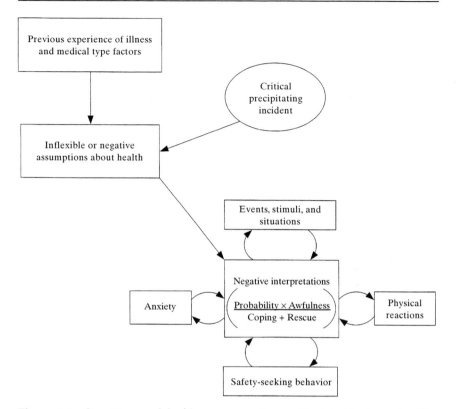

**Figure 3.2** Cognitive model of how assumptions, critical incidents, and misinterpretations interact in health anxiety.

experience of anxiety (including, but not confined to, the consequences of autonomic arousal), or the patient does *not* regard the feared catastrophe as imminent (e.g., 'these palpitations are the first sign of heart disease'), then the reaction will be more likely to be that typical of the anxious preoccupation and anxiety focused on health common to patients with a diagnosis of hypochondriasis. On the other hand, if the symptoms that are misinterpreted *are* those that occur as part of anxiety-induced autonomic arousal *and* the interpretation is that the symptoms are evidence of *immediate* catastrophe (e.g., 'these palpitations mean that I am having a heart attack right now'), a further immediate increase in symptoms will result. If this process continues unchecked, it will spiral out of control and a panic attack is the more likely response.

There are reasons to consider that the two problems often overlap. While the panic-type response is likely to be confined to sensations subject to rapid increase when anxious, both anxiety-related and anxiety-unrelated symptoms may play a part in the concerns of hypochondriacal patients. Also, although hypochondriacal patients may characteristically believe that the catastrophe will occur in the more distant future, when the problem follows a chronic course they may reach the point where they think that the time has now come, at which point panic becomes a disturbing complication of their condition.

Negative or even catastrophic interpretations of health-relevant information are commonplace. From time to time, the majority of people are liable to become briefly preoccupied with unexplained bodily variations. However, such episodes of health anxiety are usually transient. Symptoms fade, reassuring information from our doctor is absorbed with relief, and our anxiety about health declines and disappears. Clearly, the key to understanding and helping those in whom this health anxiety does not fade (or in whom it escalates to the point where it dominates their life) lies in understanding what it is that causes their anxiety to *persist*. The cognitive model makes a simple prediction. The persistence of health anxiety is a result of processes that maintain the interpretations from which the anxiety arises. As each of these factors and processes is motivated by threat beliefs, either as an automatic reaction or as strategically deployed responses to the perception of threat, a particular pattern of vicious circles form (as shown in Figure 3.2).

Although the relative contribution of each factor, and the specific details of those which are involved varies from person to person, four main types of process tend to be involved. These are information processing biases (particularly selective attention), physiological reactions (including, but not confined to, heightened experience of bodily sensations), safety-seeking behaviors (including avoidance, checking and reassurance seeking), and affective changes (particularly anxiety and depression).

## Biases in the Way Threat Information is Processed

Once people begin actively to contemplate the possibility that they are suffering from a serious physical illness, their attention understandably turns to gathering evidence relevant to this possibility. Most people will have a tendency to err on the side of caution, as the consequences of a false negative decision (e.g., mistakenly believing that one is healthy when cancer is present and, therefore, failing to take appropriate preventative action) are considerably more serious than those of a false positive decision (e.g., deciding that one has cancer when this is not so). Patients with persistent health anxiety may be particularly aware of this difference and, therefore, consider anything less than *complete certainty* that they are healthy as inadequate. Attention is selectively focused on information which *could be* consistent with illness, while information which is inconsistent with illness beliefs tends to be disregarded as, at best, insufficient, and, at worst, irrelevant. This phenomenon, often known as a confirmatory bias, is further bolstered by other assumptions prominent in health anxiety, such as 'if I do not worry about my health, then I am likely become ill' (Warwick & Salkovskis, submitted).

Selective attention is the most obvious manifestation of cognitive bias. Hypochondriacal patients notice (and attach special significance to) stimuli consistent with their health beliefs and either fail to notice or disregard inconsistent stimuli. Thus, the patients concerned about their heart may notice palpitations that occur after they have gone to bed, thinking them a sign of cardiac weakness, but failing to notice that their heart responds appropriately (and imperceptibly) to their having to run to catch a bus. Apart from resulting in increased preoccupation with bodily variations, selective attention can also operate to bias the impact of information provided by doctors in the course of medical consultation.

Once illness fears are activated, attention may be paid to previously unnoticed normal bodily changes (e.g., gastric distention after eating). The fact that these bodily variations had not previously been noticed can lead a person to conclude that they were new phenomena and, therefore, represent the effects of pathological processes. Focusing prompted by worries about health thus brings slight bodily variations to awareness at times when ideas about illness are already present, leading to a bias towards noticing information that is consistent with beliefs about being seriously ill.

## Interactions Between Misinterpretations and Bodily Sensations

Intense anxiety about the possible catastrophic meaning of health-related information and bodily variations will almost invariably result in physiological arousal as part of the normal reaction to stress. Those patients who then misinterpret an increase in symptoms as further evidence of illness will experience yet more anxiety and thus more symptoms, resulting in an upward spiral of symptoms, catastrophic misinterpretations, and anxiety. When such catastrophic interpretations are prominent, they have the effect of motivating safety-seeking behaviors which are likely to increase manifest symptoms.

This type of pattern is characteristic of patients who experience panic attacks, but also occurs at a relatively lower level of intensity in patients who do not. When panic attacks are prominent, the sequence is almost invariably that if, and only if, bodily sensations are misinterpreted as a sign of a relatively imminent catastrophe, then the resulting anxiety will increase bodily sensations (Clark, 1988; Salkovskis, 1988b; Salkovskis & Clark, 1993). In a subset of patients, this type of misinterpretation is almost immediately exacerbated by physiological processes, such as hyperventilation. The importance of processes such as hyperventilation has often been exaggerated by those keen to offer physical explanations to anxiety patients (Salkovskis, 1988a). It is clear that seeking to teach patients controlled breathing as a way of combating hyperventilation is not an appropriate target for treatment. The problem is not hyperventilation (which occurs not only when some patients become acutely anxious, but much more commonly as a normal physiological response to excitement and anger), but the catastrophic meaning which patients attach to their physiological responses.

There is often considerable specificity involved in psychophysiological reactions. For example, a patient who believed bowel disturbance indicated that he or she was developing Crohn's disease would experience abdominal symptoms as a reaction to stress, including the stress provoked by the person's health concerns. It also seems likely that some idiopathic pain problems may involve similar mechanisms (Salkovskis & Nouwen, in preparation; also see Chapter 12).

There are a further set of effects which probably combine the interpretation/physiological response and interpretation/selective attention links. The meaning that people suffering from severe health anxiety attach to bodily variations makes them attend more closely than usual to such variations. In doing so, they may develop a heightened ability to detect variations that non-health-anxious people simply would not notice. Patients suffering from severe health anxiety often say 'I'm certain that others are not plagued with a constant awareness of what their body is doing and the way it reacts'. It is likely that this is true—these people notice things that most other people simply would not. Unfortunately, this combination of somatically focused attention and heightened accuracy of bodily perception has the understandable effect of further increasing their health concerns.

## Safety-Seeking Behaviors Motivated by Illness Beliefs

Recently, it has been suggested that the avoidance and escape behaviors characteristic of people suffering from anxiety problems can best be conceptualized from a cognitive perspective as 'safety-seeking behaviors' (Salkovskis, 1991; Salkovskis, 1996a; Salkovskis, 1996b; Salkovskis, Clark, & Gelder, 1996). It is an almost universal response to threat that one takes action intended to avert or reduce the likelihood and impact of perceived threat. The person who believes that he or she may be about to experience some catastrophe will seek to prevent it. The person who is afraid of having a heart attack refrains from exercising; the person who believes that he or she is susceptible to cancer checks for early signs of disease and consults the doctor, perhaps insisting on examination or medical investigations. This type of behavior, by which the person seeks to avoid, check for, or totally exclude physical illnesses (e.g., avoiding physical exertion or contact with disease; reading medical textbooks; frequent medical consultations; bodily checking, manipulation, and inspection) will maintain anxiety by increasing symptoms and preoccupation. Such behavior serves to focus people even more on the fears about which they worry, and can thereby increase the degree of preoccupation experienced.

The safety-seeking behaviors used by patients may serve directly to increase the symptoms that form the focus of misinterpretation and, therefore, increases their anxiety. For example, patients who believe that the discomfort they are experiencing indicates incipient disease may be motivated by these concerns to repeatedly prod areas of inflammation or pain, to take inappropriate medication, to excessively focus attention on particular bodily systems, and so on (Salkovskis & Bass, 1997; Warwick & Salkovskis, 1990). Doing this increases the discomfort which the patient has interpreted as a sign of illness and therefore fears. A patient with fears of multiple sclerosis (MS) believed that tingling in the fingertips was symptomatic of the diagnosis. He held out his hand, palm up and fingers bent, while focusing on his fingertips. When he did this he was alarmed to notice that he was experiencing tingling. He checked the sensitivity of his fingertips by repeatedly brushing his fingers over his clothes, and found that the tingling got progressively more noticeable as he did this. The same patient believed that MS impaired the ability to become sexually aroused. He would initiate lovemaking in order to check whether there was any sign of this happening to him. Not surprisingly, he found that sex was less stimulating than before, reinforcing his belief that he did indeed have MS.

Likewise, pain patients may adopt unusual ways of carrying out physical activity on the basis that 'hurt = harm'. Unfortunately, some of the ways in which they seek to prevent further damage to themselves can have the effect of increasing muscle spasm and therefore pain. Paradoxically, this type of behavior often has the effect of making the person think 'it's this bad when I remember to be careful; it would be much worse if I did not'.

Probably the most prominent and troublesome safety-seeking behavior in severe health anxiety is reassurance seeking, which, as described above, is part of the definition of health anxiety. Several authors have proposed an important role for reassurance, although the possible mechanisms have seldom been discussed. Kenyon (1995) cites Wychoff who argued that hypochondriasis is largely iatrogenic in the sense of being initiated or perpetuated by doctors, particularly by those ordering further physical investigations 'just to make sure'. Subtle and persistent ways of seeking reassurance can evolve, as recognized by Leonhard (1968), who notes 'any discussion of the state of health will only be of disadvantage to the hypochondriac . . . these constant discussions must be stopped at all costs'. This view is not supported by Pilowsky or Kellner, the latter of whom states that 'treatment strategies include repeated physical examination when the patient fears he has acquired a new disease . . . and repeated reassurance'. The available data support the cognitive-behavioral view (Salkovskis & Warwick, 1986; Warwick & Salkovskis, 1985) that, although reassurance may be helpful in instances in which people have developed transient concerns about health, in people suffering from severe and persistent health anxiety it is likely at best to be useless and at worst to be counter-productive.

Reassurance seeking will undoubtedly have at least two further effects in many patients. First, it increases the likelihood of ambiguous or false positive results for medical investigations, which will be instituted by the doctor in an attempt to allay the patient's fears. Second, it will result in the patient being given slightly different information by different people as reassurance, or different information by the same person on different occasions. This usually undermines the patient's confidence in the doctors' judgement. Direct contradictions of opinion between doctors has a particularly disastrous effect in this respect.

A substantial proportion of people suffering from health anxiety endorse high levels of belief in assumptions such as 'if my doctor sends me for any further medical investigations, this means that he or she is doing so to confirm their suspicion that I am ill'. This means that such patients are likely to interpret any investigation or referral to a specialist clinic as confirmation of their fears that their doctor believes them to be ill. If the effects of medical investigation can be so counter-productive, why do patients persist in seeking reassurance of this type? We suggest that this is because of further assumptions typically held by patients suffering from health anxiety. For example, some patients believe that, because they have a history of anxiety, the doctor might withhold information about illness out of a misplaced sense of kindness. Note that this belief is often based on specific direct or indirect experience such as being involved in a decision to withhold information about a terminal diagnosis from an elderly relative. Such a thing is known to happen particularly in the context of people thought by others as psychologically vulnerable. It is, therefore, evident to the patients that they have to make sure that this is not now happening to themselves, as they are usually aware that others regard them as prone to extreme psychological reactions to potentially adverse health information.

Problematic assumptions may interact in counter-productive ways. Thus, many patients who believe that their doctor would only send them for investigation if there were good reason to believe that they were ill also believe that the only way to *really* rule out an illness is to have medical investigations. Understandably, such patients are reluctant to accept a clinical diagnosis of 'wellness' that is not backed up by a specific test or investigation for the problem they fear. Recently, we noted the possibility that there may be some overlap between the reassurance-motivating beliefs of health anxious patients and those of people suffering from obsessional problems. In obsessional problems, beliefs concerning the person's fears for being responsible for harm (including harm to themselves) appear to motivate checking and reassurance-seeking behavior (Salkovskis et al., 2000). We believe that health anxious patients have an inflated sense of responsibility for the way they interact with the physician during medical consultations. If this is so, then this may explain the way in which some patients anxious about health tend to irritate physicians by their over-inclusive descriptions of the details of the symptoms they have experienced, the circumstances in which they occur, and so on. Furthermore, such patients often express the concern that they have described things in insufficient detail for the doctor to be able to make a diagnosis.

In a recent instance, one of the authors encountered a case in which it is clear why such beliefs developed. The patient described how, as a young man, he had believed himself to be 'made of steel'. He had no worries about his health, and tended to ignore his safety in a wide range of health relevant and irrelevant situations. One day, when he was 19, he experienced intense chest pains. His family doctor reassured him it was most likely to be a pulled muscle, so he ignored it for the remainder of the day. By the evening, it was considerably worse, so he attended the Emergency Room. The doctor there diagnosed a collapsed lung, and asked why he had not sought attention sooner. When he explained that he had seen his own doctor that morning, he was told that he must have failed to provide his doctor with the appropriate information. At that point, he developed the belief that at any time he could be afflicted by a dangerous medical condition, and that it was up to him to alert doctors to *all* relevant details of his condition, otherwise the appropriate diagnosis would not be made.

The most obvious effect of behavior is seen when patients believe that their safety-seeking behavior has the immediate and direct effect of preventing the feared catastrophe (as in the instance of those who believe that they are in danger of having a heart attack if they do not succeed in taking the strain off their heart). In such instances, the patients not only experience immediate relief because of the safety they believe they have achieved, but also inadvertently 'protect' their belief of the potential for disaster associated with particular sensations. Each episode of anxiety, rather than being a disconfirmation, becomes another example of *nearly* being overtaken by a disaster: 'I have almost died of a heart attack many times. I have to be more careful, or one of these times I won't be able to catch it in time.' This, in effect, means that each episode of acute anxiety is perceived as a 'near miss' which, in itself, increases the threat belief.

## Affective-Cognitive Interactions

The interaction between negative beliefs and disturbed mood, particularly anxiety and depression, is well established (Butler & Mathews, 1983; Teasdale, 1983). Affective disturbance increases negative thinking, which further increases affective disturbance. These processes probably also prime ruminative worries about the further implications of the feared consequences. For example, a woman feared that she had terminal cancer. When preoccupation with this belief became prominent, she would become both anxious and depressed. Her low mood would then trigger ruminations about how the family would cope (or not cope, in this instance) with her illness and subsequent death. She would imagine her husband and daughter struggling with the stress of losing her, and become preoccupied with the idea that their life would be ruined by her death. Such rumination further increased her anxiety and depression, and so on.

## SPECIFICITY OF MISINTERPRETATIONS

The specificity of misinterpretations in hypochondriasis, as opposed to panic, has important implications for treatment. Panic is characterized by the enduring tendency to misinterpret bodily sensations as a sign of *imminent* catastrophes, while hypochondriasis involves the misinterpretation of a much broader range of stimuli as a sign of gradual and progressive or much more delayed catastrophes. In terms of treatment, a commonly used and particularly efficient strategy in the therapy for anxiety disorders such as panic disorder and social phobia involves helping patients to change their behavior in ways which lead to a clear disconfirmation of their threat beliefs (Clark, 1999; Salkovskis, 1991, 1996b; Salkovskis, Clark, Hackmann, Wells, & Gelder, 1999; Wells et al., 1995). It had previously been suggested (Salkovskis, 1996a) that this type of treatment strategy would not be effective if the feared catastrophe were to be located in the more distant future, as disconfirmation would, in many instances, not be an option. It is usually possible to use a brisk run with the therapist to establish that a patient's chest pain is not the sign of an impending heart attack. Such a run would not demonstrate anything of great significance for a patient who thinks the occasional cardiac irregularity experienced indicates that he or she has the early signs of a heart condition which will culminate in serious harm many years later. Consequently, the therapist has to rely on providing the sufferer with a clear non-catastrophic alternative explanation of the problem, and help to convince the patient that this alternative is true.

An example of a specific maintenance model worked out in the course of clinical assessment of a patient with fears of cancer is illustrated in Figure 3.3. Such a model would, for that patient, form the basis of the alternative account used in therapy.

If the alternative account is sufficiently convincing for the sufferer, it results in the threatening explanation previously held by the patient (e.g., 'I have the early signs of cancer') seeming less and less plausible. Clearly, alternative explanations that are based on more accurate understandings

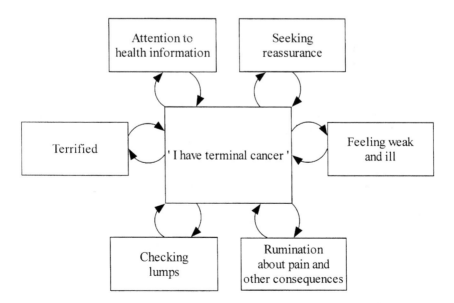

**Figure 3.3**   A specific maintenance model of a patient with fears of cancer.

of the psychopathology of the problem concerned are more likely to be convincing to the sufferer, and are particularly likely to survive the person's subsequent experience both in and out of therapy. We believe that the cognitive-behavioral approach is the best supported account of health anxiety, and currently offers the most useful and accessible way of helping people suffering from severe and persistent health anxiety to understand and deal with their problems.

## THE COGNITIVE-BEHAVIORAL MODEL

### Maintenance of Health Anxiety Indicates how Treatment can Best be Conducted

As noted above, patients suffering from severe and persistent health anxiety can be regarded a being victims of misinterpretation, in which a particularly negative or unhelpful way of looking at their experience has come to dominate their thinking. The role of the therapist is to help them to explore *alternative ways* of making sense of their experience. A plausible alternative account is negotiated (as a shared understanding which identifies how the particular beliefs and maintaining factors interact for that particular patient). The therapist and patient subsequently work out ways of evaluating this alternative, drawing on the patient's past and present experience. Specific behavioral experiments are devised and carried out when issues arise that require new information—for example, to help them to

- establish that some feared catastrophe will not happen;
- discover the importance of maintaining factors identified during assessment;
- discover the importance of negative thinking;
- find out whether using an alternative strategy will be of any value; or
- reconsider any beliefs about health and illness that are seriously distorted.

Overall, the cognitive-behavioral model highlights the importance of a particular style of therapy, in which the aim is *not* to persuade the patients that their current way of looking at the situation is wrong, irrational, or too negative. Instead, it is to allow them to identify where they may have become trapped or stuck in their way of thinking, and then to allow them to find out if there may be other ways of looking at their situation. Once this is done, the therapist then helps the patients to identify any obstacles there might be to thinking and acting in any more helpful ways that the patients might wish to choose. Thus, cognitive therapy aims to free the patients to choose other ways of interpreting their situation and reacting to it, drawing from the fullest possible range of alternatives available to them (including their current negative account). In this way, the therapist seeks to empower the patients by broadening the choices they can make about the way they react to their situation, and helping them to discover information which allows them to decide between the available choices in an informed way. It may be that the chosen alternative is more rational, it might be more positive, but it does not have to be. This philosophy highlights the importance of guided discovery where the therapist helps the patients themselves to explore alternative ways of looking at their situation.

By definition, this style of therapy also means that the alternatives arrived at are acceptable to the patient and consistent with their beliefs and values. It also means that there is no place in the model or the therapy for the idea of therapist-defined 'wrong thinking', which is inappropriately judgmental. Subsequent therapy (including discussion, behavioral experiments, and exercises in disconfirmation) are then all directed at helping the patients to distinguish between the different interpretations they have. In every instance the alternative explanation is going to be highly idiosyncratic, based on the particular pattern of symptoms and interpretations experienced by each person.

Engagement in treatment of severe anxiety about health needs to involve reaching a shared understanding with the patients concerning the *possible* psychological basis of their problem. This is crucial because, at the beginning of therapy, these patients believe that they are in danger of some terrible physical catastrophe. If this belief is held very strongly, the patients are unlikely to engage in psychologically (or psychiatrically) based treatment.

A hypochondriacal patient, for example, may believe that he has heart disease or cancer for which a psychological treatment is unlikely, in his belief, to be of any particular value. The patient, at that stage, seeks to solve his problem by paying careful attention to the symptoms he experiences, by getting the appropriate medical help, and so on. It is, therefore, necessary that in the early stages of treatment the patient is helped to see that there may be an alternative explanation of the difficulties he is experiencing. The patient is introduced to an idiosyncratically based cognitive model which offers a quite different and less threatening account of his problems. That is, it is not that he has cancer but that he is *worried about and believes* that he might have cancer, and these worries have consequences for his experience, perhaps including his symptoms. For treatment to be effective, it follows that it is crucial that this patient agrees that therapeutic strategies should be aimed at reducing such worries rather than the fruitless attempts to reduce risk. At this stage of treatment (engagement) the two possible explanations for the patient's problems are considered alongside each other rather than as mutually exclusive alternatives. The patient is invited to consider how the two alternative views match up to his experience. Once therapist and patient agree on the two alternatives, therapy proceeds as an evaluation of the relative merits of these two views. Evidence for and against each is reviewed and discussed in detail.

Discussion often reaches the point where further information, which is not currently available to the patient, has to be sought, and this is where behavioral experiments become an important part of therapy. Behavioral experiments are information-gathering exercises which help patients to reach conclusions about the beliefs they hold. For example, a patient may have noticed that his chest pain tends to worsen around the time that he exercises. During the discussion he is not certain whether this is before, during, or after exercise. In order to test this out, therapist and patient go for a brisk walk around the hospital, taking repeated ratings of chest pain intensity. There is a constant interplay between the cognitive-behavioral formulation drawn up by patient and therapist, discussion of how the patient's experience fits with that formulation, and generation of new and informative experience using behavioral experiments to further illuminate the model. Cognitive and behavioral elements are interwoven but the guiding principle is always enabling the patient to consider and adopt a more helpful and less frightening belief than the one he has held previously.

In the treatment of health anxiety, therapist and patients have to understand that many of the factors that previously triggered anxiety and discomfort may continue to occur. This is often a source of concern for the patients, who would prefer to simply get rid of the symptoms or sensations that are the focus of their misinterpretation. Given that many of the things experienced by such patients are normal bodily variations, this is unlikely to be possible. By the same token, therapists should not usually seek to construct specific accounts of why particular symptoms are innocuous; while this strategy might sometimes be effective, many of the things such patients will experience will be normal variations that are not readily explained, and to seek to do so would simply reinforce the patients' beliefs. Therapy, instead, aims to modify the *meaning* of physical variations, medically relevant information, or negative intrusive cognitions about health so that it more closely resembles that experienced by people who do not suffer from health anxiety. By the same token, no direct attempts are made to decrease the number of bodily sensations or variations experienced in the early stages of treatment (and often never). Any intention on the part of the patients to bring about such a reduction is challenged by helping them to deal with the beliefs that motivate it.

However, a fortunate and desirable side effect of cognitive therapy is that there is usually an actual decrease in such symptoms. Clearly, a 'normal' person does not constantly seek to control symptoms or thoughts; if there are any attempts made at control they tend to be indirect, because the person generally believes that there are no catastrophic consequences of failing to control symptoms. Returning patients suffering from severe and persistent health anxiety to this relatively untroubled state is, of course, the main reason for seeking to understand and treat health anxiety.

**Authors' Note:** Paul Salkovskis is Wellcome Trust Senior Research Fellow in Basic Biomedical Science.

## REFERENCES

Barsky, A.J., & Klerman, G.L. (1983). Overview: Hypochondriasis, bodily complaints, and somatic styles. *American Journal of Psychiatry*, **140**, 273–283.

Barsky, A.J., Wyshak, G., Klerman, G.L., & Latham, K.S. (1990). The prevalence of hypochondriasis in medical outpatients. *Social Psychiatry and Psychiatric Epidemiology*, **25**, 89–94.

Beck, A.T. (1976). *Cognitive therapy and the emotional disorders*. New York: International Universities Press.

Beck, A.T., Emery, G., & Greenberg, R.L. (1985). *Anxiety disorders and phobias: A cognitive perspective*. New York: Basic Books.

Butler, G., & Mathews, A. (1983). Cognitive processes in anxiety. *Advances in Behaviour Research and Therapy*, **5**, 51–62.

Clark, D.M. (1988). A cognitive model of panic. In S.J. Rachman & J. Maser (Eds.), *Panic: Psychological perspectives* (pp. 71–89). Hillsdale, NJ: Erlbaum.

Clark, D.M. (1999). Anxiety disorders: Why they persist and how to treat them. *Behaviour Research and Therapy*, **37**, s5–s28.

Hitchcock, P.B., & Mathews, A. (1992). Interpretation of bodily symptoms in hypochondriasis. *Behaviour Research and Therapy*, **30**, 223–234.

Leonhard, K. (1968). Prevention von neurosen durch rechtzeitige differenzierurig wunschneurotischer und befurzhtungsneurotischer ansatze. *Deutsche Gesundheitswesen*, **23**, 1560–1562.

Kenyon, F.E. (1995). Hypochondriasis: A clinical study. *British Journal of Psychiatry*, **110**, 478–488.

Salkovskis, P.M. (1988a). Hyperventilation and anxiety. *Current Opinion in Psychiatry*, **1**, 76–82.

Salkovskis, P.M. (1988b). Phenomenology, assessment and the cognitive model of panic. In S.J. Rachman & J. Maser (Eds.), *Panic: Psychological perspectives* (pp. 111–136). Hillsdale, NJ: Erlbaum.

Salkovskis, P.M. (1989). Somatic Problems. In K. Hawton, P.M. Salkovskis, J. Kirk, & D.M. Clark (Eds.), *Cognitive therapy for psychiatric problems: A practical guide* (pp. 235–276). Oxford: Oxford University Press.

Salkovskis, P.M. (1991). The importance of behaviour in the maintenance of anxiety and panic: A cognitive account. *Behavioural Psychotherapy*, **19**, 6–19.

Salkovskis, P.M. (1996a). The cognitive approach to anxiety: Threat beliefs, safety seeking behaviour, and the special case of health anxiety and obsessions.

In P.M. Salkovskis (Ed.), *Frontiers of cognitive therapy* (pp. 48–74). New York: Guilford.

Salkovskis, P.M. (1996b). Resolving the cognition-behaviour debate. In P.M. Salkovskis (Ed.), *Trends in cognitive-behaviour therapy.* Chichester: John Wiley.

Salkovskis, P.M., & Bass, C. (1997). Hypochondriasis. In D.M. Clark & C.G. Fairburn (Eds.), *The science and practice of cognitive-behaviour therapy* (pp. 313–339). Oxford: Oxford University Press.

Salkovskis, P.M., & Clark, D.M. (1993). Panic disorder and hypochondriasis. *Advances in Behaviour Research and Therapy*, **15**, 23–48.

Salkovskis, P.M., Clark, D.M., & Gelder, M.G. (1996). Cognition-behaviour links in the persistence of panic. *Behaviour Research and Therapy*, **34**, 453–458.

Salkovskis, P.M., Clark, D.M., Hackmann, A., Wells, A., & Gelder, M.G. (1999). An experimental investigation of the role of safety-seeking behaviours in the maintenance of panic disorder with agoraphobia. *Behaviour Research and Therapy*, **37**, 559–574.

Salkovskis, P.M., & Rimes, K.A. (1997). Predictive genetic testing: Psychological factors. *Journal of Psychosomatic Research*, **44**, 477–487.

Salkovskis, P.M., & Warwick, H.M.C. (1986). Morbid preoccupations, health anxiety and reassurance: A cognitive behavioural approach to hypochondriasis. *Behaviour Research and Therapy*, **24**, 597–602.

Salkovskis, P.M., Wroe, A.L., Gledhill, A.M., Morrison, N., Forrester, E., Richards, H.C., Reynolds, M., & Thorpe, S. (2000). Responsibility attitudes and interpretations are characteristic of obsessive-compulsive disorder. *Behaviour Research and Therapy*, **38**, 347–372.

Teasdale, J.D. (1983). Negative thinking in depression: Cause, effect or reciprocal relationship? *Advances in Behaviour Research and Therapy*, **5**, 3–26.

Warwick, H.M., & Salkovskis, P.M. (1985). Reassurance. *British Medical Journal*, **290**, 1028.

Warwick, H.M., & Salkovskis, P.M. (1990). Hypochondriasis. *Behaviour Research and Therapy*, **28**, 105–117.

Wells, A., Clark, D.M., Salkovskis, P.M., Ludgate, J., Hackmann, A., & Gelder, M.G. (1995). Social phobia: The role of in-situation safety behaviours in maintaining anxiety and negative beliefs. *Behavior Therapy*, **26**, 153–161.

Chapter 4

# PERSONALITY TRAITS AND HEALTH ANXIETY

*Erin B. McClure\* and Scott O. Lilienfeld\**

## INTRODUCTION

Individuals with certain personality characteristics appear to be at increased risk for a variety of forms of psychopathology, including mood, anxiety, substance use, and conduct disorders (Krueger, Caspi, Moffitt, Silva, & McGee, 1996; Trull & Sher, 1994). In addition, a growing body of evidence suggests that a relatively distinctive constellation of personality features is linked to somatoform disorders (see Kirmayer, Robbins, & Paris, 1994, for a review). Although much research in this area has focused on medical complaints and somatic concerns (e.g., Costa & McCrae, 1985; McCrae, 1991), accumulating findings also implicate personality factors in health anxiety within both clinical and normal ranges. In this chapter, we review the steadily accumulating literature on the relations between personality variables and clinical and non-clinical health anxiety.

According to the *Diagnostic and Statistical Manual of Mental Disorders, Fourth Edition* (DSM-IV; American Psychiatric Association, 1994), the defining feature of hypochondriasis is a preoccupation with 'fears of having, or the idea that one has, a serious disease based on misinterpretation of one or more bodily signs or symptoms' (p. 462). Although hypochondriasis shares with other somatoform conditions a core focus on somatic concerns and complaints, it occupies its own distinct nosological category. Cloninger, Sigvardsson, von Knorring, and Bohman (1984) used admixture and discriminant analysis techniques to examine clinical variation among women adoptees with prominent somatizing symptoms.

*Emory University, USA

*Health Anxiety*
Edited by G.J.G. Asmundson, S. Taylor & B.J. Cox
© 2001 John Wiley & Sons Ltd.

Their results yielded preliminary evidence for two discrete categories of somatizers, whose symptoms differed in frequency and severity. Of these categories, one ('high frequency somatization') corresponded to traditionally defined hypochondriasis, whereas the second ('diversiform somatization') more closely resembled Briquet's syndrome or somatization disorder. Kirmayer and Robbins (1991) presented further evidence that hypochondriasis constitutes a separable diagnosis. Of their sample of 685 primary care clinic patients, the majority of those with somatoform disorders met criteria for either somatization or hypochondriasis, but not both. Although hypochondriasis and somatization frequently co-occur (Barsky, Wyshak, & Klerman, 1986), they also exist independently. It therefore seems valid to focus the present review on the relation between personality and hypochondriasis and hypochondriacal concerns per se, because hypochondriasis is separable from other somatoform disorders.

Although we will examine normal range health anxiety as well as clinical hypochondriasis, it is unclear how the two constructs are related. Clinical hypochondriasis tends to be a chronic condition marked by functional impairment and frequently accompanied by one or more Axis I or Axis II disorders (Barsky, Fama, Bailey, & Ahern, 1998). Normal range health worries, in contrast, appear to be transient and tied more closely to medical morbidity (Barsky, Wyshak, & Klerman, 1990). It is possible that the two represent fundamentally different constructs, in which case personality variables would not necessarily play similar roles in their etiology or course. Hypochondriasis, for example, could be symptomatic of an underlying personality disorder (Kirmayer & Robbins, 1991). As Tyrer and colleagues (1990) pointed out, hypochondriasis can emerge early in development and continue to interfere with interpersonal functioning throughout the lifespan, as would be expected of a DSM Axis II disorder. Subclinical health anxiety, in contrast, may be more closely tied to chronic situational stressors (e.g., marital or occupational difficulties). Alternatively, the two constructs may differ in degree rather than kind, with clinical hypochondriasis representing the extreme of one or more personality dimensions (Costa & McCrae, 1985). If so, then personality characteristics may exhibit comparable correlates across the full spectrum of health anxiety. At this point, however, the question of whether clinical hypochondriasis is underpinned by a latent dimension or by a latent taxon (i.e., a non-arbitrary class existing in nature; Meehl & Golden, 1982) remains unresolved.

## TRAIT MODELS OF PERSONALITY

Efforts to uncover a comprehensive taxonomic structure of personality have yielded numerous trait models that postulate competing hierarchical representations of personality dimensions (e.g., Costa & McCrae, 1992; Eysenck, 1947, 1967; Tellegen, 1982, 1985). Prominent among these models are various 'Big Three' (Eysenck, 1947, 1967; Tellegen, 1985) and 'Big Five' (Costa & McCrae, 1992) taxonomies, comprising three to five separable higher-order factors that partly subsume an array of more specific lower-order factors. Common to most Big Three and Big Five models are two broadly overarching factors representing Neuroticism/Negative Affectivity and Extraversion/Positive Affectivity. In addition, Costa and McCrae's (1992) Big Five taxonomy identifies three further higher-order factors: Agreeableness, Conscientiousness, and Openness to Experience.

The Big Five, which has received considerable attention in the health anxiety literature, is a descriptive taxonomy originally derived from factor analyses of adjectives used to identify phenotypic human attributes. It is rooted in the 'lexical hypothesis', which postulates that single-word descriptors used in everyday conversation should capture the full range of fundamental personality characteristics (Block, 1995; Goldberg, 1993). Over the past 60 years, numerous researchers have factor analyzed lengthy lists of descriptive terms and extracted largely similar core sets of five factors (e.g., Goldberg, 1981; Norman, 1963). More recently, Costa and McCrae (1992) found evidence of consistency between the five lexical factors identified in earlier research and item sets from their Neuroticism–Extraversion–Openness (NEO) Personality Inventory that assess five dimensions that they had established a priori.

The Big Five offers an important conceptualization of personality; however, for the purposes of this chapter we have chosen to adopt Tellegen's (1985) 'Big Three' model as a heuristic framework. Although there are several closely related conceptualizations of the Big Three (e.g., Eysenck, 1967; Gray, 1982), we will limit ourselves to a discussion of Tellegen's model because his dimensions offer a useful scheme for reviewing the literature on personality and health anxiety. Notable for its consistency with dimensions of mood (Larsen & Ketelaar, 1991; Tellegen, 1982) and underlying psychobiological systems (Depue & Collins, 1999; Depue & Spoont, 1986; Tomarken, Davidson, Wheeler, & Doss, 1992), this model emerged from Tellegen's extensive research on personality structure (see Tellegen & Waller, 1994). Assessed by such measures as the Multidimensional Personality Questionnaire (MPQ; Tellegen, 1982), this model consists of three higher-order factors that Tellegen (1985) termed Negative Affectivity (Negative Emotionality), Positive Affectivity (Positive Emotionality), and Constraint.

Perhaps the best studied of these dimensions is Negative Affectivity, which has recently been relabeled Negative Emotionality (NE) or Negative Activation (Watson, Wiese, Vaidya, & Tellegen, 1999). Individuals high on this dimension tend to experience distress that manifests itself as nervousness, tension, and worry (Watson & Clark, 1984). Not surprisingly, trait anxiety is central to NE; however, this dimension also encompasses a broader array of unpleasant affects, including anger, guilt, distrust, and hostility. Additionally, individuals with high levels of NE are prone to antagonistic or adversarial interpersonal interactions and often find themselves in the roles of victim or victimizer (Tellegen & Waller, 1994). Clearly the experience of negative emotion constitutes a core element of NE. This dimension is, however, largely unrelated to the propensity to experience positive emotional states (Watson & Clark, 1984).

A second dimension encompasses the experience of positive emotion, as well as interpersonal connectedness and effectance in both social and work environments. Largely orthogonal to NE, Positive Emotionality (PE) includes four central facets: Well Being, Social Potency (ascendence or dominance), Achievement, and Social Closeness. High scorers on this dimension are prone to a range of pleasantly aroused states and typically feel actively engaged in their environments (Tellegen, 1985; Tellegen et al., 1988). More recently, Tellegen and Waller (1994) proposed dividing PE into Agentic and Communal dimensions, because PE often splits into two subfactors best defined by the Achievement and Social Closeness scales.

Tellegen describes the third dimension, Constraint, as reflecting caution, fearfulness, attention to detail, effective impulse control, and adherence to traditional values. Three subscales, Control, Harm Avoidance, and Traditionalism contribute to this factor, whose implications for psychopathology have received less attention than PE and NE.

The MPQ includes one additional scale, which reflects a fourth broad personality factor termed Absorption (Tellegen & Atkinson, 1974). Absorption has been defined as a capacity to become immersed in sensory and imaginal experiences, and has been linked to artistic creativity and peak and mystical experiences. In addition, Absorption has generally been found to be a modest predictor of hypnotic susceptibility (Tellegen & Atkinson, 1974). Absorption exhibits low to moderate loadings on both NE and PE, but does not load primarily on any single higher-order dimension (Tellegen, 1982). Because of its potential importance to health anxiety, we will review the literature on Absorption and hypochondriacal concerns in a separate section.

Although Tellegen's model is distinct from Big Five conceptualizations of personality, an empirical comparison of the two suggests that they are hierarchically related, with NE, PE, and Constraint constituting higher-order dimensions that partly encompass the Big Five dimensions of Neuroticism, Extraversion, Agreeableness, Openness to Experience, and

Conscientiousness (Church, 1994). NE appears to comprise both Neuroticism and the inverse of Agreeableness; these two dimensions fuse into a general NE factor that pervades both intrapersonal and interpersonal domains. Consistent with Tellegen's division of PE into Communal and Agentic subdimensions, this dimension subsumes both Extraversion and the achieving or surgent facets of Conscientiousness. Finally, Conscientiousness, as well as aspects of Openness to Experience (reversed), are included within the broader dimension of Constraint. Whereas Conscientiousness corresponds to the aspects of Constraint characterized by behavioral or impulse control, Openness to Experience is more closely associated with the aspects of Constraint that reflect non-traditional values, norms, and moral standards.

Thus, the Big Three and Big Five models appear to map onto roughly overlapping territories of personality, although they differ in how they divide up these territories. As Kirmayer et al. (1994) point out in their thoughtful review of somatoform disorders and their relation to personality traits, the Big Five provide one useful structure for understanding health anxiety. The Big Three, however, possess a number of substantive advantages over the Big Five that increase its value as a heuristic framework. Tellegen's (1985) three primary trait dimensions, for instance, appear to tap what Cattell (1950) termed source traits (i.e., broad underlying dispositions that can provide causal explanations for associations among behaviors, biological markers, and performance on laboratory tests). The dimensions that the Big Five comprises, in contrast, have not been clearly linked to such underlying dispositions; instead, they appear largely to reflect surface traits, which are primarily descriptive in nature and do not permit prediction of behaviors that might not superficially resemble their core aspects (Eysenck, 1993).

Additionally, NE, PE, and Constraint have been linked to underlying psychobiological systems and patterns of neural activation. PE, for instance, appears to map onto an underlying motivational system of reward-signal sensitivity and to govern approach motivation (Tellegen, 1985). This motivational system, in turn, has been theoretically and empirically associated with patterns of neurotransmitter activity and electroencephalogram activation (e.g., Depue, Luciana, Arbisi, Collins, & Leon, 1994; Tomarken et al., 1992). Specifically, researchers have found positive correlations between levels of dopamine activity and both PE (Depue & Collins, 1999; Depue et al., 1994) and an analog behavioral approach or facilitation system observed in varied animal species (Gray, 1982; Le Moal & Simon, 1991). This system appears to be underpinned largely by midbrain dopamine systems. An additional postulated marker of the behavioral approach system, anterior electroencephalogram asymmetry during a resting state, has also been shown to relate to elevated levels of PE (Tomarken et al., 1992).

NE has been linked by some authors (e.g., Tellegen, 1985) to a second motivational system driven by punishment-signal sensitivity and termed the behavioral inhibition system. The behavioral inhibition system appears to be underpinned by the septum, hippocampus, orbitofrontal cortex, and other brain structures (Cloninger, 1987; Gray, 1982). According to Gray (1982), the behavioral inhibition system inhibits behavior in response to signals of threat and frustrative non-reward and is responsible for anxiety. Nevertheless, the association between NE and the behavioral inhibition system is controversial, and some authors (e.g., Fowles, 1987) have linked behavioral inhibition system activity primarily to the third dimension of the Big Three, Constraint.

Constraint has been postulated to modulate the activity of approach and inhibitory motivational systems in response to signals of both reward and punishment (Depue & Spoont, 1986). More specifically, Constraint appears to prevent both motivational systems from becoming dysregulated or from 'overshooting' their normal ranges of functioning. To these ends, it may play both facilitative and inhibitory roles (Spoont, 1992). Measures of Constraint are positively associated with impulse control and levels of serotonin, which suggests that serotonin may act as a neurochemical substrate for this dimension (Depue & Collins, 1999; Depue & Spoont, 1986; Spoont, 1992).

Most of the research that we will discuss in this chapter focuses on dimensional personality traits as potential predictors of the Axis I diagnosis of hypochondriasis and its milder variants. Some evidence suggests that personality dimensions similar to those in Tellegen's (1985) Big Three may also explain the covariance among Axis II personality disorders. For example, based on biological, behavior-genetic, and symptomatic evidence, Siever and Davis (1991) argued that the covariation among DSM personality disorders can be accounted for largely by four dimensions: impulsivity/aggression, affective instability, anxiety/inhibition, and cognitive/perceptual disorganization. The first and second of these dimensions bear important conceptual similarities to Tellegen's (1982) Constraint (reversed) and NE dimensions, respectively. Cloninger (1987) suggested that the three dimensions of Novelty Seeking, Harm Avoidance, and Reward Dependence can explain much of the covariation among Axis II disorders. Psychometric analyses indicate that the first two of these dimensions bear close relations to two of the Big Three dimensions (Constraint, reversed, and NE, respectively), although Reward Dependence does not (Waller, Lilienfeld, Tellegen, & Lykken, 1991). Thus, the domains of abnormal personality may be underpinned by some of the same dimensions as normal personality.

## THE BIG THREE AND ITS ASSOCIATION WITH HEALTH ANXIETY

In light of the chronic, pervasive nature of many cases of hypochondriasis (Noyes et al., 1994; cf. Barsky, 1995), there is surprisingly little research on its relation to personality variables. The bulk of the existing research has focused on NE and its strong and consistent association with health anxiety and hypochondriasis (Kirmayer et al., 1994). Recently, however, a growing number of investigators have examined broader patterns of association between personality dimensions and health concerns, and a more detailed descriptive profile is gradually emerging (Cox, Borger, Asmundson, & Taylor, 2000; Hollifield, Tuttle, Paine, & Kellner, 1999; Noyes, Happel, & Yagla, 1999; Noyes et al., 1993). The present chapter will examine this literature with emphasis on several questions. First, are health anxiety and hypochondriasis simply manifestations of high NE in the somatic domain? If not, what do other personality dimensions have to offer in explaining these constructs? Second, although most research has focused on higher-order personality factors in their examinations of health anxiety, recent research has begun to examine lower-order factors as well. Do these lower-order factors contribute to the assessment and understanding of health anxiety above and beyond the higher-order factors? Third, are the personality correlates of normal-range health anxiety and hypochondriasis similar? Fourth, does the study of abnormal personality (i.e., personality disorders) shed light on the etiology of health anxiety above and beyond contributions of normal personality?

It should be borne in mind that operationalizations of the Big Three personality dimensions vary across the studies included in our review. For example, Tellegen's conceptualization of NE is somewhat broader than the neuroticism constructs of Eysenck (1947, 1967) and Costa and McCrae (1992). Consequently, studies that use measures based on different theoretical frameworks measure somewhat different, although substantially overlapping, constructs. These differences should be considered when interpreting discrepancies across studies. Nevertheless, consistencies across studies using different operationalizations of the Big Three dimensions lend support to the argument that relations between health anxiety and the Big Three are valid and meaningful.

### Negative Emotionality (NE) and Health Anxiety

Persons with hypochondriasis display marked anxiety about their well-being and are often described as irritable, angry, and resentful (Mabe, Riley, Jones, & Hobson, 1996; Starcevic, 1990). Additionally, their interpersonal interactions are frequently characterized by distrust and hostility (Kellner, Abbott, Winslow, & Pathak, 1987; Kirmayer et al., 1994). It is thus not surprising that perhaps the most consistent finding in the literature on hypochondriasis and personality traits is a moderate, statistically significant association between NE and health anxiety. High levels of NE, as measured by a variety of self-report instruments, have been shown to relate to overreporting of symptoms (Feldman, Cohen, Doyle, Skoner, & Gwaltney, 1999; Watson & Pennebaker, 1989), fear of illness or death (Cox et al., 2000; Hollifield et al., 1999; Noyes et al., 1993, 1999), and disease conviction (Cox et al., 2000). Additionally, individuals who meet diagnostic criteria for hypochondriasis consistently report higher levels of NE than do those with subthreshold or no symptoms of hypochondriasis (Noyes et al., 1994).

It is not clear whether health anxiety and somatization are independently related to NE. In one of the only studies to examine the three constructs in conjunction, Hollifield et al. (1999) used scores on the hypochondriacal beliefs and disease phobia subscales of the Illness Attitudes Scale (IAS; Kellner, 1986) and the somatization subscale of the Symptom Questionnaire (SQ; Kellner, 1987) to identify individuals with high levels of hypochondriacal worry ('hypochondriacal responders'), medically unexplained somatic symptoms ('high somatic concern'), or both. When they compared scores on the Eysenck Personality Inventory (EPI; Eysenck & Eysenck, 1968) across these groups and a normal comparison group, Hollifield and colleagues found a non-significant main effect of hypochondriacal worry on NE. Nevertheless, the interaction between somatic complaints and hypochondriacal worry significantly predicted NE at a 0.05 alpha level. The authors did not report the form of this interaction.

Results from one study suggest that the association between NE and hypochondriasis is relatively stable over time, at least in clinical samples. Noyes et al. (1994) followed a sample of individuals with clinically diagnosed hypochondriasis for an extended period of time by evaluating them at baseline and at a one-year follow-up. They found that baseline Neuroticism scores obtained using the EPI (Eysenck & Eysenck, 1968) were significantly associated with hypochondriacal symptoms at the one-year follow-up evaluation ($r = 0.36$). Regression analyses showed that the baseline measure of Neuroticism, along with baseline physician ratings of hypochondriasis and scores on the Somatic Symptom Inventory (SSI; Barsky et al., 1986), accounted for a substantial proportion of the variance in future self-reported hypochondriacal symptoms. Nevertheless, because of substantial overlap between the predictor and dependent variables in these analyses [the SSI served as both a predictor variable and, in combination with the Whiteley Index (Pilowsky, 1967), as the dependent variable], these results are difficult to interpret. In particular, it is impossible to determine whether Neuroticism accounted independently for a significant amount of variance in the dependent 'variable because the shared variance between the SSI and Neuroticism was partialled out when the two were entered as independent variables.

Although NE levels are consistently higher in clinically hypochondriacal than in non-hypochondriacal individuals, it is not clear whether a comparable degree of association exists between NE and health anxiety among individuals with normal-range health anxiety and among individuals with hypochondriasis. Most researchers who have examined associations between NE and scores on measures of hypochondriasis (typically the IAS or the Whiteley Index) have not reported separate correlations for patient and comparison groups. Correlations beween NE and hypochondriacal symptoms, however, are similar across those studies focused on non-clinical samples and those that include both clinical hypochondriasis and non-hypochondriacal groups.

Cox and colleagues (2000), for example, found a correlation of $r = 0.60$ between Neuroticism as measured by the Revised NEO Personality Inventory (NEO-PI-R; Costa & McCrae, 1992) and scores on the IAS Health Anxiety higher-order factor[1] in a sample of college students. Comparable findings ($r = 0.50$) were evident for scores on the EPI Neuroticism scale and the Whiteley Index (Pilowsky, 1967) in a sample of hypochondriacal patients' relatives, 10% of whom met DSM criteria for hypochondriasis (Noyes et al., 1999). In research on individuals with clinically significant levels of hypochondriasis, Noyes and colleagues (1993, 1994) found correlations ranging from $r = 0.36$ to $r = 0.49$ between the EPI Neuroticism scale and the Whiteley Index for combined hypochondriacal and comparison samples. Thus, although no research to date has reported separate analyses for individuals with clinical and subclinical levels of health anxiety, we can tentatively infer from the consistent findings across samples of varying composition that relations between NE and health anxiety likely do not differ substantively between normal-range and clinically significant levels of symptomatology. More research will be necessary, however, to corroborate this pattern of findings.

NE is a broad domain enacompassing numerous lower-order dimensions that include both a propensity to experience various negative affects and a tendency toward unpleasant and unsatisfying interpersonal interactions. Tellegen (1985) identified three lower-order NE dimensions in his

---

[1] Factor analysis of the IAS has revealed two higher-order dimensions (termed Health Anxiety and Health Behaviors) that explain approximately 36% and 21% of the variance in the measure. The Health Anxiety dimension comprises three IAS lower-order factors: Fear of Illness or Death, Symptom Effects, and Disease Phobia and Conviction (Cox et al., 2000; Chapter 5, this volume).

model of personality: Stress Reaction, Alienation, and Aggression. Stress Reaction correlates moderately to highly with each of the NEO-PI-R lower-order dimensions that constitute Neuroticism; the strongest correlates of Stress Reaction are the Anxiety, Hostility, and Depression scales (Church, 1994). Alienation and Aggression appear more closely related to the NEO-PI-R Agreeableness domain, but also share variance with facets of Neuroticism, particularly Hostility.

Although elevations on certain lower-order dimensions of NE may be especially relevant to hypochondriasis, little research has examined associations between health anxiety and subdomains of NE. Cox et al. (2000) conducted regression analyses using NEO-PI-R higher- and lower-order factors to predict IAS factor scores. When they entered the higher-order NEO-PI-R factors as a block, followed by a block comprising the lower-order factors, only two lower-order factors (Anxiety and Depression) emerged as significant predictors of the IAS higher-order factor, Health Anxiety. Although the zero-order correlation between IAS Health Anxiety and the Trust facet of Agreeableness was statistically significant ($r = -0.31$), Trust did not significantly predict Health Anxiety when other personality dimensions were statistically controlled.

When Cox and colleagues (2000) separated IAS Health Anxiety into its lower-order factors (Fear of Illness and Death, Symptom Effects, and Disease Phobia and Conviction), the Anxiety facet of Neuroticism was the only consistent lower-order NEO-PI-R predictor across all three IAS factors. Depression and Vulnerability to Stress aspects of Neuroticism also significantly predicted Symptom Effects, and Agreeableness and its lower-order facet of Straightforwardness were significant predictors of Disease Phobia and Conviction.

The results of this study suggest that, at least in non-clinical samples, intrapersonal rather than interpersonal aspects of NE are central to the experience of health anxiety. Only Disease Phobia and Conviction showed a significant association with more interpersonal facets of NE, particularly the tendency to communicate indirectly, when Neuroticism was statistically controlled. The negative interpersonal characteristics associated with health anxiety may only manifest themselves when concerns about health reach phobic levels. The possibility that individuals who experience more pressing fears about their health are more interpersonally unpleasant than other individuals is intuitively appealing, and others have suggested that such patterns may reflect the negative pole of Agreeableness (Kirmayer et al., 1994). The findings of Cox and colleagues (2000), however, suggest that this trait may play only a limited or peripheral role in health anxiety. Replication in both clinical and non-clinical samples will be necessary to corroborate this pattern of results.

One lower-order facet of NE that has recently received attention in the health anxiety literature is anxiety sensitivity. Anxiety sensitivity, which has generally been conceptualized as the extent to which individuals fear their own anxiety and anxiety-related sensations (see Taylor, 1999, for a comprehensive review), has been posited to be a risk factor for panic disorder and other anxiety disorders. Specifically, anxiety sensitivity may amplify individuals' responses to their own anxiety sensations (e.g., heart rate increases, breathing difficulties) and thereby produce a positive feedback cycle of anxiety. Indeed, anxiety sensitivity is a correlate and antecedent of panic attacks (McNally, 1996; Schmidt, 1999).

Anxiety sensitivity correlates moderately to highly with self-report indexes of NE and Neuroticism (see Lilienfeld, 1999, for a review). Lilienfeld, Turner, and Jacob (1993) proposed a hierarchical model in which anxiety sensitivity is posited as a lower-order facet of trait anxiety which is in turn a lower-order facet of NE, although this model has yet to be comprehensively tested (but see Taylor, 1995a). In addition, anxiety sensitivity bears important conceptual similarities to Barsky's (1992a) construct of somatosensory amplification.

Several investigators have examined the possibility that anxiety sensitivity amplifies responding to health-related complaints (see Cox, Borger, & Enns, 1999, for a review). Sigmon, Fink, Rohan, and Hotovy (1996) found that females with high scores on the Anxiety Sensitivity Index (ASI; Reiss, Peterson, Gursky, & McNally, 1986), a commonly used self-report measure of anxiety sensitivity, reported more intense menstrual symptoms (e.g., headaches, cramps, water retention) than females with low ASI scores. It is not clear, however, whether high ASI scorers simply perceived their menstrual symptoms to be more intense than low ASI scorers or whether their symptoms were actually more severe objectively. Asmundson (1999) reviewed several studies indicating that anxiety sensitivity intensifies the levels of subjective distress reported by patients with chronic pain. Interestingly, however, anxiety sensitivity appears not to be associated with ratings of pain severity.

Otto, Pollack, Sachs, and Rosenbaum (1992) examined the relation between ASI scores and hypochondriacal concerns as assessed by the IAS (Kellner, 1986) among 50 patients with panic disorder. The ASI was significantly and positively correlated with the Worry About Illness, Concern About Pain, Thanatophobia (fear of death), Disease Phobia, and Bodily Preoccupations subscales of the IAS. Moreover, in hierarchical multiple regression analyses the ASI contributed significantly to the prediction of scores on four of these five IAS subscales (Disease Phobia was the lone exception) above and beyond measures of trait anxiety and depression. Otto et al.'s findings suggest that anxiety sensitivity correlates with, and perhaps increases risk for, a broad variety of health concerns. In a recent study of 91 elderly individuals in the community, Frazier and Waid (1999) replicated Otto et al.'s (1992) finding of a significant positive correlation between the ASI and IAS ($r = 0.58$), although they did not examine the correlates of separate IAS subscales. Such an analysis would be important in view of Cox et al.'s (1999) contention that only a subset of IAS subscales are relevant to health anxiety and hypochondriasis.

Nevertheless, Otto et al.'s (1992) findings and conclusions were called into question by Taylor (1994), who pointed out that both the ASI and IAS explicitly assess fears concerning physical sensations. For example, a typical ASI item is 'When I notice that my heart is beating rapidly, I worry that I might have a heart attack', while a typical IAS item is 'Are you afraid that you may die soon?'. As Taylor noted, patients with panic disorder may endorse this and similar IAS items simply because they are reporting panic-specific fears. Panic disorder patients may report being 'afraid that [they] may die soon', for instance, because fears of dying are a frequent symptom of panic attacks (American Psychiatric Association, 1994). In other words, Otto et al.'s (1992) results may not necessarily indicate that anxiety sensitivity correlates with a broad range of health-related concerns. Instead, they may indicate only that among panic disorder patients the ASI and IAS assess very similar or identical domains of health worry, namely concerns regarding autonomic arousal (see Otto & Pollack, 1994, and Taylor, 1995b, for further discussions). If so, Otto et al.'s (1992) findings may bear relatively little relevance to hypochondriasis, which in contrast to panic disorder is typically characterized by fears of non-autonomic symptoms (McNally, 1994).

In response to Taylor's (1994, 1995b) criticisms, Otto, Demopulos, McLean, Pollack, and Fava (1998) presented data from 100 patients with major depression who had no history of panic disorder. They reported that the ASI was again moderately and significantly correlated with most IAS scales (with the exception of Health Habits). Moreover, in hierarchical multiple regression analyses the ASI exhibited statistically significant levels of incremental validity above and beyond measures of anxiety, depression, somatic symptoms, and hostility in the prediction of the IAS Concern About Pain, Hypochondriacal Beliefs, Disease Phobia, and Bodily Preoccupation scales. Although these analyses partly address the criticisms of Taylor (1994, 1995a,b), Otto et al. (1998) acknowledged that their investigation does 'not fully address the question of whether the hypochondriacal concerns endorsed by patients on the IAS are specific to, rather than just associated with, the fears of arousal-related symptoms targeted by the ASI' (p. 230). In other words, although Otto et al.'s (1998) findings exclude the possibility that the correlation between the ASI and IAS is a consequence of panic disorder, they do not exclude the possibility that the variance shared by these two measures is limited to autonomic concerns, which are not a distinguishing feature of hypochondriasis. More broadly, Otto et al.'s (1998) results do not rule out the hypothesis that the correlation between the ASI and IAS is largely a product of quasi-tautological content overlap between the items on these two measures (see Nicholls, Licht, & Pearl, 1982, for a general discussion of this problem in the self-report assessment of personality and psychopathology).

As a consequence, more information is needed regarding the relation between anxiety sensitivity measures and indexes of hypochondriacal symptoms per se (Cox et al., 1999). Furer, Walker, Chartier, and Stein (1997) compared the ASI scores of panic disorder patients with ($n = 10$) and without ($n = 11$) hypochondriasis. The ASI scores of the former group were higher, although this difference did not reach significance. This negative finding may, however, be a consequence of low statistical power. More recently, Cox, Fuentes, Borger, and Taylor (in press) compared the IAS scores of high AS persons with histories of a panic attack ($n = 24$) to high AS persons without panic ($n = 20$). The high AS group with panic reported significantly higher levels of worry about illness, hypochondriacal beliefs, and bodily preoccupation than did the panic-free high AS group.

Koszycki, Zacharko, and Bradwejn (1996) found that the ASI correlated moderately and significantly ($r = 0.54$) with the MMPI Hypochondriasis Scale in a sample of 29 panic disorder patients. Nevertheless, the extent to which the elevated scores on the MMPI Hypochondriasis Scale were attributable to common panic disorder symptoms (e.g., rapid heart beat, nausea, breathing difficulties) is unclear. This issue is important because the variance shared by the ASI and the MMPI Hypochondriasis Scale could be largely or entirely a product of panic disorder symptoms. In addition, because the MMPI Hypochondriasis Scale, like most MMPI scales, is highly saturated with NE (Tellegen, 1985), it will be important in future research to ascertain the extent to which the ASI contributes to the prediction of hypochondriacal symptoms above and beyond NE measures.

## Positive Emotionality (PE) and Health Anxiety

When reversed, the two dimensions—Community and Agency—into which PE often divides appear likely to share common ground with hypochondriasis and perhaps normal-range health anxiety. For instance, although individuals with persistent hypochondriasis are prone to reach out to others, particularly those in the medical profession, their relationships tend to be brief, frustrating to both parties, and likely to revolve around insatiable needs for reassurance rather than for social affiliation (Barsky & Klerman, 1983). Additionally, relative to non-hypochondriacal peers, they tend to limit their work and social activity on the basis of their perceived health problems (Noyes et al., 1993; Robbins & Kirmayer, 1996). Little empirical work, however, has examined whether these behavioral features relate to PE, and existing findings are inconsistent with regard to such an association.

Most research examining associations between PE and hypochondriasis has used measures of Extraversion, which tap primarily the communal and positive affective components of PE. This research has yielded mixed findings, and it remains unclear whether the experience of positive emotion or proclivity for interpersonal closeness is substantially diminished in individuals who report high levels of health anxiety. In the two studies that compared EPI Extraversion levels in individuals diagnosed with hypochondriasis and comparison participants, between-group differences were non-significant (Noyes et al., 1993, 1999). In the more recent of these two studies, however, Extraversion and Whiteley Index scores for the combined clinical and comparison samples were significantly and negatively correlated (Noyes et al., 1999). Further, in Hollifield et al.'s (1999) examination of subclinical 'hypochondriacal responders' and 'somatizers', NEO-PI-R Extraversion levels were significantly lower in both groups relative to comparison participants.

Cox et al. (2000) found that scores on the IAS Health Anxiety higher-order factor correlated significantly and negatively with NEO-PI-R Extraversion and three of its facets (Assertiveness, Activity, and Positive Emotions). When they statistically controlled for the contribution of Neuroticism, however, these associations were reduced to non-significant levels. These results suggest that health anxiety may reflect high NE, at least aspects of NE, in the somatic domain, and that health anxiety manifests itself essentially independently of PE and other personality traits. Additionally, they highlight the importance of controlling for NE when examining potential associations with other personality dimensions. Indeed, although NE and PE are theoretically orthogonal, certain lower-order facets of PE, such as Well Being, tend to be weakly to moderately negatively correlated with NE (Tellegen, 1982).

## Constraint and Health Anxiety

Kirmayer et al. (1994) postulated that elevated levels of Constraint, at least its facets characterized by behavioral or impulse control (Conscientiousness), may partly underlie hypochondriacal individuals' obsessive concerns about their health. The small body of available evidence, however, suggests that neither control-oriented (e.g., Conscientiousness) nor tradition-oriented (e.g., reversed Openness to Experience) facets of Constraint are elevated among individuals with subclinical health anxiety. In Hollifield et al.'s (1999) study, hypochondriacal responders reported comparable levels of Conscientiousness and Openness to Experience to those of non-hypochondriacal responders. Hypochondriacal responders' Conscientiousness scores were, in fact, slightly, but not significantly, lower than those of their non-hypochondriacal peers. This finding is consistent with Cox et al.'s (2000) results; among college students, IAS health anxiety was significantly and *negatively* correlated with Conscientiousness and several of its facets (Competence, Dutifulness, and Self-discipline). When Neuroticism was statistically controlled, however, none of these associations remained significant. It is important to note that Neuroticism and Conscientiousness tend to be modestly negatively correlated (Block, 1995).

High levels of Conscientiousness do appear to play a role in patterns of elevated symptom reporting in the absence of objective disease (Feldman et al., 1999). Rather than contributing to elevated health anxiety, however, they appear to facilitate an adaptive and proactive stance toward maintaining good health. Cox et al. (2000) found that Conscientiousness, particularly its deliberation facet, was a significant predictor of the IAS higher-order factor termed Health Behaviors, even when the contribution of Neuroticism was controlled statistically. Thus, although the conscientious or controlled aspect of Constraint does not appear related to the manifestation of health anxiety per se, it may play a role in adults' proclivity to engage in health-promoting behaviors. This possibility is consistent with earlier findings suggesting a positive association between Conscientiousness and wellness behavior (Booth-Kewley & Vickers, 1994).

Among individuals with clinically significant levels of health anxiety, the potential role of Constraint has yet to be adequately examined. In their study of family members of hypochondriacal patients, Noyes et al. (1999) found significantly *lower* levels of Conscientiousness among relatives who met diagnostic criteria for hypochondriasis than among non-hypochondriacal relatives, although they did not control for levels of Neuroticism. This finding provides a preliminary argument against the possibility that substantial elevations on Constraint or its facets, although absent in subclinical health anxiety, are evident in individuals whose health anxiety is extreme. Instead, it suggests that hypochondriacal individuals may be more impulsive than their non-hypochondriacal counterparts. Alternatively, as Barsky (1992b) has suggested, two different subtypes, one more strongly characterized by obsessive features than the other, may exist within the broad domain of clinical hypochondriasis. If so, then aspects of Constraint may figure more prominently in the etiology of the former subtype than the latter and studies that conflate these subtypes could obscure these patterns of association. Given the dearth of data in this area, further research examining the relations of health anxiety, particularly clinical hypochondriasis, to Constraint is clearly needed.

## ABSORPTION AND HEALTH ANXIETY

As noted earlier, Absorption does not load primarily on any one of the Big Three dimensions, although it tends to exhibit modest positive loadings on both NE and PE (Tellegen & Waller, 1994). This finding suggests the intriguing possibility that Absorption may amplify both negative and positive affective experiences. To our knowledge, however, there exists no published research examining the association between absorption and health anxiety per se. Nevertheless, two lines of research suggest that this association may be worth investigating. First, several researchers have reported that Absorption and closely related traits are positively correlated with measures of somatic symptoms. Watten, Vassend, Myhrer, and Syversen (1997), for example, found that scores on Tellegen and Atkinson's (1974) absorption scale were positively and significantly, although weakly ($r = 0.15$), correlated with a self-reported measure of somatic complaints among 411 male military recruits. Gick, McLeod, and Hulihan (1997) similarly found a significant positive correlation between absorption scale scores and self-reported somatic symptoms in a sample of 290 patients drawn from a behavioral medicine clinic (see also McGrady, Lynch, Nagel, & Zsembik, 1999; but see Wickramasekera, 1995, for data suggesting that the association between hypnotizability—a construct related to Absorption—and somatization may be curvilinear). Although these studies have focused on the relation between Absorption and self-reported somatic symptoms, they suggest that an examination of the association between absorption and health anxiety is warranted.

Second, in a study of 220 undergraduates, Lilienfeld (1997; see also Lilienfeld, 1999) reported that Absorption scale scores were positively and significantly, although weakly ($r = 0.16$), correlated with a history of panic attacks during the previous year. Although Absorption correlated nonsignificantly with a history of unexpected panic attacks, it correlated moderately and significantly ($r = 0.48$) with the proportion of panic attacks that were unexpected. This finding is intriguing given that unexpected panic attacks are the hallmark of panic disorder (American Psychiatric Association, 1994; Barlow, 1988). Moreover, Absorption was positively and significantly ($r = 0.27$) correlated with a composite measure of anxiety sensitivity derived by standardizing and summing the ASI and three other self-report anxiety sensitivity indexes. This correlation remained significant even among participants with no panic attack history, suggesting that the association between Absorption and anxiety sensitivity is not simply a consequence of previous panic attacks. Instead, absorption may be a risk factor for panic attacks and perhaps panic disorder (Lilienfeld, 1997), although longitudinal and causal modeling research will be necessary to provide stronger evidence for this conjecture. Subsidiary analyses (Lilienfeld, 1999) revealed that the correlation between Absorption and anxiety sensitivity remained significant even after statistically controlling for either trait anxiety or NE. These findings indicate that although NE is associated with hypervigilance concerning physical sensations (Pennebaker & Watson, 1991), Absorption shares variance with anxiety sensitivity that is not entirely accounted for by NE.

Although Lilienfeld's (1997) findings are not directly pertinent to health anxiety or hypochondriasis, they raise the possibility that absorption increases risk for certain anxiety-related conditions, perhaps by heightening individuals' attention to interoceptive cues. Like panic disorder, hypochondriasis is associated with a tendency to catastrophically misinterpret unexpected or ambiguous physical sensations. Indeed, hypochondriacal fears often precede panic attacks (Fava, Grandi, & Canestrari, 1988a), and both anxiety sensitivity and hypochondriacal fears tend to decrease in panic disorder patients following cognitive-behavioral therapy (Fava, Kellner, Zielezny, & Grandi, 1988b; McNally & Lorenz, 1987; Saviotti et al., 1991). In addition, hypochondriasis and panic disorder frequently co-occur (Barsky, Barnett, & Cleary, 1994). The principal differences between panic disorder and hypochondriasis are (a) the time frame for expected catastrophe (immediate in the case of panic disorder, delayed in the case of hypochondriasis); and (b) the symptom focus of anxiety (autonomic in the case of panic disorder, non-autonomic in the case of hypochondriasis) (McNally, 1994). An investigation of personality variables that panic disorder and hypochondriasis both do and do not share could assist in identifying both general and specific etiological factors for each condition.

## PERSONALITY DISORDER AND HEALTH ANXIETY

Although hypochondriasis is currently conceptualized in the DSM as a categorical Axis I disorder, several authors have contended that it may be better classified along Axis II due to its chronic course and pervasive impact on cognition and behavior (Pennebaker & Watson, 1991; Tyrer et al., 1990). According to this perspective, hypochondriasis and other somatoform disorders constitute enduring, maladaptive patterns of interaction with others in which the individual's identity revolves around playing the 'sick role' (Bass & Murphy, 1995, p. 424). Thus, interpersonal aspects of the disorder, which the current DSM criteria downplay, may be as salient as the nature of the individual's distress (Barsky, 1995). In light of the growing body of evidence indicating associations between health anxiety and personality dimensions, particularly NE (e.g., Cox et al., 2000; Hollifield et al., 1999; Noyes et al., 1993, 1994), this proposed reconceptualization of hypochondriasis as an Axis II disorder merits further attention. Such a rethinking of hypochondriasis seems especially interesting in light of recent suggestions that comparable dimensions may underlie variation in both normal and abnormal personality functioning (Livesley, Jang, & Vernon, 1998; Widiger, 1998).

Whether hypochondriasis constitutes a personality disorder in its own right is debatable. Some researchers have contended that a separate diagnostic category for hypochondriacal personality is warranted for a cluster of hypochondriacal patients who exhibit a stable constellation of characteristics including general anxiety, dependence, and conscientiousness, in addition to their health worries and preoccupations (Tyrer et al., 1990; Tyrer, Seivewright, & Seivewright, 1999). Using cluster analyses of Personality Assessment Schedule (PAS; Tyrer & Alexander, 1979) scores, Tyrer and colleagues (1999) identified individuals with this distinctive set of personality traits and then followed them for 2 years. Relative to individuals whose PAS profiles were consistent with other non-specified personality disorders, those within the hypochondriacal personality cluster were more impaired and less improved in terms of global psychopathology after 2 years. On the basis of these findings, Tyrer et al. suggested that the hypochondriacal personality is separable from other personality disorders.

Given the high levels of overlap of hypochondriasis with other personality disorders, however, it is possible that this condition instead represents a specific behavioral manifestation of a generally maladaptive personality style. Among individuals who meet DSM criteria for hypochondriasis, associated personality disorders are disproportionately common. Barsky, Wyshak, and Klerman (1992) found that vastly more participants in their hypochondriacal sample (63.4%) exceeded the cut-off for likely personality disorder caseness on a screening questionnaire than did participants in their non-hypochondriacal comparison group (17.3%). Because Barsky et al. (1992) used a screening instrument rather than a full diagnostic interview, their results likely overestimate rates of DSM-III-R syndromal personality disorder among individuals recruited from medical outpatient settings. Similarly high rates of personality disorder, however, are evident in psychiatric samples with hypochondriasis when more stringent diagnostic interviews are used. Among hypochondriacal patients drawn from two community mental health centers, 74% met DSM criteria for a personality disorder, with Cluster C disorders (i.e., Avoidant, Dependent, and Obsessive-Compulsive) being the most frequently diagnosed (Garyfallos et al., 1999).

Hypochondriacal behavior may therefore simply constitute one expression of underlying anxious and dependent traits. Why health concerns occupy a central place for some individuals with these traits but not others is unclear. Bass and Murphy (1995) suggested that a history of childhood victimization and a lack of parental care, combined with severe illness early in development, may increase the likelihood of hypochondriasis in individuals who are prone to approach their environments in an anxious, dependent manner. Without prospective, longitudinal research on community samples, however, it will be difficult to evaluate the validity of this conjecture.

## SUMMARY AND FUTURE DIRECTIONS

Although personality traits and their relations to health anxiety and hypochondriasis have received increased research attention in recent years, the literature on this topic is still in its early stages. Currently, the best-established finding is a consistent, moderate association between NE and measures of both health anxiety and clinical hypochondriasis. Preliminary evidence indicates that this association may be partly explained by lower-order facets of both NE and health anxiety. In the one study to examine the predictive value of lower-order factors while statistically controlling for higher-order personality factors, the Anxiety facet of NE emerged as the strongest predictor of health anxiety and its subdomains (Cox et al., 2000). Other lower-order facets of NE, such as anxiety sensitivity, also hold potential explanatory value for health anxiety and hypochondriasis. It remains unclear, however, whether anxiety sensitivity correlates with the type of health concerns that are central to hypochondriasis and whether it provides incremental validity above and beyond NE, although the findings of Otto et al. (1992, 1998) offer preliminary evidence for the latter possibility. More research will be necessary to examine more closely these and other lower-order NE facets and their relations to health anxiety, particularly their relevance to more severe manifestations of health anxiety, such as clinical hypochondriasis. The systematic examination of personality disorders and health anxiety is in its infancy, although preliminary evidence suggests that personality disorders ostensibly characterized by elevated NE and trait anxiety, particularly those in Cluster C, are positively associated with health anxiety (Garyfallos et al., 1999).

Although NE is clearly important to health anxiety, it is less apparent whether other personality dimensions contribute incrementally to health anxiety and hypochondriasis beyond NE. Because associations between health anxiety and personality dimensions other than NE are vastly understudied, this issue is currently difficult to evaluate. The small existing body of literature suggests that PE figures minimally in health anxiety, especially when NE is statistically controlled. Constraint and Absorption, however, may contribute to the etiology and maintenance of health anxiety above and beyond NE, although the role of Conscientiousness (which is related to Constraint) is inconsistent across studies and requires clarification. One lower-order component of Constraint that has received surprisingly little attention in the literature is fearfulness or harm avoidance. Although sometimes viewed as interchangeable with trait anxiety, fearfulness is largely or entirely uncorrelated with trait anxiety or NE (Watson & Clark, 1984). Tellegen (1982) proposed that whereas fearfulness is the perception of impending threat, anxiety is the perception that danger is present and can no longer be avoided. Moreover, an accumulating body of evidence suggests that fearfulness and trait anxiety are underpinned by different neural systems (White & Depue, 1999). Because patients with hypochondriasis often anticipate long-term threats (i.e., serious physical illness), the construct of fearfulness may be relevant to understanding the interpretations and emotional reactions of individuals with elevated levels of health anxiety. Nevertheless, only tentative statements about personality dimensions other than NE are possible on the basis of the existing literature. Much more research needs to focus on Absorption, Constraint, and PE to clarify whether and how these dimensions may enhance our understanding of health anxiety.

Additionally, although we have focused in this chapter on the Big Three, the Big Five model of personality dimensions also offers promise for explaining aspects of health anxiety. In their review of personality factors and their relation to various somatoform disorders, Kirmayer et al. (1994) suggest that the Big Five may be especially useful for understanding the problematic doctor–patient interactions that are often associated with hypochondriasis because it decomposes Tellegen's third factor, Constraint, into Conscientiousness and Agreeableness. Specifically, Kirmayer et al. conjecture that hypochondriacal patients may be low in Agreeableness, given their propensities toward interpersonal conflict and mistrust. Kirmayer et al. also speculate that individuals with either high or low levels of Openness to Experience or Absorption may be prone to hypochondriasis. Whereas high levels of Openness may relate to the enhanced suggestibility evident in some hypochondriacal patients, low levels of Openness may contribute to other patients' ineffective efforts to suppress symptoms. Only recently, however, have researchers begun to examine associations between these dimensions and health anxiety, and more research will be necessary to evaluate the strength and importance of such associations.

Correlational studies of health concerns and personality in combined normal and clinical samples suggest that associations between these two domains may be comparable among individuals with normal-range health anxiety and hypochondriasis. No research to date, however, has compared associations across the two groups, nor have many studies examining specific personality dimensions such as NE statistically controlled for the contributions of other personality dimensions. Research using hierarchical multiple regression, like that of Cox et al. (2000), that examines the incremental contributions of various personality dimensions to both clinical hypochondriasis and non-clinical health anxiety will be necessary in order to draw conclusions about similarities or differences in patterns of association at high and low levels of health anxiety.

Little is known about the developmental precursors of health anxiety. In particular, prospective designs are warranted to examine how associations between personality and health anxiety/hypochondriasis unfold over time. Although a few researchers have followed hypochondriacal patients over several years, they have selected their participants on the basis of pre-existing levels of health anxiety. These designs have thus precluded the separation of premorbid personality characteristics from behavioral and cognitive sequelae of long-term illness or perceived symptoms. Ideally, to tease apart potential precursors and consequences of high levels of health concern, large samples of children will need to be recruited prior to the emergence of health anxiety and followed through the course of development. High-risk samples, such as the offspring or other first-degree relatives of hypochondriacal patients, may prove especially useful for elucidating the developmental course of hypochondriasis and its association with long-standing personality features.

Finally, although personality traits hold promise for increasing our understanding of health anxiety, they alone cannot entirely explain this condition. Although high levels of NE, for instance, are characteristic of individuals with high levels of health anxiety, the converse of this pattern is not necessarily true. Many people with high levels of NE have neither hypochondriasis nor high levels of health anxiety. Both dispositional and environmental factors thus likely play important roles in the emergence of health anxiety, with long-standing personality characteristics combining or interacting with environmental triggers to produce elevated levels of health concern. A crucial next step will therefore be to identify environmental precipitants that lead to health anxiety in predisposed individuals.

## REFERENCES

American Psychiatric Association (1994). *Diagnostic and statistical manual of mental disorders* (4th edn.). Washington, DC: Author.

Asmundson, G.J.G. (1999). Anxiety sensitivity and chronic pain: Empirical findings, clinical implications, and future directions. In S. Taylor (Ed.), *Anxiety sensitivity: Theory, research, and treatment of the fear of anxiety* (pp. 269–285). Mahwah, NJ: Lawrence Erlbaum.

Barlow, D.H. (1988). *Anxiety and its disorders.* New York: Guilford Press.

Barsky, A.J. (1992a). Amplification, somatization, and the somatoform disorders. *Psychosomatics, 33,* 28–34.

Barsky, A.J. (1992b). Hypochondriasis and obsessive compulsive disorder. *Psychiatric Clinics of North America, 15,* 791–801.

Barsky, A.J. (1995). Somatoform disorders and personality traits. *Journal of Psychosomatic Research, 39,* 399–402.

Barsky, A.J., Barnett, M.C., & Cleary, P.D. (1994). Hypochondriasis and panic disorder: Boundary and overlap. *Archives of General Psychiatry, 51,* 918–925.

Barsky, A.J., Fama, J.M., Bailey, E.D., & Ahern, D.K. (1998). A prospective 4- to 5-year study of DSM-III-R hypochondriasis. *Archives of General Psychiatry, 55,* 737–744.

Barsky, A.J., & Klerman, G.L. (1983). Overview: Hypochondriasis, bodily complaints, and somatic styles. *American Journal of Psychiatry, 140,* 273–283.

Barsky, A.J., Wyshak, G., & Klerman, G. (1986). Hypochondriasis—an evaluation of the DSM-III criteria in medical outpatients. *General Hospital Psychiatry, 10,* 322–327.

Barsky, A.J., Wyshak, G., & Klerman, G. (1990). Transient hypochondriasis. *Archives of General Psychiatry, 47,* 746–752.

Barsky, A.J., Wyshak, G., & Klerman, G.L. (1992). Psychiatric comorbidity in DSM-III-R hypochondriasis. *Archives of General Psychiatry, 49,* 101–108.

Bass, C., & Murphy, M. (1995). Somatoform and personality disorders: Syndromal comorbidity and overlapping developmental pathways. *Journal of Psychosomatic Research, 39,* 403–427.

Block, J. (1995). A contrarian view of the five-factor approach to personality description. *Psychological Bulletin, 117,* 187–215.

Booth-Kewley, S., & Vickers, R.R. (1994). Associations between major domains of personality and health behavior. *Journal of Personality, 62,* 281–298.

Cattell, R.B. (1950). *Personality: A systematic, theoretical, and factual study.* New York: McGraw-Hill.

Church, A.T. (1994). Relating the Tellegen and five-factor models of personality structure. *Journal of Personality and Social Psychology, 67,* 898–909.

Cloninger, C.R. (1987). A systematic method for clinical description and classification of personality variants. *Archives of General Psychiatry, 44,* 573–588.

Cloninger, C.R., Sigvardsson, S., von Knorring, A., & Bohman, M. (1984). An adoption study of somatoform disorders. *Archives of General Psychiatry, 41,* 863–871.

Costa, P.T., Jr., & McCrae, R.R. (1985). Hypochondriasis, neuroticism, and aging: When are somatic complaints unfounded? *American Psychologist, 40,* 19–28.

Costa, P.T., Jr., & McCrae, R.R. (1992). *NEO-PI-R: Revised NEO Personality Inventory (NEO-PI-R).* Odessa, FL: Psychological Assessment Resources.

Cox, B.J., Borger, S.C., Asmundson, G.J.G., & Taylor, S. (2000). Dimensions of hypochondriasis and the five-factor model of personality. *Personality and Individual Differences, 29,* 99–108.

Cox, B.J., Borger, S.C., & Enns, M.W. (1999). Anxiety sensitivity and emotional disorders: Psychometric studies and their theoretical implications. In S. Taylor (Ed.), *Anxiety sensitivity: Theory, research, and treatment of the fear of anxiety* (pp. 115–148). Mahwah, NJ: Lawrence Erlbaum.

Cox, B.J., Fuentes, K., Borger, S.C., & Taylor, S. (in press). Psychopathological correlates of anxiety sensitivity: Evidence from clinical interviews and self-report measures. *Journal of Anxiety Disorders.*

Depue, R.A., & Collins, P.F. (1999). Neurobiology of the structure of personality: Dopamine, facilitation of incentive motivation, and extraversion. *Behavioral and Brain Sciences*, **22**, 491–569.

Depue, R.A., Luciana, M., Arbisi, P., Collins, P., & Leon, A. (1994). Dopamine and the structure of personality: Relation of agonist-induced dopamine activity to positive emotionality. *Journal of Personality and Social Psychology*, **67**, 485–498.

Depue, R.A., & Spoont, M.R. (1986). Conceptualizing a serotonin trait: A behavioral dimension of constraint. *Annals of the New York Academy of Sciences*, **487**, 47–62.

Eysenck, H.J. (1947). *Dimensions of personality*. New York: Praeger.

Eysenck, H.J. (1967). *The biological basis of personality*. Springfield, IL: Charles C. Thomas.

Eysenck, H.J. (1993). Comment on Goldberg. *American Psychologist*, **48**, 1299–1300.

Eysenck, H.J., & Eysenck, S.B.S. (1968). *Manual for the Eysenck Personality Inventory*. San Diego, CA: Educational and Industry Testing Service.

Fava, G.A., Grandi, S., & Canestrari, R. (1988a). Prodromal symptoms in panic disorder with agoraphobia. *American Journal of Psychiatry*, **145**, 1564–1567.

Fava, G.A., Kellner, R., Zielezny, M., & Grandi, S. (1988b). Hypochondriacal fears and beliefs in agoraphobia. *Journal of Affective Disorders*, **14**, 1564–1567.

Feldman, P.J., Cohen, S., Doyle, W.J., Skoner, D.P., & Gwaltney, J.M., Jr. (1999). The impact of personality on the reporting of unfounded symptoms and illness. *Journal of Personality and Social Psychology*, **77**, 370–378.

Fowles, D.C. (1987). Application of a behavioral theory of motivation to the concepts of anxiety and impulsivity. *Journal of Research in Personality*, **21**, 417–435.

Frazier, L.D., & Waid, L.D. (1999). Influences on anxiety in later life: The role of health status, health perceptions, and health locus of control. *Aging and Mental Health*, **3**, 213–220.

Furer, P., Walker, J.R., Chartier, M.J., & Stein, M.B. (1997). Hypochondriacal concerns and somatization in panic disorder. *Depression and Anxiety*, **6**, 78–85.

Garyfallos, G., Adamopoulou, A., Karastergiou, A., Voikli, M., Idonomidis, N., Donias, S., Giouzepas, J., & Dimitriou, E. (1999). Somatoform disorders: Comorbidity with other DSM-III-R psychiatric diagnoses in Greece. *Comprehensive Psychiatry*, **40**, 299–307.

Gick, M., McLeod, C., & Hulihan, D. (1997). Absorption, social desirability, and symptoms in a behavioral medicine population. *Journal of Nervous and Mental Disease*, **185**, 454–458.

Goldberg, L.R. (1981). Language and individual differences: The search for universals in personality lexicons. In L. Wheeler (Ed.), *Review of personality and social psychology* (Vol. 2, pp. 141–165). Beverly Hills, CA: Sage.

Goldberg, L.R. (1993). The structure of phenotypic personality traits. *American Psychologist*, **48**, 26–34.

Gray, J. (1982). *The neuropsychology of anxiety: An enquiry into the functions of the septo-hippocampal system*. Oxford: Clarendon Press.

Hollifield, M., Tuttle, L., Paine, S., & Kellner, R. (1999). Hypochondriasis and somatization related to personality and attitudes toward self. *Psychosomatics, 40,* 387–395.

Kellner, R. (1986). *Somatization and hypochondriasis.* New York: Praeger Publishers.

Kellner, R. (1987). *Manual of the Symptom Questionnaire.* Unpublished manuscript, University of New Mexico.

Kellner, R., Abbott, P., Winslow, W.W., & Pathak, D. (1987). Fears, beliefs, and attitudes in DSM-III hypochondriasis. *Journal of Nervous and Mental Disease, 175,* 20–25.

Kirmayer, L.J., & Robbins, J.M. (1991). Three forms of somatization in primary care: Prevalence, co-occurrence, and sociodemographic characteristics. *Journal of Nervous and Mental Disease, 179,* 647–655.

Kirmayer, L.J., Robbins, J.M., & Paris, J. (1994). Somatoform disorders: Personality and the social matrix of somatic distress. *Journal of Abnormal Psychology, 103,* 125–136.

Koszycki, D., Zacharko, R.M., & Bradwejn, J. (1996). Influence of personality on behavioral response to cholecystokinin-tetrapeptide in patients with panic disorder. *Psychiatry Research, 62,* 131–138.

Krueger, R.F., Caspi, A., Moffitt, T.E., Silva, P.A., & McGee, R. (1996). Personality traits are differentially linked to mental disorders: A multitrait-multidiagnosis study of an adolescent birth cohort. *Journal of Abnormal Psychology, 105,* 299–312.

Larsen, R.J., & Ketelaar, T. (1991). Personality and susceptibility to positive and negative emotional states. *Journal of Personality and Social Psychology, 61,* 132–140.

Le Moal, M., & Simon, H. (1991). Mesocorticolimbic dopaminergic network: Functional and regulatory roles. *Physiological Reviews, 71,* 155–234.

Lilienfeld, S.O. (1997). The relation of anxiety sensitivity to higher and lower order personality dimensions: Implications for the etiology of panic attacks. *Journal of Abnormal Psychology, 106,* 539–544.

Lilienfeld, S.O. (1999). Anxiety sensitivity and the structure of personality. In S. Taylor (Ed.), *Anxiety sensitivity: Theory, research, and treatment of the fear of anxiety* (pp. 149–180). Mahwah, NJ: Lawrence Erlbaum.

Lilienfeld, S.O., Turner, S.M., & Jacob, R.G. (1993). Anxiety sensitivity: An examination of theoretical and methodological issues. *Advances in Behaviour Research and Therapy, 15,* 147–183.

Livesley, W.J., Jang, K.L., & Vernon, P.A. (1998). Phenotypic and genetic structure of traits delineating personality disorder. *Archives of General Psychiatry, 55,* 941–948.

Mabe, P.A., Riley, W.T., Jones, L.R., & Hobson, D.P. (1996). The medical context of hypochondriacal traits. *International Journal of Psychiatry in Medicine, 26,* 443–459.

McCrae, R.R. (1991). The five-factor model and its assessment in clinical settings. *Journal of Personality Assessment, 57,* 399–414.

McGrady, A., Lynch, D., Nagel, R., & Zsembik, C. (1999). Application of the High Risk Model of Threat Perception to a primary care patient population. *Journal of Nervous and Mental Disease, 187,* 369–375.

McNally, R.J. (1994). *Panic disorder: A critical analysis.* New York: Guilford Press.

McNally, R.J. (1996). Anxiety sensitivity is distinguishable from trait anxiety. In R.M. Rapee (Ed.), *Current controversies in the anxiety disorders* (pp. 214–227). New York: Guilford.

McNally, R.J., & Lorenz, M. (1987). Anxiety sensitivity in agoraphobics. *Journal of Behavior Therapy and Experimental Psychiatry, 18,* 3–11.

Meehl, P.E., & Golden, R. (1982). Taxometric methods. In P. Kendall & J. Butcher (Eds.), *Handbook of research methods in clinical psychology* (pp. 127–181). New York: Wiley.

Nicholls, J.G., Licht, B.G., & Pearl, R.A. (1982). Some dangers of using personality questionnaires to measure personality. *Psychological Bulletin*, **92**, 572–580.

Norman, W.T. (1963). Toward an adequate taxonomy of personality attributes: Replicated factor structure. *Journal of Abnormal and Social Psychology*, **66**, 574–583.

Noyes, R., Jr., Happel, R.L., Yagla, S.J. (1999). Correlates of hypochondriasis in a nonclinical population. *Psychosomatics*, **40**, 461–469.

Noyes, R., Jr., Kathol, R.G., Fisher, M.M., Phillips, B.M., Suelzer, M.T., & Holt, C.S. (1993). The validity of DSM-III-R hypochondriasis. *Archives of General Psychiatry*, **50**, 961–970.

Noyes, R., Jr., Kathol, R.G., Fisher, M.M., Phillips, B.M., Suelzer, M.T., & Woodman, C.L. (1994). One-year follow-up of medical outpatients with hypochondriasis. *Psychosomatics*, **35**, 533–545.

Otto, M.W., Demopulos, C.M., McLean, N.E., Pollack, M.H., & Fava, M. (1998). Additional findings on the association between anxiety sensitivity and hypochondriacal concerns: Examination of patients with major depression. *Journal of Anxiety Disorders*, **12**, 225–232.

Otto, M.W., & Pollack, M.H. (1994). Panic disorder and hypochondriacal concerns: A reply to Taylor. *Journal of Anxiety Disorders*, **8**, 101–103.

Otto, M.W., Pollack, M.H., Sachs, G.S., & Rosenbaum, J.F. (1992). Hypochondriacal concerns, anxiety sensitivity, and panic disorder. *Journal of Anxiety Disorders*, **6**, 93–104.

Pennebaker, J.W., & Watson, D. (1991). The psychology of somatic symptoms. In L.J. Kirmayer & J.M. Robbins (Eds.), *Current concepts of somatization* (pp. 21–35). Washington, DC: American Psychiatric Press.

Pilowsky, I. (1967). Dimensions of hypochondriasis. *British Journal of Psychiatry*, **113**, 89–93.

Reiss, S., Peterson, R.A., Gursky, D.M., & McNally, R.J. (1986). Anxiety sensitivity, anxiety frequency, and the prediction of fearfulness. *Behaviour Research and Therapy*, **24**, 1–8.

Robbins, J.M., & Kirmayer, L.J. (1996). Transient and persistent hypochondriacal worry in primary care. *Psychological Medicine*, **26**, 575–589.

Saviotti, F.M., Grandi, S., Savron, G., Ermentini, R., Bartolucci, G., Conti, S., & Fava, G.A. (1991). Characterological traits of recovered patients with panic disorder and agoraphobia. *Journal of Affective Disorders*, **23**, 113–117.

Schmidt, N.B. (1999). Prospective evaluations of anxiety sensitivity. In S. Taylor (Ed.). *Anxiety sensitivity: Theory, research, and treatment of the fear of anxiety* (pp. 217–235). Mahwah, NJ: Lawrence Erlbaum.

Siever, L., & Davis, K.L. (1991). A psychobiological perspective on the personality disorders. *American Journal of Psychiatry*, **148**, 1647–1658.

Sigmon, S.T., Fink, C., Rohan, K.J., & Hotovy, L.A. (1996). Anxiety sensitivity and menstrual cycle reactivity: Psychophysiological and self-report differences. *Journal of Anxiety Disorders*, **10**, 393–410.

Spoont, M.R. (1992). Modulatory role of serotonin in neural information processing: Implications for human psychopathology. *Psychological Bulletin*, **112**, 330–350.

Starcevic, V. (1990). Role of reassurance and psychopathology in hypochondriasis. *Psychiatry*, **53**, 383–395.

Taylor, S. (1994). Comment on Otto et al. (1992): Hypochondriacal concerns, anxiety sensitivity, and panic disorder. *Journal of Anxiety Disorders*, **8**, 97–99.

Taylor, S. (1995a). Issues in the conceptualization and measurement of anxiety sensitivity. *Journal of Anxiety Disorders*, **9**, 163–174.

Taylor, S. (1995b). Panic disorder and hypochondriacal concerns: Reply to Otto and Pollack (1994). *Journal of Anxiety Disorders*, **9**, 87–88.

Taylor, S. (1999). *Anxiety sensitivity: Theory, research, and treatment of the fear of anxiety*. Mahwah, NJ: Lawrence Erlbaum.

Tellegen, A. (1982). *Brief manual for the Differential Personality Questionnaire*. Unpublished manuscript, University of Minnesota.

Tellegen, A. (1985). Structures of mood and personality and their relevance to assessing anxiety, with an emphasis on self-report. In A.H. Tuma & J.D. Maser (Eds.), *Anxiety and the anxiety disorders* (pp. 681–706). Hillsdale, NJ: Erlbaum.

Tellegen, A., & Atkinson, G. (1974). Openness to experience and self-altering experiences ('absorption'), a trait related to hypnotic susceptibility. *Journal of Abnormal Psychology*, **83**, 268–277.

Tellegen, A., Lykken, D.T., Bouchard, T.J., Jr., Wilcox, K.J., Segal, N.L., & Rich, S. (1988). Personality similarity in twins reared apart and together. *Journal of Personality and Social Psychology*, **54**, 1031–1039.

Tellegen, A., & Waller, N.G. (1994). Exploring personality through test construction: Development of the Multidimensional Personality Questionnaire. In S.R. Briggs & J.M. Cheek (Eds.), *Personality measures: Development and evaluation* (Vol. 1, pp. 133–161). Greenwich, CT: JAI Press.

Tomarken, A.J., Davidson R.J., Wheeler R.E., & Doss R.C. (1992). Individual differences in anterior brain asymmetry and fundamental dimensions of emotion. *Journal of Personality and Social Psychology*, **62**, 676–687.

Trull, T.J., & Sher, K.J. (1994). Relationship between the five-factor model of personality and Axis I disorders in a nonclinical sample. *Journal of Abnormal Psychology*, **103**, 350–360.

Tyrer, P., & Alexander, J. (1979). Classification of personality disorder. *British Journal of Psychiatry*, **135**, 163–167.

Tyrer, P., Fowler-Dixon, R., Ferguson, B., & Kelemen, A. (1990). A plea for the diagnosis of hypochondriacal personality disorder. *Journal of Psychosomatic Research*, **34**, 637–642.

Tyrer, P., Seivewright, N., & Seivewright, H. (1999). Long-term outcome of hypochondriacal personality disorder. *Journal of Psychosomatic Research*, **46**, 177–185.

Waller, N.G., Lilienfeld, S.O., Tellegen, A., & Lykken, D.T. (1991). The Tridimensional Personality Questionnaire: Structural validity and comparison with the Multidimensional Personality Questionnaire. *Multivariate Behavioral Research*, **26**, 1–23.

Watson, D., & Clark, L.A. (1984). Negative affectivity: The disposition to experience aversive emotional states. *Psychological Bulletin*, **96**, 465–490.

Watson, D., & Pennebaker, J. (1989). Health complaints, stress, and distress: Exploring the central role of negative affectivity. *Psychological Review*, **96**, 234–254.

Watson, D., Wiese, D., Vaidya, J., & Tellegen, A. (1999). The two general activation systems of affect: Structural findings, evolutionary considerations, and psychobiological evidence. *Journal of Personality and Social Psychology*, **76**, 820–838.

Watten, R.G., Vassend, O., Myhrer, T., Syversen, J. (1997). Personality factors and somatic symptoms. *European Journal of Personality*, **11**, 57–68.

White, T.L., & Depue, R.A. (1999). Differential association of traits of fear and anxiety with norepinephrine- and dark-induced pupil reactivity. *Journal of Personality and Social Psychology*, **77**, 863–877.

Wickramasekera, I.E. (1995). Somatization: Concepts, data, and predictions from the high risk model of threat perception. *Journal of Nervous and Mental Disease*, **183**, 15–23.

Widiger, T.A. (1998). Four out of five ain't bad. *Archives of General Psychiatry*, **55**, 865–866.

Part II

# ASSESSMENT AND TREATMENT

Chapter 5

# ASSESSMENT OF HEALTH ANXIETY

*Sherry H. Stewart\* and Margo C. Watt[†]*

## INTRODUCTION

The primary feature of hypochondriasis is the preoccupation with fears of having, or the belief that one has, a serious disease (e.g., cancer, heart disease, multiple sclerosis) based on the person's misinterpretation of body sensations (Warwick & Salkovskis, 1990). The most common reported body sensation is pain (Barsky & Klerman, 1983), but any benign body sensation such as rashes and swellings may become the focus of distress (Warwick & Salkovskis, 1990). The preoccupation occurs without adequate underlying organic pathology, and despite medical reassurance following negative outcomes on appropriate tests. Hypochondriasis also involves a number of safety behaviors including reassurance-seeking (frequent physician visits, 'doctor shopping', repeated discussions of the problem with relatives and friends), compulsive checking of the body for signs of the feared illness (e.g., prodding of the body, scanning stools or urine for abnormality, scanning of skin for irritation, lumps), and avoidance (i.e., avoiding anything that reminds the patient of the feared illness or increases the perceived chances of contracting it). The preoccupation causes clinically significant disruptive effects (distress or impairment) in important areas of functioning (DSM-IV; American Psychiatric Association, 1994). More detailed information on these core features of hypochondriasis can be found in Chapter 1 of this volume.

The assessment of hypochondriasis requires a careful review of the patient's medical records, and consultation with any medical profes-

\*Dalhousie University, Canada; [†]Saint Francis Xavier University, Canada

*Health Anxiety*
Edited by G.J.G. Asmundson, S. Taylor & B.J. Cox
© 2001 John Wiley & Sons Ltd.

sionals involved, to rule in/out possible organic causes, such as physical illness or injury, or the use of medications, drugs, or alcohol (Escobar, 1995). Once organic pathology is ruled out, a thorough evaluation of all aspects of the hypochondriacal syndrome should be conducted (Warwick, 1995).

The purpose of the present chapter is to provide a critical review of instruments commonly employed in the assessment of health anxiety that will be useful to clinicians and researchers alike. Our review covers structured interviews for the purpose of diagnosis of hypochondriasis, and self-report measures for assessment of levels of core and associated features of health anxiety for use in screening, treatment planning, tracking of therapy progress, and therapy outcome evaluation. A summary of primary instruments is provided in Table 5.1. In this table, we indicate which of the core (i.e., DSM-IV; American Psychiatric Association, 1994) features of hypochondriasis is assessed with each instrument. In the table and throughout the chapter, we organize these core features into four different dimensions: illness fears, illness beliefs, safety behaviors, and disruptive effects. These four dimensions are employed primarily as tools to facilitate organization of the material, although there is some limited empirical support for these particular dimensions (e.g., Stewart & Watt, 2000). We also provide a brief summary of each instrument's psychometric properties in the table.

We begin with two case examples.[1] We return to these two cases later in the chapter to illustrate how the various instruments can be useful in the assessment process.

## CASE STUDIES

### Case A

Kirsten was a 42-year-old married mother of three daughters who worked part time as a bank teller. She presented with a persistent fear of breast cancer and a preoccupation with the belief that she may have developed malignant tumors in her breasts. Prior to the onset of Kirsten's illness, a female relative had suffered breast cancer and had undergone radical mastectomy. Kirsten herself had discovered small lumps in her breasts and had consulted her physician, fearing that she herself had developed breast cancer. Medical tests

---

[1] The two cases presented in this chapter represent composites of clinical cases, rather than individual cases. As recommended by Clifft (1986), extreme care has been taken to remove all identifying characteristics in order to protect the privacy and confidentiality of the patients involved.

**Table 5.1**  Summary of hypochondriasis structured interviews and self-report questionnaires: Core features assessed by each and example psychometric properties

| Instrument | Core features assessed | | | | Examples of psychometric properties |
|---|---|---|---|---|---|
| | IF | IB | SB | DE | |
| **STRUCTURED INTERVIEWS** | | | | | |
| Composite International Diagnostic Interview | X | X | | X | Inter-rater reliability: 90% agreement ($k = 0.71$) for DSM-III-R diagnosis; convergent validity with clinical opinion |
| Structured Clinical Interview for DSM-IV | X | X | | | Reliability: $k = 0.57$ for DSM-III-R diagnosis over 24 hours to 2 weeks |
| Structured Diagnostic Interview for Hypochondriasis | X | X | | | Inter-rater reliability: 96% agreement for DSM-III-R diagnosis; convergent validity with Whiteley Index/Somatic Symptom Inventory: $r = 0.78$ |
| **SELF-REPORT QUESTIONNAIRES** | | | | | |
| Whiteley Index | X | X | | | Cronbach's alpha: 0.78; test-retest $r$: 0.90 (4 weeks); concurrent validity with Structured Diagnostic Interview for Hypochondriasis: Sensitivity: 0.87, Specificity: 0.72 |
| Illness Attitude Scales | X | X | X | X | Cronbach's alpha: 0.87 (Illness Behavior scale), 0.96 (Health Anxiety scale); test-retest $rs$ for 9 subscales: 0.75–1.00 (1 to 4 weeks); concurrent validity with Structured Diagnostic Interview for Hypochondriasis: Sensitivity: 0.79, Specificity: 0.84 (Health Anxiety scale) |
| Illness Behavior Questionnaire | X | X | | | Test-retest $rs$ for 7 subscales: 0.67–0.87 (1 to 12 weeks); convergent validity with friends'/relatives' ratings: $rs = 0.50$–0.78. |
| Health Anxiety Questionnaire | X | | X | X | Cronbach's alpa: 0.92; test-retest $r$: 0.87 (6 weeks, lay sample) and 0.95 (4 to 7 weeks in outpatient psychiatric sample); discriminative validity relative to trait anxiety and depression in distinguishing DSM-III-R hypochondriasis from anxiety disorders |

*Note:* IF = Illness fears; IB = Illness beliefs; SB = Safety behaviours; DE = Disruptive effects.

revealed that her physical symptoms were indicative of non-malignant fibroid masses and did not require intervention. For several months prior to her psychological assessment, Kirsten had been visiting her family physician two times per month for breast examinations. These tests would temporarily allay her fears, but worries that she had developed breast cancer would return within days or even hours of her visits to the physician. These concerns were exerting significant effects on her interpersonal and work life. Intrusive thoughts about breast cancer would interfere with her ability to concentrate at her bank job. She was so highly distressed by touching or looking at her own breasts, that she had her husband assist her in putting on her brassiere and in applying creams or sunscreen in any area around her chest. Kirsten reported that she avoided the news and women's magazines for fear that she would come across an article or news item on breast cancer, which she found extremely distressing. She also avoided visiting her relative who had had the mastectomy because she found such contact to be upsetting to her. Kirsten reported a strong fear of death, involving concerns that she would die from breast cancer and leave her three children motherless. Her husband was becoming exasperated with the demands she was placing on him. Her family physician was also becoming frustrated about Kristen's constant need for reassurance, and referred her for psychological assessment and possible cognitive-behavioral therapy.

## Case B

Marshall was a 36-year-old married accountant with one child aged 8 years. Marshall was referred by his general physician for panic attacks. The psychological assessment revealed that he suffered from infrequent, limited symptom, panic attacks. During the assessment, Marshall also admitted that he was constantly plagued by intrusive thoughts that he might have a serious disease. These intrusive thoughts began when one morning he suffered from an extreme episode of dizziness on arising from bed. The dizziness was so severe that he reportedly almost fainted, but did not actually lose consciousness. Marshall also complained of numerous other somatic symptoms including tension in his shoulders and neck, frequent headaches, and balance difficulties. After investigating these symptoms on the Internet and in several medical books, he became preoccupied with the idea that he might have brain cancer, or an inner ear disturbance, or have suffered a stroke or aneurysm. He took several weeks off work, consulted with his family physician and underwent a number of medical tests over several appointments. Lab tests ruled out serious illness as the cause of Marshall's symptoms. His physician thought Marshall's initial episode of dizziness was the result of a restrictive weight-loss diet he was on at the time. Medical reassurances did little to allay Marshall's preoccupation with illness and he continued to experience multiple somatic symptoms even after he had returned to a normal diet. Marshall's wife was becoming frustrated with his bodily and health preoccupations. Safety behaviors (e.g., scanning his body for signs of dizziness, searching the Internet to learn more about the source of his symptoms) were consuming a great deal of his work time. His reduced productivity and frequent sick leave were of concern to his supervisors.

These two composite cases illustrate the marked heterogeneity that can exist in the clinical presentation of hypochondriasis (e.g., Noyes, 1999). We will return to these two cases at several points later in the chapter to illustrate the utility of various measurement tools in the assessment process.

## ASSESSMENT OF CORE FEATURES

There are currently several tools available for assessing the core features of hypochondriasis as outlined in the DSM-IV (American Psychiatric Association, 1994). In this section, we review the three structured interviews available for diagnosing hypochondriasis and four standardized self-report questionnaires that can be useful in quantifying levels of certain core features (i.e., illness fears, illness beliefs, safety behaviors, and disruptive effects). We conclude this section with a discussion of the use of daily diaries and visual analogue scales in the cognitive-behavioral assessment of hypochondriasis.

### Structured Interviews

*Composite International Diagnostic Interview*

The Composite International Diagnostic Interview (World Health Organization, 1990) is a comprehensive, fully standardized diagnostic interview for the assessment of mental disorders (see review by Wittchen, 1994). The history and development of the Composite International Diagnostic Interview is described elsewhere (Robins et al., 1988). The current version of the Composite International Diagnostic Interview incorporates the necessary items to elicit characteristics and correlates of ICD-10 (World Health Organization, 1991) hypochondriacal disorder and DSM-IV (American Psychiatric Association, 1994) hypochondriasis. Four structured questions on the current version of the Composite International Diagnostic Interview tap the essential features of hypochondriasis as defined in DSM-IV. Specifically, one item asks about beliefs in or fears of having a serious disease (DSM-IV Criterion A); two other items address whether such preoccupation persists after medical reassurance (DSM-IV

Criterion B) and causes significant disruptive effects in various functional areas (DSM-IV Criterion D); and another item queries whether the disturbance has duration of at least 6 months (DSM-IV Criterion E). Additional items in the somatoform disorders section of this structured interview elicit information pertaining to other characteristics needed to make the more restrictive (Escobar et al., 1998) ICD-10 diagnosis of hypochondriacal disorder (i.e., 'preoccupation with no more than two physical diseases, one of which at least must be named by the patient' and 'persistent refusal to accept medical advice that there is no adequate physical cause for symptoms').

Wittchen, Essau, Rief, and Fichter (1993) administered the Composite International Diagnostic Interview to patients from a psychosomatic clinic. Percent agreement between two independent interviewers for a DSM-III-R hypochondriasis diagnosis was 90% and the kappa coefficient was 0.71, indicating good reliability. Reliability results for ICD-10 hypochondriacal disorder were similar (Wittchen, 1994). Wittchen et al. (1993) also found high clinical confirmation rates for ICD-10 hypochondriacal disorder diagnoses with the Composite International Diagnostic Interview, providing some preliminary evidence of its validity. This structured interview is effective for scrutinizing the characteristics of hypochondriasis in a relatively simple, quick (i.e., 10 minutes for somatoform disorders section; Wittchen, Lachner, Wunderlick, & Pfister, 1998), and unobtrusive fashion (Escobar et al., 1998).

### Structured Clinical Interview for DSM

The Structured Clinical Interview for DSM-IV (First, Spitzer, Gibbon, & Williams, 1995) includes a set of probe questions at the beginning of the somatoform disorders module (e.g., 'Do you worry much about your physical health?, Does your doctor think you worry too much?'). A symptomatic response to any of the probes prompts the interviewer to continue with the other sections within the somatoform disorders module (e.g., hypochondriasis, somatization disorder). If nothing in response to the probes suggests a current somatoform disorder, the interviewer is instructed to skip to the next module.

The hypochondriasis section of the Structured Clinical Interview for DSM-IV includes a series of structured questions covering many of the DSM-IV (American Psychiatric Association, 1994) criteria for hypochondriasis. Based on the responses to these questions, the interviewer judges whether or not the patient warrants a hypochondriasis diagnosis. For example, DSM-IV Criterion A is assessed with the following questions: 'Do you worry a lot that you have a serious disease that the doctors have not been able to diagnose?, What makes you think so? (What do you think you have?)'. However, not every DSM-IV criterion has a question associated with it in this structured interview. For example, the new criterion D in the DSM-IV (i.e., Clinically significant disruptive effects on functioning) does not have an associated question; instead, the interviewer is instructed to code Criterion D as present if both Criteria A and B are coded as present.

Williams et al. (1992) examined the reliability of the earlier version of this interview—the Structured Clinical Interview for DSM-III-R. Participants at four patient and two non-patient sites in the USA and Germany were interviewed twice independently by trained interviewers. Test–retest intervals ranged from 24 hours to 2 weeks. The kappa coefficient for a DSM-III-R diagnosis of hypochondriasis was 0.57 in the patient sample, indicating fair agreement. However, there were insufficient cases of hypochondriasis to calculate kappa for the non-patient sample. Williams et al. (1992) warned that because the Structured Clinical Interview for DSM-III-R requires clinical judgment, its reliability is highly dependent on the training and skills of the interviewer. Therefore, researchers using this structured interview should pay careful attention to adequately training their interviewers and to evaluating the reliability of their interviewers in their particular setting.

### Structured Diagnostic Interview for Hypochondriasis

The Structured Diagnostic Interview for Hypochondriasis was originally designed by Barsky et al. (1992a) to serve as a module for the Structured Clinical Interview for DSM-III-R (Spitzer, Williams, Gibbon, & First, 1992). It was not adopted in the development of the Structured Clinical Interview for DSM-III-R, however. Thus, it should be emphasized that although the two structured interviews are similar in format, their content (i.e., particular questions) differs. The Structured Diagnostic Interview for Hypochondriasis begins with a set of probe questions (e.g., 'Do you have symptoms that bother you?', 'Is your health on your mind a lot?'). An affirmative response to any of the probes triggers the rest of the interview. Negative responses to all four probes exclude the diagnosis of hypochondriasis. The remainder of the instrument consists of eight structured questions covering each of the DSM-III-R (American Psychiatric Association, 1987) diagnostic criteria. For example, DSM-III-R Criterion A-1 (Disease Fear or Conviction) is assessed by the following questions: 'Are you concerned that you might have a serious undetected illness?' and 'Do you worry about getting sick or being sick?'. Criterion A-2 (Persistent Body Sensations) is assessed by the question, 'What kinds of symptoms have you been having?', which is dichotomously coded as indicating the presence or absence of body sensation complaints. The interviewer judges whether each criterion is satisfied, based on information elicited by all questions in that section.

Inter-rater agreement with the Structured Diagnostic Interview for Hypochondriasis is 96% for a DSM-III-R diagnosis of hypochondriasis, from 88 to 97% for individual questions, and from 92 to 96% for individual diagnostic criteria (Barsky et al., 1992a). Barsky et al. (1992a) administered the Structured Diagnostic Interview for Hypochondriasis to a sample of general medical outpatients who scored above a predetermined cut-off on a self-report hypochondriasis questionnaire (i.e., the Whiteley Index [Pilowsky, 1967] and Somatic Symptom Inventory [Barsky, Wyshak, & Klerman, 1986] combined) and to a sample of comparison patients scoring below the cut-off. Structured Diagnostic Interview for Hypochondriasis interview-positive patients scored significantly higher on the two self-report hypochondriasis measures and on physician ratings of hypochondriasis than did both groups of interview-negative patients, indicating concurrent validity of the Structured Diagnostic Interview for Hypochondriasis. The total number of positive responses on the Structured Diagnostic Interview for Hypochondriasis was significantly positively correlated with both self-report hypochondriasis questionnaire scores ($r = 0.75$) and physician ratings of hypochondriasis ($r = 0.28$). Several hypothesized ancillary clinical features of hypochondriasis (e.g., number of non-specific medical complaints, degree of functional impairment, degree of utilization of medical care, degree of difficulty reported by physician in caring for patient, degree of psychiatric comorbidity) were significantly greater in interview-positive patients than in interview-negative patients, providing evidence for the convergent validity of the Structured Diagnostic Interview for Hypochondriasis.

*Summary of Structured Interviews*

All of the interviews reviewed above for the diagnosis of hypochondriasis (i.e., Composite International Diagnostic Interview, Structured Clinical Interview for DSM, Structured Diagnostic Interview for Hypochondriasis) appear to possess adequate-to-good reliability. This indicates that interviewers can generally agree on the presence or absence of clinical hypochondriasis using these instruments, and that their use leads to fairly stable diagnoses—at least over relatively short intervals. Two of these interviews have some preliminary concurrent validity data (i.e., Composite International Diagnostic Interview and Structured Diagnostic Interview for Hypochondriasis). With respect to all of these interviews, there is the need for better validation studies, particularly those examining the sensitivity and specificity of each instrument in diagnosing hypochondriasis with respect to some established 'gold standard'.

However, there continue to be controversies regarding a suitable standard (Barsky et al., 1992a; Wittchen, 1994). The empirical data available to date on each of the structured interviews is insufficient to recommend one instrument over another. Until more comparative psychometrics are available, the purpose of the assessment must be used to assist the interviewer in selecting the most appropriate interview. For example, Wittchen (1994) has suggested that, since each of the available interviews has been developed for particular purposes, some interviews (e.g., Composite International Diagnostic Interview) may be most suited for research purposes (e.g., establishing a diagnosis in community surveys), while others (e.g., Structured Clinical Interview for DSM-IV) may be better suited for clinical practice (e.g., providing clinical assessment information that can be used in treatment planning).

## Standardized Questionnaires

### Whiteley Index

The first self-report questionnaire specifically designed to assess the core features of hypochondriasis was the Whiteley Index (Pilowsky, 1967). The Whiteley Index was developed from a clinical study of hypochondriacal patients at the Department of Psychiatry, Whiteley Woods Clinic, University of Sheffield. It consists of 14 items such as 'Do you get the feeling that people are not taking your illnesses seriously enough?' and 'Do you think there is something seriously wrong with your body?'. Principal components analysis of the Whiteley Index items yielded three factors: (1) disease fear, (2) disease conviction, and (3) bodily preoccupation (Pilowsky, 1967). The three subscales can be scored separately or summed to yield a total score. Items were originally responded to in a binary (yes/no) fashion (Pilowsky, 1967). However, a modification of the instrument by Barsky et al. (1992a) calls for rating of items on an ordinal scale from 1 ('Not at all') to 5 ('A great deal').

Speckens, Spinhoven, Sloekers, Bolk, and van Hemert (1996a) reported adequate internal consistency (alpha = 0.78) and excellent test–retest reliability ($r$ = 0.90 over 4 weeks) for a Dutch version of the Whiteley Index. Its convergent validity has been established by Noyes et al. (1993), who observed a significant positive correlation with the Symptom Checklist-90-Revised Somatization subscale (Derogatis, 1975). Speckens et al. (1996a) examined convergent validity of a Dutch version of the Whiteley Index and found it to correlate significantly with Dutch versions of the Illness Attitudes Scale (Kellner, 1987) and the Somatosensory Amplification Scale (Barsky, Wyshak, & Klerman, 1990). Its concurrent validity in discriminating psychiatric patients with clinically diagnosed hypochondriasis from those without has also been demonstrated (Noyes et al., 1993; Pilowsky, 1967). Moreover, a recent study by Rief, Hiller, and Margraf (1998) showed that Whiteley Index scores were higher among those diagnosed with hypochondriasis than among those diagnosed with somatization disorder. Its convergent validity has also been evidenced by a high concordance between Whiteley Index scores and spouses' ratings of repondents' hypochondriacal attitudes, complaints, and behaviors (Pilowsky, 1967) and physician ratings of respondents' unrealistic fear of illness (Noyes et al., 1993). Whiteley Index scores also correlate with several measures of health care utilization, including the number of visits made to general practitioners (Parker & Lipscombe, 1980), 'doctor shopping' (Kasteler, Kane, Olsen, & Thetford, 1976; Noyes et al., 1993), and receiving more laboratory screening tests (Beaber & Rodney, 1984). Patients scoring high on the Whiteley Index demonstrate a diminished tolerance for experimental pain (Ziesat, 1978). In a longitudinal study by Speckens, van Hemert, Spinhoven, and Bolk (1996b), Whiteley Index scores at the initial assessment were negatively associated with recovery rate at one-year follow-up, providing evidence of its predictive validity.

Despite these overall favorable results for the Whiteley Index, some concerns should be noted. For example, the Whiteley Index may lack discriminative validity, in that misleadingly high scores could be obtained by patients with general medical conditions or certain psychiatric disorders other than hypochondriasis. For example, the item 'Do you think there is something seriously wrong with your body?' might be answered 'yes' by a person with major depression (without hypochondriasis) because he or she believes depression is due to a biological dysfunction. In fact, Noyes, Reich, Clancy, and O'Gorman (1986) observed Whiteley Index total scores among a sample of patients with panic disorder that were nearly as high as those obtained by patients with hypochondriasis, suggesting that the scale may lack discriminative validity in distinguishing hypochondriasis from panic disorder.

Moreover, Fink et al. (1999) reported results that did not support the internal consistency/homogeneity of the Whiteley Index in its original 14-item version. Thus, they constructed a reduced seven-item version of the scale with two subscales—Illness Conviction and Illness Worrying. The total Whiteley Index-7 scale and subscale scores each displayed high internal consistency. The Whiteley Index-7 and the Illness Conviction scales showed 0.71 and 0.63 sensitivity and 0.62 and 0.87 specificity, respectively, in identifying patients who fulfilled criteria for at least one DSM-IV somatoform disorder on a structured interview; sensitivity and specificity in detecting particular somatoform disorders (e.g., hypochondriasis) were not evaluated. Whiteley Index-7 total scale and subscale scores showed moderate agreement with physician ratings of (a) patients' degree of bodily preoccupation, and (b) patients' reason for consultation (well-defined somatic disorder vs. ill-defined condition or mental illness with physical symptoms). Moderate agreement was also seen between the Whiteley Index-7 total score and the score on the Symptom Checklist-90-Revised (Derogatis, 1975) Somatization subscale ($r = 0.35$).

*Illness Attitudes Scale*

The Illness Attitudes Scale purports to measure fears, beliefs, and attitudes associated with clinical hypochondriasis (Kellner, 1986, 1987). During scale development, attempts were made to limit the items to features specific to hypochondriasis (e.g., worry about illness, bodily preoccupation) and to exclude items characteristic of other psychiatric syndromes such as anxiety and depressive disorders (e.g., difficulty sleeping, depressed affect, somatic symptoms). The 27 items on the Illness Attitudes Scale were constructed from statements made by a sample of hypochondriacal patients (Kellner, 1987). Two additional items provide supplementary information (i.e., on current diagnosed illness and nature of treatment(s) received) but are not used in scoring. There are nine scales consisting of three items each: (1) Worry about Illness (e.g., 'Are you worried that you may get a serious illness in the future?'); (2) Concerns about Pain (e.g., 'If you have a pain, are you concerned that it may be caused by a serious illness?'); (3) Health Habits (e.g., 'Do you examine your body to find out whether there is something wrong?'); (4) Hypochondriacal Beliefs (e.g., 'Do you believe that you have a physical disease, but the doctors have not diagnosed it correctly?'); (5) Thanatophobia (e.g., 'Are you afraid of news which reminds you of death (such as funerals or obituary notices)?'); (6) Disease Phobia (e.g., 'Are you worried that you may have cancer?'); (7) Bodily Preoccupations (e.g., 'When you read or hear about an illness do you get symptoms similar to those of the illness?'); (8) Treatment Experience (e.g., 'How often do you see a doctor?'); and (9) Effects of Symptoms (e.g., 'Do your bodily symptoms stop you from concentrating on what you are doing?'). Each Illness Attitudes Scale item is rated on a 5-point Likert-type scale of relative frequency.

Test–retest reliability in two groups of normals over 1- to 4-week intervals has ranged from 0.62 and 0.75 (Hypochondriacal Beliefs) to 0.92 and 1.00 (Disease Phobia; see review by Kellner, 1987). The Illness Attitudes Scale shows convergent validity with the Whiteley Index and Somatosensory Amplification Scale (Speckens et al., 1996a). The Illness Attitudes Scale also appears to possess concurrent validity in detecting patients diagnosed with hypochondriasis. For example, Kellner, Abbott, Winslow, and

Pathak (1987a) compared a group of patients with DSM-III (American Psychiatric Association, 1980) hypochondriasis to three groups of age- and sex-matched controls, including psychiatric outpatients (mainly depressed or anxiety disordered outpatients with no significant hypochondriacal concerns), employees, and family practice patients. The hypochondriacal patients scored significantly higher than the other three groups on all Illness Attitudes Scale subscales save Health Habits.

With respect to internal consistency, however, the nine subscales of the Illness Attitudes Scale suggested by Kellner (1987) contain too few items to reliably assess the construct that each was designed to tap, resulting in some unacceptably low alphas (e.g., Ferguson & Daniel, 1995). In fact, recent factor analytic work in both clinical and non-clinical samples has indicated that the Illness Attitudes Scale captures a smaller number of dimensions than the nine originally proposed by Kellner (1987). Most factor analytic studies suggest that the Illness Attitudes Scale consists of either four or five factors (Cox, Borger, Asmundson, & Taylor, 2000; Ferguson & Daniel, 1995; Hadjistavropoulos & Asmundson, 1998; Hadjistavropoulos, Frombach, & Asmundson, 1999; Stewart & Watt, 2000). The most robust/replicable factors appear to be (a) Worry about Illness and Pain (illness fears), (b) Disease Conviction (illness beliefs), (c) Health Habits (safety behavior), and (d) Symptom Interference with Lifestyle (disruptive effects). Less robust dimensions include Fear of Death (thanatophobia), which sometimes loads on the illness fears factor, and Treatment Experiences, which sometimes loads on the safety behavior factor. In contrast to studies finding four to five primary Illness Attitudes Scale dimensions, Speckens et al. (1996a) found support for a two-factor structure for a Dutch version of the scale, with factors pertaining to Health Anxiety and Illness Behavior, respectively. It should be noted, however, that Speckens et al. (1996a) used a somewhat unorthodox approach to factor analysis.

The inconsistent results of these previous factor analytic studies have recently been reconciled by findings indicating a hierarchical structure for the Illness Attitudes Scale (i.e., four or five lower-order factors each of which loads on one or two higher-order factors). Cox et al. (2000) found support for a two-factor solution at the higher-order level, with higher-order factors very similar to the two factors reported by Speckens et al. (1996a): Health Anxiety (loadings from Illness Fears, Illness Beliefs, and Disruptive Effects lower-order factors) and Health Behavior (loadings from Health Habits and Treatment Experiences lower-order factors). When a single factor structure has been supported at the higher-order level (Hadjistavropoulos et al., 1999; Stewart & Watt, 2000), Illness Attitudes Scale safety behavior factors have tended to show relatively weak loadings on the global Hypochondriacal Concerns factor relative to other lower-order Illness Attitudes Scale components. In fact, Hadjistavropoulos et al.'s (1999) best-fitting model involved deletion of Health Habits items. Cox et al. (2000) suggested that the characteristics assessed on their Health Behavior factor are likely adaptive (e.g., avoidance of smoking) and therefore not part of the constellation of hypochondriasis characteristics (cf. Stewart & Watt, 2000).

There appears to be sufficient convergence across the factor analytic studies to date to suggest that the original nine-subscale scoring of the Illness Attitudes Scale suggested by Kellner (1986, 1987) may be inappropriate. Instead, factor scores representing each of the core dimensions of hypochondriasis (i.e., Illness Fears, Illness Beliefs, Safety Behaviors, and Disruptive Effects) may be more useful and appropriate in the context of clinical assessment (e.g., Stewart & Watt, 2000). In fact, internal consistency values improve with the scoring of fewer subscales for the Illness Attitudes Scale (e.g., Ferguson & Daniel, 1995; Speckens et al., 1996a).

Speckens et al. (1996b) conducted an investigation of the diagnostic and prognostic significance of the Illness Attitudes Scale. The sample consisted of patients with medically unexplained body sensations presenting at a general medical outpatient clinic. Of the self-report measures administered, the Whiteley Index and their Health Anxiety subscale of the Illness Attitudes Scale best discriminated between patients diagnosed with and without hypochondriasis using the Structured Diagnostic Interview for Hypochondriasis. The sensitivity of the Whiteley Index (0.87) was slightly better than that of their Health Anxiety subscale of the Illness Attitudes Scale (0.79), suggesting that the Whiteley Index does the better job of the two measures in correctly identifying true cases of hypochondriasis. However, specificity of the Whiteley Index (0.72) was slightly lower than that of their Health Anxiety subscale of the Illness Attitudes Scale (0.84), suggesting that it is the Illness Attitudes Scale which does the better job of the two measures in correctly identifying individuals who do not meet diagnostic criteria for hypochondriasis. Moreover, their Illness Attitudes Scale–Illness Behavior subscale was predictive of the number of visits to the physician in the 1-year follow-up (Speckens et al., 1996b). The Illness Attitudes Scale total score has also proven sensitive to treatment effects. For example, Furer, Vincent, Lander, and Walker (1999) showed that Illness Attitudes Scale scores declined significantly from pre- to posttreatment among a group of patients with DSM-IV hypochondriasis receiving cognitive-behavioral therapy for their intense illness worries.

*Illness Behavior Questionnaire*

Pilowsky (1971; Pilowsky & Spence, 1983, 1994) introduced the Illness Behavior Questionnaire to measure his conception of abnormal illness behavior. This questionnaire was designed to measure inappropriate or maladaptive modes of responding to one's state of health. In its present form (Pilowsky & Spence, 1994), the Illness Behavior Questionnaire is a 62-item self-report inventory that is an expanded version of the Whiteley Index. It measures health anxiety and illness behavior on seven primary scales: (1) General Hypochondriasis, (2) Disease Conviction, (3) Perception of Illness, (4) Affective Inhibition, (5) Affective Disturbance, (6) Denial, and (7) Irritability. The first scale, General Hypochondriasis, is characterized by anxious or phobic preoccupation with the possibility of disease (i.e., illness fears). Disease Conviction is characterized by beliefs in the presence of serious pathology and the rejection of reassurances by physicians and relatives (i.e., illness beliefs). The third scale, Perception of Illness, is bipolar and is characterized by items contrasting the attribution of illness to either somatic or psychological causes (with hypochondriacal patients being theoretically more likely to attribute illness to somatic causes). Affective Inhibition is characterized by difficulties in expressing personal feelings, especially negative ones. Affective Disturbance is characterized by feelings of anxiety or sadness. The sixth scale, Denial, involves the respondent denying that there are problems in his or her life (with hypochondriacal patients being theoretically more likely to deny the existence of current life problems/stressors that may be contributing to his or her symptoms). Finally, Irritability is characterized by the presence of hostile reactions, anger, and interpersonal friction. However, factor analyses of the Illness Behavior Questionnaire have failed to replicate Pilowsky's (1971) original 7 factors instead finding anywhere from 6 to 11 factors (see review by Zonderman, Heft, & Costa, 1985). Zonderman et al. (1985) argue that lack of an invariant factor structure threatens the construct validity of the Illness Behavior Questionnaire.

Test–retest reliability of the seven Illness Behavior Questionnaire subscales over 1 to 12 weeks has been found to range from 0.67 for Affective Inhibition to 0.87 for General Hypochondriasis and Affective Disturbance, indicating marginally acceptable-to-good stability (see review by Pilowsky & Spence, 1994). With respect to convergent validity, correlations between a patient's scores on the Illness Behavior Questionnaire subscales and a relative's or friend's ratings of the patient's behavior have ranged from 0.50 for General Hypochondriasis to 0.78 for Denial, and Affective Disturbance subscale scores have been found to correlate significantly with state ($r = 0.59$) and trait ($r = 0.76$) anxiety (see Pilowsky & Spence, 1994). Finally, in a study of headache patients, Wise, Mann, Jani, Kozachuk, and Jani (1994) found the Illness Behavior Questionnaire to have convergent validity with the Illness Effects Questionnaire (Greenberg, Peterson, & Heilbronner, 1989)—a measure assessing patients' perceptions of the overall disruptive effects of their symptoms on daily living. The Illness Behavior Questionnaire–Disease Conviction scale was most strongly associated with Illness Effects Questionnaire scores. Thus, although the Illness Behavior Questionnaire does not directly assess illness effects, it is predictive of an adverse impact of symptoms on functioning.

The Illness Behavior Questionnaire has been criticized for the high correlations of its scales with measures of anxiety, depression, and negative affectivity. For example, Zonderman et al. (1985) found that all of the Illness Behavior Questionnaire subscales are highly positively correlated with neuroticism. They concluded that this suggests poor discriminant validity and, therefore, questionable value of the Illness Behavior Questionnaire in the diagnosis of hypochondriasis. However, research does suggest that patients diagnosed with hypochondriasis are more neurotic than controls (Noyes et al., 1993) and so to take correlations between neuroticism and Illness Behavior Questionnaire scores as suggesting difficulties with the Illness Behavior Questionnaire's validity may not be warranted. Instead, research should focus on the relative degree to which various health anxiety measures assess information unique to hypochondriasis as opposed to information shared with anxiety and depression measures.

In this regard, there appear to be interesting differences in the degree to which Illness Attitudes Scale vs. Illness Behaviour Questionnaire correlate with anxiety and depression measures. In a study by Kellner et al. (1987b), the Hypochondriacal Beliefs subscale from the Illness Attitudes Scale tended to be less highly associated with anxiety and depression measures than did the Disease Conviction subscale from the Illness Behavior Questionnaire. Kellner (1987) has argued that this pattern is due to the care taken during the construction of the Illness Attitudes Scale not to include items that may be characteristic not only of hypochondriasis, but also of related disorders such as anxiety and depression. In contrast, some Illness Behavior Questionnaire–Disease Conviction items (e.g., 'Are you sleeping well?', 'Do you find that you are bothered by many different symptoms?') could be endorsed strongly by depressed or anxious patients who do not necessarily have hypochondriacal beliefs. In short, the Illness Attitudes Scale appears to do a better job of measuring attitudes unique to hypochondriasis as opposed to related states such as anxiety and depression than does the Illness Behavior Questionnaire. The relative discriminative validity of the various self-report measures of the core hypochondriasis symptoms (e.g., in distinguishing hypochondriasis from affective and anxiety disorders) remains to be investigated in future research.

A further disadvantage of the Illness Behavior Questionnaire is its extensive length relative to other self-report measures of the core features of hypochondriasis (i.e., 62 items; see Furer et al., 1999). Although the first two of the seven Illness Behavior Questionnaire dimensions (i.e., General Hypochondriasis and Disease Conviction) appear to tap core features of hypochondriasis, the other five scales add to its overall length in assessing associated features (e.g., affective disturbance) which are not core constructs in the constellation of DSM-IV (American Psychiatric Association, 1994) hypochondriasis characteristics. Moreover, the reference to illness behavior in this measure's title may be somewhat of a misnomer, since the Illness Behavior Questionnaire does not specifically assess the maladaptive safety behaviors commonly associated with hypochondriasis (e.g., bodily checking, reassurance seeking, avoidance).

Recently, Chaturvedi, Bhandari, Beena, and Rao (1996) developed an abbreviated 11-item screening version of the Illness Behavior Questionnaire (i.e., the Short Illness Behavior Questionnaire) for detection of abnormal illness behavior, using six items from the original Disease Conviction subscale and five items from the original Illness Perceptions subscale. This abbreviated version has demonstrated good sensitivity and specificity in the detection of clinically diagnosed hypochondriasis.

*Health Anxiety Questionnaire*

The Health Anxiety Questionnaire was developed based on a cognitive-behavioral model of health anxiety (Lucock & Morley, 1996). Its purpose was to identify individuals with high levels of concern about their health. Earlier health anxiety measures were developed with clinical psychiatric samples and involved claims that their items reflect the attitudes and beliefs involved in clinical hypochondriasis (e.g., Illness Attitude Scale; Kellner, 1986, 1987). No such claims are made for the Health Anxiety Questionnaire, which was developed with medical as well as psychiatric groups and was intended to tap a range of severity of health anxiety.

Twenty-two items were initially chosen to reflect important aspects of health anxiety as identified by research and theory on the cognitive-behavioral model of health anxiety. Fourteen of these initial items were derived from the Illness Attitude Scale and the remaining items were developed from discussions with patients presenting with persistent health anxiety (Lucock & Morley, 1996). One of the 22 items was dropped from the scale due to item redundancy. Each of the remaining 21 items are rated on a 4-point Likert scale with anchors ranging from 'not at all or rarely' (scored as 0 points) to 'most of the time' (scored as 3 points). Lucock and Morley (1996) conducted three studies in developing and evaluating the Health Anxiety Questionnaire. Study 1 was conducted with a large sample of 284 individuals including lay participants, student nurses, medical outpatients, and clinical psychology patients from an anxiety disorders clinic. Cluster analysis revealed four clusters of items, including health worry and preoccupation (8 items; e.g., 'Do you ever worry about your health?'); fear of illness and death (7 items; e.g., 'Are you ever worried that you may get a serious illness in the future?'); reassurance-seeking behavior (3 items; e.g., 'When you experience unpleasant feelings in your body do you tend to ask friends or family about them?'); and interference with life (3 items; e.g., 'Have your bodily symptoms stopped you from working during the past six months or so?'). Subsequent factor analysis provided partial support for the cluster analysis results in that four factors were extracted. The first factor corresponded to the fear of illness and death cluster; the second factor corresponded to the interference with life and the health worry and preoccupation clusters; and the third factor corresponded to the reassurance-seeking behavior cluster. However, the fourth factor did not correspond clearly to any of the clusters identified in the first analysis. Lucock and Morley (1996) argued that high inter-item correlations, and the fact that all items showed salient loadings on the first factor prior to rotation, suggest that the Health Anxiety Questionnaire total score can be used as a measure of overall health anxiety. Internal consistency of the entire scale was excellent (alpha = 0.92). Six-week test–retest reliability carried out on a subsample of the lay participants was good ($r = 0.87$). In Study 2, test–retest reliability with a sample of clinical psychology outpatients was excellent ($r = 0.95$ for 4–7 weeks with no intervening treatment). In Study 3, two groups of clinical psychology outpatients—patients meeting DSM-III-R (American Psychiatric Association, 1987) diagnostic criteria for hypochondriasis versus comparison patients meeting DSM-III-R criteria for an anxiety disorder (i.e., generalized anxiety disorder, social phobia, or panic disorder)—were compared. While the hypochondriasis group scored significantly higher than the anxiety disorders group on the Health Anxiety Questionnaire total score, the two groups were indistinguishable based on either State–Trait Anxiety Inventory–Trait Anxiety subscale (Spielberger, 1983) or Beck Depression Inventory (Beck, Ward, Mendelson, Mock, & Erbaugh, 1961) scores, indicating some discriminative validity for the Health Anxiety Questionnaire in specifically detecting hypochondriasis as opposed to related anxiety disorders.

The major intended purpose of the Health Anxiety Questionnaire was to identify individuals with persistent health anxiety who may be relatively unresponsive to routine medical reassurance (Lucock & Morley, 1996). In fact, the predictive validity of the Health Anxiety Questionnaire has been recently demonstrated in this respect. Lucock, White, Peake, and Morley (1998) examined the effect of health anxiety (as assessed using Health Anxiety Questionnaire total scores) on how patients perceived/recalled reassurance given by the doctor following gastroscopic evaluation. All participants' gastroscopic results were negative for serious pathology. Patients and the doctor rated the probability that something was seriously wrong after receiving reassuring feedback from the doctor. Patients scoring in the high range on the Health Anxiety Questionnaire were more likely to recall the reassurance given by the doctor as less certain that there was nothing seriously wrong (relative to doctors' ratings) than were patients scoring moderate or low in health anxiety. These group differences were evident immediately post-consult and persisted at a one-month follow-up. These data support the predictive validity of the Health Anxiety Questionnaire.

### Summary of Standardized Questionnaires

Many of the standardized self-report questionnaires of core hypochondriasis features reviewed in this chapter were derived from pre-existing questionnaires with items added or deleted as deemed useful by the authors. For example, the Illness Behavior Questionnaire is an expanded version of the Whiteley Index, and many of the Health Anxiety Questionnaire items were derived from the Illness Attitudes Scale. Thus, evidence of convergent validity between various hypochondriasis measures must always be considered in the context of item redundancy issues.

Although all four measures possess face validity in tapping aspects of hypochondriasis as defined in the DSM-IV (American Psychiatric Association, 1994), different self-report questionnaires tend to measure different features of the hypochondriasis syndrome (i.e., illness beliefs, illness fears, safety behaviors, and disruptive effects) with some being more comprehensive in this regard than others (see Table 5.1). Specifically, the Illness Attitudes Scale and the Health Anxiety Questionnaire appear more comprehensive than the Whiteley Index and the Illness Behavior Questionnaire in assessing the various core features of hypochondriasis (e.g., only the former two measures tap the safety behaviors and disruptive effects dimensions; see Table 5.1). Nonetheless, each of these two measures (Illness Attitudes Scale and Health Anxiety Questionnaire) possesses relative advantages over the other.

First, the Health Anxiety Questionnaire fails to support a distinction between a false belief in having a disease (illness beliefs) and an inordinate fear of having a disease (illness fears) which is supported by the other three measures of core symptoms. Some research suggests that illness beliefs are associated with body sensations whereas illness fears are associated with anxiety (Noyes, 1999). Given their factorial distinctiveness and different correlates, some have argued that there may be two subtypes of hypochondriasis with primary elevations in either illness fears or illness beliefs (Fava & Grandi, 1991). This distinction is exemplified in the two cases presented earlier where Case A (Kirsten) presented with hypochondriasis primarily characterized by illness fears and Case B (Marshall) presented with hypochondriasis primarily characterized by illness beliefs. This distinction was captured in the Illness Attitudes Scale scores of each patient such that Case A showed primary elevations on the items comprising Stewart and Watt's (2000) illness fears factor while Case B showed primary elevations on items comprising their illness beliefs factor. This subtype distinction may carry implications for treatment planning (see Chapters 3 and 7 for a review of psychological treatment options). For example, with the illness beliefs subtype, the patient would need to be persuaded that the conviction he or she suffers from a serious undiagnosed disease is indeed false (e.g., via cognitive-behavioral techniques). However, if illness fears are the predominating feature, exposure may be the most appropriate and adequate treatment. In fact, there is evidence that therapy based on principles of exposure may be effective for those hypochondriacal patients presenting primarily with illness fears (Warwick & Marks, 1988).

Second, although the Illness Attitudes Scale contains two scales relevant to hypochondriacal behavior (i.e., treatment experience and health habits) which have formed a separate safety behavior factor in some studies (e.g., Cox et al., 2000; Stewart & Watt, 2000), one of these scales (health habits) has been criticized for containing items that are too peripheral to the DSM-IV construct of hypochondriasis (e.g., healthy diet, avoidance of smoking; Cox et al., 2000; Furer et al., 1999; Hadjistavropoulos et al., 1999). The Health Anxiety Questionnaire appears to do a better job of assessing the types of reassurance-seeking behavior observed among those with hypochondriasis (e.g., bodily checking, seeking reassurance about symptoms from family/friends) than does the Illness Attitudes Scale. However, there are no items on either the Illness Attitudes Scale or the Health Anxiety Questionnaire pertaining to the avoidance types of safety behaviors manifested by Case A—Kirsten (e.g., avoidance of breast self-examination and all other contact with her breasts, avoidance of reading literature pertaining to breast cancer, and avoidance of contact with others who had breast cancer). In fact, no available hypochondriasis measure assesses the health-related avoidance which many authors have noted as being a characteristic safety behavior of some hypochondriacal patients (Warwick, 1995).

## Daily Diaries and Visual Analogue Scales

In her description of the cognitive-behavioral assessment of hypochondriasis, Warwick (1995) recommends the use of diaries and visual analogue scales. According to Warwick, patients should keep diaries of negative thoughts pertaining to their illness beliefs and illness fears, and of the safety behaviors in which they engage, during the assessment period. Visual analogue scale ratings of relevant hypochondriasis characteristics (e.g., need for reassurance, disease conviction) facilitate tracking of progress throughout therapy. In an outcome study on the efficacy of cognitive behavioral therapy in the treatment of hypochondriasis (Warwick, Clark, Cobb, & Salkovskis, 1996), visual analogue scales proved sensitive to treatment effects, save patient ratings of frequency of avoidance. Other psychometric properties of these single-item scales (and of the daily diary method) remain to be investigated.

## ASSESSMENT OF COGNITIVE ASPECTS OF HYPOCHONDRIASIS

Given relatively recent cognitive conceptualizations of hypochondriasis (e.g., Warwick & Salkovskis, 1990), interest has turned to the measurement of cognitive aspects of hypochondriasis in the assessment process. In this section, we review two self-report questionnaires pertaining to cognitive aspects of health anxiety.

### Somatosensory Amplification Scale

Hypochondriasis is highly correlated with a cognitive style that Barsky (1992; Barsky & Wyshak, 1990) calls 'somatosensory amplification'—the tendency to experience bodily sensations as being unusually intense, aversive, or distressing. The Somatosensory Amplification Scale (Barsky et al., 1990) is a 10-item self-report questionnaire designed to operationalize this construct. The scale assesses the individual's sensitivity to a range of mild bodily experiences (e.g., 'hunger contractions') which are uncomfortable and unpleasant, but which are not typical symptoms of disease. The Somatosensory Amplification Scale asks the respondent to indicate the degree to which each statement is characteristic of them in general, on an ordinal scale from 1 to 5. Internal consistency values for the Somatosensory Amplification Scale have ranged from alpha = 0.71 to 0.82, and test–retest reliability coefficients have ranged from $r = 0.87$ (4 weeks) to 0.79 (10 weeks) (Barsky et al., 1990; Speckens et al., 1996a). Somatosensory Amplification Scale scores have been shown to be highly correlated with Illness Attitudes Scale and Whiteley Index scores, indicating convergent validity (Speckens et al., 1996a). Whereas several studies have shown scores on the Somatosensory Amplification Scale to be significantly higher in patients with clinically diagnosed hypochondriasis than in controls (Barsky et al., 1990; Noyes et al., 1993), Speckens et al. (1996b) found that scores on the Somatosensory Amplification Scale did not differentiate patients with clinically diagnosed hypochondriasis from those without hypochondriasis. Together, these studies suggest that the assessment of the cognitive style of somatosensory amplification may be useful in the complete assessment of hypochondriasis.

## Cognitions about Body and Health Questionnaire

Rief et al. (1998) evaluated whether specific cognitive features could distinguish those with hypochondriasis from those with somatization disorder. In their first study, a sample of 493 behavioral medicine patients was employed to examine the psychometric properties of a German-language questionnaire assessing cognitions concerning interpretation of body signals, perception of minor body events, and attitudes about body, health, and health habits. Nine items from the Somatosensory Amplification Scale (Barsky et al., 1990) were included among the original 68 items piloted in the first study. The items on the Cognitions about Body and Health Questionnaire are rated on a 4-point scale with anchors ranging from 'completely wrong' (scored as 0) to 'completely right' (scored as 3). In factor analysis, a 5-factor solution produced the most stable and specific factors. Thirty-seven of the original 68 items were excluded because of insufficient or equivocal factor loadings, or inconsistency of item-to-factor allocation, resulting in a final 31-item version of the scale. The first factor pertained to a catastrophizing interpretation of bodily complaints (14 items; e.g., 'When one sweats a lot, it can be due to an overburdened heart'), the second factor to autonomic sensations (4 items; e.g., 'I often feel my heart beating because my circulatory system is very sensitive'), the third factor to bodily weakness (6 items; e.g., 'I have to avoid physical exertion in order to save my strength'), the fourth factor to intolerance of bodily complaints (4 items; e.g., 'I consult a doctor as soon as possible when I have bodily complaints'), and the fifth factor to health habits (3 items; e.g., 'I make sure that I eat healthily'). The internal consistency for the total scale was excellent (alpha = 0.90) and marginally acceptable-to-good for the five subscales (alpha range = 0.67 to 0.88 for the intolerance of bodily complaints and catastophizing cognitions subscales, respectively).

In the second study, five groups of participants, classified by structured interviews, were compared. The groups included somatization disorder only, hypochondriasis only, comorbid somatization disorder—hypochondriasis, clinical controls (i.e., major depression, dysthymia, social phobia, panic disorder, and/or drug abuse), and non-clinical controls. Significant effects of participant diagnostic group were found on four of the five sub-scales (i.e., all but health habits). For the catastrophizing cognitions and autonomic sensations subscales, the three groups with somatization and/or hypochondriasis scored significantly higher than the controls. Scores on the bodily weakness scale were significantly higher among the two groups with somatization disorder relative to controls, whereas scores on the intolerance of bodily complaints subscale were significantly higher among the two groups with hypochondriasis relative to controls. Results thus suggest that there are indeed cognitive factors that distinguish hypochondriasis from somatization disorder. Cognitions that bodily sensations should be followed immediately by safety behaviors (e.g., help-seeking, mediation-taking) are more characteristic of those with hypochondriasis than of those with somatization disorder, whereas self-concepts of being weak and of not being able to tolerate physical effort are more characteristic of the cognitions of those with somatization disorder than of those with hypochondriasis. Therefore, the relatively new Cognitions about Body and Health Questionnaire appears useful in understanding the cognitions unique to specific somatoform disorders, and shows potential for use in the differential diagnosis of hypochondriasis vs. somatization disorder.

## ASSESSMENT OF ASSOCIATED FEATURES

There are a number of characteristics associated with hypochondriasis, including unwanted bodily sensations, anxiety, depression, neuroticism, panic attacks, anxiety sensitivity, death anxiety, and alexithymia. Useful measures for tapping each of these associated features in the assessment process are reviewed below.

### Body Sensations

A complete evaluation of hypochondriasis should include an assessment of presenting body sensations using measures such as the Minnesota Multiphasic Personality Inventory–II Hypochondriasis scale (Butcher, 1990), the Symptom Checklist-90-Revised Somatization scale (Derogatis, 1975), or the Somatic Symptom Inventory (Barsky et al., 1986). The Hypochondriasis Scale is one of the original clinical scales from the Minnesota Multiphasic Personality Inventory (MMPI; McKinley & Hathaway, 1940) designed to measure a pattern of 'neurotic' concern over physical health (Butcher, 1990). The MMPI-II Hypochondriasis Scale consists of 32 true–false items intended to elicit complaints of body sensations. Sample items include 'I have a great deal of stomach trouble' and 'I feel weak all over much of the time'. Although psychometric properties such as test–retest reliability have been demonstrated (e.g., Dahlstrom, Welsh, & Dahlstrom, 1971), this scale has been criticized for containing several items unrelated to hypochondriasis (e.g., Kellner, 1987). This limitation is not surprising when one considers that the 'empirical criterion keying' method was used in its construction (Dahlstrom et al., 1971). Thus, items distinguishing between patients with clinically diagnosed hypochondriasis and those without hypochondriasis were retained, regardless of the content validity of the items with respect to the known features of hypochondriasis. Although Hypochondriasis Scale scores have been found to discriminate significantly between hypochondriacal and non-hypochondriacal patients (e.g., McKinley & Hathaway, 1940; Welsh, 1952), Edelman and Holdsworth (1993) have argued that the MMPI-II Hypochondriasis Scale does not actually assess hypochondriasis per se, but instead provides an index of somatic awareness (i.e., objective awareness of body sensations). Similarly, Kellner (1987) has pointed out that the Hypochondriasis Scale does not assess the discrepancy between objective and subjective health that typifies hypochondriasis. Both patients with organic disease and those with similar symptoms but no known organic pathology obtain equivalent Hypochondriasis Scale scores, with both groups obtaining elevated scores relative to healthy controls (e.g., Talley et al., 1990). Thus, the MMPI-II Hypochondriasis Scale should be used primarily as a measure of body sensations. Although the term hypochondriasis is used in the title of this scale, it probably applies as much (if not more) to somatization and pain disorder as it does to hypochondriasis, per se.

The Symptom Checklist-90-Revised is a widely used scale of psychopathology and distress. The 90 items of this measure are rated according to the amount of discomfort caused by each listed problem in the last week, and are scored according to nine underlying symptom dimensions. The dimensions include somatization, obsession-compulsion, interpersonal sensitivity, anxiety, depression, hostility, phobic anxiety, paranoid ideation, and psychoticism. The 12-item Somatization Scale taps body sensations such as 'pains in lower back' and 'nausea or upset stomach'. This scale shows good internal consistency and stability (Derogatis, 1975), convergent validity with the MMPI-II Hypochondriasis Scale (Derogatis, 1975; Dinning & Evans, 1977), and sensitivity to treatment effects among hypochondriasis patients treated with cognitive-behavioral therapy (Furer et al., 1999). Hypochondriacal patients have also been shown to score higher than normal controls on the Somatization Scale (e.g., Kellner, Abbott, Winslow, & Pathak, 1989; Noyes et al., 1993). However, the Somatization Scale cannot be used to assist in differential diagnosis of hypochondriasis vs. anxiety and depressive disorders (Rief, Schaefer,

Hiller, & Fichter, 1992), probably because these latter disorders are also characterized by body sensations.

The Somatic Symptom Inventory is a 26-item questionnaire drawn from the MMPI-II Hypochondriasis Scale and the Symptom Checklist-90-Revised Somatization Scale. Typical items include 'soreness in your muscles' and 'difficulty keeping your balance while walking'. The Somatic Symptom Inventory has shown excellent internal consistency and good stability (Barsky et al., 1992a). Scores on the Somatic Symptom Inventory show convergent validity with scores on the Whiteley Index (Barsky et al., 1986). Barsky et al.'s (1986) Somatic Symptoms *Inventory* should not be confused with the Somatic Symptom *Index* (Escobar, Rubio-Stipec, Canino, & Karno, 1989) which was designed to operationalize a new method of conceptualizing somatization disorder.

Any of these three measures of somatic sensations can be useful in quantifying the number of body sensations currently being experienced by the patient. A review of the particular items endorsed can also be helpful in determining whether the patient is complaining primarily of relatively benign sensations or relatively more pathological body sensations which can be helpful in the differential diagnosis of hypochondriasis vs. somatization disorder, respectively (Furer et al., 1999), and whether he or she is preoccupied primarily with arousal-reactive body sensations (e.g., symptoms immediately exacerbated by arousal such as dizziness) or arousal-non-reactive sensations (e.g., rashes, lumps) which can be helpful in the differential diagnosis of panic disorder versus hypochondriasis, respectively (Salkovskis & Clark, 1993; Taylor, 1994, 1995). [Issues pertaining to differential diagnosis are covered more fully in Chapter 6 of the current volume.] Unfortunately, none of these three measures of body sensations makes empirically supported distinctions between these various types of sensations. Additionally, a study by Barsky, Wyshak, and Klerman (1992b) showed that rates of somatization disorder were significantly elevated among patients with hypochondriasis relative to non-hypochondriacal control patients. Thus, it is recommended that a structured interview (e.g., Structured Clinical Interview for DSM-IV, Composite International Diagnostic Interview) be employed in any complete clinical assessment of hypochondriasis to rule in/out the possibility of comorbid somatization disorder in a given patient.

## Anxiety, Depression, and Neuroticism

Anxiety and depression are associated features of hypochondriasis (e.g., Kellner, 1987). Thus, an evaluation of hypochondriasis should include measures to assess current levels of both anxiety and depression. The Beck

Anxiety Inventory (Beck, Epstein, Brown, & Steer, 1988) and the Beck Depression Inventory (Beck et al., 1961) are useful measures for assessing current (i.e., over the last two weeks) levels of anxiety and depression, respectively. Beck Anxiety Inventory and Beck Depression Inventory scores have proved sensitive to treatment effects in studies of cognitive-behavioral therapy for hypochondriasis (Furer et al., 1999; Warwick et al., 1996). With respect to the assessment of anxiety, the State–Trait Anxiety Inventory (Spielberger, 1983) may also be useful as it includes separate scales for the assessment of state (current levels of anxiety) versus trait anxiety (an enduring tendency to experience anxiety under stressful circumstances). Additionally, the Symptom Checklist-90-Revised (Derogatis, 1975) includes several scales relevant to the assessment of anxiety and depression (i.e., the anxiety, depression, and phobic anxiety scales). Finally, it may be useful to assess levels of neuroticism or negative affectivity (a general tendency to experience a variety of negative emotions including anxiety and depression) since neuroticism is elevated among those with hypochondriasis (Noyes et al., 1993). Useful measures include Neuroticism subscales from the Revised NEO Personality Inventory or its briefer version—the NEO Five-Factor Inventory (Costa & McCrae, 1992)—as well as the Eysenck Personality Inventory (Eysenck & Eysenck, 1968). Chapter 4 of the current volume reviews the relationship of personality factors to hypochondriasis.

Additionally, hypochondriasis is often comorbid with certain anxiety and depressive disorders (Noyes, 1999). For example, a study by Barsky et al. (1992b) showed that rates of panic disorder, generalized anxiety disorder, phobic disorders, and obsessive-compulsive disorder, as well as major depression and dysthymic disorder were significantly elevated among patients with hypochondriasis relative to non-hypochondriacal control patients. Thus, it is recommended that a structured interview (e.g., Structured Clinical Interview for DSM-IV, Composite International Diagnostic Interview) be employed in any complete clinical assessment of hypochondriasis to rule in/out the possibility of comorbid anxiety or depressive disorders in a given patient.

## Death Anxiety

Death anxiety, or 'thanatophobia', is an associated feature of hypochondriasis (Kellner, 1986, 1987; see also Chapter 14) for a complete review of death anxiety). There are several measures available for assessing this construct (see review by Lester & Templer, 1992–93) including the Thanatophobia subscale of the Illness Attitudes Scale (Kellner, 1986, 1987) reviewed earlier in this chapter. Two of the most common measures that focus exclusively on death anxiety are the Death Anxiety Scale (Templer,

1970) and the Fear of Death Scale (Collett & Lester, 1969; Lester, 1990). The Death Anxiety Scale consists of 15 items (e.g., 'I fear dying a painful death', 'I often think about how short life really is') that are answered in a true/false fashion (Templer, 1970). The total score shows acceptable stability and internal consistency (Templer, 1970). Moreover, the Death Anxiety Scale total scores have been shown to be significantly higher among a sample of psychiatric patients who spontaneously verbalized fear of (or preoccupation with) death, as compared to a matched control group (Templer, 1970). The Death Anxiety Scale has been shown to be multifactorial (see review by Lonetto & Templer, 1986). While most Death Anxiety Scale factors have been shown to be highly correlated with anxiety and depression, the first factor (i.e., the Fear of Death and Dying factor, comprising items such as 'I am very much afraid to die') has been shown to be essentially unrelated to anxiety and depression, providing a relatively pure index of death anxiety (Gilliland & Templer, 1985–86).

Lester has criticized measures such as the Death Anxiety Scale for mixing several dimensions of death anxiety together in the same scale, such as fears of death versus dying, and whether consideration was being given to the death/dying of oneself or another person (Lester & Templer, 1992–93). Thus, in the construction of the Fear of Death Scale (Collett & Lester, 1969; Lester, 1990) four separate subscales were developed, including Fear of Death of Self, Fear of Dying of Self, Fear of Death of Others, and Fear of Dying of Others. Scores on three of these subscales (i.e., all but Fear of Dying of Others) have been shown to possess convergent validity with the Death Anxiety Scale (Templer, 1970) total score (Triplett et al., 1995). In making the conceptual distinction between fears of death versus fears of dying, the Fear of Death Scale holds promise in empirically evaluating a suggestion made by Noyes (1999) as to the aspects of death anxiety that may distinguish panic disorder from hypochondriasis. Noyes (1999) has noted that during panic attacks, patients with panic disorder often fear dying from some catastrophic event such as a heart attack, whereas patients with hypochondriasis fear death from a progressive disease such as lung cancer. If this speculation is correct, panic disorder patients should score relatively higher on the Fear of Dying of Self subscale, and hypochondriasis patients should score relatively higher on the Fear of Death of Self subscale. This possibility requires empirical investigation.

## Panic Attacks

Since panic disorder and hypochondriasis are commonly co-morbid conditions (see Chapter 6), any clinical evaluation of hypochondriasis should assess for the presence of panic attacks. Whether the patient meets diagnostic criteria for panic disorder can be determined through the use of a structured interview such as the Composite International Diagnostic Interview or the Structured Clinical Interview for DSM-IV. Detailed information on the frequency, number of symptoms, symptom severity, and whether panic attacks are spontaneous or cued can also be obtained with the self-report Revised Panic Attack Questionnaire (Cox, Norton, & Swinson, 1992).

## Anxiety Senstivity

Anxiety sensitivity, a fear of anxiety-related bodily sensations (e.g., dizziness, racing heartbeat), is elevated in patients with panic disorder (Taylor, Koch, & McNally, 1992). Anxiety sensitivity is typically assessed with the Anxiety Sensitivity Index (Peterson & Reiss, 1992). Interest has recently turned to the potential role of anxiety sensitivity in hypochondriasis (see reviews by Cox, 1996; Cox, Borger, & Enns, 1999a). In a sample of panic disorder patients, Otto, Pollack, Sachs, and Rosenbaum (1992) found that Anxiety Sensitivity Index scores were the best predictor of hypochondriacal concerns on the Illness Attitudes Scale. Otto et al. (1992) speculated that the Illness Attitudes Scale and Anxiety Sensitivity Index assess different aspects of a tendency to experience fear in response to body sensations, with the Illness Attitudes Scale targeting this tendency in terms of a proclivity to display fear in response to arousal-non-reactive body sensations and the Anxiety Sensitivity Index tapping this tendency in terms of a proclivity to fear arousal-reactive body sensations. Taylor (1994, 1995) raised concerns about whether true hypochondriacal concerns were assessed by the Illness Attitudes Scale in the Otto et al. (1992) study, or whether panic disorder patients had confounded questions about their physical health with worries and concerns associated with their panic disorder (see also reply by Otto & Pollack, 1994). More specifically, Taylor (1994) pointed out that the Illness Attitudes Scale was not designed to distinguish between fears of arousal-reactive and arousal-non-reactive symptoms, and that panic disorder patients may endorse items on both the Anxiety Sensitivity Index and Illness Attitudes Scale relative to the same fears of arousal-related sensations characteristic of their panic disorder. Since Taylor (1994, 1995) expressed these concerns, a significant association between hypochondriacal concerns and anxiety sensitivity has also been demonstrated in patients with major depression (Otto, Demopulos, McLean, Pollack, & Fava, 1998) and in a non-clinical sample (Stewart & Watt, 2000) demonstrating that these relations are not restricted to panic disorder patients.

Cox et al. (1999a) and Cox, Borger, Taylor, Fuentes, and Ross (1999b) have suggested that of the three anxiety sensitivity dimensions identified in factor analytic studies of the Anxiety Sensitivity Index (i.e., physical vs. psychological vs. social concerns; e.g., Stewart, Taylor, & Baker, 1997) only the physical concerns dimension (fears that bodily symptoms will result in physical illness) should be elevated in both panic disorder and hypochondriasis, and that social concerns should not be elevated among those with hypochondriasis. To test these propositions, Cox (1999) compared the Anxiety Sensitivity Index scores of patients with primary DSM-IV hypochondriasis to panic disorder patients and community controls. Hypochondriasis patients scored significantly higher than normal controls on every item of the Anxiety Sensitivity Index, with the smallest differences being evident on social concern items. Panic disorder patients scored higher than the hypochondriacs on the social concerns item 'Other people notice when I feel shaky' and hypochondriasis patients scored higher than panic disorder patients on the physical concerns item 'When my stomach is upset, I worry that I might be seriously ill'. Cox (1999) suggested that the Anxiety Sensitivity Index taps into a more general catastrophic style related to the misinterpretation of bodily symptoms in general, rather than anxiety-related symptoms in particular (cf. Asmundson & Norton, 1995; Asmundson & Taylor, 1996; Stewart et al., 2001; Watt & Stewart, 2000; Watt, Stewart, & Cox, 1998).

## Alexithymia

Alexithymia involves a difficulty identifying and verbalizing emotional states, and in distinguishing emotions from bodily sensations (Bagby, Parker, & Taylor, 1994a). Nemiah (1977) suggested that hypochondriacal patients should be high in alexithymia. Because of their inability to identify their own feelings and to elaborate on them (i.e., high alexithymia), hypochondriacal patients are considered to focus on the somatic manifestations of emotional arousal while minimizing the affective components of emotions, resulting in somatosensory amplification and misinterpretation of somatic sensations as signs of physical illness (Bach, Bach, & de Zwaan, 1996). One psychometrically sound measure of alexithymia is the 20-item version of the Toronto Alexithymia Scale (Bagby et al., 1994a; Bagby, Taylor, & Parker, 1994b). Using this measure, Devine, Stewart, and Watt (1999) showed that alexithymia is related to anxiety sensitivity, even after conceptually redundant items are removed. Several studies have shown alexithymia levels to be positively correlated with scores on self-report measures of hypochondriasis (e.g., Bagby, Taylor, & Ryan, 1986) and to be significantly elevated among patients diagnosed with hypochondriasis (e.g., Taylor, Bagby, & Parker, 1991). Others, however, have been highly critical of the evidence for alexithymia as an associated feature of hypochondriasis (e.g., Warwick & Salkovskis, 1990).

For example, if hypochondriacal patients minimize affective components of emotions as in alexithymia (Bach et al., 1996), it is difficult to explain why they also have elevated scores on anxiety and depression scales (e.g., Kellner, 1987). It may be that the alexithymia construct is more relevant for somatization and pain disorder than for hypochondriasis per se.

## ISSUES IN DIFFERENTIAL DIAGNOSIS

Hypochondriasis shares a number of features in common with certain anxiety disorders including panic disorder, generalized anxiety disorder, obsessive-compulsive disorder, and simple phobia (i.e., illness phobia; Noyes, 1999) as well as with somatization disorder (another somatoform disorder). Chapter 6 of the current volume provides a thorough review of issues in differential diagnosis. In this section we return to the two cases presented earlier to illustrate how the various measures described throughout this chapter can be useful in the process of differential diagnosis.

Panic disorder is similar to hypochondriasis in that both disorders involve the catastrophic misinterpretation of body sensations. A differential diagnosis of hypochondriasis versus panic disorder was an important consideration in Marshall's case (Case B). Salkovskis and Clark (1993) have suggested that the types of body sensations with which the patient is preoccupied, and the types of catastrophic physical outcomes feared, help to distinguish panic disorder patients from hypochondriacal patients. An examination of Marshall's responses on the MMPI-II Hypochondriasis Scale revealed that he reported preoccupations with both arousal-reactive sensations as is typical of panic disorder patients, and arousal-non-reactive sensations as is more commonly reported by hypochondriacal patients. Reviews of Marshall's responses to structured questions on the Structured Clinical Interview for DSM-IV and of his responses on the Illness Attitudes Scale and Anxiety Sensitivity Index showed that he misinterpreted his body sensations as being possibly indicative of both immediate (e.g., stroke) and relatively more delayed (e.g., brain cancer) catastrophic physical outcomes. Thus, the first two distinguishing features offered by Salkovskis and Clark (1993; i.e., type of body sensations, type of feared outcome) were not particularly helpful in determining whether this client was suffering from panic disorder or hypochondriasis. However, Marshall's elevations on the Anxiety Sensitivity Index physical concerns (but not social concerns) items was consistent with a diagnosis of hypochondriasis (cf. Cox, 1999). Moreover, his frequent checking-type safety behavior (e.g., searching the Internet for information on the cause of his symptoms, frequent visits to the physician, seeking reassurance from his spouse), as opposed to safety behaviors involving avoidance, was more consistent with a diagnosis of hypochondriasis than of panic disorder (cf. Salkovskis & Clark, 1993). In fact, Marshall showed elevated scores on items from the safety behavior factor of the Illness Attitudes Scale (Stewart & Watt, 2000). Finally, the anxiety disorders section of the Structured Clinical Interview for DSM-IV and the self-report Revised Panic Attack Questionnaire (Cox et al., 1992) were helpful in determining that Marshall suffered from limited-symptom, infrequent panic attacks that did not meet full DSM-IV (American Psychiatric Association, 1994) diagnositic criteria for panic disorder.

Specific phobia of illness (i.e., illness phobia) is also similar to hypochondriasis—both disorders involve fears about illness or disease. A differential diagnosis of simple phobia vs. hypochondriasis was an important consideration in Kirsten's case (Case A). Kirsten reported fears that she had already contracted breast cancer (as in hypochondriasis) and fears that she would develop breast cancer in the future (as in illness phobia) (see Noyes, 1999). Moreover, she displayed some of the characteristics which Marks (1987) has suggested are more likely indicative of illness phobia than of hypochondriasis (e.g., severe avoidance behavior relating to her fear of breast cancer, a primary focus on a single body sensation and a single feared disease—lumps in her breasts and breast cancer, respectively). However, other of her maladaptive safety behaviors were more of the checking variety characteristic of hypochondriasis (Furer et al., 1999), particularly her very frequent visits to her physician for breast examinations, which served a short-term anxiety-reducing function. In fact, Kirsten showed elevated scores on items from the safety behavior factor (Stewart & Watt, 2000) of the Illness Attitudes Scale, reflecting high levels of reassurance seeking and her endorsement of the importance of bodily checking (through frequent physician visits rather than breast self-examinations). Scores on the MMPI-II Hypochondriasis Scale and Somatosensory Amplification Scale were also revealing in that Kirsten scored above normative values on both, suggesting multiple complaints involving body sensations and a tendency toward somatosensory amplification consistent with a diagnosis of hypochondriasis. The entire picture obtained through the assessment process suggested that the most useful diagnosis for Case A would be the proposed illness fears subtype of hypochondriasis (Fava & Grandi, 1991).

## CONCLUSION

A thorough assessment of hypochondriasis involves the exclusion of organic and other psychiatric disorders (e.g., anxiety, depression) which may better account for the presenting picture, as well as a complete evaluation of all core dimensions of psychopathology directly relevant to hypochondriasis—illness fears, illness beliefs, safety behavior, and disruptive effects. The development and evaluation of structured interviews for diagnosing hypochondriasis has tended to lag behind that for other psychiatric disorders (Escobar, 1995). At present, no widely agreed upon 'gold standard' exists for diagnosing this relatively prevalent and extremely disabling psychiatric disorder. Whereas each of the structured diagnostic interviews reviewed herein (i.e., Composite International Diagnostic Interview, Structured Clinical Interview for DSM-IV, Structured Diagnostic Interview for Hypochondriasis) could facilitate the diagnostic process, none has demonstrated the psychometric properties required to recommend it above the others. We recommend the use of a structured interview for both researchers and clinicians interested in diagnosing hypochondriasis; however, the choice of the particular interview should depend on the purpose of the assessment (Wittchen, 1994).

With respect to self-report measures, none of the questionnaires described above provides a simultaneous assessment of all four sets of core hypochondriacal symptoms (i.e., illness fears, illness beliefs, safety behaviors, and disruptive effects), and of important associated features (e.g., body sensations, anxiety sensitivity, alexithymia, death anxiety). Thus, we recommend the combining of various tools in the clinical assessment process (cf. Noyes, Holt, Happel, Kathol, & Yagla, 1997) to assist in treatment planning with a given patient. The following set of measures would tentatively appear to provide maximum information with minimal overlap: (1) the Illness Attitudes Scale (for assessment of the four core dimensions of DSM-IV hypochondriasis symptoms, as well as the associated feature of death anxiety); (2) the Somatosensory Amplification Scale (for assessment of the cognitive style of somatosensory amplification); (3) the Cognitions about Body and Health Questionnaire (for the assessment of cognitive features unique to hypochondriasis); as well as (4) the Anxiety Sensitivity Index; (5) the Revised Panic Attack Questionnaire; (6) the 20-item Toronto Alexithymia Scale; and (7) the Symptom Checklist-90-Revised (for the assessment of the associated features of anxiety sensitivity, panic attacks, alexithymia, and body sensations, anxiety, and depression, respectively). However, there is currently no empirical support for this particular recommended set of tools. Thus, we suggest that future research focus on determining which particular combination of self-report measures is most useful in the clinical assessment of hypochondriasis.

**Authors' Note:** All correspondence concerning this manuscript should be addressed to Dr. S. H. Stewart at the Department of Psychology, Dalhousie University, Life Sciences Centre, 1355 Oxford Street, Halifax, Nova Scotia,

Canada, B3H 4J1. The first author can also be reached by telephone (902-494-3793), FAX (902-494-6585), or Internet (*sstewart@is.dal.ca*). The authors would like to thank Ms. Heather Lee Loughlin for her research assistance in preparing this manuscript.

## REFERENCES

American Psychiatric Association (1980). *Diagnostic and statistical manual of mental disorders* (3rd edn.). Washington, DC: American Psychiatric Press.

American Psychiatric Association (1987). *Diagnostic and statistical manual of mental disorders* (3rd edn., rev.). Washington, DC: American Psychiatric Press.

American Psychiatric Association (1994). *Diagnostic and statistical manual of mental disorders* (4th edn.). Washington, DC: American Psychiatric Press.

Asmundson, G.J.G., & Norton, G.R. (1995). Anxiety sensitivity in patients with physically unexplained chronic back pain: A preliminary report. *Behaviour Research and Therapy*, **33**, 771–777.

Asmundson, G.J.G., & Taylor, S. (1996). Role of anxiety sensitivity in pain-related fear and avoidance. *Journal of Behavioral Medicine*, **19**, 573–582.

Bach, M., Bach, D., & de Zwaan, M. (1996). Independency of alexithymia and somatization: A factor analytic study. *Psychosomatics*, **37**, 451–458.

Bagby, R.M., Parker, J.D.A., & Taylor, G.J. (1994a). The twenty-item Toronto Alexithymia Scale. I: Item selection and cross-validation of the factor structure. *Journal of Psychosomatic Research*, **38**, 23–32.

Bagby, R.M., Taylor, G.J., & Parker, J.D.A. (1994b). The twenty-item Toronto Alexithymia Scale. II. Convergent, discriminant, and concurrent validity. *Journal of Psychosomatic Research*, **38**, 33–40.

Bagby, R.M., Taylor, G.J., & Ryan, D. (1986). Toronto Alexithymia Scale: Relationship with personality and psychopathology measures. *Psychotherapy and Psychosomatics*, **45**, 207–215.

Barsky, A.J. (1992). Amplification, somatization, and the somatoform disorders. *Psychosomatics*, **33**, 28–34.

Barsky, A.J., Cleary, P.D., Wyshak, G., Spitzer, R.L., Williams, J.B.W., & Klerman, G.L. (1992a). A structured diagnostic interview for hypochondriasis: A proposed criterion standard. *The Journal of Nervous and Mental Disease*, **180**, 20–27.

Barksy, A.J., & Klerman, G.L. (1983). Overview: Hypochondriasis, bodily complaints, and somatic styles. *American Journal of Psychiatry*, **140**, 273–281.

Barsky, A.J., & Wyshak, G. (1990). Hypochondriasis and somatosensory amplification. *British Journal of Psychiatry*, **157**, 404–409.

Barsky, A.J., Wyshak, G., & Klerman, G.L. (1986). DSM-III hypochondriasis in medical outpatients. *Archives of General Psychiatry*, **43**, 493–500.

Barsky, A.J., Wyshak, G., & Klerman, G.L. (1990). The Somatosensory Amplification Scale and its relationship to hypochondriasis. *Journal of Psychiatric Research*, **24**, 323–334.

Barsky, A.J., Wyshak, G., & Klerman, G.L. (1992b). Psychiatric comorbidity in DSM-III-R hypochondriasis. *Archives of General Psychiatry*, **49**, 101–108.

Beaber, R.J., & Rodney, W.M. (1984). Underdiagnosis of hypochondriasis in family practice. *Psychosomatics*, **24**, 39–45.

Beck, A.T., Ward, C.H., Mendelson, M., Mock, J., & Erbaugh, J. (1961). An inventory for measuring depression. *Archives of General Psychiatry*, **4**, 53–63.

Beck, A.T., Epstein, N., Brown, G., & Steer, R.A. (1988). An inventory for measuring clinical anxiety: Psychometric properties. *Journal of Consulting and Clinical Psychology*, **56**, 893–897.

Butcher, J.N. (1990). *The MMPI-2 in psychological treatment.* New York: Oxford University Press.

Chaturvedi, S.K., Bhandari, S., Beena, M.B., & Rao, S. (1996). Screening for abnormal illness behavior. *Psychopathology*, **29**, 325–330.

Clifft, M.A. (1986). Writing about psychiatric patients: Guidelines for disguising case material. *Bulletin of the Menninger Clinic*, **50**, 511–524.

Collett, L., & Lester, D. (1969). The fear of death and the fear of dying. *Journal of Psychology*, **72**, 179–181.

Costa, P.T., & McCrae, R.R. (1992). *Revised NEO Personality Inventory (NEO-PI-R) and NEO Five Factor Inventory (NEO-FFI) professional manual.* Odessa, FL: Psychological Assessment Resources.

Cox, B.J. (1999, March). *The role of anxiety sensitivity in panic and other disorders.* Paper presented at the 19th National Conference of the Anxiety Disorders Association of America, San Diego, CA.

Cox, B.J. (1996). The nature and assessment of catastrophic thoughts in panic disorder. *Behaviour Research and Therapy*, **34**, 363–374.

Cox, B.J., Borger, S.C., Asmundson, G.J.G., & Taylor, S. (2000). Dimensions of hypochondriasis and the five-factor model of personality. *Personality and Individual Differences*, **29**, 99–108.

Cox, B.J., Borger, S.C., & Enns, M.W. (1999a). Anxiety sensitivity and emotional disorders: Psychometric studies and their theoretical implications. In S. Taylor (Ed.), *Anxiety sensitivity: Theory, research and treatment of the fear of anxiety* (pp. 115–148). Mahwah, NJ: Erlbaum.

Cox, B.J., Borger, S.C., Taylor, S., Fuentes, K., & Ross, L.M. (1999b). Anxiety sensitivity and the five-factor model of personality. *Behaviour Research and Therapy*, **37**, 633–641.

Cox, B.J., Norton, G.R., & Swinson, R.P. (1992). *The Panic Attack Questionnaire, revised.* Toronto, ON: Clarke Institute of Psychiatry.

Dahlstrom, W.A., Welsh, G.S., & Dahlstrom, L.E. (1971). *An MMPI handbook, Vol. I: Clinical interpretation* (rev. ed.). Minneapolis, MN: University of Minnesota Press.

Derogatis, L.R. (1975). *SCL-90-R: Administration, scoring and procedures manual—II for the revised version and other instruments of the psychopathology rating scale series.* Towson, MD: Clinical Psychometric Research.

Devine, H., Stewart, S.H., & Watt, M.C. (1999). Relations between anxiety sensitivity and dimensions of alexithymia. *Journal of Psychosomatic Research*, **47**, 145–158.

Dinning, W.D., & Evans, R.G. (1977). Discriminant and convergent validity of the SCL-90 in psychiatric inpatients. *Journal of Personality Assessment*, **41**, 304–310.

Edelman, R.J., & Holdsworth, S. (1993). The Minnesota Multiphasic Personality Inventory Hypochondriasis Scale: Its relation to bodily awareness and irrational beliefs. *Personality and Individual Differences*, **14**, 369–370.

Escobar, J.I. (1995). Transcultural aspects of dissociative and somatoform disorders. *Psychiatric Clinics of North America*, **18**, 555–569.

Escobar, J.I., Gara, M., Waitzkin, H., Silver, R.C., Holman, A., & Compton, W. (1998). DSM-IV hypochondriasis in primary care. *General Hospital Psychiatry*, **20**, 155–159.

Escobar, J.I., Rubio-Stipec, M., Canino, G., & Karno, M. (1989). Somatic Symptom Index (SSI): A new and abridged somatization construct. *Journal of Nervous and Mental Disease*, **177**, 1140–1146.

Eysenck, H.J., & Eysenck, S.B.S. (1968). *Manual for the Eysenck Personality Inventory*. San Diego, CA: Educational and Industrial Testing Service.

Fava, G.A., & Grandi, S. (1991). Differential diagnosis of hypochondriacal fears and beliefs. *Psychotherapy and Psychosomatics*, **55**, 114–119.

Ferguson, E., & Daniel, E. (1995). The Illness Attitudes Scale (IAS): A psychometric evaluation on a non-clinical population. *Personality and Individual Differences*, **18**, 463–469.

Fink, P., Ewald, H., Jensen, J., Sorensen, L., Engberg, M., Holm, M., & Munk-Jorgensen, P. (1999). Screening for somatization and hypochondriasis in primary care and neurological in-patients: A seven-item scale for hypochondriasis and somatization. *Journal of Psychosomatic Research*, **46**, 261–273.

First, M.B., Spitzer, R.L., Gibbon, M., & Williams, J.B.W. (1995). *Structured Clinical Interview for DSM-IV*. New York: New York State Psychiatric Institute, Biometrics Research Department.

Furer, P., Vincent, N., Lander, M., & Walker, J. (1999, March). *Hypochondriasis or intense illness worry: Assessment, treatment, and research*. Workshop presented at the 19th National Convention of the Anxiety Disorders Association of America, San Diego, CA.

Gilliland, J.C., & Templer, D.I. (1985–86). Relationship of Death Anxiety Scale factors to subjective states. *Omega: Journal of Death and Dying*, **16**, 155–167.

Greenberg, G.D., Peterson, R.A., & Heilbronner, G.D. (1989). *Manual: Illness Effects Questionnaire*. Unpublished manual, Department of Psychology, George Washington University, Washington, DC.

Hadjistavropoulos, H.D., & Asmundson, G.J.G. (1998). Factor analytic investigation of the Illness Attitudes Scale in a chronic pain sample. *Behaviour Research and Therapy*, **36**, 1185–1195.

Hadjistavropoulos, H.D., Frombach, I.K., & Asmundson, G.J.G. (1999). Exploratory and confirmatory factor analytic investigations of the Illness Attitudes Scale in a nonclinical sample. *Behaviour Research and Therapy*, **37**, 671–684.

Kasteler, J., Kane, R.L., Olsen, D.M., & Thetford, C. (1976). Issues underlying prevalence of 'doctor-shopping' behavior. *Journal of Health and Social Behavior*, **17**, 328–339.

Kellner, R. (1986). *Somatization and hypochondriasis*. New York: Praeger-Greenwood.

Kellner, R. (1987). *Abridged manual of the Illness Attitude Scales*. Unpublished manual, Department of Psychiatry, School of Medicine, University of New Mexico, Albuquerque.

Kellner, R., Abbott, P., Winslow, W.W., & Pathak, D. (1987a). Fears, beliefs, and attitudes in DSM-III hypochondriasis. *The Journal of Nervous and Mental Disease*, **175**, 20–25.

Kellner, R., Abbott, P. Winslow, W.W., & Pathak, D. (1989). Anxiety, depression, and somatization in DSM-III hypochondriasis. *Psychosomatics*, **30**, 57–64.

Kellner, R., Slocumb, J.C., Wiggins, R.J., Abbott, P., Romanik, R., Winslow, W.W., & Pathak, D. (1987b). The relationship of hypochondriacal fears and beliefs to anxiety and depression. *Psychiatric Medicine*, **4**, 15–24.

Lester, D. (1990). The Collett–Lester Fear of Death Scale. *Death Studies*, **14**, 451–468.

Lester, D., & Templer, D.I. (1992–93). Death anxiety scales: A dialogue. *Omega: Journal of Death and Dying*, **26**, 239–253.

Lonetto, R., & Templer, D.I. (1986). *Death anxiety*. Washington, DC: Hemisphere.

Lucock, M.P., & Morley, S. (1996). The Health Anxiety Questionnaire. *British Journal of Health Psychology*, **1**, 137–150.

Lucock, M.P., White, C., Peake, M.D., & Morley, S. (1998). Biased perception and recall of reassurance in medical outpatients. *British Journal of Health Psychology*, **3**, 237–243.

Marks, I.M. (1987). *Fears, phobias, and rituals*. New York: Oxford University Press.

McKinley, J.C., & Hathaway, S.R. (1940). A Multiphasic Personality Schedule (Minnesota): II. A differential study of hypochondriasis. *Journal of Psychology*, **10**, 255–268.

Nemiah, J.C. (1977). Alexithymia. *Psychotherapy and Psychosomatics*, **28**, 199–206.

Noyes, R. (1999). The relationship of hypochondriasis to anxiety disorders. *General Hospital Psychiatry*, **21**, 8–17.

Noyes, R., Holt, C.S., Happel, R.L., Kathol, R.G., & Yagla, S.J. (1997). A family study of hypochondriasis. *The Journal of Nervous and Mental Disease*, **185**, 223–232.

Noyes, R., Kathol, R.G., Fisher, M.M., Phillips, B.M., Suelzer, M.T., & Holt, C.S. (1993). The validity of DSM-III-R hypochondriasis. *Archives of General Psychiatry*, **50**, 961–970.

Noyes, R., Reich, J., Clancy, J., & O'Gorman, T.W. (1986). Reduction in hypochondriasis with treatment of panic disorder. *British Journal of Psychiatry*, **149**, 631–635.

Otto, M.W., Demopulos, C.M., McLean, N.E., Pollack, M.H., & Fava, M. (1998). Additional findings on the association between anxiety sensitivity and hypochondriacal concerns: Examination of patients with major depression. *Journal of Anxiety Disorders*, **12**, 225–232.

Otto, M.W., & Pollack, M.H. (1994). Panic disorder and hypochondriacal concerns: A reply to Taylor. *Journal of Anxiety Disorders*, **8**, 101–103.

Otto, M.W., Pollack, M.H., Sachs, G.S., & Rosenbaum, J.F. (1992). Hypochondriacal concerns, anxiety sensitivity, and panic disorder. *Journal of Anxiety Disorders*, **6**, 93–104.

Parker, G., & Lipscombe, P. (1980). The relationship of early parental experiences to adult dependency, hypochondriasis, and utilization of primary physicians. *British Journal of Medical Psychology*, **53**, 355–363.

Peterson, R.A., & Reiss, S. (1992). *Anxiety Sensitivity Index manual* (2nd edn., rev.). Worthington, OH: International Diagnostic Services.

Pilowsky, I. (1967). Dimensions of hypochondriasis. *British Journal of Psychiatry*, **113**, 89–93.

Pilowsky, I. (1971). The diagnosis of abnormal illness behavior. *Australia and New Zealand Journal of Psychiatry*, **5**, 136–138.

Pilowsky, I., & Spence, N.D. (1983). *Manual for the Illness Behavior Questionnaire* (2nd edn.). Unpublished manual, Department of Psychiatry, University of Adelaide, Adelaide, South Australia.

Pilowsky, I., & Spence, N.D. (1994). *Manual for the Illness Behavior Questionnaire* (3rd edn.). Unpublished manual, Department of Psychiatry, University of Adelaide, Adelaide, South Australia.

Rief, W., Hiller, W., & Margraf, J. (1998). Cognitive aspects of hypochondriasis and the somatization syndrome. *Journal of Abnormal Psychology*, **107**, 587–595.

Rief, W., Schaefer, S., Hiller, W., & Fichter, M.M. (1992). Lifetime diagnoses in patients with somatoform disorders: Which came first? *European Archives of Psychiatry and Clinical Neuroscience*, **241**, 236–240.

Robins, L.N., Wing, J., Wittchen, H.-U., Helzer, J.E., Babor, T.F., Burke, J., Farmer, A., Jablenski, A., Pickens, R., Regier, D.A., Sartorius, N., & Towle, L.H. (1988). The Composite International Diagnostic Interview. *Archives of General Psychiatry*, **45**, 1069–1077.

Salkovskis, P.M., & Clark, D.M. (1993). Panic disorder and hypochondriasis. *Advances in Behaviour Research and Therapy*, **15**, 23–48.

Speckens, A.E.M., Spinhoven, P., Sloekers, P.P.A., Bolk, J.H., & van Hemert, A.M. (1996a). A validation study of the Whiteley Index, the Illness Attitude Scales, and the Somatosensory Amplification Scale in general medical and general practice patients. *Journal of Psychosomatic Research*, **40**, 95–104.

Speckens, A.E.M., van Hemert, A.M., Spinhoven, P., & Bolk, J.H. (1996b). The diagnostic and prognostic significance of the Whiteley Index, the Illness Attitude Scales, and the Somatosensory Amplification Scale. *Psychological Medicine*, **26**, 1085–1090.

Spielberger, C.D. (1983). *Manual for the State-Trait Anxiety Inventory (Form Y)*. Palo Alto, CA: Consulting Psychologists Press.

Spitzer, R.L., Williams, J.B.W., Gibbon, M., & First, M.B. (1992). The Structured Clinical Interview for DSM-III-R. I: History, rationale, and description. *Archives of General Psychiatry*, **49**, 624–629.

Stewart, S.H., Taylor, S., & Baker, J.M. (1997). Gender differences in dimensions of anxiety sensitivity. *Journal of Anxiety Disorders*, **11**, 179–200.

Stewart, S.H., Taylor, S., Jang, K.L., Cox, B.J., Watt, M.C., Fedoroff, I.C., & Borger, S.C. (2001). Causal modeling of relations among learning history, anxiety sensitivity, and panic attacks. *Behaviour Research and Therapy*, **39**, 443–456.

Stewart, S.H., & Watt, M.C. (2000). Illness Attitude Scale dimensions and their association with anxiety-related constructs in a non-clinical sample. *Behaviour Research and Therapy*, **38**, 83–99.

Talley, N.J., Phillips, S.F., Bruce, B., Twomey, C.K., Zinsmeister, A.R., & Melton, L.J., III (1990). Relation among personality and symptoms in nonulcer dyspepsia and the irritable bowel syndrome. *Gastroenterology*, **99**, 327–333.

Taylor, G.J., Bagby, R.M., & Parker, J.D.A. (1991). The alexithymia construct: A potential paradigm for psychosomatic medicine. *Psychosomatics*, **32**, 151–164.

Taylor, S. (1994). Comment on Otto et al. (1992): Hypochondriacal concerns, anxiety sensitivity, and panic disorder. *Journal of Anxiety Disorders*, **8**, 97–99.

Taylor, S. (1995). Panic disorder and hypochondriacal concerns: Reply to Otto and Pollack (1994). *Journal of Anxiety Disorders*, **9**, 87–88.

Taylor, S., Koch, W.J., & McNally, R.J. (1992). How does anxiety sensitivity vary across the anxiety disorders? *Journal of Anxiety Disorders*, **6**, 249–259.

Templer, D.I. (1970). The construction and validation of a Death Anxiety Scale. *The Journal of General Psychology*, **82**, 165–177.

Triplett, G., Roshdieh, S., Cohen, D., Stanczak, E.M., Reimer, W., Siscoe, K., Rinaldi, S., Templer, D.I., & Hill, C. (1995). Death discomfort differential. *Omega: Journal of Death and Dying*, **31**, 295–304.

Warwick, H.M.C. (1995). Assessment of hypochondriasis. *Behaviour Research and Therapy*, **33**, 845–853.

Warwick, H.M.C., & Marks, I.M. (1988). Behavioral treatment of illness phobia. *British Journal of Psychiatry*, **152**, 239–241.

Warwick, H.M.C., Clark, D.M., Cobb, A.M., & Salkovskis, P.M. (1996). A controlled trial of cognitive-behavioral treatment of hypochondriasis. *British Journal of Psychiatry*, **169**, 189–195.

Warwick, H.M.C., & Salkovskis, P.M. (1990). Hypochondriasis. *Behaviour Research and Therapy*, **28**, 105–117.

Watt, M.C., & Stewart, S.H. (2000). Anxiety sensitivity mediates the relationships between childhood learning experiences and elevated hypochondriacal concerns in young adulthood. *Journal of Psychosomatic Research*, **49**, 107–118.

Watt, M.C., Stewart, S.H., & Cox, B.J. (1998). A retrospective study of the learning history origins of anxiety sensitivity. *Behaviour Research and Therapy*, **36**, 505–525.

Welsh, G.S. (1952). A factor study of the MMPI using scales with item overlap eliminated. *American Psychologist*, **7**, 341–347.

Williams, J.B.W., Gibbon, M., First, M.B., Spitzer, R.L., Davies, M., Borus, J., Howes, M.J., Kane, J., Pope, H.G., Rounsaville, B., & Wittchen, H.-U. (1992). The Structured Clinical Interview for DSM-IIII-R (SCID): II. Multisite test-retest reliability. *Archives of General Psychiatry*, **49**, 630–636.

Wise, T.N., Mann, L.S., Jani, N., Kozachuk, W., & Jani, S. (1994). Convergent validation of the Illness Effects Questionnaire. *Psychological Reports*, **75**, 248–250.

Wittchen, H.-U. (1994). Reliability and validity studies of the WHO-Composite International Diagnostic Interview (CIDI): A critical review. *Journal of Psychiatric Research*, **28**, 57–84.

Wittchen, H.-U., Essau, C.A., Rief, W., & Fichter, M.M. (1993). Assessment of somatoform disorders and comorbidity pattern with the CIDI: Findings in psychosomatic patients. *International Journal of Methods in Psychiatric Research*, **3**, 87–100.

Wittchen, H.-U., Lachner, G., Wunderlick, U., & Pfister, H. (1998). Test–retest reliability of the computerized DSM-IV version of the Munich-Composite International Diagnostic Interview (M-CIDI). *Social Psychiatry and Psychiatric Epidemiology*, **33**, 568–578.

World Health Organization (1990). *Composite International Diagnostic Interview (CIDI)*. Geneva, Switzerland: World Health Organization.

World Health Organization (1991). *Tenth revision of the International Classification of Diseases Chapter V (F): Mental and behavioral disorders (including disorders of psychological development). Clinical descriptions and diagnostic guidelines*. Geneva, Switzerland: World Health Organization, Division of Mental Health.

Ziesat, H.A. (1978). Correlates of the tourniquet ischemia pain ratio. *Perceptual and Motor Skills*, **47**, 147–150.

Zonderman, A.B., Heft, M.W., & Costa, P.T. (1985). Does the Illness Behavior Questionnaire measure abnormal illness behavior? *Health Psychology*, **4**, 425–536.

Chapter 6

# HYPOCHONDRIASIS: BOUNDARIES AND COMORBIDITIES

*Russell Noyes, Jr.**

## INTRODUCTION

The modern description of hypochondriasis is credited to Gillespie (1928), but the disorder first appeared in the DSM classification under the heading of hypochondriacal neurosis (American Psychiatric Association, 1968). There it was defined as a 'condition dominated by preoccupation with the body and with fear of presumed diseases of various organs. Though the fears are not of delusional quality . . . , they persist despite reassurance.' DSM-III added that the disorder is based upon unrealistic interpretation of physical signs or sensations and is not due to any other mental disorder (American Psychiatric Association, 1980). Thus, somatic symptoms were incorporated without specifying type, and the disorder was relegated to the bottom of the diagnostic hierarchy. Also, an impairment criterion was included. With DSM-III-R, a 6-month duration requirement was added, and consistent with removal of most hierarchical rules from this revision, hypochondriasis might exist in the presence of other mental disorders as long as the symptoms were not simply those of panic attacks and were not delusional in nature (American Psychiatric Association, 1987). The DSM-IV (American Psychiatric Association, 1994) criteria are shown in Table 6.1. By rewording criterion A, emphasis is placed on disease conviction, or preoccupation with a disease that is already present. Disease conviction is distinguished from disease phobia, or fear of developing or being exposed to a disease. The latter, according to these

---

*University of Iowa College of Medicine, USA

*Health Anxiety*
Edited by G.J.G. Asmundson, S. Taylor & B.J. Cox
© 2001 John Wiley & Sons Ltd.

criteria, is more characteristic of another category, namely specific phobia of illness. Also according to criterion E, the diagnosis is not made if the symptoms of hypochondriasis are better accounted for by most anxiety, depressive, and somatoform disorders.

The ICD-10 criteria, shown in Table 6.2, are similar with notable differences (World Health Organization, 1993). They specify a persistent belief in the presence of a serious physical disease that is specifically named by the patient. Persistent refusal to accept medical reassurance is specified, but short-term acceptance does not exclude the diagnosis. Persistent preoccupation with a presumed deformity or disfigurement (body dysmorphic disorder) qualifies under ICD-10, but is specifically excluded under DSM-IV (American Psychiatric Association, 1994). Finally, the diagnosis is not made if the symptoms occur only during schizophrenia or related disorders or any mood disorders. As may be seen, changes in the DSM criteria and differences between DSM-IV and ICD-10 indicate uncertainty about the classification of hypochondriasis (Cote et al., 1996). In reviewing the phenomenology and comorbidity of hypochondriasis, I will examine the boundaries of the disturbance and its overlap with other disorders within the current classification.

Questions about classification reflect uncertainty about how hypochondriasis should be conceptualized. Some look upon it as a personality trait

Table 6.1 DSM-IV criteria for hypochondriasis

A. Preoccupation with fears of having, or the idea that one has, a serious disease based on the person's misinterpretation of bodily symptoms.

B. The preoccupation persists despite appropriate medical evaluation and reassurance.

C. The belief in Criterion A is not of delusional intensity (as a Delusional Disorder, Somatic Type) and is not restricted to a circumscribed concern about appearance (as in Body Dysmorphic Disorder).

D. The preoccupation causes clinically significant distress or impairment in social, occupational, or other important areas of functioning.

E. The duration of the disturbance is at least 6 months.

F. The preoccupation is not better accounted for by Generalized Anxiety Disorder, Obsessive-Compulsive Disorder, Panic Disorder, a Major Depressive Episode, Separation Anxiety, or another Somatoform Disorder.

Specify if:

  *With Poor Insight*: If, for most of the time during the current episode, the person does not recognize that the concern about having a serious illness is excessive or unreasonable.

**Table 6.2**   ICD-10 criteria for hypochondriacal disorder

A. Either of the following must be present:

   (1) a persistent belief, of at least 6 months' duration, of the presence of a maximum of two serious physical diseases (of which at least one must be specifically named by the patient);

   (2) a persistent preoccupation with a presumed deformity or disfigurement (body dysmorphic disorder).

B. Preoccupation with the belief and the symptoms causes persistent distress or interference with personal functioning in daily living, and leads the patient to seek medical treatment or investigations (or equivalent help from local healers).

C. There is persistent refusal to accept medical reassurance that there is no physical cause for the symptoms or physical abnormality. (Short-term acceptance of such reassurance, i.e., for a few weeks during or immediately after investigations, does not exclude this diagnosis.)

D. *Most commonly used exclusion clause.* The symptoms do not occur only during any of the schizophrenic and related disorders or any of the mood [affective] disorders.

---

(Tyrer, Fowler-Dixon, Ferguson, & Kelemen, 1990). Its early onset and long-term stability in some patients fit this conception. Others view it as a dimension of psychopathology (Barsky & Klerman, 1983; Brown & Vaillant, 1981; Costa & McCrae, 1985). Hypochondriacal symptoms accompany many psychiatric disorders in which their occurrence appears to be a matter of degree (Demopulos et al., 1996; Noyes, Reich, Clancy, & O'Gorman, 1986). For those who take a categorical approach, the issue of whether hypochondriasis is primary or secondary remains unsettled. In psychiatric populations, it is commonly a secondary feature of other disorders (Kellner, 1992; Kenyon, 1964). Also, high rates of comorbidity have created doubt about its independent status (Barsky, Wyshak, & Klerman, 1992a; Noyes et al., 1994a). Beyond this, there is, according to Starcevic (1988), a lack of consensus about the definition of hypochondriasis. Some emphasize fear of developing a disease, while others view the disorder as an unfounded belief that one is currently suffering from physical disease. For instance, various authors view disease or illness phobia as a dimension of hypochondriasis (Pilowsky, 1967), a subtype of hypochondriasis (Marks, 1987), or a separate disorder, in this case specific phobia of illness (Cote et al., 1996). Still, most experts agree that patients whose beliefs are delusional should not receive the diagnosis of hypochondriasis (Kellner, 1992). In fact, delusions of disease are often the main or only manifestation of delusional disorder, somatic type (American Psychiatric Association, 1994). Such delusions are often bizarre or unrealistic, whereas the beliefs of the individual with hypochondriasis are overvalued (McKenna, 1984).

However, recent empirical research, especially in primary care, has shown hypochondriasis to be a reliable and valid diagnosis. This work was based on factor analytic studies, beginning with that of Pilowsky (1967). These studies showed consistent features of hypochondriasis that were correlated with one another (Bianchi, 1973; Hanbach & Revelle, 1978; Pilowsky, 1967; Pilowsky & Spence, 1975). Barsky, Wyshak, and Klerman (1986) found that, in general medical patients, distinguishing characteristics of the disorder aggregated in certain individuals and were less common in others. Specifically, the core features of bodily preoccupation, disease phobia, disease conviction, and somatic symptoms were highly correlated with one another. These same hypochondriacal individuals also had other clinical features that gave hypochondriasis external validity, and follow-up studies showed that the diagnosis remains stable over time (Barsky, Fama, Bailey, & Ahern, 1998; Noyes et al., 1994b). Using a structured interview, Barsky et al. (1992b) demonstrated high inter-rater agreement and positive correlations between interview and physician ratings of hypochondriasis (concurrent validity). Patients identified by this interview more frequently had ancillary features of hypochondriasis (e.g., more non-specific somatic complaints, greater functional impairment, and higher utilization of medical care) than did non-hypochondriacal patients (external validity). Other clinical features (e.g., medical morbidity, psychiatric comorbidity, and physician's view of them) distinguished interview-positive from interview-negative patients, indicating a degree of discriminant validity. Similar evidence for validity has been reported by others (Noyes et al., 1993).

I would like to review evidence, where it exists, concerning the phenomenology of hypochondriasis and its boundaries with other disorders. In doing so, I will touch upon certain issues having to do with the classification of the disorder, which I have listed in Table 6.3 (1–4). Likewise, evidence concerning overlap and comorbidity has a bearing on the classification and upon our understanding of relationships between disorders. I have also listed several important questions regarding these topics in Table 6.3 (5–8).

## ANXIETY DISORDERS

In DSM-IV, hypochondriasis is defined as a preoccupation with fears of having, or the idea that one has a serious disease based on misinterpretation of bodily symptoms (American Psychiatric Association, 1994). The fears and ideas about life-threatening circumstances in this definition

**Table 6.3** Issues involving the phenomenology and comorbidity of hypochondriasis

1. Should the diagnostic criteria for hypochondriasis include somatic symptoms?
2. Should hypochondriasis be classified among the somatoform or the anxiety disorders?
3. Can hypochondriasis be distinguished from specific (illness) phobia?
4. Are there disease phobia and disease conviction subtypes of hypochondriasis?
5. Is hypochondriasis a primary or secondary disorder?
6. Are hypochondriasis and panic disorder independent disorders?
7. What is the relationship between hypochondriasis and major depressive disorder?
8. Are hypochondriasis and somatization disorder variants of the same underlying condition?

suggest that hypochondriasis bears a phenomenological resemblance to the anxiety disorders, and that the boundaries between it and various anxiety disorders may be important in defining hypochondriasis (Schafer, 1982; Cote et al., 1996). The framers of DSM-IV wondered whether hypochondriasis might even warrant classification among the anxiety disorders (American Psychiatric Association Task Force on DSM-IV, 1991). They noted that individuals with the disorder frequently have comorbid anxiety and that it is difficult to draw clear boundaries between hypochondriasis, generalized anxiety disorder, and specific phobias. It is currently classified among the somatoform disorders because, according to the above definition, the preoccupation is based upon misinterpretation of bodily symptoms. However, the American Psychiatric Association Task Force on DSM-IV (1991) considered removing this requirement because it excludes individuals whose fears are not accompanied by physical symptoms (e.g., fear of being HIV positive) and blurs the distinction between hypochondriasis and other disorders with prominent somatic presentations (e.g., panic disorder, somatization disorder).

A number of studies have identified anxious characteristics among hypochondriacal patients. Indeed, many investigators have observed a cluster of anxious features, confirming Pilowsky's original factor analysis that identified disease phobia as one of three dimensions (Bianchi, 1973; Hanbach & Revelle, 1978; Kellner et al., 1987a; Pilowsky, 1967; Pilowsky & Spence, 1975). Associated anxious or phobic features have included fear of death, fear of aging, and a sense of vulnerability to illness or injury

(Kellner, 1986; Kellner, Abbott, Winslow, & Pathak, 1987b; Barsky & Wyshak, 1990). Also, a number of authors have reported high correlations between hypochondriacal symptoms and both anxiety and depression (Baker & Merskey, 1983; Kreitman, Sainsbury, Pearce, & Costain, 1965; Stenback & Jalava, 1962; Timsit, Dugardin, Adam, & Sabatier, 1973). Some have observed stronger associations with anxiety, others with depression. In one study of psychiatric patients, Kellner, Abbott, Winslow, and Pathak (1989) found anxiety and somatic symptoms higher in hypochondriacal than in non-hypochondriacal patients. In another they found—this time among general practice patients—a high correlation between fear of disease and anxiety (Kellner, Hernandez, & Pathak, 1992).

## Phenomenology and Boundaries

There are, in fact, at least four anxiety disorders with phenomenological resemblance to hypochondriasis, including specific phobia, generalized anxiety disorder, panic disorder, and obsessive-compulsive disorder. Each of these is discussed below.

### Specific Phobia

Specific phobia of illness was originally described by Ryle (1948) and Bianchi (1971). It receives little mention in DSM-IV, but individuals with the disorder are said to fear being exposed to or contracting a disease they do not as yet have, whereas persons with hypochondriasis are preoccupied with fears of having, or the idea that one has, a disease that is already present (American Psychiatric Association, 1994; Craske et al., 1996). Marks (1970) originally separated phobias of illness from other phobias, noting that the feared objects were internal. Such phobias, although prevalent in the general population, have received little study (Agras, Sylvester, & Oliveau, 1969).

The distinction between illness phobia and hypochondriasis has received little attention (Cote et al., 1996). According to Marks (1987), illness phobia may be a subtype of hypochondriasis in which fears are persistently focused on a specific illness rather than on multiple bodily symptoms as is the case in hypochondriasis. The idea of subtypes has also arisen from findings of distinct components, namely disease phobia and disease conviction, in factor analytic studies and controlled group comparisons (Kellner, 1985; Kellner et al., 1987a; Pilowsky, 1967). Salkovskis, Warwick, and Clark (1990) compared hypochondriacal patients who had high disease phobia with those who had high disease conviction. In contrast to those with high disease phobia, those with high disease conviction scored higher on the core aspects of hypochondriasis, such as misinterpretation of bodily symptoms and checking behaviors. Anxiety symptoms were also associated with disease conviction. These authors concluded that hypochondriasis, as currently defined, includes two phenomenologically distinct entities: disease phobia and disease conviction.

Whether specific (illness) phobia represents a separate diagnostic entity remains uncertain (Cote et al., 1996). According to DSM-IV, persons with specific phobia of illness fear developing or being exposed to an illness, whereas those with hypochondriasis believe they already have a serious disease. Other distinguishing characteristics may include avoidance of internal and external stimuli associated with the feared illness (illness phobia) and multiple diffuse somatic symptoms attributed to serious illness (hypochondriasis; Fava & Grandi, 1991; Noyes, Wesner, & Fisher, 1992; Salkovskis et al., 1990). Also, treatments based on exposure may be more effective for illness phobia, whereas treatments based on change in beliefs may be more effective for patients with hypochondriasis (Salkovskis & Warwick, 1986; Warwick & Marks, 1988).

*Generalized Anxiety Disorder*

Generalized anxiety disorder, like hypochondriasis, involves excessive worry, and hypochondriacal patients may also have other anxiety symptoms. In DSM-IV, the boundary between these disorders receives mention. The criteria for hypochondriasis state that the preoccupation with serious disease is not better accounted for by generalized anxiety disorder, and the criteria for generalized anxiety disorder state that the focus of anxiety and worry is not confined to features of another Axis I disorder (e.g., having a serious illness; American Psychiatric Association, 1994). However, according to Starcevic, Fallon, Uhlenhuth, and Pathak (1994) worry about health or illness is a relatively unimportant feature of generalized anxiety disorder. In their study, comparing hypochondriacal phenomena in patients with generalized anxiety and panic disorders, these authors noted that worry about illness and hypochondriasis appears to be a distinct phenomenon. They observed that worry about illness in patients with generalized anxiety often lacks the intrusive quality of hypochondriacal fears. They further observed that several features that contribute to hypochondriasis in panic disorder patients, such as catastrophic misinterpretation of symptoms and autonomic hyperactivity, are lacking in patients with generalized anxiety.

*Panic Disorder*

The phenomenological distinction between panic disorder and hypochondriasis is one of considerable importance. This is, in part, because excessive fear of bodily disease, hypochondriacal worry and believing that one is physically ill despite medical reassurance are found in a substantial proportion of patients with panic disorder and agoraphobia (Buglass, Clarke, Henderson, Kreitman, & Presley, 1977; Noyes, Clancy, Hoenk, & Slymen, 1980; Roth & Harper, 1962; Sheehan, Ballenger, & Jacobsen, 1980). In addition, similar mechanisms have been theorized to underlie panic disorder and hypochondriasis, including distorted cognitive assessment of health status, and heightened awareness of physiological processes and physiological arousal (Hoehn-Saric & McLeod, 1993; Katon, 1984; McLeod & Hoehn-Saric, 1993; Warwick & Salkovskis, 1990; Warwick, Clark, Cobb, & Salkovskis, 1996). According to DSM-IV, a diagnosis of hypochondriasis should not be made if hypochondriacal symptoms are better accounted for by panic disorder (American Psychiatric Association, 1994). In this regard, the manual specifies that a hypochondriacal syndrome or some aspects of it that first appears during the course of panic disorder, but disappears after successful treatment of that disorder, must be considered secondary (American Psychiatric Association, 1994). Although there is no provision for it in DSM-IV, Kellner (1992) favors retaining the primary vs. secondary distinction because of its theoretical interest and treatment implications for some patients. Secondary hypochondriasis occurs during the course of disorders such as major depression and panic disorder and is focused upon the bodily symptoms of those disorders (Baker & Merskey, 1983).

Phenomenologically, hypochondriasis appears to resemble panic yet is distinct from it. During panic attacks, patients often experience intense fear and feel as though they are dying from some catastrophic event (e.g., heart attack, stroke). Patients with hypochondriasis, on the other hand, fear death from progressive disease (e.g., cancer, multiple sclerosis). One fears dying and the other death (Warwick & Salkovskis, 1990). Otto, Pollack, Sachs, and Rosenbaum (1992) found that panic disorder patients who have hypochondriacal concerns also score high on anxiety sensitivity, which is a fear of anxiety symptoms and a tendency to respond anxiously to arousal. Although this study has been criticized (Taylor, 1995), it suggests that the abnormal cognitive style characteristic of panic may also contribute to hypochondriasis and have explanatory significance for both (Clark, 1986).

The distinguishing feature of panic disorder is recurring panic attacks. However, panic attacks may also occur in patients with hypochondriasis. In fact, Fava, Grandi, Saviotti, and Conti (1990) described a series of cases in which hypochondriasis preceded the onset of attacks by years. In these patients, attacks were prompted by fearful hypochondriacal cognitions, and pharmacological treatment, while reducing panic, had little effect on hypochondriacal fears or beliefs. Other studies have also found hypochondriacal concerns or illness phobic symptoms in a substantial proportion of panic and agoraphobic patients prior to their first attacks (Benedetti et al., 1997; Fava, Grandi, & Canestrari, 1988; Fava et al., 1990). Such symptoms may represent predisposing factors, prodromes, or early manifestations of panic but, as indicated earlier, they may also constitute separate disorders (Fava & Kellner, 1993).

Although the literature suggests that there is phenomenological similarity, only one study directly contrasted patients with hypochondriasis and panic disorder. In that study, Barsky, Barnett, and Cleary (1994) compared large consecutive series of primary care patients with these disorders and concluded that they are distinct illnesses. On direct comparison, patients with pure hypochondriasis had more severe hypochondriacal symptoms and somatized more. In addition, hypochondriacal patients were consistently more impaired in social and occupational functioning. Primary care physicians also distinguished patients with these two disorders—they judged patients with hypochondriasis to be more hypochondriacal, more anxious, more demanding, and more help-seeking. Consistent with these ratings, the hypochondriacal patients themselves were less satisfied with the medical care they had received.

### Obsessive-Compulsive Disorder

Patients with obsessive-compulsive disorder, like those with hypochondriasis, may be preoccupied with distressing ideas about health and have obsessions involving fears of illness, injury, or contamination (Fallon, Javitch, Hollander, & Liebowitz, 1991; Khanna, Kaliaperunnal, & Channabasavanna, 1990). According to the DSM-IV criteria, a diagnosis of hypochondriasis requires that preoccupation with serious disease not be better accounted for by obsessive-compulsive disorder. On the other hand, a diagnosis of obsessive-compulsive disorder should not be made if obsessions are restricted to preoccupation with having a serious illness (American Psychiatric Association, 1994). Rasmussen and Eisen (1992) state that patients with somatic obsessions are indistinguishable from patients with hypochondriasis except for having other obsessions and compulsions. Barsky (1992a), on the other hand, reviewed a number of potentially distinguishing characteristics. He stated that, in contrast to patients with hypochondriasis, those with obsessive-compulsive disorder view their ideas and fears as unrealistic and try to resist them. However, some patients with hypochondriasis have wavering insight and a few may avoid acting upon their fears. He also noted that the ideas of the hypochondriacal patient constitute an interpretive schema (i.e., a way of viewing health, thinking about disease, and interpreting bodily sensations), whereas the ideas of the obsessive-compulsive patient lack an organizing principle (i.e., they are disconnected, discrete, and intrusive thoughts).

Hypochondriacal behaviors and compulsive rituals also have similarities, according to Barsky (1992a). Hypochondriacal behaviors include self-checking, self-examination, reassurance-seeking and medical care-seeking. Like compulsions, they have a driven and irresistible quality, are excessive, and are intended to relieve anxiety. However, while the hypochondriac views his or her behavior as sensible and makes little effort to resist, the person with obsessive-compulsive disorder may attempt to hide his or her behavior from others. Barsky (1992a) also noted that hypochondriasis, unlike obsessive-compulsive disorder, includes bodily sensations which are an important feature of the disorder. However, there have been no studies directly comparing patients with these disorders.

## Overlap and Comorbidity

Two studies have examined in detail the prevalence of psychiatric disorders among primary care outpatients with DSM-III-R hypochondriasis (Barsky et al., 1992a; Noyes et al., 1994a). These studies used structured interviews for current and lifetime psychiatric diagnoses to compare hypochondriacal and non-hypochondriacal patients, and they yielded similar results as shown in Table 6.4. The proportion of hypochondriacal and control patients having one comorbid Axis I disorder, or more, was 88% versus 51% in one study and 62% versus 30% in the other (Barsky et al., 1992a; Noyes et al., 1994a). Anxiety disorders contributed to the overall excess among the hypochondriacal groups. In fact, Barsky et al. (1992a) found generalized anxiety, the most frequently diagnosed disorder, in 71% of hypochondriacal patients. Odds ratios for lifetime generalized anxiety disorder (10.1), phobias (3.3), and any anxiety disorder (5.9) were statistically significant, but that for panic disorder (3.8) was not. Odds ratios for current disorders were similarly increased.

These results indicate that comorbidity of DSM-III-R hypochondriasis with anxiety disorders is high, although not clearly higher than that with depressive or somatoform disorders. Comorbid generalized anxiety disorder was especially frequent in one study but was not diagnosed in the other. Such inconsistency may be due to low diagnostic reliability. Generalized anxiety disorder and normal anxiety appear to fall on a continuum and distinguishing between the two can be difficult. Nevertheless, such extensive comorbidity raises the question of what the relationship between coexisting disorders may be.

**Table 6.4**  Comorbidity identified in patients with DSM-III-R hypochondriasis

| | Barsky et al. (1992) | | | Noyes et al. (1994) | | |
|---|---|---|---|---|---|---|
| | Hypochondriasis $n = 42$ (%) | Control subjects $n = 76$ (%) | $p$ | Hypochondriasis $n = 50$ (%) | Control subjects $n = 50$ (%) | $p$ |
| Major depression | 43 | 18 | 0.005 | 38 | 16 | 0.005 |
| Dysthymic disorder | 45 | 9 | 0.0001 | 8 | 2 | ns |
| Panic disorder | 17 | 3 | 0.01 | 16 | 6 | ns |
| Generalized anxiety | 71 | 28 | 0.0001 | 0 | 0 | ns |
| Phobic disorders | 43 | 21 | 0.05 | 6 | 2 | ns |
| Obsessive-compulsive disorder | 10 | 2 | 0.05 | 0 | 0 | ns |
| Alcohol abuse/dependence | 10 | 18 | ns | 14 | 12 | ns |
| Drug abuse/dependence | 12 | 4 | ns | 8 | 10 | ns |
| Somatization disorder | 21 | 0 | 0.0001 | 7 | 0 | — |
| Any depressive disorder | 55 | 20 | 0.0001 | 44 | 18 | 0.005 |
| Any anxiety disorder | 86 | 36 | 0.01 | 22 | 6 | 0.05 |
| Any substance use | 17 | 20 | ns | 20 | 18 | ns |

As Barsky et al. (1992a) note concerning such comorbidity, we still need to ascertain which disorder is the more pervasive or predominant and which came first (suggesting a causal relationship). Being anxious may lead persons to worry about their health. On the other hand, hypochondriacal concerns together with somatic distress may give rise to anxiety. Noyes et al. (1994a) observed that hypochondriacal patients with coexisting anxiety disorders (mostly panic disorder with agoraphobia) were younger and had an onset of anxiety before that of hypochondriasis. This was in contrast to hypochondriacal subjects with depressive disorders who did not differ from patients without depressive disorders in terms of demographic or illness characteristics. Also, in these cases, the onset of depression usually followed that of hypochondriasis and was associated with more severe hypochondriacal symptoms and impairment in functioning. Such data might suggest, if confirmed, that hypochondriasis is often a secondary manifestation of panic disorder.

*Specific Phobia*

There are almost no data on the overlap or comorbidity of specific phobia of illness and hypochondriasis. Illness phobia is a neglected subject and few case series have been reported. However, in one such series, Bianchi (1971) found no increase in other phobias except for fear of dying and agoraphobia. Noyes et al. (1992) found Whiteley Index scores (a measure of hypochondriasis) among a series of illness phobics that were comparable to scores obtained by hypochondriacal psychiatric patients. An epidemiologic study that included illness phobia estimated the prevalence at 3.1% of in the general population but did not determine how many of these persons might have had hypochondriacal features as well (Agras et al., 1969).

Prior to DSM-IV, illness phobia had consistently been identified as one of the core features or dimensions of hypochondriasis, and disease phobia had been the label given to one subscale of the Whiteley Index. Studies of hypochondriacal patients using this measure have consistently yielded high scores on this subscale (Pilowsky, 1967; Pilowsky & Spence, 1983). In addition, Warwick and Salkovskis (1990) described a number of typically phobic behaviors among patients with hypochondriasis. These included a phobic response to bodily sensations; avoidance of illness stimuli; vigilance toward the body, its appearance and its functioning; ritualistic checking for abnormalities; and persistent seeking of reassurance. Also, associated features of hypochondriasis have included fears of aging and death, as well as a sense of vulnerability to illness or injury (Kellner et al., 1987b; Barsky & Wyshak, 1989). Consequently, despite the lack of study, there is evidence of considerable overlap between illness phobia and hypochondriasis.

*Generalized Anxiety Disorder*

As noted earlier, worry about health or illness appears to be a relatively unimportant feature of generalized anxiety disorder. Starcevic et al. (1994) found that, although 31% of their generalized anxiety patients worried about health or illness, only 18% met criteria for hypochondriasis. Likewise, Borkovec, Shadick, & Hopkins (1991) found that family was the most frequent sphere of worry and that illness was the least frequent at only 3%. Worries about health, illness, and injury were present in 14% and 31% of generalized anxiety patients in two other studies (Craske, Rapee, Jackel, & Barlow, 1989; Sanderson & Barlow, 1990). Thus, worry about health occurs in a minority of these patients. As previously stated, the rate of generalized anxiety appeared to be high in two studies of hypochondriacal patients, but the reliability of this diagnosis has been questioned. Bianchi (1971) reported that nearly two-thirds of patients with disease phobia had such anxiety, and Barsky et al. (1992a) identified generalized anxiety disorder in 71% of hypochondriacal patients. On the other hand, Noyes et al. (1994a) failed to diagnose the disorder in 50 patients with hypochondriasis.

*Panic Disorder*

The overlap of panic and agoraphobia with hypochondriasis appears to be both extensive and specific, at least in psychiatric populations. Both Noyes et al. (1986) and Fava et al. (1988) reported that patients with panic disorder and agoraphobia scored nearly as high on measures of hypochondriasis as hypochondriacal psychiatric patients. Also, Starcevic, Kellner, Uhlenhuth, and Pathak (1992) found that half of the panic patients they examined scored in the hypochondriacal range on the Illness Attitude Scales. In addition, three groups of investigators—Bach, Nutzinger, and Hartl (1996), Benedetti et al. (1997), and Furer, Walker, Chartier, and Stein (1997)—found that between 45% and 51% of their patients with panic and agoraphobia met DSM-III-R or DSM-IV criteria for hypochondriasis. Also, Furer et al. (1997) found hypochondriasis in a greater proportion of patients with panic disorder (48%) than with social phobia (17%) or controls (14%).

Most studies of the occurrence of hypochondriasis in panic disorder patients have involved psychiatric populations, and with the exception of the most recent investigations, they did not employ diagnostic criteria. When the relationship was examined in a primary care population, the findings were somewhat different. Barsky et al. (1994) compared comorbidity of DSM-III-R panic disorder and hypochondriasis in a general medicine clinic. They found that only 25% of panic patients had current hypochondriasis and only 13% of hypochondriasis patients had current panic disorder. Thus, although the disorders coexisted more often than might have been expected by chance, they more often occurred separately than concurrently. Also, patients with the two disorders differed demographically; specifically, those with hypochondriasis were older and more often women than those with panic disorder. In addition, the authors observed distinguishing clinical features and a different pattern of comorbidity for panic and hypochondriacal patients. Panic disorder patients more often had major depressive disorder, phobic disorders, and obsessive-compulsive disorder and less often had generalized anxiety disorder than hypochondriacal patients. Consequently, these appear to be separate disorders and their coexistence varies with the population studied.

To explore the relationship between panic disorder and hypochondriasis further, several authors have sought to determine what features of panic were most closely associated with hypochondriasis. Starcevic et al. (1992) found a strong relationship between hypochondriacal concerns and agoraphobia in a series of panic patients. They speculated that hypochondriasis might be attributed to greater severity or might be associated with a separate disorder, namely agoraphobia. The finding by Argyle, Solyom, and Solyom (1991) of an illness phobia dimension within the structure of agoraphobic fears supports their suggestion. However, other investigators (Bach et al., 1990; Benedetti et al., 1997; Fava et al., 1988; Otto et al., 1992) failed to find such an association. Instead, Otto et al. (1992) found that, of the symptom characteristics they examined, hypochondriacal concerns were most strongly associated with anxiety sensitivity. Thus, they related hypochondriasis to the abnormal cognitive style characteristic of panic disorder (Beck, Lande, & Bohnert, 1974; Hibbert, 1984).

Several studies have examined the temporal relationship of panic and hypochondriasis in an effort to understand the relationship between them. In three of these, Fava et al. (1988), Fava, Grandi, Rafanelli, and Canestrari (1992), and Benedetti et al. (1997) found hypochondriacal or illness phobic symptoms in a substantial proportion of panic and agoraphobic patients prior to their first attacks. As mentioned earlier, these symptoms might represent predisposing factors, prodromes, or early manifestations of panic (Fava & Kellner, 1993; Perugi et al., 1998). Of course, they might also constitute separate disorders. As indicated, Fava et al. (1990) identified a series of cases in which hypochondriasis preceded the onset of panic attacks.

*Obsessive-Compulsive Disorder*

With respect to obsessive-compulsive disorder, there is documentation of extensive comorbidity especially with depressive and anxiety disorders (Black & Noyes, 1990). Obsessions may involve fears of illness, injury or contamination, and compulsions may involve checking the body for signs of illness, as well as cleaning to prevent infection or toxic exposure. In one series of obsessive-compulsive clinic patients, 33% had somatic obsessions and 50% had obsessions involving contamination (Rasmussen & Eisen, 1992). There is, however, only one estimate of the prevalence of hypochondriasis in such patients. Using the Illness Attitude Scales, Savron et al. (1996) identified only 10% of patients with obsessive-compulsive disorder as having the response characteristics of hypochondriasis and 27% as having the characteristics of disease phobia. Neither percentage was significantly greater than that observed in healthy controls.

## Hypochondriasis: An Anxiety Disorder?

As indicated above, there is evidence of phenomenological similarities between hypochondriasis and several anxiety disorders, including specific phobia, panic disorder, and, to a lesser extent, generalized anxiety and obsessive-compulsive disorder. Like the anxiety disorders, hypochondriasis appears most fundamentally to be a disorder of cognitive misinterpretation. Even though the boundaries between these disorders are specifically addressed in DSM-IV, there is evidence of anxiety and phobic symptoms among hypochondriacal patients and of hypochondriacal concerns among patients with the various anxiety disorders. Beyond that, there appears to be considerable shared comorbidity, especially with panic disorder. However, the data remain limited and few direct comparisons have been made. Also, it is not clear whether subtypes of hypochondriasis exist. An illness phobia subtype has been suggested but may be difficult to distinguish from specific phobia of illness. Regardless, subgroups have received little study. Thus, hypochondriasis appears to be distinct, but because of phenomenological similarity and extensive comorbidity, it may in the future warrant classification with the anxiety disorders (Noyes, 1999).

## DEPRESSIVE DISORDERS

The DSM-IV definition of hypochondriasis also suggests a relationship to depression. It includes preoccupation with fears of having, or the idea that one has, a serious disease. While 'fears of having' anticipates future danger, 'the idea that one has' refers to a loss that has already occurred. These contrasting cognitions correspond to the dimensions of disease phobia and disease conviction that have been identified in hypochondriacal patients (Bianchi, 1973; Marks, 1987; Mayou, 1976). In some patients, disease fear appears prominent and in others, disease conviction dominates the clinical picture (Cote et al., 1996; Kellner, 1985). As noted above, patients with disease phobia may be more closely related to the anxiety disorders, but those with disease conviction may be closer to depression.

In fact, Barsky (1992a) presented prototypical examples of these possible subtypes, noting several differences between them. The patient with prominent disease phobia presented more like a patient with an anxiety disorder and appeared to have more insight into the psychological nature of his disturbance. The patient with predominant disease conviction had more of a depressive picture. This patient was preoccupied with somatic symptoms and was more convinced of being ill than afraid of developing illness. He lacked insight and had unsatisfying, antagonistic relationships with physicians. These differences correspond to differences between anxiety and depression.

A number of studies have shown strong associations between depressive symptoms and hypochondriasis in clinical populations. For example, Barsky et al. (1986) reported a positive correlation ($r = 0.58$) between depression scores and hypochondriacal concerns among medical outpatients. Similarly, Noyes et al. (1993) reported higher Symptom Checklist-90 depression subscale scores among hypochondriacal than among non-hypochondriacal general medical outpatients ($32.4 \pm 11.2$ vs. $22.3 \pm 8.4$; $p < 0.0001$). Also, Gureje, Üstün, and Simon (1997) observed higher mean General Health Questionnaire scores among these patients with abridged hypochondriasis than patients without. The subscale measuring depression was significantly higher in their hypochondriacal vs. non-hypochondriacal patients ($2.1 \pm 2.4$ vs. $1.0 \pm 1.8$; $p < 0.0001$). However, in these and other studies, correlations with other psychological and somatic symptoms were also high. For example, Barsky et al. (1986) reported positive correlations with anxiety ($r = 0.55$) and somatic symptoms ($r = 0.52$), and Gureje et al. (1997) observed higher anxiety ($3.4 \pm 2.4$ vs. $2.4 \pm 2.3$; $p < 0.0001$) and somatization ($4.0 \pm 2.1$ vs. $2.6 \pm 2.1$) in hypochondriacal versus control primary care patients. Consequently, the association with depressive symptoms does not appear to be specific.

Three studies of primary care outpatients with hypochondriasis have shown that this diagnosis increases the risk of depressive disorders. Both Barsky et al. (1992a) and Noyes et al. (1994a) found comparable increases in the prevalence of lifetime and current major depressive disorder among patients with hypochondriasis compared to control patients (see Table 6.5). Both also reported an increased prevalence of dysthymia although significantly higher rates were found only by Barsky et al. (1992a). In their study, the odds ratio for any lifetime depressive disorder was 4.9. Likewise, Gureje et al. (1997) observed ICD-10 major depression in a greater percentage of hypochondriacal than non-hypochondriacal primary care patients (36.9% vs. 9.8%). Similar findings were reported from a general population survey by Faravelli et al. (1997). These investigators found that the diagnosis of hypochondriasis increased the risk for dysthymia (3.8),[1] major depression (4.2), and cyclothymia (10.0), although in their small sample (N = 30), only the risk for cyclothymia achieved statistical significance. The last study suggests that the relationship with depression is not simply based on treatment seeking.

## Phenomenology and Boundaries

According to DSM-IV, a diagnosis of hypochondriasis should not be made if the preoccupation with fears of having, or the idea that one has, a serious disease is better accounted for by a major depressive episode (American Psychiatric Association, 1994). This hierarchical rule, which was added to the latest edition of the DSM classification, reflects early debate about the status of hypochondriasis as an independent disorder. According to Kenyon (1964), who studied psychiatric patients, hypochondriasis is almost always secondary to other psychiatric illness, especially depression. On the other hand, Pilowsky (1970) observed important differences in the demographic and clinical characteristics of patients with primary and secondary hypochondriasis and concluded that the disorder has independent status. The proportion of general medical patients identified as having hypochondriasis, in the absence of other psychiatric illness, has ranged from 12% to 38% in recent studies, indicating that, at least among clinical populations, comorbidity is high but that a significant minority have the disorder alone (Barsky et al., 1992a; Noyes et al., 1994a). This also speaks for independence.

Depressed patients often present with a variety of somatic symptoms and preoccupation with their health. They may also experience a sense of loss and negative beliefs that may become focused on physical health (Bech, 1992). This preoccupation with bodily symptoms can develop into a conviction on the part of the patient that he or she is suffering from severe physical illness. An example is that of Sutherland (1976) who became convinced that he was suffering from lung cancer even though negative physical examinations and tests afforded him brief reassurance. Thus, just as the physiological and cognitive features of anxiety contribute to hypochondriasis, the corresponding features of depression may do likewise. And, in patients with psychotic depression, such beliefs may reach delusional proportions (Lewis, 1934).

---

[1] Indicates number of observed cases divided by the number expected by chance.

## Overlap and Comorbidity

As just mentioned, hypochondriasis has been viewed by some as a manifestation of depression. This view prompted surveys of its prevalence among depressed patients and examination of the relationship between these disorders. Among depressed inpatients, estimates based on clinical assessment have ranged from 18% to 69% (Bianchi, 1973; El-Islam, Malasi, Suleiman, & Mirza, 1988; Kellner, Fava, Lisansky, Perini, & Zielezny, 1986; Lewis, 1934; Stenback & Jalava, 1962). In addition, studies reported especially high rates of 60% to 64% among the elderly (de Alarcon, 1964; Kramer-Ginsberg, Greenwald, Aisen, & Brod-Miller, 1989). These studies of inpatients included those with psychotic depression, and the criteria for hypochondriasis varied widely from one study to the next. When Demopulos et al. (1996) examined depressed outpatients they found that hypochondriacal symptoms were prominent but that only 2% met DSM-III-R criteria for hypochondriasis.

Various authors have examined the temporal relationship between hypochondriasis and depression to learn which might be primary. De Alarcon (1964) found that hypochondriacal symptoms usually developed during the course of a depressive syndrome. According to this author, only 19.5% of patients had lifelong hypochondriacal concerns. Also, Burns and Nichols (1972) reported that many depressed patients with chest symptoms had fear or conviction of disease (sometimes of delusional proportions) that remitted after treatment with antidepressants or electrotherapy. Similarly, Kellner et al. (1986) observed that, while over a third of their melancholic patients were hypochondriacal, only 5% remained so after treatment. However, both Kramer-Ginsberg et al. (1989) and Demopulos et al. (1996) observed some persistence of hypochondriacal concerns after antidepressant treatment and concluded that such features are a mixture of state and trait phenomena.

Few differences have been found between hypochondriacal and non-hypochondriacal depressed patients to explain the relationship. Neither Kramer-Ginsberg et al. (1989) nor Demopolus et al. (1996) found any relationship between hypochondriacal features and severity of depression, but both found associations with anxiety and somatic symptoms. Likewise, few variables contributing to hypochondriasis in depressed patients have been identified. A high frequency of hypochondriasis and somatic symptoms among elderly depressives has suggested that age might be a factor. In fact, Gurland (1976) observed more hypochondriacal symptoms in older than in younger depressives. Brown and Vaillant (1981) observed more hypochondriasis, as well as agitation and initial insomnia in depressed patients over age 50 than in those under 50. Also, most recently, Wallace and Pfohl (1995) found hypochondriasis, as measured by the

Hamilton Rating Scale for Depression, the only item positively correlated with age in both female ($r = 0.25$) and male ($r = 0.29$) depressed inpatients.

However, the data on this point have not been consistent and, as Herrmann (1996) noted in his review of late life depression, the studies referred to above did not assess physical illness that might have accounted for somatic symptoms even in the absence of depression. In two studies, no differences in somatic symptoms or hypochondriasis were found in old compared to young depressives. Neither Blazer, Barchar, and Hughes (1987), who studied psychiatric inpatients, nor Musetti et al. (1989) were able to confirm common clinical stereotypes among depressed out-patients. Koenig, Cohen, Blazer, Krishnan, and Sibert (1993) found that the number of somatic complaints distinguished depressed and non-depressed patients from a medically ill population. However, the large number of somatic complaints among these elderly depressives appeared to be due mostly to severe physical illness. The clinical impression that late life depression is associated with hypochondriasis may have stemmed from contact with patients who had such coexisting physical and mental illness (Baldwin, 1991).

According to Ball and Clare (1990), cultural factors may be important with the occurrence of hypochondriasis in depressed patients (Kenyon, 1964). These authors found hypochondriasis more common in Jewish compared to non-Jewish depressives, confirming earlier observations.

## Hypochondriasis, Primary or Secondary

Kenyon's belief that hypochondriasis is a secondary manifestation of depression was based on his study of psychiatric inpatients (Kenyon, 1964). Even among psychiatric outpatients, hypochondriasis is commonly secondary to anxiety and depressive disorders. However, among general medical patients, there are many who have no current or past mood disorder. Also, the natural histories of these disorders, even when they coexist, appear to differ. Patients with hypochondriasis experience fluc-tuating symptoms and a chronic course, whereas depression is episodic (Noyes et al., 1994b; Barsky et al., 1998). If major depressive disorder and hypochondriasis are separate, when, if ever, should a hierarchical rule apply (Starcevic, 1988)? This may depend upon the temporal relationship. If hypochondriasis occurs only within an episode of major depression and is the result of somatic symptoms of depression, then hypochondriacal symptoms should perhaps be regarded as secondary (Kellner, 1992). But, if hypochondriasis precedes the onset of depression or persists after resolution of the mood disorder, then hypochondriasis is not 'better accounted for' by depression and should be considered primary (American Psychiatric Association, 1994). Comparisons of these two groups of patients in terms of family history and course of illness may help answer this question.

## SOMATOFORM DISORDERS

According to DSM-IV, hypochondriasis is not to be diagnosed if preoccupation with illness occurs exclusively during the course of somatization disorder. However, this hierarchical rule—which appeared in DSM-III, disappeared from DSM-III-R, then reappeared in DSM-IV—has been challenged by Murphy (1990). This author notes that while hypochondriasis is defined by a set of beliefs, attitudes, and fears, somatization disorder is defined by past medical history. Since these definitions are not mutually exclusive, patients might be assigned both diagnoses were it not for this exclusionary rule. But, as Murphy (1990) observes, it seems logically suspect to say, when both disorders are present, that hypochondriasis is due to or better accounted for by somatization disorder or vice versa.

### Phenomenology and Boundaries

Differences in the diagnostic criteria and associated features of hypochondriasis and somatization disorder are shown in Table 6.5 (adapted from

**Table 6.5** Summary of differences between hypochondriasis and somatization disorder

| Somatization disorder | Hypochondriasis |
| --- | --- |
| Emphasis on multiple unexplained physical symptoms | Preoccupation with fear or conviction about serious disease |
| Specified number and type of symptoms | Unspecified symptoms |
| Pathophysiologic mechanisms not known | Symptoms arise from normal sensations, minor abnormalities |
| Chronic, onset before 30, usually in teens | Duration at least 6 months, can occur at any age |
| Predominantly women | Sex ratio equal |
| Associated with borderline and antisocial personalities | Associated with obsessive-compulsive personality |
| Familial associations reported | Familial associations not present |

Murphy, 1990). According to ICD-10, the distinction between these disorders is based upon the focus of concern. The patient with hypochondriasis is preoccupied with 'the presence of the disorder itself and its future consequences', whereas the patient with multiple somatization disorder is concerned about individual symptoms. It also states that, in a person with hypochondriasis, there is 'likely to be a preoccupation with only one or two possible physical disorders which will be named consistently, rather than the more numerous and often changing possibilities in multiple somatization disorder' (World Health Organization, 1987). Also, according to Murphy (1990), there are differences in cognitive set or attitude; specifically, the patient with hypochondriasis seeks reassurance that he or she is free of serious disease, whereas the person with somatization disorder seeks sanction for the sick role by way of diagnosed physical disease.

## Overlap and Comorbidity

Several studies of patients from primary care have shown that only a small proportion of hypochondriacal patients qualify for a diagnosis of somatization disorder, but that a much larger proportion meet criteria for the subsyndromal disorder. Rates for somatization disorder (requiring 14 symptoms for women and 12 for men) ranged from 7% to 21%, but for the subsyndromal disorder (requiring 6 and 4 symptoms) they ranged from 32% to 83% (Barsky et al., 1992a; Escobar et al., 1998; Garcia-Campayo, Lobo, Perez-Echeverria, & Campos, 1998; Kirmayer and Robbins, 1991; Noyes et al., 1994a). Barsky et al. (1992a) found that the symptoms of somatization disorder were not correlated with hypochondriasis, but that somatic symptoms associated with hypochondriasis (assessed by the Somatic Symptom Inventory) were significantly correlated with the Whiteley Index ($r = 0.36$, $p = 0.019$). Based on this finding, they suggested that these disorders may be distinguishable on the basis of the type of somatic symptoms. Also, Escobar et al. (1998) found patients with hypochondriasis to have fewer somatic symptoms than those with somatization disorder.

Differences in demographic and clinical features tend also to support the distinction between these two somatoform disorders. For example, Kirmayer and Robbins (1991) reported that the hypochondriacal somatizers they studied had somewhat less income and fewer years of education than non-somatizers but were no more likely to be female than male. By contrast, their functional somatizers (subsyndromal somatization disorder) tended to be women, unmarried, and of lower socioeconomic status. Garcia-Campayo et al. (1998), in a similarly designed study, also found differences between functional and hypochondriacal somatizers. Their hypochondriacal somatizers had fewer somatic symptoms, higher depression and anxiety scores, and shorter duration of illness than functional somatizers. Findings such as these support the belief expressed by a number of authors that hypochondriasis differs from somatization disorder in terms of age of onset, gender distribution, personality type, and psychiatric comorbidity (Barsky et al., 1992a; Cloninger, von Knorring, Sigvardsson, & Bohman, 1986; Yates, 1991). The existence of two somatoform disorders is supported by Cloninger et al. (1986) who identified two distinct symptom patterns among somatizing women, one of which resembled hypochondriasis and the other somatization disorder.

If hypochondriasis and somatization disorder often coexist, then what is the relationship between them? A preliminary family study suggests that hypochondriasis may be a variant of somatization disorder (Noyes et al., 1997). In that study, the first-degree relatives of 19 probands meeting DSM-III-R criteria for hypochondriasis were compared with the relatives of 24 non-hypochondriacal probands obtained from the same primary care clinic. The relatives were interviewed blindly using the Structured Diagnostic Interview for DSM-IV. There were no significant differences in the frequency of lifetime or current psychiatric diagnoses, except for somatization disorder which was more frequent among relatives of hypochondriasis probands. The hypochondriacal relatives also differed from control relatives on a number of interrelated symptoms, traits, and attitudes often associated with somatization, including mistrust and antagonism in interpersonal relationships.

## Hypochondriasis and Somatization Disorder

The findings of this family study suggest that hypochondriasis and somatization disorder, as defined in DSM-IV, are closely related. The question is, how are they related and how might future studies address this relationship. It may simply be one of definitional overlap (Schmidt, 1994). For instance, few studies have compared the somatic symptoms of hypochondriasis (once located in the hypochondriacal region below the costal cartilages) and somatization disorder, and while attitudinal differences have been proposed, few studies have examined them (Murphy, 1990). Another possibility is that these disorders represent variable or contrasting expressions of an inherited vulnerability which are influenced by gender, personality, and perhaps physiological variables. Needed are studies comparing clinical and related features, such as personality traits, as well as family, follow-up, and treatment studies comparing the two disorders.

Also, further efforts are needed to identify distinct patterns of somatization in the general population (Cloninger et al., 1986).


## CONCLUSION

There is increasing evidence that, in many instances, hypochondriasis is a primary disorder. In other instances, it coexists with anxiety, depressive, or somatoform disorders and, as in the case of panic disorder, is best regarded as secondary or as an associated feature of the primary illness. However, much uncertainty remains concerning the boundaries of the condition and relationships with coexisting disorders. There are reasons to consider classifying hypochondriasis among the anxiety disorders. On the other hand, patients typically present with somatic symptoms, and traditionally hypochondriasis and somatization disorder have been viewed as gender specific counterparts of the same disease process (Ladee, 1966). It, therefore, may be too soon to change the placement of hypochondriasis in the classification. The differentiation from specific phobia of illness has received little study and is related to the question of hypochondriacal subtypes. Comparisons of groups with predominant disease phobia and disease conviction will be especially useful here. Considerable progress has been made in defining hypochondriasis; however, more work is needed in clarifying its boundaries and relationships to coexisting disorders.


## REFERENCES

Agras, S., Sylvester, D., & Oliveau, D. (1969). The epidemiology of common fears and phobias. *Comprehensive Psychiatry*, **10**, 151–156.

American Psychiatric Association (1968). *Diagnostic and statistical manual of mental disorders* (2nd edn.). Washington, DC: Author.

American Psychiatric Association (1980). *Diagnostic and statistical manual of mental disorders* (3rd edn.). Washington, DC: Author.

American Psychiatric Association (1987). *Diagnostic and statistical manual of mental disorders* (3rd edn., rev.). Washington, DC: Author.

American Psychiatric Association (1994). *Diagnostic and statistical manual of mental disorders* (4th edn.). Washington, DC: Author.

American Psychiatric Association Task Force on DSM-IV (1991). *DSM-IV options book: Work in progress.* Washington, DC: American Psychiatric Association.

Argyle, N., Solyom, C., & Solyom, L. (1991). The structure of phobias in panic disorder. *British Journal of Psychiatry*, **159**, 378–382.

Bach, M., Nutzinger, D.O., & Hartl, L. (1996). Comorbidity of anxiety disorders and hypochondriasis considering different diagnostic systems. *Comprehensive Psychiatry*, **37**, 62–67.

Baker, B., & Merskey, H. (1983). Classification and association of hypochondriasis in patients from a psychiatric hospital. *Canadian Journal of Psychiatry*, **28**, 629–634.

Baldwin, R.C. (1991). Depressive illness. In R. Jacoby & C. Oppenheimer (Eds.), *Psychiatry in the elderly* (pp. 676–719). Oxford: Oxford University Press.

Ball, R.A., & Clare, A.W. (1990). Symptoms and social adjustment in Jewish depressives. *British Journal of Psychiatry*, **156**, 379–383.

Barsky, A.J. (1992a). Amplification, somatization, and the somatoform disorder. *Psychosomatics*, **33**, 28–34.

Barsky, A.J. (1992b). Hypochondriasis and obsessive-compulsive disorder. *Psychiatric Clinics of North America*, **15**, 791–801.

Barsky, A.J., Barnett, M.C., & Cleary, P.D. (1994). Hypochondriasis and panic disorder: Boundary and overlap. *Archives of General Psychiatry*, **51**, 918–925.

Barsky, A.J., Cleary, P.D., Wyshak, G., Spitzer, R.L., Williams, J.B.N., & Klerman, G.L. (1992b). A structured diagnostic interview for hypochondriasis: A proposed criterion standard. *Journal of Nervous and Mental Disease*, **180**, 20–27.

Barsky, A.J., Fama, J.M., Bailey, E.D., & Ahern, D.K. (1998). A prospective 4- to 5-year study of DSM-III-R hypochondriasis. *Archives of General Psychiatry*, **55**, 737–744.

Barsky, A.J., & Klerman, G.L. (1983). Overview: Hypochondriasis, bodily complaints and somatic styles. *American Journal of Psychiatry*, **140**, 273–283.

Barsky, A.J., & Wyshak, G. (1989). Hypochondriasis and related health attitudes. *Psychosomatics*, **30**, 412–420.

Barsky, A.J., & Wyshak, G. (1990). Hypochondriasis and somatosensory amplification. *British Journal of Psychiatry*, **157**, 404–409.

Barsky, A.J., Wyshak, G., & Klerman, G.L. (1986). Hypochondriasis: An evaluation of the DSM-III criteria in medical outpatients. *Archives of General Psychiatry*, **43**, 493–500.

Barsky, A.J., Wyshak, G., & Klerman, G.L. (1992a). Psychiatric comorbidity in DSM-III-R hypochondriasis. *Archives of General Psychiatry*, **49**, 101–108.

Bech, P. (1992). Symptoms and assessment of depression. In E.S. Paykel (Ed.), *Handbook of affective disorders* (2nd edn., pp. 3–14). New York: Guilford Press.

Beck, A.T., Lande, R., & Bohnert, M. (1974). Ideational components of anxiety neurosis. *Archives of General Psychiatry*, **31**, 319–325.

Benedetti, A., Perugi, G., Toni, C., Simonetti, B., Mata, B., & Cassano, G.B. (1997). Hypochondriasis and illness phobia in panic-agoraphobic patients. *Comprehensive Psychiatry*, **38**, 124–131.

Bianchi, G.N. (1971). Origins of disease phobia. *Australian & New Zealand Journal of Psychiatry*, **5**, 241–257.

Bianchi, G.N. (1973). Patterns of hypochondriasis: A principal components analysis. *British Journal of Psychiatry*, **122**, 541–548.

Black, D.W., & Noyes, R. (1990). Comorbidity and obsessive-compulsive disorder. In J.D. Maser & C.R. Cloninger (Eds.), *Comorbidity of mood and anxiety disorders* (pp. 305–316). Washington, DC: American Psychiatric Press.

Blazer, D., Barchar, J.R., & Hughes, D.C. (1987). Major depression with melancholia: A comparison of middle-aged and elderly adults. *Journal of the American Geriatrics Society*, **35**, 927–932.

Borkovec, T.D., Shadick, R.N., & Hopkins, M. (1991). The nature of normal and pathological worry. In R.M. Rapee & D.H. Barlow (Eds.), *Chronic anxiety: Generalized anxiety disorder and mixed anxiety-depression* (pp. 29–51). New York: Guilford Press.

Brown, H.N., & Vaillant, G.E. (1981). Hypochondriasis. *Archives of Internal Medicine*, **141**, 723–726.

Buglass, D., Clarke, J., Henderson, A.S., Kreitman, N., & Presley, A.S. (1977). A study of agoraphobic housewives. *Psychological Medicine*, **7**, 73–86.

Burns, B.H., & Nichols, M.A. (1972). Factors related to the localization of symptoms to the chest in depression. *British Journal of Psychiatry*, **121**, 405–409.

Clark, D.M. (1986). A cognitive approach to panic. *Behaviour Research and Therapy*, **24**, 461–470.

Cloninger, C.R., von Knorring A.-L., Sigvardsson, S., & Bohman, M. (1986). Symptom patterns and causes of somatization in men. II. Genetic and environmental independence from somatization in women. *Genetic Epidemiology*, **3**, 171–185.

Costa, P.T., & McCrae, R.R. (1985). Hypochondriasis, neuroticism, and aging. *American Psychologist*, **40**, 19–28.

Cote, G., O'Leary, T., Barlow, D.H., Strain, J.J., Salkovskis, P.M., Warwick, H.M.C., Clark, D.M., Rapee, R., & Rasmussen, S.A. (1996). Hypochondriasis. In T.A. Widiger, A.J. Frances, & H.A. Pincus (Eds.), *DSM-IV source book* (Vol. 2, pp. 933–947). Washington, DC: American Psychiatric Association.

Craske, M.G., Barlow, D.H., Clark, D.M., Curtis, G.C., Hill, E.M., Himle, J.A., Lee, Y. -J., Lewis, J.A., McNally, R.J., Ost, L. -G., Salkovskis, P.M., & Warwick, H.M.C. (1996). Specific (simple) phobia. In T.A. Widiger, A.J. Frances, & H.A. Pincus (Eds.), *DSM-IV source book* (Vol. 2, pp. 473–506). Washington, DC: American Psychiatric Association.

Craske, M.G., Rapee, R.M., Jackel, L., & Barlow, D.H. (1989). Qualitative dimensions of worry in DSM-III-R generalized anxiety disorder subjects and non-anxious controls. *Behaviour Research Therapy*, **27**, 397–402.

de Alarcon, R. (1964). Hypochondriasis and depression in the aged. *Gerontology Clinics*, **6**, 266–277.

Demopulos, C., Fava, M., McLean, N.E., Alpert, J.E., Nierenberg, A.A., & Rosenbaum, J.F. (1996). Hypochondriacal concerns in depressed outpatients. *Psychosomatic Medicine*, **58**, 314–320.

El-Islam, M.F., Malasi, T.A., Suleiman, M.A., & Mirza, I.A. (1988). The correlates of hypochondriasis in depressed patients. *International Journal of Psychiatry in Medicine*, **18**, 253–261.

Escobar, J.I., Gara, M., Waitzkin, H., Silver, R.C., Holman, A., & Compton, W. (1998). DSM-IV hypochondriasis in primary care. *General Hospital Psychiatry*, **20**, 155–159.

Fallon, B.A., Javitch, J.A., Hollander, E., Liebowitz, M.R. (1991). Hypochondriasis and obsessive compulsive disorder: Overlaps in diagnosis and treatment. *Journal of Clinical Psychiatry*, **52**, 457–460.

Fava, G.A., & Grandi, S. (1991). Differential diagnosis of hypochondriacal fears and beliefs. *Psychotherapy and Psychosomatics*, **55**, 114–119.

Fava, G.A., Grandi, S., & Canestrari, R. (1988). Prodromal symptoms in panic disorder with agoraphobia. *American Journal of Psychiatry*, **145**, 1564–1567.

Fava, G.A., Grandi, S., Rafanelli, C., & Canestrari, R. (1992). Prodromal symptoms in panic disorder with agoraphobia: A replication study. *Journal of Affective Disorders*, **26**, 85–88.

Fava, G.A., Grandi, S., Saviotti, F.M., & Conti, S. (1990). Hypochondriasis with panic attacks. *Psychosomatics*, **31**, 351–353.

Fava, G.A., & Kellner, R. (1993). Staging: A neglected dimension in psychiatric classification. *Acta Psychiatrica Scandinavica*, **87**, 225–230.

Faravelli, C., Salvatori, S., Galassi, F., Aiazzi, L., Drei, C., & Cabras, P. (1997). Epidemiology of somatoform disorders: A community survey in Florence. *Social Psychiatry and Psychiatric Epidemiology*, **32**, 24–29.

Furer, P., Walker, J.R., Chartier, M.J., & Stein, M.B. (1997). Hypochondriacal concerns and somatization in panic disorder. *Depression and Anxiety*, **6**, 78–85.

Garcia-Campayo, J., Lobo, A., Perez-Echeverria, J., & Campos, R. (1998). Three forms of somatization presenting in primary care settings in Spain. *Journal of Nervous and Mental Disease*, **186**, 554–560.

Gillespie R.D. (1928). Hypochondria: Its definition, nosology, and psychopathology. *Guy's Hospital Report*, **8**, 408–460.

Gureje, O., Üstün, T.B., & Simon, G.E. (1997). The syndrome of hypochondriasis: A cross-national study in primary care. *Psychological Medicine*, **27**, 1001–1010.

Gurland, B. (1976). The comparative frequency of depression in various adult age groups. *Journal of Gerontology*, **31**, 283–292.

Hanbach, J.W., & Revelle, W. (1978). Arousal and perceptual sensitivity in hypochondriacs. *Journal of Abnormal Psychology*, **87**, 523–530.

Herrmann, N. (1996). Clinical features and pathogenesis of depression in old age. In K.L. Shulman, M. Tohen, & S.P. Kutcher (Eds.), *Mood disorders across the life span* (pp. 341–360). New York: Wiley-Liss.

Hibbert, G.A. (1984). Ideational components of anxiety: Their origin and content. *British Journal of Psychiatry*, **144**, 618–624.

Hoehn-Saric, R., & McLeod, D.R. (1993). Somatic manifestations of normal and pathological anxiety. In R. Hoehn-Saric & D.R. McLeod (Eds.), *Biology of anxiety disorders* (pp. 177–222). Washington, DC: American Psychiatric Press.

Katon, W. (1984). Panic disorder and somatization: Review of 55 cases. *American Journal of Medicine*, **77**, 101–106.

Kellner, R. (1985). Functional somatic symptoms and hypochondriasis. *Archives of General Psychiatry*, **42**, 821–833.

Kellner, R. (1986). *Somatization and hypochondriasis*. New York: Praeger.

Kellner, R. (1992). Diagnosis and treatment of hypochondriacal syndromes. *Psychosomatics*, **33**, 278–289.

Kellner, R., Abbott, P.J., Winslow, W.W., & Pathak, D. (1987b). Fears, beliefs and attitudes in DSM-III hypochondriasis. *Journal of Nervous and Mental Disease*, **175**, 20–25.

Kellner, R., Abbott, P.J., Winslow, W.W., & Pathak, D. (1989). Anxiety, depression, and somatization in DSM-III hypochondriasis. *Psychosomatics*, **30**, 57–64.

Kellner, R., Fava, G.A., Lisansky, J., Perini, G.I., & Zielezny, M. (1986). Hypochondriacal fears and beliefs in DSM-III melancholia: Changes with amitriptyline. *Journal of Affective Disorders*, **10**, 21–26.

Kellner, R., Hernandez, J., & Pathak, D. (1992). Hypochondriacal fears and beliefs, anxiety, and somatization. *British Journal of Psychiatry*, **160**, 525–532.

Kellner, R., Slocumb, J.C., Wiggins, R.J., Abbott, P.J., Romanik, R.L., Winslow, W.W., & Pathak, D. (1987a). The relationship of hypochondriacal fears and beliefs to anxiety and depression. *Psychiatriatric Medicine*, **4**, 15–24.

Kenyon, F.E. (1964). Hypochondriasis: A clinical study. *British Journal of Psychiatry*, **110**, 478–488.

Khanna, S., Kaliaperunnal, V.G., & Channabasavanna, S.M. (1990). Clusters of obsessive-compulsive phenomena in obsessive-compulsive disorder. *British Journal of Psychiatry*, **156**, 51–54.

Kirmayer, L.J., & Robbins, J.M. (1991). Three forms of somatization in primary care: Prevalence, co-occurrence and sociodemographic characteristics. *Journal of Nervous and Mental Disease*, **179**, 647–655.

Koenig, H.G., Cohen, H.J., Blazer, D.G., Krishnan, K.R.R., & Sibert, T.E. (1993).

Profile of depressive symptoms in younger and older medical inpatients with major depression. *Journal of the American Geriatrics Society*, **41**, 1169–1176.

Kramer-Ginsberg, E., Greenwald, B.S., Aisen, P.S., & Brod-Miller, C. (1989). Hypochondriasis in the elderly depressed. *Journal of the American Geriatric Society*, **37**, 507–510.

Kreitman, N., Sainsbury, P., Pearce, K., & Costain, W.R. (1965). Hypochondriasis and depression in outpatients at a general hospital. *British Journal of Psychiatry*, **111**, 607–615.

Ladee, G.A. (1966). *Hypochondriacal syndromes*. New York: Elsevier.

Lewis, A. (1934). Melancholia: A clinical survey of depressive states. *Journal of Mental Science*, **80**, 277–378.

Marks, I.M. (1987). *Fears, phobias, and rituals*. New York: Oxford University Press.

Marks, I.M. (1970). The classification of phobic disorders. *British Journal of Psychiatry*, **116**, 377–386.

Mayou, R. (1976). The nature of bodily symptoms. *British Journal of Psychiatry*, **129**, 55–60.

McKenna, P.J. (1984). Disorders with overvalued ideas. *British Journal of Psychiatry*, **145**, 579–585.

McLeod, D.R., & Hoehn-Saric, R. (1993). Perception of physiological changes in normal and pathological anxiety. In R. Hoehn-Saric & D.R. McLeod (Eds.), *Biology of anxiety disorders* (pp. 223–244). Washington, DC: American Psychiatric Press.

Murphy, M.R. (1990). Classification of the somatoform disorders. In C.M. Bass (Ed.), *Somatization: Physical symptoms and psychological illness* (pp. 10–39). London: Blackwell Scientific.

Musetti, L., Perugi, G., Soriani, A., Ross, V.M., Cassano, G.B., & Akiskal, H.S. (1989). Depression before and after age 65: A re-examination. *British Journal of Psychiatry*, **155**, 330–336.

Noyes, R. (1999). The relationship of hypochondriasis to anxiety disorders. *General Hospital Psychiatry*, **21**, 8–17.

Noyes, R., Clancy, J., Hoenk, P.R., & Slymen, D.J. (1980). The prognosis of anxiety neurosis. *Archives of General Psychiatry*, **37**, 173–178.

Noyes, R., Holt, C.S., Happel, R.L., Kathol, R.G., & Yagla, S.J. (1997). A family study of hypochondriasis. *Journal of Nervous and Mental Disease*, **185**, 223–232.

Noyes, R., Kathol, R., Fisher, M., Phillips, B., Suelzer, M., & Woodman, C. (1994a). Psychiatric comorbidity among patients with hypochondriasis. *General Hospital Psychiatry*, **16**, 78–87.

Noyes, R., Kathol, R., Fisher, M., Phillips, B., Suelzer, M., & Woodman, C. (1994b). A one-year follow-up of medical outpatients with hypochondriasis. *Psychosomatics*, **35**, 533–545.

Noyes, R., Kathol, R., Fisher, M., Phillips, B., Suelzer, M., & Holt, C. (1993). The validity of DSM-III-R hypochondriasis. *Archives of General Psychiatry*, **50**, 961–970.

Noyes, R., Reich, J., Clancy, J., & O'Gorman, T.W. (1986). Reduction in hypochondriasis with treatment of panic disorder. *British Journal of Psychiatry*, **149**, 631–635.

Noyes, R., Wesner, R.B., & Fisher, M.M. (1992). A comparison of patients with illness phobia and panic disorder. *Psychosomatics*, **23**, 92–99.

Otto, M.W., Pollack, M.H., Sachs, G.S., & Rosenbaum, J.F. (1992). Hypochondriacal concerns, anxiety sensitivity, and panic disorder. *Journal of Anxiety Disorders*, **6**, 93–104.

Perugi, G., Toni, C., Benedetti, A., Simonetti, B., Simoncini, M., Torti, C., Musetti, L., & Akiskal, H.S. (1998). Delineating a putative phobic-anxious temperament in 126 panic-agoraphobic patient: Toward a rapprochement of Euopean and US views. *Journal of Affective Disorders*, **47**, 11–23.

Pilowsky, I. (1967). Dimensions of hypochondriasis. *British Journal of Psychiatry*, **113**, 89–93.

Pilowsky, I. (1970). Primary and secondary hypochondriasis. *Acta Psychiatrica Scandinavica*, **46**, 273–285.

Pilowsky, I., & Spence, N.D. (1975). Patterns of illness behavior in patients with intractable pain. *Journal of Psychosomatic Research*, **19**, 279–287.

Pilowsky, I., & Spence, N.D. (1983). *Manual of the Illness Behavior Questionnaire (IBQ)* (2nd edn.). Adeliade, South Australia: Department of Psychiatry, University of Adelaide.

Rasmussen, S.A., & Eisen, J.L. (1992). The epidemiology and differential diagnosis of obsessive compulsive disorder. *Journal of Clinical Psychiatry*, **53** (Suppl. 4), 4–10.

Roth, M., & Harper, M. (1962). Temporal lobe epilepsy and the phobic-anxiety depersonalization syndrome. *Comprehensive Psychiatry*, **3**, 215–226.

Ryle, J.A. (1948). Nosophobia. *Journal of Mental Science*, **94**, 1–17.

Salkovskis, P.M., & Warwick, H.M.C. (1986). Morbid preoccupations, health anxiety and reassurance: A cognitive behavioural approach to hypochondriasis. *Behaviour Research and Therapy*, **24**, 597–602.

Salkovskis, P.M., Warwick, H.M.C., & Clark, D.M. (1990). *Hypochondriasis, illness phobia and other anxiety disorders* (Review paper for the DSM-IV subgroup on hypochondriasis). Oxford, UK: Department of Psychiatry, University of Oxford.

Sanderson, W.C., & Barlow, D.H. (1990). A description of patients diagnosed with DSM-III-R generalized anxiety disorder. *Journal of Nervous and Mental Disease*, **178**, 588–591.

Savron, G., Fava, G.A., Grandi, S., Rafanelli, C., Raffi, A.R., & Belluardo, P. (1996). Hypochondriacal fears and beliefs in obsessive-compulsive disorder. *Acta Psychiatrica Scandinavica*, **93**, 345–348.

Schafer, M.L. (1982). Phenomenology and hypochondria. In A.J.J. De Konig & F.A. Jenner (Eds.), *Phenomenology and psychiatry*. London: Grune & Stratton.

Schmidt, A.J.M. (1994). Bottlenecks in the diagnosis of hypochondriasis. *Comprehensive Psychiatry*, **35**, 306–315.

Sheehan, D.V., Ballenger, J., & Jacobsen, G. (1980). Treatment of endogenous anxiety with phobic, hysterical, and hypochondriacal symptoms. *Archives of General Psychiatry*, **37**, 51–59.

Starcevic, J. (1988). Diagnosis of hypochondriasis: A promenade through the psychiatric nosology. *American Journal of Psychotherapy*, **52**, 197–211.

Starcevic, J., Fallon, S., Uhlenhuth, E.H., & Pathak, D. (1994). Generalized anxiety disorder, worries about illness, and hypochondriacal fears and beliefs. *Psychotherapy and Psychosomatics*, **61**, 93–99.

Starcevic, J., Kellner, R., Uhlenhuth, E.H., & Pathak, D. (1992). Panic disorder and hypochondriacal fears and beliefs. *Journal of Affective Disorders*, **24**, 73–85.

Sutherland, S. (1976). *Breakdown. A personal crisis and a medical dilemma*. London: Weidenfeld & Nicolson.

Stenback, A., & Jalava, J. (1962). Hypochondria and depression. *Acta Psychiatrica Scandinavica*, **37** (Suppl. 162), 240–246.

Taylor, S. (1995). Panic disorder and hypochondriacal concerns: Reply to Otto and Pollack (1994). *Journal of Anxiety Disorders*, **9**, 87–88.

Timsit, M., Dugardin, J.C., Adam, A., & Sabatier, J. (1973). La neurose hypochondriaque a-t-elle-droit de cité? *Acta Psychiatrica Belgica*, **73**, 458–483.

Tyrer, P., Fowler-Dixon, R., Ferguson, B., & Kelemen, A. (1990). A plea for the diagnosis of hypochondriacal personality disorder. *Journal of Psychosomatic Research,* **34**, 637–642.

Wallace, J., & Pfohl, B. (1995). Age-related differences in the symptomatic expression of major depression. *Journal of Nervous and Mental Disease,* **183**, 99–102.

Warwick, H.M.C., Clark, D.M., Cobb, A.M., & Salkovskis, P.M. (1996). A controlled trial of cognitive-behavioral treatment of hypochondriasis. *British Journal of Psychiatry,* **169**, 189–195.

Warwick, H.M.C., & Marks, I.M. (1988). Behavioural treatment of illness phobia. *British Journal of Psychiatry,* **152**, 239–241.

Warwick, H.M.C., & Salkovskis, P.M. (1990). Hypochondriasis. *Behaviour Research Therapy,* **28**, 105–117.

World Health Organization (1993). *The ICD-10 classification of mental and behavioral disorders: Diagnostic criteria for research.* Geneva, Switzerland: Author.

Yates, W.R. (1991). Transient hypochondriasis: A new somatoform diagnosis? *Archives General Psychiatry,* **48**, 955–956.

Chapter 7

# APPROACH TO INTEGRATED COGNITIVE-BEHAVIOR THERAPY FOR INTENSE ILLNESS WORRIES

*Patricia Furer\*, John R. Walker\*, and Mark H. Freeston[†]*

## INTRODUCTION

Previous chapters have provided a detailed description of the theoretical and research rationale for the cognitive-behavioral treatment (CBT) of hypochondriasis. In this chapter we will describe a practical approaches to treatment. First, a few words about terminology are in order. The terms *hypochondriasis* and *hypochondriac* have negative connotations and are often misunderstood and misused. In developing the treatment materials used in our clinic we generally use *intense illness worry* to substitute for the term hypochondriasis as clients seem more comfortable with this. In addition, intense illness worry can include a number of problems beyond what is traditionally considered to be hypochondriasis, such as specific phobia of illness and some other forms of somatoform disorder, and it is more easily understandable to persons unfamiliar with technical medical language.

Most of the treatment studies published in this area provide relatively brief descriptions of the procedures involved. In this chapter we will provide a session-by-session outline of an approach that we have used in individual and group treatment in our clinic. This will include detailed descriptions of the procedures and examples of the materials (Furer & Walker, 1998) used in treatment. Hopefully, this will make it easier for the clinician familiar with the principles of CBT to implement these

\*St Boniface General Hospital, Winnipeg MB, Canada; [†]Newcastle Centre for Cognitive and Behaviour Therapies, New Castle Upon Tyne, UK

*Health Anxiety*
Edited by G.J.G. Asmundson, S. Taylor & B.J. Cox
© 2001 John Wiley & Sons Ltd.

procedures with hypochondriasis and related problems such as fear of medical procedures and fear of mental illness.

## OVERVIEW OF APPROACH USED IN OUR PROGRAM

Our clinical service is based in a specialty anxiety disorders program in the outpatient service of a teaching hospital. We have been treating people with anxiety disorders for many years and have been aware of the high frequency with which these people also present with intense illness worries which often reach the proportion of hypochondriasis (see for example, Furer, Walker, Chartier, & Stein, 1997). The approach, outlined in detail later in the chapter, builds on the work by previous research groups (e.g., Bouman & Visser, 1998; Clark et al., 1998; Warwick, Clark, Cobb, & Salkovskis, 1996) but has expanded the areas targeted by the cognitive-behavioral procedures. Some of these changes have been based on our earlier work with panic disorder, obsessive-compulsive disorder (Freeston et al., 1997; Freeston, Rhéaume, & Ladouceur, 1996), and intense fear of death. In developing this treatment protocol we have been guided by the research which has demonstrated the tremendous importance of exposure to feared situations in the treatment of anxiety disorders. We have also been guided by research on the importance of cognitive factors in the development and maintenance of anxiety disorders. To date, the research evaluating the relative importance of these factors is not completely clear. We have found that both types of procedures are well accepted by clients when adequately explained. While the protocol includes a range of procedures, we recognize that they are not all equally important. The procedures which are emphasized for a particular client will depend on the behaviors and thoughts displayed by that individual.

Four treatment components that we have emphasized in our approach to intense illness worry are cognitive modification strategies, response prevention, exposure to feared health problems, and exposure to themes related to death. These components will be briefly described here. More detail is provided in the treatment protocol description.

### Cognitive Modification Strategies

Cognitive modification strategies play a prominent role in most of the treatments for hypochondriasis (see, for example, the work of the group at Oxford, including Salkovskis, Warwick, Clark, and others). We have found that helping individuals identify their illness-related thoughts and learning how to dispute them can reduce anxiety and facilitate response prevention and exposure-related tasks.

## Response Prevention

The individuals we have seen for treatment of hypochondriasis often repeatedly check their bodily symptoms or repeatedly check for signs of illness. Following on the large literature on the role of checking in maintaining obsessive-compulsive disorder, our program evaluates the degree of bodily checking and reassurance seeking reported by each participant and emphasizes the importance of response prevention. Likewise, excessive information seeking in medical encyclopaedias, newspapers and other similar sources is also targeted for response prevention. Finally, excessive or stereotyped use of health foods, vitamin supplements, and other prohealth behaviors should also be considered for response prevention if behavioral analysis suggests that they play an anxiety-reducing rather than a health-promoting role. These procedures are well accepted by most participants and when implemented effectively often result in a significant reduction in anxiety. We implement this treatment component early in the program.

## Exposure to Feared Health Problems

Many individuals with intense illness worries are fearful that they will develop the illness that they fear the most, even during periods without somatic symptoms or when disease conviction is low. They may be extremely vigilant for signs and symptoms of the illness and experience a great deal of dread about developing the illness in the future. Drawing from the work on exposure to feared situations in obsessive-compulsive disorder, especially work with pure obsessions (Freeston & Ladouceur, in press), we have developed procedures to provide imaginal and in vivo exposure to feared health problems. We also use attentional focus procedures to produce exposure to uncomfortable bodily symptoms which may be interpreted as signs of severe illness.

## Exposure to Themes Related to Death

Not surprisingly, most individuals who report high levels of illness fears usually also report high levels of fear of death. Previously described cognitive-behavioral approaches have tended not to emphasize this aspect of the problem. Illness and eventual death are inevitable parts of life and occasional exposure is unavoidable when family, friends, colleagues, acquaintances, or public figures have health problems or die. Such experiences can lead to an exacerbation of illness worries, so considerable emphasis is given to work on coping with fear of death. The main approach used in our program has been homework assignments to promote exposure to death-related themes. For example, assignments included later in the program involve writing one's own obituary, reviewing funeral plans, considering one's will, and facing situations related to death which have been avoided. These assignments can also be expanded to coping with the death of a close friend or family member. Rather than reassuring participants that they do not have a health problem, we emphasize that we will all have to face illnesses and death in the natural course of life. Part of the challenge here is coping with uncertainty about when these events will occur. Individuals who are able to face the reality of death seem best equipped to appreciate and enjoy life.

## Preliminary Outcome Data

We have been collecting treatment outcome data in a pilot study of our treatment protocol for individuals with DSM-IV (American Psychiatric Association, 1994) hypochondriasis (Furer, Walker, & Vincent, 1999) and we have started a larger-scale controlled evaluation of the group program. Our preliminary results are very promising, with significant reductions in hypochondriacal symptoms (i.e., fears and beliefs), depression, and anxiety occurring by post-treatment. For example, clients reported a significant change on the Illness Attitude Scale (Kellner, 1986) with mean scores dropping from 71.9 at pretreatment to 49.7 at post-treatment ($p < 0.001$). Global ratings of improvement completed by an independent assessor were consistent with the self-report measures, with group participants showing significant decreases in their illness concerns after CBT and 83% no longer meeting criteria for hypochondriasis.

## WHICH TREATMENT FOR WHICH INDIVIDUAL?

In planning treatment, it is essential to have a comprehensive assessment of the problem (see Chapter 5). Once the initial assessment has been completed, most clients will wish to discuss the clinician's recommendations for treatment. The majority of people come to treatment with some idea about what they want in the way of treatment. Usually we explore the individual's initial preferences first. We then provide information about the two types of treatment that have been evaluated for intense illness worry: pharmacotherapy and CBT. We try to provide a balanced description of each of these treatment approaches, outlining the advantages and disadvantages of each, with an emphasis on the positive aspects of treatment. We indicate that the client is likely to see considerable improvement in the problem with either approach, provided that he or she participates fully in the treatment. A brief description of the advantages and disadvantages of each treatment approach is provided in Table 7.1. It is important for the clinician to describe all the major treatments that have some scientific support to enable the patient or client to provide truly informed consent for treatment. If the client prefers a treatment not provided by the clinician, an appropriate referral should be made.

Initially, we did not know how receptive individuals would be to CBT. We explored this question when we were recruiting persons simultane-

**Table 7.1** Advantages and disadvantages of medication treatment and CBT

| Factor | Medication Treatment | CBT |
| --- | --- | --- |
| Efficacy | Early indications (A/D), efficacy with related problems (A) | More indications of efficacy (A), efficacy with related problems (A) |
| Availability | Prescribed by a family doctor, or a specialist in psychiatry (A) | Treatment provided by a specialist in CBT—may be more difficult to obtain (D) |
| Complexity of treatment | Medication may be taken on a reasonably simple schedule (A) | Requires more time and effort, individuals with limited education may find the treatment difficult (D) |
| Side effects | Side effects are not uncommon, may wear off over the weeks (D) | No indication of side effects (A) |
| Duration of treatment | Treatment should continue for at least 6 to 12 months (D) | Treatment is usually time limited—in the range of 3 to 4 months (A) |
| Effect of discontinuing treatment | Limited evidence on long-term effectiveness, return of symptoms is not uncommon with other problems treated with medication (D) | More evidence on long-term effectiveness, maintenance of gains when treatment is completed is common (A) |
| Cost of treatment | May be more costly in the long run (D) | May be more costly in short run, less costly in long run (A) |
| Effect on related problems | Likely to be helpful with related anxiety and depression problems (A) | Likely to be helpful with related anxiety and depression problems (A) |
| Safety during pregnancy | Limited evidence, usually patients are encouraged not become pregnant while on treatment (D) | No problem (A) |

*Note*: (A), Advantage; (D), Disadvantage. Adapted from Furer and Walker (1998).

ously for two studies of treatment of intense illness worries, one with pharmacological treatment and one with CBT (Walker, Vincent, Furer, Cox, & Kjernisted, 1999). Brief descriptions of each treatment were provided to potential participants before they met with a member of the staff for an initial assessment. Each participant completed ratings of opinions about the acceptability and likely short- and long-term effectiveness of each of the treatments. When individuals were asked to rank order choice of treatment, as their first choice 74% chose CBT and 4% chose medication; 22% indicated equal preference. The CBT was also rated highly in terms of acceptability and likely short-term and long-term effectiveness. CBT also has the advantage of being less costly than pharmacological treatment in many settings in the medium and long term.

For clients who indicate a preference for CBT, there is then the question of whether to provide individual or group therapy. Group treatments have a number of advantages, including generally being less costly than individual treatments. In addition, persons with intense illness worries often find it embarrassing to speak about their fears to people who may not be sympathetic to their concerns, so the opportunity in group treatment to talk to others who have encountered similar difficulties can be a tremendous relief.

There are, however, some challenges in making group treatments easily available. Unless a large number of individuals with intense illness worry are seen in a setting, it may be difficult to assemble enough people who are ready to start treatment at one time. Furthermore, some clients prefer individual therapy because they fear that they may learn about and acquire new worries and symptoms from other group members. We have not found this to be a problem in our groups. Some clients prefer the privacy of individual treatment, although we have never experienced difficulty with breeches of confidentiality in our group programs. Treatment may be more clearly individualized in one-to-one therapy and at times this may allow for treatment to be briefer in length or to be adjusted to unique problems.

Some consideration should also be given to the suitability of an individual for a group program. One rule of thumb that we use is to consider the impact of the participation of a specific individual on the functioning of the group. If an individual's presence is likely to seriously distract other group members from the task at hand or to slow down their progress, we may direct that person toward individual therapy. Examples would be people who have limited literacy (since our group program involves a good deal of reading and writing), people with unstable living situations or personal crises (e.g., current suicidal intent), and individuals who would have difficulty sharing the floor with others in the group. Persons with a high degree of disease conviction who do not see the problem as being related to their own pattern of worry and anxiety may not fit well in a group. Similarly, individuals who express a great deal of frustration and anger directed toward the health care system may cause some distraction for other group members if they are not able to focus on the content of the group program. Individuals in these situations may require the greater flexibility possible in individual therapy. To date, our experience has been that we have rarely had to recommend that people should not attend a group program because of these problems. The demands of work schedules and family responsibilities are the main factors that have made group participation difficult for a few individuals. In our setting we tend to emphasize group treatment because of its lower cost and we have found that the program has been well received.

Some authors have recommended offering CBT for hypochondriasis in a non-medical health setting. We have only been able to provide our group and individual treatment in a mental health setting and have not found this to be a problem. It remains an empirical question whether consumers would prefer treatment in a medical, mental health, or community setting, and whether the setting influences treatment efficacy.

## TREATMENT PROTOCOL

Our CBT program for intense illness worry consists of 14 weekly treatment sessions. A treatment manual (Furer & Walker, 1998) provides educational material about the problem, descriptions of the treatment components, many clinically-based examples, and detailed homework assignments. Participants are encouraged to make session attendance and homework assignments a priority in their lives while they are in treatment. It is suggested that they spend 30 to 60 minutes per day working on treatment-related material.

This program was developed for either group or individual treatment. The description provided here uses the terminology used in our group program but can be easily adapted to individual treatment. We generally include 8 to 10 participants in each group. When possible, we prefer to have co-leaders for the group, with one experienced group leader and one leader in training.

Typical session structure involves introduction and discussion of new material, review of the previous week's homework assignments, and preparation of homework assignments for the subsequent week. A brief description of each session is provided below. Some excerpts from the treatment manual are included and common challenges that arise during treatment are discussed.

## Session 1: Introduction

*Session Content*

The focus of the first session is to provide the outline of the goals of the program and to begin developing therapeutic rapport. The treatment manual and the structure of its contents are reviewed. When this program is administered in group treatment format, the first session also provides opportunity for group cohesion to develop as group members describe their experiences with illness fears. Every group member is encouraged to speak in every group meeting (social anxiety is a common problem). Questions that participants address in the discussion in the first meeting include:

What was it like to start the group today? Did anyone feel nervous about attending the group for the first time? What kind of difficulties have you been having with fears about illness? Which illnesses do you worry about the most?

*Special Issues*

A central issue that needs to be addressed very early in treatment is the message that many clients have received from their doctors and from significant others—that the physical symptoms and fears about disease are 'all in their head'. Many individuals come into our program feeling embarrassed and misunderstood. They feel that their concerns have not been taken seriously in the health care system. It is important to clarify that the symptoms that the person reports are real physical experiences and that the therapist does not think that the client is 'making up' these symptoms. The therapists also need to demonstrate that they recognize and are respectful of the amount of emotional pain and suffering that intense illness fears can cause.

## Session 2: Understanding Intense Illness Worry

*Session Content*

Each individual's current illness worries and the triggers for these concerns are reviewed. This provides the group leader(s) with information about the presenting problems for each group member and is a good exercise for further development of group cohesiveness. Terminology and definitional issues can also be addressed at this point. The 'hypochondriac' label is discussed and other less stigmatizing terms are presented:

You may have heard the terms *hypochondriasis* or *hypochondriac* which are sometimes used instead of *intense illness worry*. Hypochondriasis is a medical term with which some people are uncomfortable because it has developed negative connotations and is often misunderstood and misused. Some people may feel insulted if they are called a *hypochondriac* as they feel that they are being labelled as a complainer. When used properly, the term *hypochondriasis* is simply another way to label the experience of having intense worries and fears about disease that continue despite medical reassurance.

The first of several relaxation strategies to be employed in the program—paced (or diaphragmatic) breathing—is introduced in this session and group members are asked to practice this skill on a daily basis. Simple instructions for paced breathing are available in many detailed anxiety treatment manuals (e.g., Clum, 1990). A rationale for how this relaxation strategy can be helpful is provided:

Essentially, paced breathing involves breathing from your diaphragm rather than from your upper chest. This is important because when you breathe primarily from your upper chest, you increase the risk of hyperventilating. Most people think of hyperventilation as panting, or gasping for air. Panting is only one form of hyperventilation, however. Other forms include sighing, yawning, holding your breath, or any forceful deep breath. Shallow, chest-level breathing may cause you to chronically hyperventilate.

Hyperventilation produces changes in the balance of oxygen and carbon dioxide in your blood. These changes are not harmful to your body but they do produce various physical sensations that you may find unpleasant. Shortness of breath, lightheadedness, and tingling or numbness in your fingers and toes are some of the physical symptoms that result from hyperventilation. You may find that paced breathing helps to relieve many of these physical symptoms.

Childhood factors and life events that may contribute to the development of illness fears are also reviewed. Topics discussed include experience with childhood illnesses, parental illness fears, family members with chronic or life-threatening illnesses, death experiences in childhood, adverse life events (e.g., abuse experiences, familial alcoholism, poverty), and temperament. We emphasize that many factors may be involved in the development of illness worries. While some individuals may have had very difficult life experiences related to illness, others may have had very few experiences like this. There is no need to search in child-

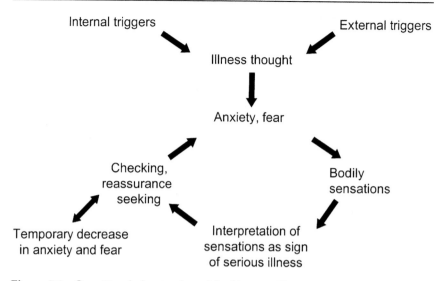

**Figure 7.1** Cognitive-behavioral model of intense illness concern (adapted from Furer & Walker, 1998).

hood or later life for events of this type if the individual does not easily recall them.

*Special Issues*

The therapist will recognize that the discussion about childhood factors and life events can be intensely emotional and can give rise to unresolved grief and bereavement issues for some participants. Generally, these issues can be effectively dealt with in the group treatment and often add to group cohesion. However, the therapist should be sensitive to the possibility that additional support for the individual may be required.

## Session 3: Cognitive-Behavioral Model

*Session Content*

The CBT model of intense illness worry (shown in Figure 7.1) is discussed. In brief, this model suggests that:

Intense illness worries are the result of a tendency to misinterpret bodily symptoms as signs of a serious disease. This misinterpretation is what causes the fear and worry. People often try to cope with this fear and worry by doing things like checking their bodies or getting reassurance from family members, doctors, or other health practitioners. This may help temporarily but most people find that the anxiety returns before long.

Each of the components of the model are reviewed and examples from group members are used to illustrate the application of the model. We emphasize the role of bodily sensations, interpretation of these sensations as signs of serious illness, and other illness-related thoughts in creating the fear and anxiety. We also discuss the effects of checking the body for symptoms and seeking reassurance from others. This is an opportunity for clients to look at their illness worries from a new perspective and to consider different alternatives with respect to how the illness worry cycle can be broken.

Clients are asked to experiment with focusing deliberately on their bodily symptoms to observe the effect on their anxiety. To illustrate how focusing on the body can intensify normal bodily sensations, clients are asked to do the following:

Swallow three times as quickly as you can. What happened? Did this feel awkward and uncomfortable? Were you able to swallow three times? Or did you feel unable to swallow properly by the third time? Some people find this exercise a bit scary at first because it can make you feel that your throat is not working normally. In fact, swallowing three times in quick succession is difficult for everyone because we simply don't produce enough saliva to do this. You can see how focusing on swallowing (or any other body sensation) can quickly lead to the feeling that something is wrong with your body. We also find that by continuously focusing on body sensations, you are training yourself to become very skilled at noticing even the slightest changes in your body. This can set off new fears and worries.

### Special Issues

We had anticipated that at least some individuals would be resistant to a psychological model of their illness worries. Thus far, however, this has rarely been the case. We have found our clients to be very receptive to considering the role of their thoughts, their reactions to body sensations, checking behaviors, and avoidance in the development and maintenance of their illness fears. Even individuals with significant disease conviction seem willing to consider this model.

## Session 4: Catastrophic Thoughts and Checking for Symptoms

*Session Content*

Clients are encouraged to examine their illness-related thoughts. The steps involved in modifying thinking patterns include learning to identify negative thoughts as they occur, disputing the negative thoughts by questioning how realistic they are, and using the challenges of the negative thoughts to develop more positive coping thoughts. In this session, the focus is on the first step, that is, identifying negative thoughts related to the illness fears. Examples of negative thoughts are discussed in the session.

The second major topic covered in Session 4 is the impact of checking the body for signs of illness. This follows logically from the previous topic, as body checking is a typical response to catastrophic thoughts. Clients are prompted to consider how they monitor their bodies. Typical examples of checking behaviors include checking the pulse rate, checking skin irregularities (e.g., moles, bumps) for signs of cancer, weighing oneself to see if weight has decreased, and frequent breast self-examinations. Clients are asked to consider both the short-term and long-term effects of checking on the illness worry cycle. At this point, clients are asked to monitor their checking behaviors for one week using the diary form illustrated in Figure 7.2. This information is used to further the client's understanding of how the illness worry is maintained and to select targets for response prevention.

Clients are also taught Progressive Muscle Relaxation (PMR), which they practice on a daily basis as homework. Simple instructions for PMR are available in many anxiety treatment manuals (e.g., Suinn, 1990).

*Special Issues*

As clients are monitoring their illness thoughts and checking behaviors, we help them identify patterns and connections between thoughts, behaviors, and anxiety levels. Our goal is to provide each individual with analysis skills that will facilitate maintenance of treatment gains.

## Session 5: Coping Thoughts

*Session Content*

Clients are encouraged to focus on developing coping thoughts. For each negative thought, the client is asked to consider the probability that this

| Date/Time | Situation and anxious thought | Beginning anxiety level (0–10) | Description of reassurance-seeking or checking | Ending anxiety level (0–10) |
|---|---|---|---|---|
| Sept. 2, 1 p.m. | Looking at mole on my arm. Is it getting bigger? Is it a bit darker? Maybe it's skin cancer. | 7 | Compared mole to other moles on both arms. Asked my wife if the mole has changed. | 5 |
| Sept. 3, 8 p.m. | Read news story about symptoms of Alzheimer's. Oh no! That's just like me. I can't remember anything these days. And I think my aunt might have had Alzheimer's so I'll probably get it too. | 9 | Went through mental checklist of the birthdays of everyone in my family to see if my memory is OK. | 10 |
| Sept. 4, 9 a.m. | Stomach pain: Why do I keep getting stomach aches? This must be something serious. Do I have a bleeding ulcer or stomach cancer? | 8 | Probed my stomach to look for lumps and sore areas. Checked medical text to look at list of symptoms of ulcers and stomach cancer. Asked my wife if I should make an appointment to see the doctor. | 5 |

**Figure 7.2**  Checking and reassurance-seeking diary form (adapted from Furer & Walker, 1998).

negative event, such as getting cancer, will happen. The client is prompted to think about how often they have had this anxious thought in the past and whether the feared event happened on those occasions. The client is also asked to consider other issues such as what the frequency is of cancer diagnoses for people of their age. Clients are encouraged not to focus on whether this event will happen in their lifetime (because we are all likely to have serious illnesses, including cancer, in our lifetime) but rather to think about how likely it is that the feared event will happen *in the near future*. They are also encouraged to consider their ability to cope if difficult things do happen. It is important that the coping thoughts also suggest the behavioral implications of the new way of looking at illness fears. Some examples of coping thoughts which clients have found to be helpful include:

I have a bad headache, but I've had lots of headaches before and it has never turned out to be a brain tumour. I can treat this headache like everyone else does.

I may get cancer some day, but the chances of this happening this week are very slim. I can just get on with my life.

This rash is probably a simple skin irritation, not skin cancer. I will wait for two or three weeks and see if this rash is getting better. If it is still a problem I can go see my doctor then.

The numbness in my arms and hands is due to anxiety and how I am breathing. It is not a sign that I am having a stroke. I just need to slow my breathing down and focus on what I am doing right now.

This lump will heal quicker if I leave it alone, so I won't keep touching it.

Another important topic is the role of reassurance-seeking. Clients are asked to self-monitor the frequency with which they seek out reassurance from others that their bodily symptoms are not signs of serious illness. Typical examples of reassurance seeking include asking a family member or friend about one's symptoms, going to the doctor to ask about symptoms, and reviewing a list of symptoms in a medical book. Clients use the same diary to monitor reassurance-seeking and other checking behaviors (see Figure 7.2).

*Special Issues*

Coping thoughts are useful for many people. However, some individuals, especially those who experience a lot of obsessional thinking, may use the coping thoughts as a form of cognitive ritual by repeating the coping thought over and over in an excessive fashion. Emphasizing the importance of acting coherently with the coping thought, rather than merely repeating the coping thought, will maximize the therapeutic value of this intervention.

## Session 6: Reducing Checking and Reassurance-Seeking

*Session Content*

The central focus in this session is continued work on response prevention, for both checking and reassurance seeking behaviors. Clients are encouraged to select several behaviors that they wish to decrease. Various strategies are suggested to assist with this goal, including postponing these behaviors, gradually decreasing their frequency, or simply stopping the selected behaviors. It is suggested that response prevention may lead to a short-term increase in anxiety. This increased anxiety generally does not last and, in the long run, decreasing the checking and reassurance-seeking behaviors results in less anxiety. Our experience has been that many clients are surprised by how quickly the response prevention strategies can reduce their focus on their body and lessen illness worries.

*Special Issues*

One of the challenges for clients when they begin working on response prevention is deciding on the appropriate frequency for certain types of body checking and reassurance seeking. Not all such behaviors should occur with zero frequency. It is generally recommended, for example, that breast self-examinations be conducted once per month. Similarly, it is appropriate to go to the doctor if one has a sore throat that lasts longer than a week. Group discussion and therapist input is often very helpful in establishing normative frequencies for health behaviors.

Another important issue to consider when working on decreasing checking and reassurance-seeking is the involvement of the client's significant others in these behaviors. We do not routinely have significant others attend treatment sessions because of the scheduling difficulties this can involve. However, clients are encouraged to discuss their response prevention goals with their partner and to decide how they would like their partner to respond when they engage in body checking and reassurance seeking. If this strategy is insufficient, it is a good idea to arrange a session with the client and the significant other to discuss these issues and plan a cooperative approach to reducing reassurance-seeking.

## Session 7: Exposure to Illness Worries

*Session Content*

Clients use a model *illness story* to develop a written narrative related to their anxious thoughts about illness and death. They are encouraged to make the story as real and strongly emotional as possible as they describe their worst fear coming true. The narrative includes the bodily feelings and possible signs of illness that cause them worry. Clients describe in vivid terms the stages of the illness and their worries at each point along the way, such as being extremely sick, being helpless, and dying. The narrative describes worries they have about other people close to them.

Some clients are concerned that they already obsess about their fears and wonder why we are asking them to think about their fears even more. Providing a clear explanation is very important:

We have found over the years that one of the most powerful ways of overcoming anxiety is to directly face the things that you fear. The more that a person faces even difficult fears, the more the anxiety about them is reduced. Facing your fears in a planned way may also help to increase your confidence that you will be able to handle other fears. It is helpful to apply this approach to fears of illness and death. The goal is not to be happy about these sad events. Rather the goal is to face the reality of illness and death as a part of life calmly and without excessive anxiety. You may say to yourself that you are already facing your fears by worrying about illness. However, worry tends to come to us at times and in ways that we feel little control over. When people are worrying about illness, they tend to do things to try and get rid of the worry or to reassure themselves. Often, after worrying for a while, they will try to do something to 'get the worry out of their mind' or to escape from their fear.

The approach of facing your fears directly is different. It involves actually regularly scheduling time to face your worry. You learn to take control of your worrying rather than having the worry come at times that you do not control. Rather than struggling to reassure yourself that the terrible things you fear won't happen, you face the reality that these things can and do happen. You accept the thoughts of illness and death rather than fighting them. With repeated practice in facing fears it is normal for the anxiety to decline and for the individual to face even unpleasant possibilities more calmly. One way that has been developed to face fears of illness and death is to write out a story that includes the most important things that you fear. You can then practice facing your fears by repeatedly reviewing the story and imagining that it is really happening to you.

Clients typically create two or three stories addressing their major illness fears. They then practice facing their fears by repeatedly reviewing the story and imagining that it is really happening. A sample illness story about developing cancer is outlined below.

I notice a feeling of discomfort and bloating in my abdomen. I can also feel the pain that has been worrying me. I feel very stressed about this. I wonder if this could be an early sign of cancer. I have had some check-ups and tests but maybe they couldn't detect these early signs. Cancer is something that can happen at my age. People can have very few symptoms and then suddenly it is there and then a few months later they are gone. I feel so scared and worried about this.

If I have cancer, what will happen? How will I cope? Will I be able to go through all the tests and treatment that are necessary? Will I feel mutilated after the surgery? How will my family cope? How will the children do if their mother is gone? I find it so difficult to cope with these fears. My stomach feels sick just thinking about it. What if the cancer treatments do not help? What if they make me very sick but before long the cancer comes back anyway? First I have surgery, then the radiation treatment, and then chemotherapy. It takes me a long time to feel better afterward. How will I cope with the worry and the fear? And after going through all of that, what if the symptoms come back before long? At that point I will know I am going to die. I don't know if I can face all of the things that lead up to dying. Will the pain and sickness be more than I can handle? Can I cope with actually knowing that I am dying? I will be so scared about going through that. As I get closer to dying, I will feel so guilty that I didn't do more to prevent myself from getting cancer. There is more that I could have done to prevent it, but I didn't do those things. I just focus on all of these worries. I feel so full of uncertainty and doubt about what will happen in the future. I feel so worried about my health.

We have found this exposure exercise to be a very powerful tool in helping individuals take control of their worrying and their fears. Clients report that the experience of writing the narratives is typically very emotional and intense. We ask group members to share their illness stories in the therapy session, which also has significant impact. Clients continue to work on this exposure exercise for several weeks, developing new narratives as their ability to manage their initial exposures increases.

*Special Issues*

We generally ask clients to repeatedly read (either out loud or to themselves) their illness stories for exposure practice as we have found this to be simpler and as effective as the traditional strategy of tape recording on a loop tape. Letting clients experiment with these different approaches (reading versus audiotape) may be helpful if the client is having difficulty with this exposure technique.

## Session 8: Overcoming Avoidance

*Session Content*

Clients begin working to overcome avoidance of illness-related situations. They are encouraged to select one or more situations that they find challenging and have avoided in the past. Examples of homework assignments selected might include visiting a sick friend, watching a TV show about hospitals, surgery, or characters with life-threatening illnesses, and going to a doctor's appointment. The client is encouraged to approach these situations on a daily basis without checking their bodies or seeking reassurance from others (i.e., exposure with response prevention).

*Special Issues*

It can be very challenging for clients to identify areas of avoidance. In some cases, the avoidance can be so well established that the client no longer attributes the fact that they do not engage in a certain activity to anxiety. Providing examples of avoidance behavior (e.g., going to funerals, going to the cemetery, visiting a person who is ill, going to the doctor, reading stories about cancer) and group discussion on this topic can be very helpful. If a client is uncertain whether they do not engage in a certain behavior due to anxiety or for another reason, such as lack of interest, the best strategy is for the client to engage in the behavior at least once to see if the avoidance is anxiety-related.

Often clients assume that exposure involves facing fears on one or two occasions. We emphasize the importance of *repeated* exposure until anxiety is reduced to a low level. Any reemergence of anxiety should be followed by additional repeated exposure practice.

## Session 9: Coping with Fear of Death

*Session Content*

Here we focus on death-related issues. In helping people come to terms with death we have found two general strategies which are helpful. One approach is to resolve to live life to its fullest and to get as much enjoy-ment and satisfaction as possible from each precious day of life:

Enjoyment of life involves an openness and commitment to seeing and appre-ciating the beauty around us. It involves a willingness to enjoy the everyday experiences in life that may bring us a lot of pleasure if we let them. This enjoyment is something that need not wait for your retirement years, your vacation, or even for late in the day when your work is done. It is something that can come frequently throughout every day. There are probably many things you do every day that you could enjoy more if you paid more atten-tion to the satisfaction and enjoyment that can come from these things. Enjoy-ment of life helps to give you the strength to deal with the challenges that life brings.

We ask clients to make a list of the things that have given them feelings of satisfaction and enjoyment in life over the last few years. An important goal for many clients later in the program is to engage in these activities more frequently.

The second approach in dealing with fear of death is to face the reality of loss and death. By directly facing fears and accepting the inevitability of serious illness and death, the anxiety, distress, and loss of satisfaction caused by fear of death can be reduced. Clients are asked to consider any ways in which they may avoid thoughts or experiences related to death. They are also encouraged to identify their anxious thoughts about death and to develop coping thoughts which can assist them in manag-ing their fears. For homework, clients are asked to write their own obitu-ary (as if they were going to die in the immediate future). The experience of writing their obituary, that is summarizing the highlights of their lives to date, their contributions to family and society, and considering who would mourn their death, may be a very emotionally powerful experience.

### Special Issues

Some clients find this material to be the most useful in the program. Clearly, fear of death is a central concern for many individuals with illness fears (also see Chapter 14). Some clients express concern, however, that they already are preoccupied with death and wonder how much more they can face their fears. They also may wonder how thinking about death would make them feel better. Making a clear distinction between being preoccupied with death and facing and accepting it is very helpful.

## Session 10: Establishing Personal Goals

*Session Content*

Clients work on establishing goals for themselves by completing a goal sheet. They are encouraged to start by considering their life goals. Selecting long-term goals and articulating these in specific and concrete terms can assist clients in developing more immediate goals. Clients are encouraged to consider what they would want from their life if they were not hampered by illness worries. They then work on developing medium-term goals and short-term goals that will help them achieve their long-term goals. Medium-term goals are goals that the client can imagine working on in the next year while short-term goals are ones they are willing to start working on in the next three months. They are asked to make their goals specific and concrete. It is also important to ensure that the short-term goals are things that will move them closer to their medium-term goals which, in turn, will move them closer to their life goals. Group members find the discussion of goals in the session to be very helpful as they often obtain helpful ideas from other group members.

Imagery-induced relaxation (the third and final relaxation technique covered) is introduced in this session and clients are also encouraged to continue using paced breathing and progressive muscle relaxation in their daily lives. Specific instructions are available in many commonly available treatment manuals.

Homework assignments for this section include writing a will (or updating their will) and discussing funeral wishes with their partner or other family member. Clients are given reading material on these topics from a local funeral-planning organization. This reading also serves as an exposure exercise as it provides detailed explanations of various funeral options including cremation and burial. Making a will and planning funeral arrangements is often very difficult for clients (as it is for many people) and they may need considerable support and encouragement in working in these tasks.

*Special Issues*

The importance of selecting clear and specific goals should be emphasized. Some clients select goals such as 'being happy' or 'living without anxiety' which are so general and non-specific that it is 'hard to know when you get there'. Life goals may be quite broad but medium- and short-term goals should be specific and behaviorally based. The goals need to be such that you can tell exactly what you want to do and exactly when you have achieved it. Clients are encouraged to set goals that involve doing things in spite of anxiety and managing any anxious feelings that arise.

## Session 11: More Work on Overcoming Avoidance and Building Life Satisfaction

*Session Content*

The central focus in the remaining sessions of the program is continued work on overcoming avoidance. Clients are encouraged to engage in daily exposure practice in working toward their short-term goals, breaking these down into smaller tasks as necessary. More exposure homework addressing fear of death issues is also encouraged. Typical homework assignments include visiting the hospital, getting information about the local cancer society, and reading obituaries of people of similar age as themselves.

Clients are also asked to keep track of the activities they do that give them a sense of satisfaction or pleasure. They are then asked to consider whether they have enough fun in their lives and, if not, to schedule more activities on a daily basis that give them satisfaction and pleasure.

*Special Issues*

We have noted that increasing pleasurable activities often has a significant positive impact on clients' worries about illness and death, so we emphasize the importance of this exercise. As clients shift their focus to having more fun and satisfaction in their lives they often find that they have less time to worry about illness. They also find that as their lives become more fulfilling, they are less threatened by the certainty of dying.

## Session 12: Dealing with Health Information

*Session Content*

For some clients, reading or hearing health information in the media can be a trigger for health worries. Clients report that they find it very challenging to know how to interpret the often conflicting information presented in the media about health and illness. Group discussion generally turns into a lively debate when this topic is introduced. We have found it helpful to encourage clients to handle negative thoughts triggered by health information in the media in the same way they handle other catastrophic illness-related thoughts. In other words, we suggest they consider the likely accuracy of the news story and the probability that the feared events will happen, and develop coping thoughts that they can use when the anxious thoughts occur. For homework, clients are asked to read whatever news articles about health they can find and to develop coping thoughts to handle any worries triggered by this information.

*Special Issues*

We have found it important to ensure that clients continue to practice the response prevention techniques discussed earlier in the program. It is crucial to ensure that as clients are facing their fears about illness and death they are *not* increasing their checking and reassurance-seeking behaviors.

## Session 13: Coping with Setbacks and Relapse Prevention

*Session Content*

Material on identifying triggers for setbacks and strategies for coping with setbacks is introduced. We point out that most people working on recovering from problems with intense illness worry have periods where they experience increased anxiety and worry. Clients are given information on types of experiences often related to setbacks. These include:

1. Experiencing a new physical symptom or the return of a physical symptom previously experienced.
2. Facing a situation related to illness worries that has been avoided for a long time.
3. A serious illness, either in themselves or someone close.
4. Losing someone close (e.g., through death, life changes, moves to other cities).
5. A threat to an important relationship or the end of an important relationship.
6. Increased life stress beyond a level that they feel readily able to cope with.

Strategies for coping with setbacks are summarized as follows:

It is important to remember that setbacks are a normal part of recovery. Rather than giving up when you have a setback, it is important to keep applying the coping strategies you have learned and keep working toward your goals. If the increased worry and fear persist, you may want to go back to a easier level in working on some of your goals to build up your confidence again. Accept that if you keep working steadily, you will continue to make progress. Be willing to give yourself time and encouragement to get your confidence back.

At this point in the program, clients are also encouraged to consider the broader context of their illness worries:

It is important to place your illness worries into the context of the rest of your life. You may have observed that your worries and fears started at a time when you were experiencing increased life stresses. Similarly, you may find that your worries increase at times when you are experiencing additional demands or stresses. Stress and anxiety are normal parts of a healthy life. Life without stress is neither possible nor desirable. Positive stress means that you are facing challenges and accepting life changes. Negative stress means that you are feeling overwhelmed and unable to cope easily with negative and difficult life changes and demands. The key to a happy life is learning how to manage stress and solve problems. Most of us are able to manage stress better in one area if we are happy with other areas of our lives.

Many people come to view increased anxiety as a 'red flag' which signals that they may be under increasing stress or experiencing increasing demands or challenges. Anxiety can remind you to pay attention to what is happening in your life and to work on effective stress management and problem-solving strategies.

We ask clients to think about their general personal wellness and physical health. Do they eat well? Exercise regularly? Refrain from smoking? Manage their time well or always feel rushed? Are they pleased with the quality of their interpersonal relationships? Clients are asked to consider issues such as stress and anger management, sleep patterns, alcohol consumption, maintaining satisfying interpersonal relationships, and use of leisure time.

### Special Issues

If clients identify numerous areas in their life which they feel they need to change they may become overwhelmed and discouraged. It is important to identify small areas of change that can be targeted initially and to note that lifestyle changes need to be established in a gradual fashion over significant periods of time in order to be durable.

## Session 14: Review of the Program

*Session Content*

No new material is introduced in the final session of the program. Clients are asked to review their goals and to determine which goals they have achieved and which goals they plan to work on next. Relaxation strategies, cognitive coping strategies, response prevention, and the importance of continued regular exposure practice are reviewed. Opportunity for clients and the therapist to say their farewells is, of course, provided. Follow-up treatment options are also discussed.

At the conclusion of treatment, we meet with each client to evaluate their progress and whether there is need for further treatment, either for the intense illness worry or for other problems (e.g., marital issues, depression). Many individuals simply continue to work on their illness worries and coping strategies independently.

*Special Issues*

It is important to ensure that any termination concerns are addressed by this session. Some group members experience considerable sadness at finishing the group because they value the experience of being able to share their fears and worries with others who are empathic and supportive. Some clients are very excited about 'graduating'. All clients need to be encouraged to continue working on overcoming their illness worries, practicing their coping techniques, and facing the challenges related to health (for oneself and significant others) that are an inevitable part of life.

## VARIATIONS ON A THEME: OTHER PROBLEMS IN WHICH ILLNESS WORRY IS PROMINENT

Many individuals have difficulty with illness worries which do not meet the full criteria for hypochondriasis. Intrusive thoughts about health are common in the general population and are reported by up to 60% of university students (Freeston et al., 1994). The situational nature of intrusive thoughts is also evident in that 75% of patients in hospital waiting rooms and 55% of their escorts reported obsessive thoughts (Freeston et al., 1994). As a worry theme, health worries are reported by 40% of adults (Dugas, Freeston, Doucet, Lachance, & Ladouceur, 1995), 62% of older adults (Doucet, Ladouceur, Freeston, & Dugas, 1998), and 26% of adolescents (Freeston et al., 1998). Thus, health- or illness-related thoughts are frequent in the general population and may cause difficulties in some circumstances. These worries about illness may be seen to lie on a continuum from the degree of concern which most people experience about health, illness, and mortality from time to time to the intense preoccupation with illness seen in hypochondriasis. A number of common presentations of clinically significant intense illness worry which may not meet the criteria for hypochondriasis are outlined below. These include fear of medical procedures, fear of persons with chronic medical conditions or risks, fear of unexplained somatic symptoms, fear of thoughts or worries triggering illness, and fear of mental illness. Other chapters in this volume provide a detailed description of approaches to pain (Chapter 12), heart-focused anxiety (Chapter 11), and death anxiety (Chapter 14). Most of the techniques described in the treatment protocol above may be adapted to deal with various types or levels of illness worry. Treatment planning should start with a careful behavioral assessment of the problem experienced by the individual and the history of the problem.

## Fear of Medical Procedures or Surgery

At some time most of us will experience medical procedures or surgeries that involve considerable discomfort and often considerable anxiety. These procedures range from very routine services such as injections and dental treatment to increasingly common but more complex medical investigations such as upper gastric endoscopy, colonoscopy, and coronary angiography. Anticipation of these procedures may result in concerns ranging from fears about pain, discomfort, or embarrassment, to apprehension about the results of medical tests, to worries about injuries arising from the procedures. Some individuals who are generally healthy and not unusually anxious avoid procedures which help in early identification of treatable problems because of concerns of this type.

There is an extensive body of research on preparation of individuals for medical procedures and surgery. Reviews of this literature (e.g., Mathews & Ridgeway, 1984; O'Halloran & Altmaier, 1995; Schultheis, Peterson, & Selby, 1987; Whelan & Kirby, 1998) and meta-analytic reviews (e.g., Devine, 1992; Hathaway, 1986; Johnston & Vögele, 1993) generally conclude that procedures designed to prepare individuals for these situations have the potential to reduce distress before, during, and after the procedures; reduce recovery time; and possibly reduce some of the costs associated with the procedures. As described briefly by Horne, Vatmanidis, and Careri (1994a, 1994b), commonly used approaches include: (a) providing procedural information; (b) providing brief instruction in relaxation approaches including muscle, breathing, or imagery relaxation; (c) cognitive coping procedures (involving coping statements); cognitive rehearsal (a type of imaginal exposure involving repeatedly visualizing the procedure and imagining coping with it in spite of the discomfort); (d) observing a model (often on videotape) as that person moves through the situation; and (e) preparing significant others—such as parents of young children—for the situation. Approaches which go beyond simple education appear to have some advantage in terms of the magnitude of the effect of the intervention. In spite of the potential of these approaches to improve quality of care and reduce costs, the consensus is that they are not yet widely used in our health care systems (Wilson-Barnett, 1994). In fact, there is some indication that financial pressure in health care systems has led to a reduction in the availability of this service in some areas (Whelan & Kirby, 1998).

Individuals who have been experiencing difficulty with anxiety often experience particular difficulty with the challenge of preparing for medical procedures or surgery. For these individuals it may be particularly beneficial to prepare in advance for anxiety arousing procedures. Many of the procedures described in our protocol for decreasing intense illness worry may be used. The goal here is not to remove all anxiety about the procedure but rather to decrease the amount of disruption in the person's life caused by the procedure and increase confidence that he or she can cope.

## Fear in Persons with Chronic Medical Conditions or Risks

People with chronic, intermittent, or degenerative conditions such as multiple sclerosis and rheumatoid arthritis may be particularly at risk for developing health-related anxiety. This anxiety may, in part, be due to the uncertainty in these conditions (e.g. Léger, Freeston, Ladouceur, 1998; Robbins, Kirmayer, & Kapusta, 1990; Smeltzer, 1994). Medical conditions without clearly recognized causes such as chronic pain, fibromyalgia, and chronic fatigue may also result in worry (e.g. Robbins et al., 1990). Survivors of cancer or other life threatening conditions may also report ongoing worry and intrusive thoughts about disease (Easterling & Leventhal, 1989; Weigers, Chesler, Zebrack, & Goldman, 1998). Finally, people with objective risk factors for disease may report worry. Although some people may cope very well, others may become excessively preoccupied with their medical condition or risk. The preoccupation may impact on their medical condition through the increased arousal and/or muscle tension associated with anxiety. It may also impact on quality of life through distress and through unnecessary or premature reduction of current activities and future plans.

When people with chronic medical conditions or risks report excessive worry, two levels of intervention can be considered. Problem-focused solutions obviously have a role to play in increasing activity and engaging fully in living to counter distress and reduction in activities or plans. In addition, the excessive preoccupations may also be targeted in therapy with great sensitivity and appropriate modification of the techniques. First, it must be clear that the target is to reduce the *excessive* preoccupation with illness and its consequences and not to convince them that the feared illness or consequences will never occur. Second, it is normal that people remain realistically concerned with their health. Third, it is helpful to encourage individuals to take charge of their health care and to pursue all normal medical care or investigations that are generally indicated for the condition. The benefits of such interventions are to reduce preoccupation and anxiety and to improve quality of life through the pursuit of normal activities.

## Fear of Thoughts or Worries Triggering Illness

People with illness-related fears may believe that thinking about illness triggers the illness. It is important to investigate the exact causal chain that the person believes may be responsible, as the intervention will vary as a result. A first form of causal belief may be a relatively realistic explanation that thinking about illness causes stress, that stress is harmful, and that this may lead to a variety of medical conditions. In this case, it is important to demonstrate that trying not to think about illness (or about anything for that matter) does not ultimately work (see Freeston & Ladouceur, in press). Thus, it may be more useful to try a different approach.

A second form of causal belief may be based on widely held views that positive thinking can cure or help cure diseases such as cancer. Unfortunately, many people also believe, by implication, that negative thinking may cause cancer. Here it is important to make the distinction that deliberate positive thinking or imagery may help illness but it is an ineffective means of dealing with anxious thinking. Thus, positive thinking or imaging techniques may be used when the person is not anxious (response delay or non-contingent use of positive thinking or other strategies; see Freeston & Ladouceur, 1997), but exposure based techniques are the most effective means of reducing the negative thinking.

A third form of causal belief may be based more on magical thinking rather than any more medically plausible explanation. This is the belief that thoughts, by some unknown mechanism, can trigger events (or that other thoughts can prevent events) and that illness is an event like any other. In this case, strategies developed for obsessive-compulsive disorder (OCD) are likely to be effective to challenge the beliefs about magical thinking and open the way for exposure (e.g. Freeston & Ladouceur, in press; Freeston et al., 1996; Rachman, 1998).

## Fear of Mental Illness

In the ICD-10 diagnostic system (World Health Organization, 1993) a diagnosis of hypochondriasis is limited to individuals who have concern about a *physical* illness. Although the DSM-IV is less specific, this diagnostic system also implies that hypochondriasis relates to fears of physical illness. In any case, fear of serious mental illness may be similar to other forms of illness worry and may share common features of intrusive thoughts or worry, reassurance-seeking, avoidance, and attempts to control the thinking. Such fears are quite common in OCD and may also appear in other anxiety disorders as the perceived loss of mental control or strange bodily sensations (such as depersonalization) that may be interpreted as signs that one is going crazy. First, it is important to identify what mental or bodily event the person is misinterpreting. Next, an alternative account can be offered that provides a more benign explanation. If it is the occurrence of particular thoughts or loss of mental control that leads to misinterpretation, the standard approach for obsessions or worry may be used that normalizes the occurrence of thoughts and emphasizes that attempts to control thinking are counterproductive and lead to decreased control.

## Fear of Illness in Individuals with Other Psychiatric Disorders

As noted in Chapter 6, illness worries are also commonly seen in a number of DSM-IV disorders including panic disorder (Furer et al., 1997), generalized anxiety disorder (GAD), OCD, specific phobia of illness such as fear of vomiting or choking (Curtis, Magee, Eaton, Wittchen, & Kessler, 1998; Himle, Crystal, Curtis, & Fluent, 1991), and major depression. There is a small literature examining the effect of treatment for the primary disorder on the accompanying illness fears. Langlois, Dugas, Léger, and Ladouceur (1998) found, for example, that health worries in GAD respond well to worry-focused treatments. Post-hoc analyses of results from 57 people who had completed treatment for GAD showed that the 25% who reported predominant worries about health showed significantly superior improvement on some clinical indicators than the other 75%. In OCD, health worries are often related to a possible consequence of contamination and in many cases the fear of transmitting the illness, with implications of personal responsibility for harm to others, is even worse than the fear of becoming ill. If overt compulsions such as washing or systematic preventive measures are present, standard exposure and response prevention treatment is likely to be successful. If there are few overt compulsions or less concern with contamination, treatment can be focused on the obsessive thoughts related to illness which generally respond very well to both cognitive therapy techniques and imaginal exposure and response prevention (Freeston et al., 1997; Ladouceur, Freeston, Gagnon, Thibodeau, & Dumont, 1993). It is important to address the responsibility issues (especially for sexually transmitted diseases), as well as the consequences of the disease.

Fears around illness and death have not been a major focus in most of the cognitive-behavioral treatments evaluated for the common anxiety disorders. Attention to illness worries that frequently accompany other anxiety disorders may help improve the effectiveness of treatment and reduce the risk of relapse. There has been little research in this area to date and specific recommendations await additional research.

## COMBINED TREATMENT WITH MEDICATION AND CBT

Earlier in this chapter we discussed the importance of informing clients about all empirically supported treatments so that they may make an informed choice. At this point the research on the advantages and disadvantages of routinely combining psychological and pharmacological treatment is very limited. Research on combined treatment with anxiety disorders suggests that combined pharmacotherapy and CBT produces no greater effect than either treatment provided alone (see Westra & Stewart, 1998). Likewise, meta-analyses of behavior therapy and pharmacotherapy for OCD have generally concluded that combined treatment is not superior to behavior therapy alone (e.g. Abramowitz, 1997; Kobak, Greist, Jefferson, Katzelnick, & Henk, 1998). Combined treatments are generally more costly and specialists in CBT have had concerns that routinely combining treatments, rather than having a positive additive effect, will bring together the disadvantages of each treatment.

In our setting, we encourage clients to chose their preferred treatment and to implement it conscientiously. If at the end of an adequate trial the individual is of the opinion that there has not been sufficient improvement, he or she is free to augment the first treatment (with greater duration of treatment or some added elements) or to add the alternative treatment. This could be described as sequential treatment.

When they begin CBT, some clients wish to reduce or discontinue medication at the early stages. Our usual practice is to encourage clients to maintain the medication they are taking at a stable level to allow an evaluation of the effectiveness of CBT against a stable background. It may be more appropriate to reduce medication (if the client expresses a desire to do this) late in the course of CBT so that the person has developed coping strategies to use if there is an increase in anxiety or decrease in mood triggered by changes in the medication treatment. Naturally, any changes in medication treatment should take place gradually and only after consultation with the prescribing physician. With antidepressant medication there may be an advantage, in terms of reducing the likelihood of return of symptoms, to maintaining the treatment for at least 6 to 12 months after the client has seen considerable improvement.

## CONCLUSION

CBT appears to have much to offer to individuals dealing with intense illness worry. CBT is an effective approach for this problem and is generally positively viewed by these individuals. Much research remains to be done, however, especially with regards to larger-scale controlled treatment trials. We are hopeful that the detailed descriptions of our treatment protocol will encourage further evaluations of CBT for intense illness worry.

## REFERENCES

Abramowitz, J. (1997). Effectiveness of psychological and pharmacological treatments for obsessive-compulsive disorder: A quantitative review. *Journal of Consulting and Clinical Psychology*, **65**, 44–52.

American Psychiatric Association (1994). *Diagnostic and statistical manual of mental disorders* (4th edn.). Washington, DC: Author.

Bouman, T.K., & Visser, S. (1998). Cognitive and behavioural treatment of hypochondriasis. *Psychotherapy and Psychosomatics*, **67**, 214–221.

Clark, D.M., Salkovskis, P.M., Hackmann, A., Wells, A., Fennell, M., Ludgate, J., Ahmad, S., Richards, H.C., & Gelder, M. (1998). Two psychological treatments for hypochondriasis. *British Journal of Psychiatry*, **173**, 218–225.

Clum, G.A. (1990). *Coping with panic: a drug-free approach to dealing with anxiety attacks*. Pacific Grove, CA: Brooks/Cole Publishing Company.

Curtis, G.C., Magee, W.J., Eaton, W.W., Wittchen, H.-U., & Kessler, R.C. (1998). Specific fears and phobias. Epidemiology and classification. *British Journal of Psychiatry*, **173**, 212–217.

Devine, E.C. (1992). Effects of psychoeducational care for adult surgical patients: A meta-analysis of 191 studies. *Patient Education and Counselling*, **19**, 129–142.

Doucet, C., Ladouceur, R., Freeston, M.H., & Dugas, M. (1998). Themes d'inquietudes et tendavice as inquieter chez les aines. / Worry themes and the tendency to worry in older adults. *Canadian Journal on Aging*, **17**, 361–371.

Dugas, M., Freeston, M.H., Doucet, C., Lachance, S., & Ladouceur, R. (1995). Structured versus free-recall measures: Effect on report of worry themes. *Personality and Individual Differences*, **18**, 355–361.

Easterling, D.V., & Leventhal, H. (1989). Contribution of concrete cognition to emotion: Neutral symptoms as elicitors of worry about cancer. *Journal of Applied Psychology*, **74**, 787–796.

Freeston, M.H., Gagnon, F., Ladouceur, R., Thibodeau, N., Letarte, H., & Rhéaume, J. (1994). Health-related intrusive thoughts. *Journal of Psychosomatic Research*, **38**, 203–215.

Freeston, M.H., & Ladouceur, R. (1997). What do patients do with their obsessive thoughts? *Behaviour Research and Therapy*, **35**, 335–348.

Freeston, M.H., & Ladouceur, R. (in press). Exposure and response prevention for obsessive thoughts. *Cognitive and Behavioural Practice*.

Freeston, M.H., Ladouceur, R., Gagnon, F., Thibodeau, N., Rhéaume, J., Letarte, L., & Bujold, A. (1997). Cognitive-behavioural treatment of obsessional thoughts: A controlled study. *Journal of Consulting and Clinical Psychology*, **65**, 405–413.

Freeston, M.H., Langlois, F., Ladouceur, R., Lemay, D., Laberge, M., & Gosselin, P. (1998, March). Towards understanding worry: What do high-school students worry about and why do they keep on worrying? In *The young and the old*, Paper session presented at the Annual Meeting of the Anxiety Disorders Association of America, Boston, MA.

Freeston, M.H., Rhéaume, J., & Ladouceur, R. (1996). Correcting faulty appraisals of obsessive thoughts. *Behaviour Research and Therapy*, **34**, 443–446.

Furer, P., & Walker, J.R. (1998). *Intense illness worry: Client treatment manual*. Unpublished manuscript, University of Manitoba.

Furer, P., Walker, J.R., Chartier, M., & Stein, M.B. (1997). Hypochondriacal concerns and somatization in panic disorder. *Depression and Anxiety*, **6**, 78–85.

Furer, P., Walker, J.R., & Vincent, N. (1999, November). *Cognitive behavioral group treatment for hypochondriasis*. Poster session presented at the meeting of the Association for Advancement of Behavior Therapy, Toronto, Canada.

Hathaway, D. (1986). Effect of preoperative instruction on postoperative outcomes: A meta-analysis. *Nursing Research*, **35**, 269–275.

Himle, J.A., Crystal, D., Curtis, G.C., & Fluent, T.E. (1991). Mode of onset of simple phobia subtypes: Further evidence of heterogeneity. *Psychiatry Research*, **36**, 37–43.

Horne, D.J., Vatmanidis, P., & Careri, A. (1994a). Preparing patients for invasive medical and surgical procedures 1: Adding behavioural and cognitive interventions. *Behavioural Medicine*, **20**, 5–13.

Horne, D.J., Vatmanidis, P., & Careri, A. (1994b). Preparing patients for invasive medical and surgical procedures 2: Using psychological interventions with adults and children. *Behavioural Medicine*, **20**, 15–21.

Johnston, M., & Vögele, C. (1993). Benefits of psychological preparations for surgery: A meta-analysis. *Annals of Behavioral Medicine*, **15**, 245–256.

Kellner, R.J. (1986). *Somatization and hypochondriasis*. New York: Praeger.

Kobak, K.A., Greist, J.H., Jefferson, J.W., Katzelnick, D.J., & Henk, H.J. (1998). Behavioral versus pharmacological treatments of obsessive-compulsive disorder: A meta-analysis. *Psychopharmacology*, **136**, 205–216.

Ladouceur, R., Freeston, M.H., Gagnon, F., Thibodeau, N., & Dumont, J. (1993). Idiographic considerations in the cognitive-behavioural treatment of obsessional thoughts. *Journal of Behavior Therapy and Experimental Psychiatry*, **24**, 301–310.

Langlois, F., Dugas, M.J., Léger, E., & Ladouceur, R. (1998, November). *Investigat-*

*ing the impact of health-related worry in the treatment of GAD: A pilot study.* Communication presented at the Annual Meeting of the Association for Advancement of Behaviour Therapy, Washington.

Léger, E., Freeston, M.H., & Ladouceur, R. (1998). Cognitive behavioural treatment of GAD in a patient with multiple sclerosis: A case study. *Behavioural and Cognitive Psychotherapy*, **26**, 261–270.

Mathews, A., & Ridgeway, V. (1984). Psychological preparations for surgery. In A. Steptoe & A. Mathews (Eds.), *Health care and human behaviour*. London: Academic Press.

O'Halloran, C.M., & Altmaier, E.M. (1995). The efficacy of preparation for surgery and invasive medical procedures. *Patient Education and Counseling*, **25**, 9–16.

Rachman, S. (1998). A cognitive theory of obsessions. *Behaviour Research and Therapy*, **36**, 385–402.

Robbins, J.M., Kirmayer, L.J., & Kapusta, M.A. (1990). Illness worry and disability in fibromyalgia syndrome. *International Journal of Psychiatry in Medicine*, **20**, 49–63.

Schultheis, K., Peterson, L., & Selby, V. (1987). Preparation for stressful medical procedures and person x treatment interactions. *Clinical Psychology Review*, **7**, 329–352.

Smeltzer, S.C. (1994). The concerns of women with multiple sclerosis. *Qualitative Health Research*, **4**, 480–502.

Suinn, R.M. (1990). *Anxiety management training: A behavior therapy*. New York: Plenum Press.

Walker, J.R., Vincent, N., Furer, P., Cox, B.J., & Kjernisted, K.D. (1999). Treatment preference in hypochondriasis. *Journal of Behavior Therapy and Experimental Psychiatry*, **30**, 251–258.

Warwick, H.M.C., Clark, D.M., Cobb, A.M., & Salkovskis, P.M. (1996). A controlled trial of cognitive-behavioural treatment of hypochondriasis. *British Journal of Psychiatry*, **169**, 189–195.

Weigers, M.E., Chesler, M.A., Zebrack, B.J., & Goldman, S. (1998). Self-reported worries among long-term survivors of childhood cancer and their peers. *Journal of Psychosocial Oncology*, **16**, 1–23.

Westra, H.A., & Stewart, S.H. (1998). Cognitive behavioural therapy and pharmacotherapy; complementary or contradictory approaches to the treatment of anxiety? *Clinical Psychology Review*, **18**, 307–340.

Whelan, T.A., & Kirby, R.J. (1998). Advantages for children and their families of psychological preparation for hospitalization and surgery. *Journal of Family Studies*, **4**, 35–51.

Wilson-Barnett, J. (1994). Preparing patients for invasive medical and surgical procedures 3: Policy implications for implementing specific psychological interventions. *Behavioural Medicine*, **20**, 23–26.

World Health Organization (1993). *The ICD-10 classification of mental and behavioural disorders: Diagnostic criteria*. World Health Organization: Geneva.

Chapter 8

# PHARMACOLOGICAL MANAGEMENT OF HYPOCHONDRIASIS AND RELATED DISORDERS

*Murray W. Enns\*, Kevin Kjernisted\*, and Mark Lander\**

## INTRODUCTION

Several different medications have been investigated for the treatment of hypochondriasis and related disorders. Pharmacological treatments for delusional forms of hypochondriasis (categorized as 'delusional disorder somatic type' in DSM-IV) have been studied for at least 25 years. Studies of pharmacological treatments for neurotic illness worry (categorized as 'hypochondriasis', a somatoform disorder, in DSM-IV) have principally been published in the last 10 years. The present chapter will review available evidence of the effectiveness of pharmacotherapy for hypochondriasis and delusional hypochondriasis. In addition, we will discuss possible mechanisms of action of the drug treatments, the implications of comorbidity and the practical aspects of pharmacological management of these conditions.

The existing literature on the treatment of hypochondriasis provides preliminary evidence of the effectiveness of antidepressant pharmacotherapy, particularly the selective serotonin reuptake inhibitors (SSRIs). However, the literature is small and only one placebo-controlled trial has been reported (Fallon et al., 1996). Several published studies have reported that DSM-III-R defined hypochondriasis commonly coexists with various emotional disorders and substance abuse disorders (Bach,

---

\*University of Manitoba, Canada

*Health Anxiety*
Edited by G.J.G. Asmundson, S. Taylor & B.J. Cox
© 2001 John Wiley & Sons Ltd.

Nutzinger, & Hartl, 1996; Barsky, Wyshak & Klerman, 1992; Noyes et al., 1994). As such, patients with hypochondriasis may require treatments directed at more than one Axis I disorder. Since the SSRI antidepressants have a broad spectrum of action on mood and anxiety symptoms, it is possible that a patient with a comorbid condition could experience improvement in both conditions during SSRI treatment. The diagnostically non-specific action of the SSRI antidepressants limits the conclusions that can be drawn regarding any presumed physiological abnormalities associated with hypochondriasis.

For the purposes of the present chapter, we consider 'delusional hypochondriasis' to be equivalent to DSM-IV defined delusional disorder–somatic type. The essential feature of this disorder is a non-bizarre delusion with a central theme involving health, bodily functions, or sensations. The most common themes in this form of delusional disorder are infestation (such as parasites or foreign bodies under the skin), being ugly or misshapen, or emitting a foul odor (Munro & Chmara, 1982; also see Chapter 13).

A large number of reports have indicated that pimozide, a unique diphenylbutylpiperidine antipsychotic medication, is effective in treating delusional hypochondriasis. Our review of this literature indicates that delusions of parasites may be a subtype of delusional hypochondriasis that is particularly responsive to pimozide treatment. In fact, only two small placebo-controlled studies demonstrating the effectiveness of pimozide in delusional hypochondriasis have been reported, and both studies involved patients with delusions of parasites (Hamann & Avnstorp, 1982; Ungvari & Vladar, 1986). It is possible that an antipruritic effect of pimozide related to opiate receptor blockade contributes to the effectiveness of pimozide in delusional parasitosis.

The evidence that other forms of delusional hypochondriasis are responsive to pimozide is considerably weaker. Delusional hypochondriasis involving imagined defects in appearance may represent the upper end of a continuum of appearance preoccupations sharing features with obsessive-compulsive disorder (OCD; Hollander, 1998; Phillips, McElroy, Keck, Hudson, & Pope, 1994). Such preoccupations (whether of delusional or non-delusional intensity) are classified in DSM-IV as Body Dysmorphic Disorder (BDD), a condition which appears to respond to fluvoxamine (an SSRI agent with demonstrated anti-obsessional effects; Phillips, Dwight, & McElroy, 1998).

The clinical care of patients with hypochondriasis can be challenging. Whether these patients are offered pharmacotherapy, cognitive-behavioral therapy, or neither, their overall health care needs to be carefully managed, preferably by an interested and empathic primary care physician. The establishment of regular appointments that are not contingent upon symptoms, and restraint from the ordering of excessive diagnostic tests and treatments, especially invasive ones, are fundamental to the management of hypochondriasis. Psychoeducation about the nature of hypochondriasis and the potential effects of treatment should allow patients to develop realistic diagnostic and treatment expectations.

# HYPOCHONDRIASIS

## Review of Pharmacotherapy Studies

The psychiatric literature on the pharmacologic treatment of hypochondriasis is small and is dominated by case reports and case series. Perhaps this is because, until recently, hypochondriasis was viewed by many as a primarily psychological disorder related to personality. As recently as 1985 a major psychiatric textbook, Kaplan and Saddock's *Comprehensive Textbook of Psychiatry*, stated that 'unless hypochondriasis is part of a depressive disorder with an overt affective disturbance, medications and ECT are without effect'. The evidence reviewed below is certainly sufficient to refute such therapeutic nihilism. The studies reported to date suggest that antidepressant medications may provide significant relief of hypochondriacal anxiety, even in the absence of overt depressive illness.

Kamlana and Gray (1988) authored the first report of successful treatment of hypochondriasis with an antidepressant agent. Their patient had 'obsessive ruminations' about having acquired AIDS. The patient was treated successfully with intravenous clomipramine and maintained his improvement on oral clomipramine. Wesner and Noyes (1991) treated 10 subjects with 'illness phobia' using up to 150 mg of imipramine per day. All of the eight patients who received imipramine for at least 4 weeks achieved moderate or greater improvement. Viswanathan and Paradis (1991) reported a single case of 'cancer phobia' that responded very well to 40 mg per day of fluoxetine but was unresponsive to adequate trials of several alternative treatments including buspirone, desipramine, and behavioral psychotherapy. A group from Columbia University reported a series of six patients with hypochondriasis, of whom two received a trial of treatment with fluoxetine (Fallon, Javitch, Hollander, & Liebowitz, 1991). Both patients showed marked improvement on 60 mg per day of fluoxetine. Stone (1993) reported one patient who achieved a full remission of hypochondriasis with 225 mg per day of clomipramine. This patient's response was particularly impressive in view of the chronicity of his illness (10 years) and his unresponsiveness to multiple previous medication treatments (benzodiazepines, tricyclic antidepressants, neuroleptics, and fluoxetine). In 1993 Fallon and colleagues reported a relatively large open-label trial of high-dose fluoxetine for hypochondriasis (Fallon et al., 1993). In this trial, 10 of 16 patients were much improved at the end of 12 weeks of treatment with 20 to 80 mg per day of fluoxetine.

To date, only a single randomized, placebo-controlled trial of pharmacotherapy for hypochondriasis has been reported (Fallon et al., 1996). The authors indicated that this was a preliminary mid-study report but, to our knowledge, no final publication on this study has followed. Twenty patients were randomized to receive either placebo or fluoxetine. Half of the patients had failed to benefit from prior psychotherapy and 85% had had unsatisfactory responses with prior pharmacotherapy. The results of the study favored fluoxetine, but failed to achieve statistical significance. Eight of 12 patients (67%) who received fluoxetine were responders versus four of eight (50%) on placebo. Four patients dropped out during the first few weeks, either because of side-effects or because of a desire to no longer participate. However, the investigators observed that there had been noteworthy improvement among eight of the 10 patients who completed 12 weeks of acute-phase treatment with fluoxetine and considered this result encouraging.

Our group has recently completed an open-label trial of nefazodone (200 to 500 mg per day) in 11 patients with DSM-IV hypochondriasis. Two patients dropped out of the trial and nine patients completed 8 weeks of treatment. Five out of nine patients who completed the trial were rated as 'much improved' at the end of the trial (Kjernisted, Enns, & Lander, submitted).

Studies of pharmacologic treatment of hypochondriasis have predominantly used fluoxetine (the first of the SSRIs available in North America). The side-effects associated with fluoxetine use are generally mild (to moderate) and the drug is typically well tolerated. Fairly common side-effects include headache, nausea or other gastrointestinal complaints, insomnia (or less frequently, sedation), and sexual side-effects, most notably delayed orgasm. In general, the side-effects associated with other SSRIs (fluvoxamine, sertraline, paroxetine, and citalopram) are closely comparable to the side-effects of fluoxetine. However, individual patients may experience differential tolerance of, or response to, the different SSRI agents. In contrast, clomipramine (a serotonin selective tricyclic antidepressant) has a fairly typical tricyclic-like side-effect profile including anticholinergic effects (e.g., dry mouth, constipation, possible urinary retention), antihistaminic effects (e.g., sedation, increased appetite, weight gain), tremor, orthostatic hypotension, and EKG changes.

In summary, there is preliminary evidence that antidepressant medications, particularly the serotonin-selective agents (fluoxetine and clomipramine), may be effective for the treatment of hypochondriasis in a substantial proportion of patients. The number of patients reported in the existing literature is very small. However, the favorable response to pharmacotherapy in some patients has been noteworthy in view of the severity and chronicity of illness, the absence of comorbidity with major depression, and the prior history of treatment refractoriness. While further controlled trials of medication treatment are clearly needed, the SSRIs should be considered a reasonable treatment option for hypochondriasis.

## Comorbidity in Hypochondriasis— Implications for Treatment

Studies of patients with DSM-III-R defined hypochondriasis have demonstrated that this diagnosis frequently coexists with other mood, anxiety, somatoform, and substance abuse disorders (Barsky et al., 1992; Noyes et al., 1994). Barsky and colleagues (1992) found a lifetime history of major depression in 43%, dysthymic disorder in 45%, generalized anxiety disorder in 71%, panic disorder in 17%, phobias in 43%, OCD in 10%, somatization disorder in 21%, and substance abuse or dependence in 17% of 42 patients with hypochondriasis. Similarly, Noyes and colleagues (1994) found a history of any depressive disorder in 44%, any anxiety disorder in 22%, and any substance use disorder in 20% of 50 patients with hypochondriasis. Bach and colleagues (1996) examined this issue from a different perspective. They examined 82 outpatients with anxiety disorders using a polydiagnostic interview (including DSM-III, DSM-III-R, and ICD-10 criteria) and found that about half of their patients exhibited the diagnostic features of hypochondriasis, regardless of the diagnostic system used. Noyes (1999) has noted that there is considerable phenomenological overlap between hypochondriasis and several anxiety disorders. Also, it is well known that depressed patients frequently experience hypochondriacal concerns as part of their depressive illness (Demopulos et al., 1996; Kellner, Fava, Lisansky, Perini, & Zielezny, 1986; Kramer-Ginsberg, Greenwald, Aisen, & Brod-Miller, 1989).

These observations emphasize the importance of comprehensiveness in the phenomenological assessment of patients with hypochondriasis. Patients with hypochondriasis may benefit from psychotherapeutic or pharmacologic treatment directed at more than one disorder simultaneously. Hypochondriacal symptoms occurring with melancholic depression (Kellner et al., 1986) or panic disorder (Noyes, Reich, Clancy, &

O'Gorman, 1986) appear to improve with the treatment of the associated disorder. In the case of pharmacotherapy, patients may benefit from the broad spectrum of therapeutic effects that the SSRI antidepressants have been demonstrated to possess; indeed, controlled studies have demonstrated that SSRI antidepressants are effective in major depression, dysthymia, panic disorder, social phobia, and OCD.

## DELUSIONAL HYPOCHONDRIASIS

### Review of Pharmacotherapy Studies

There are a large number of published reports on the treatment of delusional hypochondriasis with various psychotropic medications. Delusional hypochondriasis has been identified by a variety of terms in the psychiatric literature including 'delusional disorder—somatic type' (DSM-III-R and DSM-IV), 'monosymptomatic hypochondriacal psychosis' (e.g., Munro & Chmara, 1982), 'monosymptomatic hypochondriasis' (e.g., Brotman & Jenike, 1984), 'delusional dysmorphosis' (e.g., Fernandez, 1988), 'delusional parasitosis' (e.g., Reilly, Jopling, & Beard, 1978), and 'delusions of infestation' (e.g., Hamann & Avnstorp, 1982). Using these search terms we were able to identify a total of 50 reports through a combination of MEDLINE and bibliography-driven literature searches. A summary of these studies is presented in Table 8.1 and Table 8.2.

Although there have been a large number of published reports on the pharmacologic treatment of delusional hypochondriasis, the great majority of these reports are single cases or small case series. This introduces a substantial problem in the interpretation of the results. In most instances the authors of the reports have not operationalized the terms used to describe the degree of improvement of their patients. As a result, it is difficult to make comparisons between reports. Whenever possible in the present chapter (including Tables 8.1 and 8.2), patient outcomes have been reported using the terms selected by the authors. In general, the terms 'remission', 'complete response', and 'excellent response' have been used to describe recovery to an asymptomatic state. The terms 'response', 'good response', 'positive response', and 'improved' have been used to describe clinically substantial improvement, but with residual symptoms.

One of the most influential authors in this literature, Alistair Munro, published several reports on a large case series describing the treatment of 'monosymptomatic delusional hypochondriasis' with the antipsychotic medication pimozide (Munro, 1988a, 1988b; Munro & Chmara, 1982).

**Table 8.1** Pimozide treatment of delusional hypochondriasis

| Authors | Number of patients | Study design | Assessment methods | Content of delusion | Outcome | Comments |
|---|---|---|---|---|---|---|
| Riding & Munro (1975a, b) | 5 | Case series | Clinical | Odor, parasites, appearance | 5/5 responded | |
| Reilly (1975) | 1 | Single case | Clinical | Several symptoms in the throat | Very good response | Amitriptyline, clomipramine and minor tranquilizers not helpful |
| Munro (1978a) | 1 | Single case | Clinical | Parasites | Positive but incomplete response | |
| Munro (1978b) | 1 | Single case | Clinical | Parasites | Very good response | |
| Munro (1978c) | 4 | Case series | Clinical | Parasites | 4/4 positive response | |
| Reilly et al. (1978) | 1 | Single case | Clinical | Parasites | Very positive response | |
| Dorian (1979) | 1 | Single case | Clinical | Parasites | Very good response | Rapid response (few days) |
| Munro (1980) | 26 | Case series | Clinical | Appearance, odor, parasites | Excellent response 19/26; fair response 7/26 | Author prescribed 2–12 mg of pimozide/day. |
| Hamann (1982) | 1 | Single case | Clinical | Parasites in nails 'onychotillomania' | Good response | |
| Hamann & Avnstorp (1982) | 11 | Double blind crossover trial vs. placebo | BPRS | Parasites | 10/11 improved with pimozide (significant on BPRS ratings) | |

*continued overleaf*

**Table 8.1** (*continued*)

| Authors | Number of patients | Study design | Assessment methods | Content of delusion | Outcome | Comments |
|---|---|---|---|---|---|---|
| Munro & Chmara (1982) Munro (1988a, b) | 43 | Case series | Clinical | Appearance, odor, parasites | Excellent response 32/43; partial response 9/43; no response 2/43 | Based on a mail-out survey of dermatologists |
| Lyell (1983) | 66 | Case series | Clinical | Parasites | 44/66 improved | |
| Lindskov & Baadsgaard (1985) | 14 | Case series with longitudinal follow-up | Clinical | Parasites | 10/14 responded 7/10 stayed well without pimozide | 3/10 successfully maintained with intermittent treatment |
| Ungvari & Vladar (1986) | 10 | Double-blind crossover trial | 7-Point rating scale | Parasites | 10/10 better with pimozide and worse during placebo | |
| Reilly & Batchelor (1986) | 21 | Case series | Clinical | Parasites | 17/21 responded | |
| Rapp (1986) | 1 | Single case | Clinical | Parasites | Dramatic remission | Improvement persisted after drug discontinuation |
| Sheppard et al. (1986) | 2 | Case series | Clinical | Parasites | One good and one partial response | |
| Renvoize et al. (1987) | 1 | Single case | Clinical | Parasites | Very good response | Case associated with dementia of Alzheimer type |

| | | | | | | |
|---|---|---|---|---|---|---|
| Fernandez (1988) | 1 | Single case | Clinical | Appearance | Very good response | Patient had kidney failure due to glomerulonephritis |
| Matas & Robinson (1988) | 1 | Single case | Clinical | Parasites | Partial response | |
| Bond (1989) | 1 | Single case | Clinical | Parasites | Good response | Patient had AIDS, and some 'organic' mental signs |
| Holmes (1989) | 1 | Single case | Clinical | Parasites | Remitted | |
| Mitchell (1989) | 1 | Single case | Clinical | Parasites | Good response | Patient had a 6 year history of symptoms |
| Damiani et al. (1990) | 1 | Single case | Clinical | Parasites | Good response | |
| Chiu et al. (1990) | 1 | Single case | Clinical | Sexually transmitted disease | Good response | Comorbid depression |
| Ulzen (1993) | 1 | Single case | Clinical | Odor and appearance | Remission | Adolescent case similar to adult descriptions |
| Wang & Lee (1997) | 1 | Single case | Clinical | 'Toxic root in forehead' | Partial responses to both pimozide & haloperidol | Medical complications—self injury/infection |
| Zomer et al. (1998) | 18 | Case series | Clinical | Parasites | Remission 6/18; improved 5/18; no change 7/18 | Pimozide dose (1–5mg) may have been too low |
| Maeda et al. (1998) | 1 | Single case | Clinical | Parasites (oral) | Remission | First reported case of oral parasitosis |

*Notes*: Descriptions of patient outcomes were based on the authors' reports and were not necessarily applied consistently. BPRS = Brief Psychiatric Rating Scale.

**Table 8.2**   Delusional hypochondriasis—treatment with other agents

| Authors | Agent(s) used (no. of patients) | Study design | Assessment methods | Content of delusion | Outcome | Comments |
|---|---|---|---|---|---|---|
| Gould & Gragg (1976) | Trifluoperazine (2) | Case series | Clinical | Parasites | Moderately good response in both | |
| Frithz (1979) | Fluphenazine (10) Flupenthixol (5) | Case series | Clinical | Parasites (14) Fungal infection (1) | Remitted (11); improved (3); no response (1) | |
| Cashman & Pollock (1983) | Imipramine (1) | Single case | Clinical | Appearance | 'Encouraging and dramatic response' | Did not respond to pimozide |
| Brotman & Jenike (1984) | Doxepin (1) Imipramine (1) | Case series | Clinical | Appearance (1) Odor (1) | Both improved | Neuroleptics no help for either patient |
| Tollefson (1985) | Amoxapine (1) | Single case | Clinical | 'Bones crackling and valves bursting' | Remission | Patient also had major depression; no response to phenelzine |
| Pylko & Sicignan (1985) | Nortriptyline (1) | Single case | Clinical | Parasites | Remitted | Haloperidol and chlorpromazine were not helpful |
| Andrews et al. (1986) | Haloperidol (3) | Case series | Clinical | Parasites | 3/3 responded | 2/3 maintained improvement |
| Ross et al. (1987) | Clomipramine (1) | Single case | Clinical | Odor | Complete response | Only partial response to pimozide |
| Sondheimer (1988) | Clomipramine (1) | Single case | Clinical | Appearance (Koro-like) | Partial response | Adolescent case; haldol was unhelpful |

| Study | Treatment | Design | Setting | Focus | Outcome | Comments |
|---|---|---|---|---|---|---|
| Fernando (1988) | Clomipramine (1) | Single case | Clinical | Appearance (Koro-like) | Marked improvement | Pimozide had not been helpful |
| Shah (1988) | Haloperidol (1) | Single case | Clinical | Parasites | Considerable improvement | |
| Scarone & Gambini (1991) | Thioridazine (4) | Case series | Clinical | Various general illnesses (1 AIDS) | Response in 3/4 | |
| Srinivasan et al. (1994) | ECT (8) Haldol (2) Chlorpromazine (3) Trifluoperazine (6) | Case series | Clinical | Parasites (ears & skin) | Improvement: ECT 7/8 Haldol 2/2 Chlorpromazine 2/3 Trifluoperazine 5/6 | |
| Gallucci & Beard (1995) | Risperidone (1) | Single case | Clinical | Parasites | Considerable improvement | |
| Brooke et al. (1996) | Trifluoperazine (1) | Single case | Clinical | Appearance | Good response | Comorbid learning disability |
| Songer & Roman (1996) | Risperidone (1) Clozapine (1) | Case series | Clinical | Other | Risperidone 1/1 much improved; clozapine 1/1 improved | |
| Kalivas & Kalivas (1997) | Sertraline (14) | Case series | Clinical | Parasites | 11/14 unimproved | 2 sertraline non-responders got better with neuroleptics |
| Perkins (1999) | Sertraline (2) | Case series | Clinical | Appearance/brain tumor | Good response | Limited description of cases |

*Notes:* Descriptions of patient outcomes were based on the authors' reports and were not necessarily applied consistently. ECT = Electroconvulsive Therapy.

Munro's case series included 50 patients, of whom 43 complied with prescribed treatment using pimozide in doses of 2 to 12 mg per day. Thirty-two of 43 treated patients were judged to have had an 'excellent' response, including return to full function and total or near-total remission of symptoms (Munro, 1988a). Unfortunately, Munro did not report a breakdown of response rates for different types of delusions.

In a postal survey of 374 dermatologists, Lyell (1983) obtained information about 282 patients with delusions of parasitic skin infestation. A total of 66 patients had been prescribed pimozide (2 to 12 mg per day), of whom 44 responded to treatment. As a rule, relapse occurred upon stopping the drug. A subsequent report by Reilly and Batchelor (1986) was also based on a postal survey of dermatologists (N = 386). Fifty-three patients were identified as meeting the authors' criteria for delusional parasitosis. Thirty-four patients received psychopharmacologic treatment (with a variety of agents), of whom 20 were described as having a good response. Of note was the observation that 17 out of 20 good responders had received pimozide. The 14 non-responders to psychopharmacologic treatment had received a number of different agents including antidepressants, anxiolytics and antipsychotics, and only four patients who received pimozide were considered non-responsive.

Only two small placebo-controlled studies of the effectiveness of psychotropic medication in delusional hypochondriasis have been reported (Hamann & Avnstorp, 1982; Ungvari & Vladar, 1986). Both studies evaluated the effectiveness of pimozide in the treatment of delusions of infestation. The first of these studies (Hamann & Avnstorp, 1982) compared pimozide to placebo in 11 patients using a double-blind cross-over technique and the Brief Psychiatric Rating Scale to assess outcome. Ten of the 11 patients experienced considerable improvement during pimozide treatment, while two patients experienced partial improvement during placebo treatment. Ungvari and Vladar (1986) compared pimozide to placebo in 10 patients using a double-blind on/off/on study design and a reliable 7-point rating scale developed for the study. All 10 patients showed improvement of their condition during pimozide treatment and worsening of symptoms during placebo substitution. None of the patients showed complete remission of symptoms.

Published case reports have suggested that alternative classes of antipsychotic medications may also be useful in the treatment of delusional hypochondriasis. For example, there have been reports of the effectiveness of trifluoperazine in delusional parasitosis (Gould & Gragg, 1976—two cases) and in the treatment of dysmorphic delusions (Brooke, Collacott, & Bhaumik, 1996—one case). Haloperidol has been reported to be effective in treating delusional parasitosis (Andrews, Bellard, & Walter-

Ryan, 1986—three cases). Thioridazine was evaluated in a series of four patients with a variety of hypochondriacal delusions, and three patients showed at least a partial response (Scarone & Gambini, 1991). One report of the use of depot-injections of fluphenazine or flupenthixol suggested a favorable response in 14 out of 15 cases of delusions of infestation (Frithz, 1979). Finally, two recent reports involving a total of three cases observed positive responses of somatic delusions to 'atypical' antipsychotic agents (i.e., risperidone, clozapine; Songer & Roman, 1996; Gallucci & Beard, 1995). Unfortunately, since there are no published trials comparing the effectiveness of different antipsychotic agents, it is impossible to definitively conclude that pimozide is *uniquely* effective in the treatment of delusional hypochondriasis.

The mechanism of action of pimozide in delusional hypochondriasis has been the subject of speculation in a number of reports (Bond, 1989; Opler & Feinberg, 1991; Reilly, 1988). Like other neuroleptic antipsychotic agents, pimozide potently blocks postsynaptic dopamine receptors. Pimozide also has a number of pharmacologic effects that distinguish it from other antipsychotic drugs including a relative lack of alpha-adrenergic receptor blocking effects, blockade of calcium channels, and selective, competitive antagonism of endogenous opiates at opiate receptor sites (Creese, Feinberg, & Snyder, 1976; Opler & Feinberg, 1991). If, indeed, pimozide has specific efficacy in delusional hypochondriasis, then some of these properties may be of relevance. The most intriguing speculation has been that the opiate receptor-blocking properties of pimozide (shared, to a lesser degree, with haloperidol) may account for an antipruritic effect which enhances the action of the drug in delusional parasitosis (Bond, 1989; Reilly, 1988). Thus, pimozide's apparently dramatic effect in many patients with this subtype of delusional hypochondriasis may result from the combination of effects on delusional thinking and suppression of central nervous system recognition of abnormal skin sensations.

Pimozide has a relatively favorable side-effect profile, and most patients tolerate the drug well. Relatively common side-effects include extrapyramidal symptoms (akathisia or parkinsonism which generally respond to anticholinergic medications), drowsiness or insomnia, and mild anticholinergic effects (Bond, 1989; Hamann & Avnstorp, 1982; Munro, 1988a, 1988b). As with other dopamine receptor-blocking drugs, the potential for tardive dyskinesia exists. At high doses there is a potential for significant cardiovascular effects including QT interval prolongation, which has been attributed to calcium channel-blocking properties of the drug (Opler & Feinberg, 1991). Munro (Munro & Chmara, 1982; Munro, 1988) noted that a significant minority of patients develop postpsychotic depression while on pimozide; however, most of these patients respond to the addition of an antidepressant medication.

## Delusional Content: Implications for Treatment

As noted, a variety of delusional themes may be manifested in delusional hypochondriasis. The majority of reports documenting the effectiveness of pimozide in this condition have involved patients with delusions of infestation. Two important questions arise from this observation. First, do delusions of infestation respond to other classes of psychotropic medication? Second, does delusional hypochondriasis respond to pimozide when other delusional themes are present?

There have been a small number of reports of the treatment of delusional hypochondriasis with several different antidepressant agents. The agents used have included SSRIs, tricyclic antidepressants, and amoxapine (an atypical antidepressant that also has some antipsychotic properties). Two of these reports have dealt with delusions of parasitosis (Kalivas & Kalivas, 1997; Pylko & Sicignan, 1985). The earlier of these two reports describes a single case of a non-depressed woman who failed to respond to chlorpromazine and haloperidol, but was successfully treated with nortriptyline (a tricyclic antidepressant). In contrast, Kalivas and Kalivas (1997) treated a series of 14 patients using 50 to 100 mg per day of sertraline (an SSRI) and found that 11 of the 14 did not improve. The remaining case reports of antidepressant medication treatment of delusional hypochondriasis have described the treatment of delusions with themes *not* involving parasites (Brotman & Jenike, 1984; Fernando, 1988; Perkins, 1999; Tollefson, 1985; Ross, Siddiqui, & Matas, 1987; Sondheimer, 1988). These case reports, predominantly involving delusions about dysmorphic appearance or bodily odor, are consistent with the early observations of Riding and Munro (1975a, 1975b) who noted that some patients with 'neurotically determined' dysmorphophobias may have a different variety of illness which is unresponsive to pimozide.

'Dysmorphophobia' is categorized in DSM-IV as BDD, a somatoform disorder. The essential feature of BDD is a preoccupation with an imagined defect in appearance. When this preoccupation is of delusional intensity, DSM-IV notes that both delusional disorder–somatic type and BDD may be diagnosed (Phillips & Hollander, 1996). Several reports have been published evaluating the response of BDD to pharmacotherapy. In contrast to the literature on delusional hypochondriasis, the dominant class of psychotropic agents that have been studied in BDD is antidepressants, emphasizing the SSRIs. Three groups of investigators have reported the results of open-label treatment of BDD in fair-sized case series (Hollander et al., 1994; Perugi et al., 1996; Phillips, 1996; Phillips et al., 1998; Phillips et al., 1994). These studies provide preliminary evidence of the effectiveness of fluvoxamine (an SSRI). Phillips and colleagues (1994) reported that none of eight patients treated for BDD with pimozide had shown a positive outcome. Significantly, this study also reported a comparison of delusional and non-delusional forms of BDD and found no major systematic differences between these two groups. Both delusional and non-delusional forms of BDD appeared to be responsive to SSRI antidepressants and unresponsive to pimozide.

It has been suggested that BDD may be an obsessive-compulsive spectrum disorder (Hollander, 1998). Hollander noted that the features of OCD and BDD overlap in a number of respects including clinical features (e.g., repetitive, intrusive thoughts or behaviors), demographics, and response to pharmacological therapy. The level of insight observed in BDD parallels the situation in OCD; patients vary from obsessive uncertainty to overvalued ideas to delusional conviction about their dysmorphic features (Hollander et al., 1990). The relationship among these disorders (BDD, delusional disorder–somatic type, and OCD) clearly requires further study. Caution is certainly needed when response to the same treatment (in this case SSRI antidepressants) is considered in psychiatric nosology (Vitiello & De Leon, 1990).

In summary, the available literature on the treatment of delusional hypochondriasis is limited in a number of respects. These limitations include the failure in most instances to distinguish between delusional illnesses with different themes, the small number of patients who have been treated in controlled trials, and the complete lack of randomized trials comparing active treatments. Nevertheless, the consistency of reports on the effectiveness of pimozide, the frequent observation of patient non-responsiveness to other agents, and the dramatic and lasting effects of pimozide treatment in anecdotal reports provide support for the use of this possibly specific treatment. The existing literature most convincingly supports the use of pimozide for a particular subgroup of patients with delusional hypochondriasis, namely delusions of infestation/parasites. Available evidence suggests that dysmorphic delusions may represent the upper end of a continuum of disorders classified as BDD, and sharing some features with OCD. These disorders appear to be responsive to SSRI antidepressants.

## CLINICAL APPROACH TO THE PATIENT WITH HYPOCHONDRIASIS

Hypochondriasis and related conditions offer the interested health care professional an opportunity to practice elements of the true art of medicine. These patients present a potentially rewarding experience for those who are ready to take up the challenge. Tremendous disability, at times even invalidism, where the individual is bedridden by all consuming worry and preoccupation with illness (rather than by the relatively mild physical symptoms they may be suffering; Moore & Jefferson, 1996), can be transformed into a healthy, meaningful, and productive existence.

Pharmacological and cognitive behavioral treatment approaches to excessive illness worry offer hope to patients, their families, and their primary care physicians. In our experience, the key to success is a biopsychosocial approach[1] (Engel, 1978; Moore & Jefferson, 1996). A review of the literature and our own clinical management, which has integrated many of the recommendations by pioneers in the field of hypochondriasis, will be outlined in the following paragraphs. We acknowledge the writings of several authors in formulating our approach: Adler (1981); Rosen, Kleinman, and Kabon (1982); Lipowski (1988); Kellner (1991, 1992); Bass & Benjamin (1993); Lipsitt (1995); Barsky (1996); and Escobar (1996).

## Treatment Strategies

A general approach to treating the patient with hypochondriasis is guided by a principle elucidated by Adler (1981), who stated

> The hypochondriacal patient does not seek cure but palliation through a long-term relationship with the physician. If cure is the goal of physicians they will almost certainly be disappointed (p. 1395).

## Right to a Relationship

Many patients with hypochondriacal anxiety do not feel they have the right to a relationship. This is difficult to imagine given how demanding of the physician's time some of these patients can be. The sick role appears to help some patients feel worthy of the attention of others. For whatever reason, they have developed a style of communication using symptoms as common ground for relating to others. Unfortunately, this tends to distance others, including physicians who are not able to effectively eradicate their symptoms or worries. In some instances friends and family avoid or abandon the patient and the only acquaintances left may be other people with hypochondriasis. Later in the therapeutic process, these individuals may benefit from approaches such as group therapy (e.g., groups focusing on stress management) or other interventions to assist them in improving the quality of their relationships. The establishment of a

---

[1] The biopsychosocial approach refers to a comprehensive approach to a patient's difficulties that takes into account biological, psychological, behavioral, interpersonal, and social factors.

relationship and therapeutic alliance with a single primary care physician who is responsible for coordinating all of the patient's medical care is an essential first step in managing hypochondriasis (Barsky, 1996). This physician becomes the 'gatekeeper' through which all specialist consultation and care must flow. This role prevents redundant and excessive medical care and provides the patient with a 'stable, long-term relationship that is dependable, consistent, and not manipulable' (Barsky, 1996, p. 49).

## Regular Appointments

The optimal management of the patient with hypochondriasis requires regularly scheduled appointments with a primary care physician which are not contingent on symptoms. The length of time between visits and the duration of appointments should be discussed and agreed upon by both parties. During the initial visits, a review of medical history and previous investigations along with any additional steps to rule out significant medical illness are required. Once pharmacotherapy (if indicated) is established, scheduling a half-hour appointment once a month is probably reasonable. The physician must make every effort to maintain the agreed upon schedule. Patients needs to know that they can depend upon the physician for emergency care and be reassured that the physician will be there for them in the future. At the same time, boundaries around such things as phone calls must be established early on. We have found it helpful to explain to patients that frequent phone calls are a disservice to them, in that this promotes excessive dependency and does not allow them to learn their own ways to manage anxiety.

Regular appointments can form the foundation for a new type of relationship that does not depend on the presence of physical illness. Instead, the focus can gradually shift towards a discussion of psychosocial issues, such that the patients feel that the physician is interested in them as individuals, not just their symptoms. Before this process can begin though, the patients must feel they have been both listened to and heard. The thorough medical history and careful review of previously performed diagnostic tests thus serves both an important medical function and an important function in establishing a therapeutic alliance.

## Real Suffering and Rapport

The validation of a patient's symptoms is vital to the development of rapport and a therapeutic alliance with mutual trust and respect. Patients must know that the doctor realizes that their suffering is real and is not 'all in their head'. New symptoms must be taken seriously. These patients are not exempt from serious medical illness.

## Restraint from Over-Investigation and Over-Treatment

Managing the patient with hypochondriasis requires discipline on the part of the physician who quite naturally derives considerable satisfaction from solving a medical conundrum. In response to patient's demands, clinicians are obliged to practice restraint when ordering diagnostic tests and treatments, especially if these are invasive. Well-meaning intentions can culminate in disastrous complications and very real iatrogenic illness. Ordering of tests should be guided by objective findings from a physical examination focused on the body system(s) pertaining to the physical complaint(s) of that particular visit. Many of the tests one might be considering may already have been done and the results known to the patient or readily available in old records. One should also keep in mind that the more tests a patient undergoes, the more invested he or she may become in the idea that there is truly something physically wrong that the doctors keep missing. 'The most powerful therapeutic tool is the physician himself, his or her attention, concern, interest, and careful listening' (Barsky, 1996, p. 49).

## Rationale for Instillation of Confidence and Hope

For a patient with hypochondriasis to tolerate the withholding of unwarranted diagnostic tests and procedures, he or she must have trust and confidence in the physician's knowledge about the illness (Martin & Yutzy, 1994, 1997). Patients are often frustrated and disappointed with past experiences where either an unsatisfactory or no explanation has been offered as a cause for their distress. Education, which provides an acceptable model to explain their distress and a rationale for its treatment, is another important element of optimal management (Barsky, 1996). Telling the patient that he or she suffers from a medically recognized disorder about which a fair amount is known can offer some immediate relief (Pilowsky, 1967). Also, this can instill hope and set the stage for improved adherence to a treatment plan. Once educated, the patient should be encouraged to collaborate with the physician and take some responsibility for his or her long-term medical care. This may return some sense of control to the lives of individuals who have been rendered powerless by their illness.

## Readiness for a Trial of Medication Treatment

In our experience, preparation for a trial of pharmacotherapy involves educating the patient about possible mechanisms involved in their illness. We have found two particular concepts to be heuristically useful, namely, 'somatosensory amplification' (Barsky, Wyshak, & Klerman, 1990) and intense 'illness worry' (Blackwell & De Morgan, 1996). Without labeling the patient as a 'hypochondriac' (a term which has definite pejorative connotations) or using medical jargon, the physician can suggest that the source of the problem may lie in the manner in which the nervous system processes bodily sensations (Barsky, 1996). Most patients will be only too familiar with the experience of supersensitivity to internal (e.g., palpitations, bowel symptoms) or external (e.g., unusual sensitivity to light, sound, touch, smell, and taste) stimuli. Blackwell and De Morgan (1996) recommend using the term 'symptom sensitivity' rather than 'somatization'. They also suggest asking the patient, 'Does it feel as if the amplifier is always turned up in your body?' as a way of eliciting this phenomenon. We have found it helpful to relate the sensitivity to symptoms and intense illness worry with a hypothesized increased sensitivity at the neurochemical receptor level. This model provides a general and simplified explanation of how serotonergic antidepressants may benefit the individual whose nervous system 'volume has been turned up so high, that background static has become disturbing and noxious' (Barsky, 1996, p. 50).

The model is also valuable in explaining why unwanted side effects are immediate while therapeutic benefit is delayed. Before a therapeutic effect can be realized the 'supersensitive receptors' must be exposed to increased synaptic serotonin, sometimes for 8 to 12 weeks, in order to turn down their sensitivity (down regulation). It is the initial increased availability of serotonin that causes the side-effects. One can use this explanation to encourage the patient to stay on the medication because the serotonergic side-effects only confirm that the medication is acting as intended.

Patients with hypochondriasis can be quite reluctant to take psychotropic medication because of their fear of side-effects, their concern about possible long-term adverse effects of medication, or both. We reassure patients that every attempt will be made to minimize side-effects by starting with very low doses of the medication until they have time to adjust. The dose will be tailored to the response of their symptoms and their tolerance of side-effects. In order to optimize the tolerability of the therapeutic trial, the dose can be gradually titrated upward over 6 to 8 weeks or even longer. Case reports and open trials with SSRIs suggest that some patients with hypochondriaisis may respond preferentially to the higher doses often required to treat OCD (e.g., Fallon et al., 1993). As such, a generous amount of time for gradual dosage titration will enhance treatment tolerability and compliance. Maximum adherence to the treatment regime requires anticipation of and education about possible side-effects. Frequent office visits (e.g., weekly) and availability by telephone for support and reassurance during the initial upward titration of medication will also help to prevent premature discontinuation and a failed treatment trial. Some patients find written instructions as to how they should take the medication reassuring and helpful.

For those patients who have had intolerable side-effects from antidepressants that started at a dose that was too high, the physician needs to explain that these were not allergic reactions but rather what one would expect physiologically. These patients may be very anxious about taking the first dose of any newly prescribed medication. A strategy that we have found particularly helpful is to have the patient take the first dose of medication in the doctor's office, then sit in the waiting room for an hour or so until he or she feels confident that no reaction will occur.

## Realistic Expectations

When embarking on a trial of medication, the physician must set realistic expectations for the likely outcome. The physician should explain that recent studies are showing some positive results and the only way to know if medication will be of benefit for an individual is an adequate trial of one or more appropriately chosen agents. Explain that there is interindividual variability in the toleration of, and the response to, different agents. Even a 50% to 60% improvement in symptoms can provide appreciable relief and reduction in disability. Although there is no systematic evidence to support switching among the various SSRIs, clinical experience suggests that as with OCD and depression, if one serotonergic antidepressant is not effective, it is worth trying another. Because it is unlikely that serotonin is the only neurochemical involved in hypochondriasis and its comorbid conditions, one should also consider a trial of an SNRI (serotonin norepinephrine reuptake inhibitor) or a MAOI (monoamine oxidase inhibitor) for those who do not respond to an SSRI. This has proven beneficial in our clinic.

Clinical studies have not yet provided guidelines as to how long pharmacotherapy for hypochondriasis should be maintained. Our experience supports a minimum period of one year of maintenance pharmacotherapy during which time the patient can engage in rehabilitation.

## Rehabilitation

A significant number of patients with hypochondriasis tend to oppose psychiatric referral and reject psychological interventions (Barsky, 1996; Martin & Yutzy, 1997). For patients who believe their problem to be physical, psychological treatment may seem inappropriate. Reassurance that referral or consultation does not mean abandonment of regular visits with the primary care physician is imperative. Reasons for psychiatric consultation may include the need for an expert opinion to optimize the use of psychotropic medication. Most realize that 'stress' can adversely affect their well-being and will welcome psychological intervention if it is presented as 'stress management' (Barsky, 1996). Some patients with hypochondriasis who fully appreciate that their worries about illness are excessive and unproductive find the cognitive-behavioral approach to be intuitively appealing. However, the availability of expert cognitive-behavioral therapy for hypochondriasis is limited in many areas at present.

## Cognitive-Behavioral Therapy or Medication?

At our clinic, both cognitive-behavioral therapy and pharmacotherapy are available for hypochondriasis (see Chapter 7). In this setting, patient preference is the primary basis on which selection of treatment is made. If a balanced presentation of the relative merits and drawbacks of each form of treatment is given, most patients are able to express a clear preference for one of these approaches. We do not ordinarily begin by combining these treatment strategies, but patients who have experienced partial benefit from one approach often continue it while the second approach is introduced. Patients who do not respond to their treatment of first choice can be offered the alternative treatment; in our experience this cross-over of treatments can frequently be very helpful.

## TREATMENT APPROACH FOR DELUSIONAL HYPOCHONDRIASIS

Patients with delusional hypochondriasis will benefit from the application of many of the principles outlined above. However, they are distinguished by definition from non-delusional patients by their lack of insight. It has been frequently noted that these patients are resistant to psychiatric referral, and in the case of delusions of parasitosis, a number of authors have advocated that dermatologists provide treatment including the use of psychotropic drugs such as pimozide (e.g., Gould & Gragg, 1976; Zomer, De Wit, Van Bronswijk, Nabarro, & Van Vloten, 1998).

Although non-pharmacologic treatments for delusional hypochondriasis may have merit, existing studies are more strongly supportive of pharmacotherapeutic approaches. The rationale for medication treatment needs to be explained carefully and without dismissing the patient's concerns as invalid. Attempts to directly challenge the patient's unshakable belief generally frustrate the physician and risk losing any therapeutic alliance with the patient. Patients may accept the rationale that people differ in their sensitivity to skin sensations (in the case of delusions of parasitosis) or in their sensitivity to odor (in the case of delusions of odor) and that the medication will help to increase their 'threshold' to these stimuli. They may also accept that some relief of their anxiety about their condition would be beneficial. Patients who experience substantial relief of symptoms have a significant likelihood of long-term compliance with pharmacologic treatment.

## SUMMARY AND CONCLUSION

The above review confirms that there are a wide variety of pharmacological alternatives for the treatment of hypochondriasis and related conditions, and that, in many instances, these medication approaches can be remarkably helpful. Other chapters of this volume also attest to the growing evidence for the effectiveness of non-pharmacologic treatments, particularly cognitive-behavioral therapy. It is abundantly clear that careful assessment and diagnosis of hypochondriacal concerns are essential in selecting the appropriate treatment. There is a need for a range of additional studies including comparative studies of different pharmacological and non-pharmacological alternatives, longer-term maintenance treatment studies, and studies of treatment combinations. Further studies of comorbidity and its implications for treatment are also necessary. While the evidence for some of the treatments for 'illness worry' described in this chapter must still be considered preliminary, available treatments can already offer hope of significant benefit for these patients and their health care providers.

## REFERENCES

Adler, G. (1981). The physician and the hypochondriacal patient. *New England Journal of Medicine*, **304**, 1394.

Andrews, E., Bellard, J., & Walter-Ryan, W.G. (1986). Monosymptomatic hypochondriacal psychosis manifesting as delusions of infestation: Case studies of treatment with haloperidol. *Journal of Clinical Psychiatry*, **47**, 188–190.

Bach, M., Nutzinger, D.O., & Hartl, L. (1996). Comorbidity of anxiety disorders and hypochondriasis considering different diagnostic systems. *Comprehensive Psychiatry*, **37**, 62–67.

Barsky, A.J. (1996). Hypochondriasis: Medical management and psychiatric treatment. *Psychosomatics*, **37**, 48–56.

Barsky, A.J., Wyshak, G., & Klerman, G.L. (1990). The somatosensory amplification scale and its relationship to hypochondriasis. *Journal of Psychiatry Research*, **24**, 323–334.

Barsky, A.J., Wyshak, G., & Klerman, G.L. (1992). Psychiatric comorbidity in DSM-III-R hypochondriasis. *Archives of General Psychiatry*, **49**, 101–108.

Bass, C., & Benjamin, S. (1993). The management of chronic somatization. *British Journal of Psychiatry*, **162**, 472–480.

Blackwell, B., & De Morgan, N.P. (1996). The primary care of patients who have bodily concerns. *Archives of Family Medicine*, **5**, 457–463.

Bond, W.S. (1989). Delusions of parasitosis: A case report and management guidelines. *DICP*, **23**, 304–306.

Brooke, S., Collacott, R.A., & Bhaumik, S. (1996). Monosymptomatic hypochondriacal psychosis in a man with learning disabilities. *Journal of Intellectual Disability Research*, **40**, 71–74.

Brotman, A.W., & Jenike, M.A. (1984). Monosymptomatic hypochondriasis treated with tricyclic antidepressants. *American Journal of Psychiatry*, **141**, 1608–1609.

Cashman, F.E., & Pollock, B. (1983). Treatment of monosymptomatic hypochondriacal psychosis with imipramine. *Canadian Journal of Psychiatry*, **27**, 85–87.

Chiu, S., McFarlane, A.H., & Dobson, N. (1990). The treatment of monodelusional psychosis associated with depression. *British Journal of Psychiatry*, **156**, 112–115.

Creese, I., Feinberg, A.P., & Snyder, S.H. (1976). Butyrophenone influences on the opiate receptor. *European Journal of Pharmacology*, **36**, 231–235.

Damiani, T.J., Flowers, F.P., & Pierce, D.K. (1990). Pimozide in delusions of parasitosis. *Journal of the American Academy of Dermatology*, 312–313.

Demopulos, C., Fava, M., McLean, N.E., Alpert, J.E., Nierenberg, A.A., & Rosenbaum, J.F. (1996). Hypochondriacal concerns in depressed outpatients. *Psychosomatic Medicine*, **58**, 314–320.

Dorian, B.J. (1979). Monosymptomatic hypochondriacal psychosis. *Canadian Journal of Psychiatry*, **24**, 377.

Engel, G.L. (1978). The biopsychosocial model and the education of health professionals. *Annals of the New York Academy of Sciences*, **310**, 169–181.

Escobar J.I. (1996). Overview of somatization: Diagnosis, epidemiology, and management. *Psychopharmacology Bulletin*, **32**, 589–596.

Fallon, B.A., Javitch, J.A., Hollander, E., & Liebowitz, M.R. (1991). Hypochondriasis and obsessive compulsive disorder: Overlaps in diagnosis and treatment. *Journal of Clinical Psychiatry*, **52**, 457–460.

Fallon, B.A., Liebowitz, M.R., Salman, E., Schneier, F.R., Jusino, C., Hollander, E., & Klein, D.F. (1993). Fluoxetine for hypochondriacal patients without major depression. *Journal of Clinical Psychopharmacology*, **13**, 438–441.

Fallon, B.A., Schneier, F.R., Marshall, R., Campeas, R., Vermes, D., Goetz, D., & Liebowitz, M.R. (1996). The pharmacotherapy of hypochondriasis. *Psychopharmacology Bulletin*, **32**, 607–611.

Fernandez, A. (1988). Pimozide in delusional dysmorphosis. *Canadian Journal of Psychiatry*, **33**, 425–426.

Fernando, N. (1988). Monosymptomatic hypochondriasis treated with a tricyclic antidepressant. *British Journal of Psychiatry*, **152**, 851–852.

Frithz, A. (1979). Delusions of infestation: Treatment by depot injections of neuroleptics. *Clinical and Experimental Dermatology*, **4**, 485–488.

Gallucci, G., & Beard, G. (1995). Risperidone and the treatment of delusions of parasitosis in an elderly patient. *Psychosomatics*, **36**, 578–580.

Gould, W.M., & Gragg, T.M. (1976). Delusions of parasitosis. An approach to the problem. *Archives of Dermatology*, **112**, 1745–1748.

Hamann, K., & Avnstorp, C. (1982). Delusions of infestation treated by pimozide: A double-blind crossover clinical study. *Acta Dermato-Venereologica*, **62**, 55–58.

Hamann, K. (1982). Onychotillomania treated with pimozide (Orap). *Acta Dermato-Venereologica*, **62**, 364–366.

Hollander, E. (1998). Treatment of obsessive-compulsive spectrum disorders with SSRIs. *British Journal of Psychiatry*, **173** (Suppl. 35), 7–12.

Hollander, E., Cohen, L., Simeon, D., Rosen, J., DeCarla, C., & Stein, D.J. (1994). Fluvoxamine treatment of body dysmorphic disorder. *Journal of Clinical Psychopharmacology*, **14**, 75–77.

Hollander, E., Neville, D., DeCaria, C., Mullen, L., Schneier, F.R., & Liebowitz, M.R. (1990). On dysmorphophobia misdiagnosed as obsessive-compulsive disorder. *Psychomatics*, **31**, 468–469.

Holmes, V.F. (1989). Treatment of monosymptomatic hypochondriacal psychosis with pimozide in an AIDS patient. *American Journal of Psychiatry*, **146**, 554–555.

Kalivas, J., & Kalivas, L. (1997). Sertraline: Lack of therapeutic efficacy in patients with delusions of parasitosis and dermatitis artefacta. *International Journal of Dermatology*, **36**, 473–478.

Kamlana, S.H., & Gray, P. (1988). Fear of AIDS. *British Journal of Psychiatry*, **153**, 129.

Kaplan, H.I., & Saddock, B.J. (1985). *Comprehensive textbook of psychiatry* (4th edn.). Baltimore: Williams and Wilkins.

Kellner, R., Fava, G.A., Lisansky, J., Perini, G.I., & Zielezny, M. (1986). Hypochondriacal fears and beliefs in DSM-III melancholia. Changes with amitriptyline. *Journal of Affective Disorders*, **10**, 21–26.

Kellner, R. (1991). *Psychosomatic syndromes and somatic symptoms*. Washington, DC: American Psychiatric Press.

Kellner, R. (1992). Diagnosis and treatment of hypochondriacal syndromes. *Psychosomatics*, **33**, 278–289.

Kjernisted, K., Enns, M.W., & Lander, M. (submitted). Nefazodone treatment of DSM-IV hypochondriasis.

Kramer-Ginsberg, E., Greenwald, B.S., Aisen, P.S., & Brod-Miller, C. (1989). Hypochondriasis in the elderly depressed. *Journal of the American Geriatric Society*, **37**, 507–510.

Lindskov R., & Baadsgaard, O. (1985). Delusions of infestation treated with pimozide: A follow-up study. *Acta Dermato-Venereologica*, **65**, 267–270.

Lipowski, Z.J. (1988). An inpatient programme for persistent somatizers. *Canadian Journal of Psychiatry*, **33**, 275–278.

Lipsitt, D.R. (1995). Hypochondriasis and body dysmorphic disorder. In G.P. Gabbard (Ed.), *Treatment of psychiatric disorders* (pp. 1783–1803). Washington, DC: American Psychiatric Press.

Lyell, A. (1983). Delusions of parasitosis. *British Journal of Dermatology*, **108**, 485–499.

Matas, M., & Robinson, C. (1988). Diagnosis and treatment of monosymptomatic hypochondriacal psychosis in chronic renal failure. *Canadian Journal of Psychiatry*, **33**, 748–750.

Maeda, K., Yamamoto, Y., Yasuda, M., & Ishii, K. (1998). Delusions of oral parasitosis. *Progress in Neuro-Psychopharmacology and Biological Psychiatry*, **22**, 243–248.

Martin, R.L., & Yutzy, S.H. (1994). Hypochondriasis. In R.E. Hales, S.C. Yudofsky, & J.A. Talbot (Eds.), *American psychiatric textbook of psychiatry* (2nd edn., pp. 591–622). Washington, DC: American Psychiatric Press, Inc.

Martin, R.L., & Yutzy, S.H. (1997). Somatoform disorders. In A. Tasman, J. Kay, & J.A. Lieberman (Eds.), *Psychiatry* (pp. 1119–1155). Philadelphia: W.B. Saunders.

Mitchell, C. (1989). Successful treatment of chronic delusional parasitosis. *British Journal of Psychiatry*, **155**, 556–557.

Moore, D.P., & Jefferson, J.W. (1996). *Handbook of medical psychiatry.* St. Louis, MO: Mosby-Year Book Inc.

Munro, A. (1978a). Monosymptomatic hypochondriacal psychosis. A diagnostic entity which may respond to pimozide. *Canadian Psychiatric Association Journal*, **23**, 497–500.

Munro, A. (1978b). Two cases of delusions of worm infestation. *American Journal of Psychiatry*, **135**, 234–235.

Munro, A. (1978c). Monosymptomatic hypochondriacal psychosis manifesting as delusions of parasitosis. A description of four cases successfully treated with pimozide. *Archives of Dermatology*, **114**, 940–943.

Munro, A. (1980). Monosymptomatic hypochondriacal psychosis. *British Journal of Hospital Medicine*, 34–38.

Munro, A., & Chmara, J. (1982). Monosymptomatic hypochondriacal psychosis: A diagnostic checklist based on 50 cases of the disorder. *Canadian Journal of Psychiatry*, **27**, 374–376.

Munro, A. (1988a). Delusional (paranoid) disorders: Etiologic and taxonomic considerations, II: A possible relationship between delusional and affective disorders. *Canadian Journal of Psychiatry*, **33**, 175–178.

Munro, A. (1988b). Monosymptomatic hypochondriacal psychosis. *British Journal of Psychiatry*, **153** (Suppl. 2), 37–40.

Noyes, R. (1999). The relationship of hypochondriasis to anxiety disorders. *General Hospital Psychiatry*, **21**, 8–17.

Noyes, R., Reich, J., Clancy, J., & O'Gorman, T.W. (1986). Reduction in hypochondriasis with treatment of panic disorder. *British Journal of Psychiatry*, **149**, 613–635.

Noyes, R., Jr., Kathol, R.G., Fisher, M.M., Phillips, B.M., Suelzer, M.T., & Woodman, C.L. (1994). Psychiatric comorbidity among patients with hypochondriasis. *General Hospital Psychiatry*, **16**, 78–87.

Opler, L.A., & Feinberg, S.S. (1991). The role of pimozide in clinical psychiatry: A review. *Journal of Clinical Psychiatry*, **52**, 221–233.

Perkins, R.J. (1999). SSRI antidepressants are effective for treating delusional hypochondriasis. *Medical Journal of Australia*, **170**, 140–141.

Perugi, G., Giannotti, D., Di Vaio, S., Frare, F., Saettoni, M., & Cassano, G.B. (1996). Fluvoxamine in the treatment of body dysmorphic disorder (dysmorphophobia). *International Clinical Psychopharmacology*, **11**, 247–254.

Phillips, K.A. (1996). Pharmacologic treatment of body dysmorphic disorder. *Psychopharmacology Bulletin*, **32**, 597–605.

Phillips, K.A., McElroy, S.L., Keck, P.E., Hudson, J.I., & Pope, H.G. (1994). A comparison of delusional and nondelusional body dysmorphic disorder in 100 cases. *Psychopharmacology Bulletin*, **30**, 179–186.

Phillips, K.A., Dwight, M.M., & McElroy, S.L. (1998). Efficacy and safety of fluvoxamine in body dysmorphic disorder. *Journal of Clinical Psychiatry*, **59**, 165–171.

Phillips, K.A., & Hollander, E. (1996). Body dysmorphic disorder. In T.A. Widiger, A.J. Frances, H.A. Pincus, R. Ross, M.B. First, & W.W. Davis (Eds.), *DSM-IV source book* (Vol. 2, pp. 949–960). Washington, DC: American Psychiatric Association, Inc.

Pilowsky, I., (1967). Dimensions of hypochondriasis. *British Journal of Psychiatry,* **113**, 89–93.

Pylko, T., & Sicignan, J. (1985). Nortriptyline in the treatment of a monosymptomatic delusion. *American Journal of Psychiatry,* **142**, 1223.

Rapp, M.S. (1986). Monosymptomatic hypochondriasis. *Canadian Journal of Psychiatry,* **31**, 599.

Reilly, T.M. (1988). Delusional infestation. *British Journal of Psychiary,* **153** (Suppl. 2), 44–46.

Reilly, T.M. (1975). Pimozide in monosymptomatic psychosis. *Lancet,* **1**, 1385–1386.

Reilly, T.M., & Batchelor, D.H. (1986). The presentation and treatment of delusional parasitosis: A dermatological perspective. *International Clinical Psychopharmacology,* **1**, 340–353.

Reilly, T.M., Jopling, W.H., & Beard, A.W. (1978). Successful treatment with pimozide of delusional parasitosis. *British Journal of Dermatology,* **98**, 457–459.

Renvoize, E.B., Kent, J., & Klar, H.M. (1987). Delusional infestation and dementia: A case report. *British Journal of Psychiatry,* **150**, 403–405.

Riding, J., & Munro, A. (1975a). Pimozide in monosymptomatic psychosis. *Lancet,* **1**, 400–401.

Riding, J., & Munro, A. (1975b). Pimozide in the treatment of monosymptomatic hypochondriacal psychosis. *Acta Psychiatrica Scandinavica,* **52**, 23–30.

Rosen, G., Kleinman, A., & Kabon, W. (1982). Somatization in family practice: A biopsychosocial approach. *Journal of Family Practice,* **14**, 493–502.

Ross, C.A., Siddiqui, A.R., & Matas, M. (1987). DSM-III: Problems in diagnosis of paranoia and obsessive-compulsive disorder. *Canadian Journal of Psychiatry,* **32**, 146–148.

Scarone, S., & Gambini, O. (1991). Delusional hypochondriasis: Nosographic evaluation, clinical course and therapeutic outcome of 5 cases. *Psychopathology,* **24**, 179–184.

Shah, P.A. (1988). Delusions of parasitosis. *Southern Medical Journal,* **81**, 939–940.

Sheppard, N.P., O'Loughlin, S., & Malone, J.P. (1986). Psychogenic skin disease: A review of 35 cases. *British Journal of Psychiatry,* **149**, 636–643.

Sondheimer, A. (1988). Clomipramine treatment of delusional disorder–somatic type. *Journal of the American Academy of Child and Adolescent Psychiatry,* **27**, 188–192.

Songer, D.A., & Roman, B. (1996). Treatment of somatic delusional disorder with atypical antipsychotic agents. *American Journal of Psychiatry,* **153**, 578–579.

Srinivasan, T.N., Suresh, R.R., Jayaram, V., & Fernandez, M.P. (1994). Nature and treatment of delusional parasitosis: A different experience in India. *International Journal of Dermatology,* **33**, 851–855.

Stone, A.B. (1993). Treatment of hypochondriasis with clomipramine. *Journal of Clinical Psychiatry,* **54**, 200.

Tollefson, G. (1985). Delusional hypochondriasis, depression and amoxapine. *American Journal of Psychiatry,* **142**, 1518–1519.

Ulzen, R.P.M. (1993). Pimozide-responsive monosymptomatic hypochondriacal psychosis in an adolescent. *Canadian Journal of Psychiatry,* **38**, 153–154.

Ungvari, G., & Vladar, K. (1986). Pimozide treatment for delusion of infestation. *Activitas Nervosa Superior,* **28**, 103–107.

Viswanathan, R., & Paradis, C. (1991). Treatment of cancer phobia with fluoxetine. *American Journal of Psychiatry,* **148**, 1090.

Vitiello, B., & De Leon, J. (1990). Dysmorphophobia misdiagnosed as obsessive-compulsive disorder. *Psychosomatics,* **31**, 220–222.

Wang, C.-K., & Lee, J.Y.-Y. (1997). Monosymptomatic hypochondriacal psychosis complicated by self-inflicted skin ulceration, skull defect and brain abscess. *British Journal of Dermatology*, **137**, 299–302.

Wesner, R.B., & Noyes, R. (1991). Imipramine an effective treatment for illness phobia. *Journal of Affective Disorders*, **22**, 43–48.

Zomer, S.F., De Wit, R.F.E., Van Bronswijk, J.E.H.M., Nabarro, G., & Van Vloten, W.A. (1998). Delusions of parasitosis. A psychiatric disorder to be treated by dermatologists? An analysis of 33 patients. *British Journal of Dermatology*, **138**, 1030–1032.

Chapter 9

# GENERAL AND CROSS-CULTURAL CONSIDERATIONS IN A MEDICAL SETTING FOR PATIENTS PRESENTING WITH MEDICALLY UNEXPLAINED SYMPTOMS

*Javier I. Escobar\*, Lesley A. Allen\*,*
*Constanza Hoyos Nervi\*, and Michael A. Gara\**

## INTRODUCTION

Worldwide, patients with psychological ailments have a tendency to use general medical services far more often than they use mental health services. In the United States, the primary care sector has been defined as the 'de facto' mental health system (Regier et al., 1993). This tendency has been reinforced recently by new service delivery models that place the primary care physician in the role of 'gatekeeper'.

Patients with psychological problems often express their distress by presenting to primary care doctors with an assortment of somatic symptoms and concerns that remain medically unexplained after detailed clinical and laboratory assessments. This form of illness behavior, known as 'somatization' or 'hypochondriasis' in psychiatric circles, is often missed by the primary care physician. While a small proportion of these cases may be accurately identified as depression or anxiety syndromes, too often the psychological nature of these patients' distress goes unrecog-

*Department of Psychiatry, University of Medicine and Dentistry of New Jersey—Robert Wood Johnson Medical School, USA

*Health Anxiety*
Edited by G.J.G. Asmundson, S. Taylor & B.J. Cox
© 2001 John Wiley & Sons Ltd.

nized, and the patients are referred to specialists for further testing of their 'functional' syndromes. For the average 'somatizer', the subjective experience of having a physical illness is a compelling reality that tends to persist despite reassurance from the physician that there is nothing physically wrong. Typically, somatizing patients cannot be reassured, their symptoms become refractory to treatment, and they are left dissatisfied with their medical care.

Somatizing patients do not conform to the allopathic medicine model in which symptoms are quickly resolved by specific medical interventions. Instead, somatizers' symptoms are refractory to treatment and frustrating to family physicians, internists, obstetricians, and other primary care practitioners. Historically, somatizing syndromes have baffled the medical establishment. These syndromes frequently metamorphose as cultures evolve and medical paradigms shift (Shorter, 1994). For example, neurasthenia and hysteria, mainstays of medical discourse at the turn of the 20th century, are no longer mentioned. Instead, these diagnoses have been replaced by newer ones, such as chronic fatigue syndrome.

While the exact mechanisms mediating the conversion from the psychological to the physical are poorly understood, it is assumed that psychological, biological, and cultural elements may all play a role and need to be taken into account in treating somatizers. We believe that outcomes of care can be enhanced by, first, a thorough clinical assessment that considers psychological, cultural, and biological factors and, second, a rational therapeutic management that facilitates integration rather than fragmentation of medical care. Successful outcomes with somatizers should entail a significant decrease in their use of health care services and prevention of the iatrogenic complications that often ensue. In current medical practice, the obstacles to rational and effective therapeutic management of these patients are:

- the nebulous diagnostic status of hypochondriasis and related somatoform disorders
- the polymorphous presentation of somatizing patients
- the tendency in somatizing patients to overuse specialty services
- the tendency in each medical specialty, reminiscent of the biblical story of the Tower of Babel, to coin its own convenient nomenclature (e.g., chronic fatigue, irritable bowel) for such patients
- the recent trend by payers to 'carve out' mental health care from the bulk of health care services.

The goal of this chapter is to highlight important issues in the assessment and management of patients who present to primary care physicians with unreasonable health concerns, multiple unexplained physical symptoms, or both. We will also address cross-cultural considerations that may have practical value in the recognition and management of these syndromes. Somatization as well as health anxiety will be covered because they frequently co-occur in primary practice. The chapter begins with a description of the significance, clinical characteristics, classifications, prevalence, and cultural relevance of these conditions in primary care. The second and third sections of the chapter address assessment and treatment, respectively, and include clinical vignettes to illustrate techniques. Cross-cultural issues will also be addressed in the assessment and treatment sections.

## UNEXPLAINED PHYSICAL SYMPTOMS IN PRIMARY CARE

### Significance to Medical Care

Recognition of somatization and underlying psychiatric illness is important not only for quality of life/quality of care purposes, but also because addressing psychopathology may have a favorable impact on medical outcomes. Thus, it is crucial to scrutinize psychiatric comorbidity even for patients who have primary medical diseases. For example, research has shown that:

- depression worsens outcomes in patients with diabetes mellitus (Tun, Nathan, & Perlmutter, 1990)
- untreated depression leads to higher mortality rates after myocardial infarction (Musselman, Evans, & Nemeroff, 1998)
- psychosocial and psychopharmacological interventions may improve disease outcomes in several malignancies (Evans et al., 1988; Spiegel, Bloom, Kraemer, & Gottheil, 1989)
- stress and depression are associated with more rapid progression of infections such as HIV (Evans et al., 1997).

### Clinical Characteristics of Somatization in Primary Care

It is estimated that 25% to 50% of primary care visits are for medically unexplained physical complaints (Katon, Ries, & Kleinman, 1984; Kirmayer & Robbins, 1991; Kroenke, 1992; McLeod & Budd, 1997; Noyes, Holt, & Kathol, 1995). 'Functional' conditions, such as medically unexplained low back pain, pelvic pain, premenstrual syndrome, tinnitus, dizziness, atypical chest pain, hyperventilation, dyspnea, temporomandibular joint syndrome, irritable bowel syndrome, and hypoglycemia are common reasons for referral to specialists for whom these patients often become problematic (Katon & Walker, 1998). In the United States, a handful of these somatic symptoms (e.g., chest pain, fatigue, dizziness, headache, back pain, dyspnea, abdominal pain, insomnia, edema, numbness) account for about one half of all visits to primary care. Moreover, only about 10% of these symptoms can be attributed to a diagnosable physical illness (Katon & Walker, 1998). In England, psychiatric disorder accompanies 40% of cases with multiple physical symptoms such as arthritis/rheumatism, backache, chest pain, dizziness, headache, and abdominal pain (Hotopft, Mayou, Wadsworth, & Wessely, 1998). This work in Europe and also that of Kroenke et al. (1994) in the United States have documented that, overall, patients complaining of several unexplained symptoms are more likely to have a psychiatric disorder. The relationship between numerous physical symptoms and the manifestation of psychiatric disorder is bidirectional. That is, patients with physical complaints are more likely to develop a psychiatric disorder at a future date, and patients with a psychiatric disorder are more likely to develop multiple new physical symptoms (Hotopft et al., 1998).

## When Are Unexplained Somatic Symptoms Psychiatric In Nature?

Criteria have previously been proposed that seem useful for deciding whether or not a medically unexplained somatic symptom is likely to have a psychiatric etiology (Escobar, 1995). In Escobar's opinion, a psychiatric etiology is very likely if any of the following criteria are met:

- The symptom is associated with other psychiatric syndromes (e.g., depression or anxiety).
- The symptom(s) appears in close proximity with psychological events (e.g., traumatic experiences).
- The symptom(s) provides psychological gratification (secondary gain).
- The symptom(s) coexist with a prominent personality trait or style (e.g., frequent medical help-seeking in a dependent personality).
- The symptom(s) becomes persistent, or joins a conglomerate of other unexplained symptoms.
- The persistence of an amalgam of somatic symptoms and marked concomitant distress results in the extensive use of health care services and, frequently, chronic dissatisfaction with medical care.

## Unexplained Symptoms: Medical and Psychiatric Classifications

*Functional Somatic Syndromes*

In medical settings, 'somatizing' patients often fall under the label 'functional syndromes'—a category that includes such entities as irritable bowel syndrome, hypoglycemia, atypical chest pain, hyperventilation syndrome, chronic fatigue syndrome, fibromyalgia, and the like.

### Symptom-based Conditions

This is a rather new, and perhaps a more precise way to classify these syndromes. The phrase, 'symptom-based conditions' was recently used by Hyams (1998) in a review that compiled a comprehensive list of more than 40 'postulated organic diseases'. According to Hyams, these symptom-based disorders can be grouped as follows:

- conditions associated with pain or fatigue (e.g., fibromyalgia, chronic fatigue syndrome)
- conditions associated with food or environmental toxins (e.g., multiple chemical sensitivity)
- conditions attributed to yeast sensitivity (e.g., chronic candidiasis).
- conditions attributed to silicone in prosthetic devices (e.g., silicone implant associated syndrome)
- conditions related to modern office buildings (e.g., sick building syndrome)
- conditions resulting from service in recent wars (e.g., Gulf War syndrome).

### Somatoform Disorders

In modern psychiatric nomenclature, most patients with medically unexplained symptoms are classified among the 'somatoform' disorders. In DSM-IV and ICD-10, this category includes somatization disorder, undifferentiated somatoform disorder, conversion disorder, pain disorder, body dysmorphic disorder, and hypochondriasis. Of these, somatization disorder and hypochondriasis are perhaps the most distinctive, at least in terms of their clinical phenomenology and diagnostic stability. However, a majority of patients seeking services in primary care do not meet criteria for these diagnoses. Instead, they tend to be lumped into such broad categories as pain disorders and undifferentiated somatoform disorders. The 'functional syndromes' and 'symptom-based conditions' of medical nomenclature and the somatoform disorders in psychiatry share many common elements. These include the presence of numerous somatic complaints attributable to many organ systems that remain unexplained after physical and laboratory assessments, and are accompanied by high levels of psychological distress and disability. In addition, in neither general medicine nor psychiatry is there a 'gold standard' for confirming or refuting these diagnoses.

*Abridged Somatization*

To facilitate research on these phenomena, Escobar has proposed a sub-threshold or abridged construct of somatization that identifies a large portion of patients with unexplained physical symptoms in communities, medical settings, or psychiatric settings. A diagnosis of 'abridged somatization' is given to men with four or more, and women with six or more, unexplained physical symptoms. This construct has been shown to predict associated psychopathology, use of health care services, and disability. Also, this notion has been found to be of practical utility for primary care studies in the United States and abroad (Escobar, Rubio, Canino, & Karno, 1989; Kapoor, Fortunato, Hanusa, & Schulberg, 1997; Katon, Lin & Von Korff, 1991; Kirmayer & Robbins, 1991; Labott, Preisman, Torosian, Popovich, & Iannuzzi, 1996; Rief et al., 1996; Schulberg, 1991; Smith, Rost, & Kashner, 1995; Sullivan, Clark, & Katon, 1993).

Several groups of investigators have used the abridged somatization construct to systematically examine primary care patients with medically unexplained physical symptoms both in the United States and abroad. These studies have targeted 'functional' syndromes referred for specialty care such as patients referred to an otolaryngology practice because of persistent dizziness (Sullivan et al., 1993), patients presenting with syncope (Kapoor et al., 1995), and patients with respiratory problems seen at a pulmonary clinic (Labott et al., 1996). Other reports have underlined the usefulness of the abridged construct for case definition prior to research studies or therapeutic interventions in general medical settings (Katon et al., 1991; Schulberg, 1990; Smith et al., 1995). A study of a multi-ethnic primary care sample in Southern California showed that somatization in immigrants was strongly related to the premigration experience of overwhelming stressors such as war exposure (Holman et al., 1996).

*Three Forms of Somatization in Primary Care*

Another classification that may have utility in primary care is that proposed by Kirmayer and Robbins (1991). Working with a Canadian primary care sample, these authors derived three subtypes of somatization, namely 'functional somatization', 'hypochondriacal somatization', and 'presenting somatization'. According to these investigators, 'functional' or 'primary somatization' is akin to Escobar's abridged somatization concept (high levels of unexplained symptoms). 'Hypochondriacal' somatization primarily denotes health worry or symptom amplification. 'Presenting' somatization refers to somatic presentations of underlying depression/anxiety syndromes. The results of a recent study in western Spain have endorsed the value of this classification, suggesting that it may transcend cultural boundaries (Garcia-Campayo, Lobo, Perez-Echeverria, & Campos, 1998).

## Prevalence and Risk Factors of Somatization in Primary Care

There is little information available on the prevalence of diagnosable (DSM-IV or ICD-10) somatoform disorders in primary care settings. A WHO-sponsored international study in 14 countries reported ICD-10 prevalence rates of 3% for somatization disorder and 20% for abridged somatization (Gureje, Simon, Ustun, & Goldberg, 1997). We recently reported DSM-IV prevalence rates of 1% for somatization disorder, 3% for hypochondriasis, and 22% for abridged somatization in a large multi-ethnic primary care sample in California (Escobar, Waitzkin, Cohen Silver, Gara, & Holman, 1998) and confirmed that high levels of psychopathology and physical disability are associated with these conditions. In a carefully designed primary care study in a southern U.S. state, de Gruy, Dickingson, Dickinson, and Candib (1999) found that Escobar's abridged somatization construct coincided with an overall burden of suffering and care that exceeded the burden of most psychiatric conditions (including somatization disorder) and also most physical conditions except chronic lung disease.

## Cultural Aspects of Somatization in Primary Care

Throughout the years, data from cross-cultural studies has documented considerable cultural variation in the expression of somatizing syndromes. The available evidence further elaborates the well-accepted tenet that the presentation of personal/social distress in the form of somatic complaints appears to be the norm for most cultures (Kleinman, 1986).

Cross-cultural studies have demonstrated an excess of somatic presentations for depressed patients in Asia, Africa, and Latin America. Moreover, clinical and epidemiological studies have shown that Chinese, African-American, Puerto Rican, and other Latin-American respondents tend to present higher levels of medically unexplained symptoms than other groups (Escobar, Rubio, Canino, & Karno, 1989; Kleinman, 1977; Mezzich & Raab, 1980; Swartz, Landerman, George, Blazer, & Escobar, 1991). The WHO-sponsored international study in primary care (reported above) also found that both somatization disorder and abridged somatization were significantly more common in the two Latin-American sites (Chile and Brazil) than in the other 13 countries studied (Gureje et al., 1997).

Our primary care study, conducted in California, included four ethnic groups (US-born whites, US-born Mexican-Americans, Mexican, and Central-American immigrants). We found that while recent immigrants from Latin America had a healthier mental health profile than those born in the United States, their rates of somatization appeared to be higher (Holman et al., 1996). In addition, immigrant patients evidenced greater levels of 'pure' somatization, defined as the presentation of multiple somatic symptoms without other major coexistent psychopathology. Thus, it appears that somatization emerges as a prominent idiom of distress for Hispanics upon their arrival to the United States, but becomes less so, presumably as they become acculturated to a more psychologically minded American culture.

A review of the cross-cultural literature conducted by Escobar (1995) suggested that cultures may also vary with respect to the different symptom clusters emphasized in expressing distress. For example, some cultures may emphasize specific gastrointestinal symptoms (excessive concern about constipation in the UK); others, cardiopulmonary symptoms (poor blood circulation and low blood pressure in the so-called 'German disease'); and others, immunologically based symptoms ('viruses', 'environmental disease', and 'multiple chemical sensitivity' in the United States and Canada).

## Stability of Somatic Symptoms, Official Diagnoses and Syndromes

Simon and Gureje (1999) recently provided data suggesting that lifetime somatic symptoms and the diagnosis of somatization disorder are not stable over time. They used data collected with the Composite International Diagnostic Interview (CIDI; Wittchen et al., 1991) in the WHO's collaborative study of mental health problems in primary care. The authors found significant discrepancies in somatic symptom reporting between wave one and wave two of their study and concluded that the assessment of lifetime somatic symptoms may not be a particularly useful strategy for making a somatization disorder diagnosis. For example, the authors found that about one half of lifetime somatic symptoms reported at baseline were not reported at follow-up 12 months later, thus making somatization disorder diagnoses extremely unstable.

Because we have theorized that somatization as a syndrome may be a more stable construct than the 'full' somatization disorder diagnosis, we reanalyzed the data reported by the authors using a Monte Carlo method (StatXact4 software) for the estimation of three different measures of association (Kendall's Tau-b, Somer's D, Spearman r). According to these

secondary analyses, the level of concordance between 'full' DSM-IV somatization disorder criteria met at baseline and at follow-up by the same
patient cohort was rather small (range 0.18–0.37; 95% confidence interval;
see first row of Table 9.1). We next used the same statistical estimation
procedures and measures to examine 'number of lifetime somatization
symptoms' reported at the follow-up assessment versus the number
reported at baseline (Simon and Gureje's Table 2). We found that the stability estimates were strikingly higher in this case, ranging between 0.49
and 0.58 (95% confidence interval).

To examine how an alternative (syndromic) conceptualization of somatization fared under these conditions, we reconfigured the authors' data on
lifetime symptoms, originally presented as a 4 × 4 array, into a 2 × 2 array,
collapsing 0–2 and 3–6 symptoms as one category and 7–11 and 12 or more
symptoms as the other category. The level of association for this reconfigured table was estimated to be between 0.44 and 0.53 (95% confidence
interval).

The conclusion one may draw from these analyses is that while the 'full'
somatization disorder diagnosis is easily influenced by the reporting or
underreporting of individual symptoms, somatization qua phenomenon seems unwavering, particularly when more broadly defined. Thus,
despite the volatility of individual somatic symptoms, their clustering as
multiple somatic complaints in clinical presentations seems a relatively
stable clinical phenomenon.

Using this syndromic approach, we propose another useful way to assess
somatization. The primary care physician scrutinizes the physical symptoms listed in instruments such as the CIDI and tallies the number of
symptoms for which there is no medical explanation. Using Escobar's
abridged criteria, somatization is considered as a diagnosis if four such

**Table 9.1**  95% Confidence intervals for three different association statistics for the data reported by Simon
and Gureje (1999) in their Tables 1 and 2

| Table | Kendall's Tau-$b$ | Somer's $D$ | Spearman $r$ |
|---|---|---|---|
| Table 1 (2 × 2) | 0.18–0.37 | 0.18–0.37 | 0.18–0.37 |
| Table 2 (4 × 4) | 0.49–0.55 | 0.49–0.54 | 0.52–0.58 |
| Table 2* | 0.44–0.53 | 0.44–0.53 | 0.44–0.53 |

*Re-analyzed as a 2 × 2 array.

symptoms are found for males, or six such symptoms for females. This approach is relatively straightforward for established patients (a simple chart review may suffice in many cases using a time frame of one year) but might require a somewhat lengthy interview in the case of relatively new patients. Of course, there is no need for the physician to conduct such an interview personally. In addition, Gara, Cohen Silver, Escobar, Holman, and Waitzkin (1998) propose that this interview could be considerably streamlined by restricting scrutiny to the 15 pseudoneurological symptoms listed in the CIDI, as opposed to assessing all 41 symptoms. These 15 pseudoneurological symptoms are (medically unexplained) blindness, blurred vision, deafness, anesthesia, paralysis, aphonia, seizures, fainting, amnesia, double vision, dizziness, numbness/tingling, unconsciousness, lump in throat, and trouble walking. Gara et al. (1998) found that the presence of three or more of these symptoms predicted in the past year by Escobar's abridged criteria for somatization quite well (point biserial correlation = 0.74. $p < 0.001$), and identified a subset of primary care patients (7.6%) who were highly disabled, both in terms of physical functioning as well as psychiatric comorbidity. In fact, these 'pseudoneurological somatizing' patients were found to be just as disabled as patients with full-blown somatization disorder, even though the former were 14 times more prevalent than the latter.

## ASSESSING UNEXPLAINED PHYSICAL SYMPTOMS IN PRIMARY CARE

A particularly user-friendly and well-studied tool for the assessment of somatization and other mental disorders in primary care is the PRIME-MD, an acronym for Primary Care Evaluation of Mental Disorders (Spitzer et al., 1994). The PRIME-MD, is a two-stage screening and interview procedure that facilitates the rapid diagnosis of somatoform disorders as well as mood, anxiety, alcohol, and eating disorders. In the first stage of the process, patients complete a brief screening questionnaire which contains 25 yes–no items concerning symptoms (e.g., 'During the past month were you bothered a lot by back pain?') and a single item assessing overall health on a 5-point scale. In the second stage, the physician examines the patient's responses, and renders either no diagnosis or probes further using one or more of five highly structured interview modules (mood, anxiety, alcohol, eating, and somatoform modules). For example, if the patient reports being bothered by three or more (of 15 listed) somatic symptoms (e.g., back pain, chest pain, fainting spells) the physician enters the somatoform module.

In a carefully designed study of 1,000 primary care patients using the PRIME-MD, Spitzer et al. (1994) found that PRIME-MD disorders were diagnosed in 39% of the patients. Of these, 26% had a mood disorder and 14% a somatoform disorder. The authors also found that mental disorders in primary care, including somatization, were associated with more impairment on the Short-Form General Health Survey than were many common medical disorders, including hypertension, arthritis, and diabetes.

## Assessing Somatization in Patients from Diverse Cultures

Cultural factors and language barriers may complicate the assessment of somatizing patients from diverse backgrounds. Cultural factors may influence a patient's monitoring of and perception of physical or emotional symptoms (Angel & Guarnaccia, 1989), his or her labeling of symptoms (as physical or psychological), interpretation of symptoms (as dangerous or benign), and responses to these symptoms (Angel & Thoits, 1987).

Language barriers create obvious difficulties in the health care setting in particular, where translation requires the knowledge of specific medical terminology (Putsch, 1985). In the medical setting, careful and accurate translation requires the communication of sometimes unfamiliar terminology to patients in an understandable manner (Putsch, 1985). While the use of interviewers who are well trained in medical terminology is preferable, often such interviewers are not available in the general medical setting. Instead, it is common for patients to bring family members with them to serve as their interpreters. Unfortunately, these translators are often children or adults who are not well prepared to translate and communicate specific symptom terminology to the physician. In addition, the patients may not feel comfortable reporting certain symptoms to the physician in the presence of their kin interpreter.

## Clinical Vignette: Striving for a Culturally Sensitive Assessment

The following clinical vignette illustrates some of the above-mentioned issues.

A woman presented to her primary care physician with her 11-year-old son serving as the interpreter. She had been experiencing difficulty swallowing, headaches, diarrhea, joint pain and muscle pain, sexual indifference, and excessive menstrual bleeding. She was able to describe only headache, vomiting, and pain to her physician for three reasons. First, she felt uncomfortable describing her sexual symptoms through her son. Second, her son was unable to differentiate between joint and muscle pain. Third, her son did not consider her swallowing difficulty an important symptom.

Compounding the communication problem is the inability of the physicians to describe, in the patient's native tongue, the causal nature of the symptoms. In instances where physical symptoms are of concern but remain unexplained, the patient needs to trust that the physician has accurately understood and adequately assessed his or her physical symptoms. In cultures that consider the physician role to be directive, a patient may hesitate to question the physician or ask for clarification of the physician's recommendations. When a child is the interpreter, he or she may have difficulty translating the physician's feedback to the patient, or the parent or child might consider it inappropriate to ask the physician to clarify feedback or answer further questions. This interferes with both feedback to the patient and gathering an accurate medical history during the assessment process.

The use of properly translated and validated instruments, including structured interviews such as the CIDI or patient questionnaires such as the PRIME-MD, serves a valuable function in the assessment of patients from different language backgrounds. These instruments are available in many different languages and can be administered by lay interviewers.

Finally, it is important that the primary care physician be prepared to explain somatization in a manner that can be easily understood or easily translated. Clinicians can facilitate interpretation by using short questions and comments, avoiding jargon, breaking up lengthy explanations into parts, using lay person's terminology, and making allowances for terms that may not exist in the patient's language (Putsh, 1985).

## TREATMENT OF UNEXPLAINED PHYSICAL SYMPTOMS IN PRIMARY CARE

Both pharmacological and psychosocial treatments for patients with somatoform disorders have been examined in well-designed, controlled treatment trials. Despite the prevalence of somatoform disorders in primary care, few treatment studies have been conducted in primary care settings. We will briefly review the treatment outcome literature on somatoform disorders in order to highlight the treatment interventions with demonstrated efficacy. Afterwards, we will discuss ways to incorporate these interventions into primary care settings.

## Hypochondriasis

Psychosocial treatments for hypochondriasis have been examined in a number of controlled studies. These studies show cognitive and behavioral interventions such as group cognitive behavior therapy (Avia et al., 1996), individual cognitive behavior therapy (Warwick, Clark, Cobb, & Salkovskis, 1996), individual cognitive therapy, and individual behavioral stress management (Clark et al., 1998) more effectively reduce hypochondriacal concerns than waiting list control conditions. One other investigation with hypochondriacal patients found that a behavioral treatment (in vivo exposure with response prevention) was equally effective in reducing hypochondriacal concerns as was individual cognitive therapy (Bouman & Visser, 1998). Patients in each of these studies were referred to mental health clinics by their general practitioner or mental health professional. Thus, not one of these treatments was specifically designed to be conducted in a medical setting. Not one pharmacological treatment for hypochondriasis has been adequately investigated in a placebo-controlled trial (see Chapter 8).

## Somatization Disorder

Two behavioral (and no pharmacological) interventions have been examined in controlled studies with somatization disorder patients. The first intervention was a psychiatric consultation letter written to the patients' physicians, describing somatization disorder and providing recommendations to guide primary care (Smith et al., 1995; Rost, Kashner, & Smith, 1994). The recommendations to physicians included the following: (a) schedule appointments every 4–6 weeks instead of 'as needed' appointments; (b) at each visit conduct a physical examination focusing on the body part where the complaint is; (c) avoid diagnostic procedures and surgeries unless clearly indicated; and (d) avoid telling patients their symptoms are 'all in your head'. In two separate trials, the investigators found that patients who received this 'enhanced medical care' had better health outcomes (i.e., physical functioning and cost of medical care) than those who received standard medical care (Rost et al., 1994; Smith et al., 1995). The only other treatment approach for somatization disorder that has been tested against a control intervention is group psychotherapy (Kashner, Rost, Cohen, Anderson, & Smith, 1995). In this study, half of the patients were randomly assigned to receive no treatment besides their standard medical treatment and the other half were assigned to a group therapy condition, geared toward enhancing emotional expression as well as providing peer support, coping methods, and psychoeducation to participants. For the year following the intervention, patients treated with group therapy reported better physical and mental health than did those treated with standard medical care (Kashner, Rost, Cohen, Anderson, & Smith, 1995).

## Functional Somatic Syndromes

*Irritable Bowel Syndrome*

One of the most common diagnoses given by gastroenterologists (Langeluddecke, 1985)—irritable bowel syndrome—is characterized by persistent abdominal pain or cramping along with altered bowel habits. At present, psychotherapeutic approaches appear to have provided more relief to irritable bowel syndrome patients than have pharmacological approaches. In a somewhat dated review of the literature, Klein (1988) concluded that not one medication was superior to another or to placebo for ameliorating irritable bowel symptoms. Agents examined have, for the most part, fallen into one of the following classes: (a) antispasmodics, (b) bulking agents, (c) antidepressants, or (d) tranquilizers. More recent medication trials have been no more successful than those reviewed by Klein (Francis & Whorwell, 1994).

Several psychological interventions have been shown to have some efficacy in reducing irritable bowel syndrome symptoms when compared with standard medical treatment, waiting list, or another control condition. There are successful trials of short-term dynamic therapy (Guthrie, Creed, Dawson, & Tomenson, 1991; Svedlund, Sjodin, Ottosson, & Dotevall, 1983), stress management (Shaw et al., 1991), cognitive therapy (Greene & Blanchard, 1994; Payne & Blanchard, 1995), cognitive-behavior therapy (Lynch & Zamble, 1989), group cognitive-behavior therapy (Van Dulmen, Fennis, & Bleijenberg, 1996) and hypnotherapy (Whorwell, Prior, & Farragher, 1984). In most of these studies patients were referred by primary physicians or gastroenterologists and treated in mental health facilities. While the hypnotherapy and stress management treatments were administered in medical settings these were different from the patients' original primary care facility.

*Fibromyalgia*

As many as 20% of the patients treated by rheumatologists have fibromyalgia (Wolfe et al., 1990). Characterized by chronic widespread pain and multiple tender points, fibromyalgia is typically diagnosed after other medical conditions with similar symptoms, such as arthritis and lupus, have been ruled out. Other associated symptoms include non-restorative sleep, fatigue, and malaise. At present, no treatment has been proven effective in randomized controlled trials.

Controlled drug trials with fibromyalgia patients outnumber psychotherapeutic trials by a substantial margin. Tricyclics, especially amitriptyline and cyclobenzaprine, have produced clinically meaningful change in about 25% to 45% of patients within the first two months of treatment (Carette et al., 1994). However, follow-up results after six months of treatment show tricyclics to be no more beneficial than placebo (Carette et al., 1994). Other medications examined in short-term controlled studies with this population include zolpidem (Moldofsky, Lue, Mously, Roth-Schecheter, & Reynolds, 1996), fluoxetine (Wolfe, Cathey, & Hawley, 1994), and prednisone (Clark, Tindall, & Bennett, 1985). The efficacy of antidepressant drugs, though modest, appears more promising than that of other agents.

Non-pharmacological approaches with fibromyalgia patients have included hypnotherapy (Haanen et al., 1991), biofeedback (Ferraccioli et al., 1987), physical exercise (Burckhardt, Mannerkorpi, Hedenberg, & Bjelle, 1994), and cognitive-behavioral/educational groups (Vlaeyen et al., 1996). These studies suggest that small reductions in somatic discomfort or modest increases in pain-coping results from hypnotherapy, physical exercise, or cognitive-behavioral/educational groups. In all of these studies, rheumatologists and family practitioners referred patients to the specialized medical settings where treatment was conducted.

*Chronic Fatigue Syndrome*

Chronic fatigue syndrome (CFS) is diagnosed when there is a new onset of fatigue lasting at least six months, that causes at least a 50% reduction in activity. Concomitant symptoms include memory impairment, sore throat, tender lymph nodes, muscle pain, joint pain, headache, non-restorative sleep, and postexertional fatigue. No controlled study to date demonstrates the efficacy of medication with CFS patients. Antiviral agents (Straus et al., 1988), monoamine oxidase inhibitors (Natelson et al., 1996), and serotonin reuptake inhibitors (Vercoulen et al., 1996) have all been applied without success. In contrast, psychosocial treatments appear to have promise with this population. Treatment approaches used in controlled experimental designs have included graded exercise (Fulcher & White, 1997; Wearden et al., 1998) and cognitive-behavior therapy (Deale, Chalder, Marks, & Wessely, 1997; Sharpe et al., 1996), both of which reduced patients' reports of fatigue. In each of the medication and behavioral studies, patients were treated at specialized medical clinics.

## Undifferentiated Somatoform Disorder

Three groups of investigators have conducted controlled treatment trials with patients complaining of one or more 'psychosomatic' symptoms.

Speckens et al. (1995) showed that patients treated with individual cognitive-behavior therapy experienced greater improvements in their psychosomatic complaints than patients treated with standard medical care. This study was conducted in a general outpatient clinic where physicians trained in cognitive-behavior therapy conducted the treatment. Hellman, Budd, Borysenko, McClelland, and Benson (1990) found two different cognitive-behavioral group interventions to reduce health-care utilization as well as physical and psychological stress more effectively than a stress management information group did. All treatments were carried out in a behavioral medicine clinic with patients who had been referred by their primary physicians. Finally, Lidbeck (1997) demonstrated greater efficacy for group cognitive-behavior therapy (conducted by a physician trained in cognitive-behavior therapy) than for a waiting list control condition. Patients were referred to the study by their general practitioners and hospital physicians. Those in the cognitive-behavioral group reported greater reductions in physical distress, somatic preoccupation, and hypochondriacal beliefs than those in the waiting list group.

## Effective Treatments in Primary Care

A variety of treatment approaches appear beneficial to patients experiencing unexplained physical symptoms and hypochondriasis. Cognitive-behavior therapy, short-term dynamic therapy, hypnotherapy, and enhanced medical care have received the strongest empirical support. Pharmacological interventions, especially antidepressant medications, have also received some empirical support for ameliorating unexplained physical symptoms.

Only two of the treatment approaches described above, specifically individual cognitive-behavior therapy (Speckens et al., 1995) and enhanced medical care (Rost et al., 1994; Smith et al., 1995), have been proven effective when used in the patients' primary care setting. All other interventions were provided at outside medical or mental health settings. The treatment setting may influence the selection of patients in these studies. If a psychosocial treatment is provided in the primary care setting, primary care physicians will be familiar with the treatment and, thus, may be more likely to encourage patients to undergo the treatment. Also, if the psychosocial treatment appears to be a part of the primary care practice, patients may be more willing to engage in the treatment than if it were in a separate, unfamiliar setting. For example, primary care patients participating in the Speckens et al. (1995) study may differ from those who accepted their primary care physician's referral to seek treatment at a mental health clinic. Because the literature supports the use of enhanced medical care and individual cognitive-behavior therapy conducted in the primary care physician's office, we will examine both of these treatments in greater depth.

Enhanced medical care (Rost et al., 1994; Smith et al., 1995) was initially developed to reduce inpatient health care costs of somatizers. The goal is to minimize the need for inpatient care by improving the quality of out-patient care. Physicians providing enhanced medical care attempt to treat patients sympathetically without reinforcing patients' abnormal illness behavior. In particular, physicians meet with somatizers on a regular basis (possibly every four to six weeks) so that patients do not acquire symptoms in order to meet with their physician. Brief physical examinations are performed at each visit to avoid taking patients' physical complaints at face value. Expensive diagnostic procedures, surgeries, and hospitalizations are avoided to ensure that iatrogenic diseases and excessive surgery are not created. Physicians respond sympathetically to patients' physical discomfort in the hope of making patients feel understood and in the hope of minimizing doctor shopping. Research on this treatment approach suggests that somatizers benefit when their primary physicians receive a brief psychiatric consultation regarding the identification and treatment of somatizers.

Cognitive-behavior therapy aims to reduce physical discomfort and psychological distress of somatizers. In the Speckens et al. (1995) study, patients received between 6 and 16 individual treatment sessions that were carried out in an examination room at the primary physician's office. The cognitive-behavioral techniques used were similar to those described by Salkovskis (1989) and Sharpe, Peveler, and Mayou (1992). Specifically, patients were taught to identify and modify dysfunctional automatic thoughts and to conduct 'behavioral experiments aimed at breaking the vicious cycle of the symptoms and their consequences' (Speckens et al., 1995). While numerous investigators have demonstrated the efficacy of cognitive-behavior therapy for somatization and hypochondriasis (see Chapters 3 and 7), the Speckens study is unique in its use of the primary physician's examination room as the treatment setting.

## Treatments for Latinos with Unexplained Physical Symptoms

Positive results have been reported for the use of cognitive behavior therapy with Latino populations. Outcome studies have shown that cognitive behavior therapy benefits Puerto Rican women from low SES (Comas-Diaz, 1981), Latino medical outpatients (Organista, Munoz, &

Gonzalez, 1994), and Latinos in primary care settings (Miranda and Munoz, 1994). Miranda suggests that cognitive-behavior therapy is well-suited for Hispanics. When seeking medical care, Hispanics typically have specific expectations for the treatment and the treatment provider. First, they expect the focus of treatment to be concrete with the aim of solving the presenting problem. Immediate relief is the goal. Second, Hispanics expect the treatment provider to be reliable, responsive, and culturally sensitive, as well as to offer advice and guidance. These features are syntonic with the goals and techniques of cognitive-behavior therapy, making it an appropriate method of intervention.

A patient's cultural beliefs regarding the origin of illness is an important consideration for the clinician. Such beliefs are likely to impact the treatment process. Just as certain syndromes have become common in particular cultures, for example, 'nervios' in Puerto Rican culture, and 'susto' in Mexican culture, these cultures have established explanations for such symptoms. Particularly when working with patients from more traditional cultures, it is important to gather information about the patient's understanding of what is causing the symptoms. The patient should be queried about the existence of similar somatic syndromes in his or her culture and about his or her beliefs concerning the origin and treatment of these symptoms.

Many traditional cultures apply folk medicine to treat physical symptoms. It is important to be aware of and sensitive to the use of traditional healing practices. Explaining and treating somatization may involve educating patients in another way of understanding their physical sensations. Thus, successful treatment requires imparting new skills while maintaining respect for cultural beliefs and practices.

## Case Study: Coordinating Medical and Psychiatric Care

Given the success of Smith et al. (1995) and Speckens et al. (1995) in devising strategies for coordinating primary and psychiatric care, we have developed a therapeutic strategy for treatment of primary care patients diagnosed with somatoform disorders. A major innovation of this intervention is that it is administered at the primary care site. The following is an overview of a 10-session cognitive behavioral/primary care treatment that we recently implemented successfully in the case of a woman meeting criteria for abridged somatization and hypochondriasis.

The patient, Elaine (fictitious name) was a 44-year-old married Caucasian female who lived with her husband, their 2-year-old adopted son, and her mother who had Alzheimer's disease. Elaine was a former history teacher who had stopped working to care for her son and mother.

In 1997 Elaine switched primary care physicians to Dr. D. because of changes in her health care plan. At that time she was experiencing periods of chest pain and palpitations which she feared indicated cardiovascular disease. Dr. D. referred Elaine to a cardiologist who found no organic pathology and prescribed alprazolam. Elaine reported trying the alprazolam once or twice. She discontinued it because it made her drowsy and 'spaced out'.

A few months later, Elaine returned to Dr. D. with new complaints. She said she had been experiencing severe headaches for the previous six months and was worried about a possible brain tumor. Dr. D., who had been trained in identifying and treating somatizers, examined Elaine and queried her about stressors in her life. After learning about her recent adoption and her mother's condition, Dr. D. asked if Elaine would be interested in participating in a stress management treatment program. He explained that Elaine had been experiencing an enormous amount of stress and that stress can exacerbate physical symptoms. Dr. D. stated that he would meet with Elaine in two months and, in the meantime, she could try the stress management program. Elaine hesitantly agreed and scheduled an appointment with a psychologist in Dr. D.'s practice for the following week.

Treatment with the psychologist began with a diagnostic evaluation and a variety of questionnaires assessing the patient's physical and emotional health. Also, Elaine was asked to complete for the following week a daily diary in which she would record the severity of her physical discomfort at its worst. The evaluation revealed that Elaine met criteria for abridged somatization and hypochondriasis. She reported a history of irregular and painful menstruation, diarrhea, abdominal bloating, as well as the chest pain, palpitations, and headaches described earlier. Her questionnaires showed that she was experiencing high levels of physical discomfort (average daily diary score = 3.0 on a 1 to 5-point Likert scale), hypochondriacal beliefs (Whiteley Index = 11), and anxiety (Beck Anxiety Inventory score = 21).

The week after the psychological evaluation, Elaine began our 10-session cognitive-behavioral treatment. Although Elaine reported doubts about the potential benefits to her from this treatment, she agreed to give it a try because she recognized that her life had become increasingly stressful over the previous 18 months. Treatment began by teaching Elaine to monitor her physical symptoms and related thoughts and emotions. She quickly recognized that she often experienced headaches and chest pain after difficult interactions with her son and mother. She was taught an abbreviated version of progressive muscle relaxation (Bernstein & Borkovec, 1973) and diaphragmatic breathing, which she was instructed to practice daily. Over time, she began taking three relaxation breaks per day in order to eliminate muscular tension and to soothe herself. She also began to use relaxation techniques when she felt angry with her son or mother.

The next focus of treatment was teaching Elaine sleep hygiene and stimulus control techniques. She said that even though she felt exhausted at the end of the day, she experienced early insomnia (at least one hour) every night. In order to address the insomnia, the therapist taught her to regulate her sleep schedule and restrict her time in bed to sleeping. Also, Elaine used her relaxation skills just prior to bedtime. After a few weeks, she began falling asleep within 30 minutes on most nights.

Elaine's daily activities were addressed next. She reported spending her days working so hard to take care of her son, mother, and the housework that she was too tired to do anything in the evenings except rest on the couch. She and her therapist problem-solved about reducing her responsibilities and increasing her pleasurable activities. After examining the advantages and disadvantages of enrolling her mother in a day treatment program, she decided the potential benefits outweighed the costs. Once she had freed up a part of each day, she began taking increasingly long walks with a friend in the afternoons. Also, she and her husband began scheduling 'date night' once every week.

At session six, Elaine and her therapist began disputing some of her hypochondriacal beliefs. She learned to look for evidence supporting and contradicting her beliefs about having cardiovascular disease and a brain tumor. The fact that Elaine had been experiencing a substantial improvement in her chest pain and headaches was some of the most convincing evidence that she did not have a progressive and fatal disease. In addition, she would remind herself that her physicians had found no sign of organic pathology. Learning to create the symptoms on her own (i.e., running up her staircase to create palpitations and grinding her teeth to create headaches) also helped her to remind herself that the existence of physical symptoms was not sufficient proof of the presence of a serious illness.

At the final session, Elaine and her therapist delineated a relapse prevention plan. Elaine agreed to continue using each of her newly acquired skills (i.e., relaxation exercises, engaging in pleasurable activities/exercise, sleep hygiene, and cognitive disputation). In addition, Elaine continued to meet with Dr. D. every two months for a check-up. She reported that these brief physical exams helped her to remind herself that she was physically healthy. At this final session with the therapist, Elaine reported a significant improvement in her headaches and chest pain. Her posttreatment questionnaires showed improvements in her daily diary scores (pretreatment average = 3.0, posttreatment average = 1.3; scale range = 0–5), hypochondriacal beliefs (pretreatment Whiteley Index = 11; posttreatment Whiteley Index = 5; scale range = 0–14), and anxiety (pretreatment Beck Anxiety Inventory score = 21; posttreatment Beck Anxiety Inventory score = 2; scale range = 0–63).

Once the cognitive-behavioral treatment was complete, the therapist gave Dr. D. a report on Elaine's progress. The therapist encouraged Dr. D. to continue seeing Elaine every two months for brief physical examinations and to check in with her on her relapse prevention plan.

## CONCLUSION

Health anxiety and medically unexplained physical symptoms are frequently encountered in primary care offices. Too often patients presenting with these problems are referred to medical specialists and receive unnecessary and unsuccessful health care services. This chapter aims to improve the identification, assessment, and treatment of health anxiety and somatoform disorders in primary care. The high prevalence and costs of these disorders argues for heightened awareness of and improved treatment for them.

The chapter reminds clinicians that unexplained physical symptoms are a common form of personal and social distress in most cultures. It is recommended that assessments of primary care patients include inquiries into psychiatric and cultural factors as well as biological factors that may contribute to the presenting problem. In managing a hypochondriacal or somatizing patient, clinicians are encouraged to integrate treatment recommendations from all the patient's physicians. Patients may also benefit significantly from stress management or cognitive-behavioral treatments.

## REFERENCES

Angel, R., & Guarnaccia, P. (1989). Mind, body and culture: Somatization among Hispanics. *Social Science and Medicine*, **28**, 1229–1238.

Angel, R., & Thoits, P. (1987). The impact of culture on the cognitive structure of illness. *Culture Medicine and Psychiatry*, **11**, 465–494.

Avia, M.D., Ruiz, M.A., Olivares, E., Crespo, M., Guisado, A.N., Sanchez, A., & Varela, A. (1996). The meaning of psychological symptoms: Effectiveness of a group intervention with hypochondriacal patients. *Behaviour Research and Therapy*, **34**, 23–31.

Bernstein, D.A., & Borkovec, T.D. (1973). *Progressive relaxation training: A manual for the helping professions*. Champaign, IL: Research Press.

Bouman, T.K., & Visser, S. (1998). Cognitive and behavioural treatment of hypochondriasis. *Psychotherapy and Psychosomatics*, **67**, 214–221.

Burckhardt, C.S., Mannerkorpi, K., Hedenberg, L., & Bjelle, A. (1994). A randomized, controlled clinical trial of education and physical training for women with fibromyalgia. *Journal of Rheumatology, 21,* 714–720.

Carette, S., Bell, M., Reynolds, W.J., Haraoui, B., McCain, G.A., Bykerk, V.P., Edworthy, S.M., Baron, M., Koehler, B.E., & Fam, A.G. (1994). Comparison of amitriptyline, cyclobenzaprine, and placebo in the treatment of fibromyalgia: A randomized, double-blind clinical trial. *Arthritis and Rheumatism, 37,* 32–40.

Clark, D.M., Salkovskis, P.M., Hackmann, A., Wells, A., Fennell, M., Ludgate, J., Ahmad, S., Richards, H.C., & Gelder, M. (1998). Two psychological treatments for hypochondriasis. A randomised controlled trial. *British Journal of Psychiatry, 173,* 218–225.

Clark, S., Tindall, E., & Bennett, R.M. (1985). Double-blind crossover trial of prednisone versus placebo in the treatment of fibrositis. *Journal of Rheumatology, 12,* 980–983.

Comas-Diaz, L. (1981). Effects of cognitive and behavioral group treatment on the depressive symptomatology of Puerto Rican women. *Journal of Consulting and Clinical Psychology, 49,* 627–632.

Deale, A., Chalder, T., Marks, I., & Wessely, S. (1997). Cognitive behavior therapy for chronic fatigue syndrome: A randomized, controlled trial. *American Journal of Psychiatry, 154,* 408–414.

de Gruy, F.V., Dickingson, L.M., Dickinson, W.P., & Candib, L.M. (1999). *The burden of somatization in primary care.* Unpublished manuscript.

Escobar, J.I. (1995). Transcultural aspects of dissociative and somatoform disorders. *The Psychiatric Clinics of North America, 18,* 555–569.

Escobar, J.I., Rubio, M., Canino, G., & Karno, M. (1989). Somatic Symptom Index (SSI): A new and abridged somatization construct: Prevalence and epidemiological correlated in two large community samples. *Journal of Nervous and Mental Disease, 177,* 140–146.

Escobar, J.I., Waitzkin, H., Cohen Silver, R., Gara, M., & Holman, A. (1998). Abridged somatization: A study in primary care. *Psychosomatic Medicine, 60,* 466–472.

Evans, D.L., Leserman, J., Perkings, D.O., Stern, R.A., Murphy, C., Zheng, B., Gettes, D., Longmate, J.A., Silva, S.G., van der Horst, C.M., Hall, C.D., Folds, J.D., Golden, R.N., & Petitto, J.M. (1997). Severe life stress predicts early disease progression in HIV infection. *American Journal of Psychiatry, 154,* 630–634.

Evans, D.L., McCartney, C.F., Haggerty, J.J., Jr., Nemeroff, C.B., Golden, R.N., Simon, J.B., Quade, D., Holmes, V., Droba, M., & Mason, G.A. (1988). Treatment of depression in cancer patients is associated with improved life adaptation: Preliminary findings. *Psychosomatic Medicine, 50,* 72–76.

Ferraccioli, G., Ghirelli, L., Scita, F., Nolli, M., Mozzani, M., Fontana, S., Scorsonelli, M., Tridenti, A., & De Risio, C. (1987). EMG-biofeedback training in fibromyalgia syndrome. *Journal of Rheumatology, 14,* 820–825.

Francis, C.Y., & Whorwell, P.J. (1994). Bran and irritable bowel syndrome: Time for reappraisal. *Lancet, 344,* 39–40.

Fulcher, K.Y., & White, P.D. (1997). Randomised controlled trial of graded exercise in patients with the chronic fatigue syndrome. *British Medical Journal, 341,* 1647–1652.

Gara, M., Cohen Silver, R., Escobar, J.I., Holman, A., & Waitzkin, H. (1998). A hierarchical classes analysis (HICLAS) of primary care patients with medically unexplained somatic symptoms. *Psychiatry Research, 81,* 77–86.

Garcia-Campayo, J., Lobo, A., Perez-Echeverria, J., & Campos, R. (1998). Three forms of somatization presenting in primary care settings in Spain. *Journal of Nervous and Mental Disease, 186,* 554–560.

Greene, B., & Blanchard, E.B. (1994). Cognitive therapy for irritable bowel syndrome. *Journal of Consulting and Clinical Psychology*, **62**, 576–582.

Gureje, O., Simon, G.E., Ustun, T.B., & Goldberg, D.P. (1997). Somatization in cross-cultural perspective: A World Health Organization study in primary care. *American Journal of Psychiatry*, **154**, 989–995.

Guthrie, E., Creed, F., Dawson, D., & Tomenson, B. (1991). A controlled trial of psychological treatment for the irritable bowel syndrome. *Gastroenterology*, **100**, 450–457.

Haanen, H.C.M., Hoenderdos, H.T.W., van Romunde, L.K.J., Hop, W.C.J., Mallee, C., Terwiel, J.P., & Hekster, G.B. (1991). Controlled trial of hypnotherapy in the treatment of refractory fibromyalgia. *Journal of Rheumatology*, **18**, 72–75.

Hellman, C.J.C., Budd, M., Borysenko, J., McClelland, D.C., & Benson, H. (1990). A study of the effectiveness of two group behavioral medicine interventions for patients with psychosomatic complaints. *Behavioral Medicine*, **16**, 165–173.

Holman, E.A., Waitzkin, H., Silver, R., Castillo, R., Villasenor, I., & Escobar, J.I. (1996). Interethnic differences in somatization: Study in primary care. In H. Visotsky, F. Lieh Mak, & J.J. Lopez-Ibor (Eds.), *Abstracts of the X World Congress of Psychiatry* (Vol.1, p. 206).

Hotopft, M., Mayou, R., Wadsworth, M., & Wessley, S. (1998). Temporal relationships between physical symptoms and psychiatric disorder: Results from a national birth cohort. *British Journal of Psychiatry*, **173**, 255–261.

Hyams, K.C.(1988). Developing case definitions for symptom-based conditions: The problem of specificity. *Epidemiologic Reviews*, **20**, 148–56.

Kapoor, W., Fortunato, M., Hanusa, B.H., & Schulberg, H.C. (1995). Psychiatric illness in patients with syncope. *American Journal of Medicine*, **99**, 505–512.

Kashner, T.M., Rost, K., Cohen, B., Anderson, M., & Smith, G.R. (1995). Enhancing the health of somatization disorder patients: Effectiveness of short-term group therapy. *Psychosomatics*, **36**, 462–470.

Katon, W., Lin, E., & Von Korff, M. (1991). Somatizion: A spectrum of severity. *American Journal of Psychiatry*, **148**, 34–40.

Katon, W., Ries, R.K., & Kleinman, A. (1984). The prevalence of somatization in primary care. *Comprehensive Psychiatry*, **25**, 208–15.

Katon, W.J., & Walker, E.A. (1998). Medically unexplained symptoms in primary care. *Journal of Clinical Psychiatry*, **59**, 15–21.

Kirmayer, L.J., & Robbins, J.M. (1991). Three forms of somatization in primary care: Prevalence, co-occurrence and sociodemograohic characteristics. *Journal of Nervous and Mental Disease*, **179**, 647–655.

Klein, K.B. (1988). Controlled treatment trials in the irritable bowel syndrome: A critique. *Gastroenterology*, **95**, 232–241.

Kleinman, A. (1977). Culture, depression and the new cross-cultural psychiatry. *Social Science and Medicine*, **11**, 3–11.

Kleinman, A. (1986). *Social origins of distress and disease*. New Haven, CT: Yale University Press.

Kroenke, K. (1992). Symptoms in medical patients: An untended field. *The American Journal of Medicine*, **92**, 3S–6S.

Kroenke, K., Spitzer, R.L., Willams, J.B., Linzer, M., Hahn, S.R., deGruy, F.V., 3rd & Brody, D. (1994). Physical symptoms in primary care: Predictors of psychiatric disorders and functional impairment. *Archives of Family Medicine*, **3**, 774–779.

Labott, S.M., Preisman, R.C., Torosian, T., Popovich, J., Jr., & Iannuzzi, M.C. (1996). Screening for somatizing patients in the pulmonary subspecialty clinic. *Psychosomatics*, **37**, 327–338.

Langeluddecke, P.M. (1985). Psychological aspects of irritable bowel syndrome. *Australian and New Zealand Journal of Psychiatry*, **19**, 218–226.

Lidbeck, J. (1997). Group therapy for somatization disorders in general practice: Effectiveness of a short cognitive-behavioural treatment model. *Acta Psychiatrica Scandinavica*, **96**, 14–24.

Lynch, P.M., & Zamble, E. (1989). A controlled behavioral treatment study of irritable bowel syndrome. *Behavior Therapy*, **20**, 509–523.

McLeod, C.C., & Budd, M.A. (1997). Treatment of somatization in primary care. *HMO Practice*, **11**, 88–94.

Mezzich, J.E., & Raab, E. (1980). Depressive symptomatology across the Americas. *Archives of General Psychiatry*, **37**, 818–823.

Miranda, J., & Munoz, R. (1994). Intervention for minor depression in primary care patients. *Psychosomatic Medicine*, **56**, 136–142.

Moldofsky, H., Lue, F.A., Mously, C., Roth-Schechter, B., & Reynolds, W.J. (1996). The effect of zolpidem in patients with fibromyalgia: A dose ranging, double-blind, placebo controlled, modified crossover study. *Journal of Rheumatology*, **23**, 529–533.

Musselman, D.L., Evans, D.L., & Nemeroff, C.B. (1998). The relationship of depression to cardiovascular disease. *Archives of General Psychiatry*, **55**, 580–592.

Natelson, B.H., Cheu, J., Pareja, J., Ellis, S.P., Policastro, T., & Findley, T.W. (1996). Randomized, double-blind, controlled placebo-phase in trial of low dose phenelzine in the chronic fatigue syndrome. *Psychopharmacology*, **124**, 226–230.

Noyes, R., Holt, C.S., & Kathol, R.G. (1995). Somatization: Diagnosis and management. *Archives of Family Medicine*, **4**, 790–795.

Organista, K.C., Munoz, R.F., & Gonzalez, G. (1994). *Cognitive behavioral therapy for depression in low-income and minority medical outpatients: Description of a program and exploratory analysis.* Unpublished manuscript.

Payne, A., & Blanchard, E.B. (1995). A controlled comparison of cognitive therapy and self-help support groups in the treatment of irritable bowel syndrome. *Journal of Consulting and Clinical Psychology*, **63**, 779–786.

Putsch, R.W. (1985). Cross-cultural communication: The special case of interpreters in health care. *Journal of the American Medical Association*, **254**, 3344–3348.

Regier, D.A., Narrow, W.E., Rae, D.S., Manderscheid, R.W., Locke, B.Z., & Goodwin, F.K. (1993). The de facto US mental and addictive disorders service system. *Archives of General Psychiatry*, **50**, 85–94.

Rief, W., Heuser, J., Mayrhuber, F., Stelzer, I., Hiller, W., & Fichter, M.M. (1996). The classification of multiple somatoform symptoms. *Journal of Nervous and Mental Disease*, **184**, 680–687.

Rost, K., Kashner, T.M., & Smith, G.R. (1994). Effectiveness of psychiatric intervention with somatization disorder patients: Improved outcomes at reduced costs. *General Hospital Psychiatry*, **16**, 381–387.

Salkovskis, P.M. (1989). Somatic problems. In K. Hawton, P.M. Salkovskis, J. Kirk, & D.M. Clark (Eds.), *Cognitive behavior therapy for psychiatric problems* (pp. 235–276). Oxford: Oxford Medical Publications.

Schulberg, H.C. (1991). Mental disorders in the primary care setting. Research priorities for the 1990s. *General Hospital Psychiatry*, **13**, 156–164.

Sharpe, M., Hawton, K., Simkin, S., Surawy, C., Hackmann, A., Klimes, I., Peto, T., Warrell, D., & Seagroatt, V. (1996). Cognitive behaviour therapy for the chronic fatigue syndrome: A randomised controlled trial. *British Medical Journal*, **312**, 22–26.

Sharpe, M., Peveler, R., & Mayou, R. (1992). The psychological treatment of patients with functional somatic symptoms: A practical guide. *Journal of Psychosomatic Research*, **36**, 515–529.

Shaw, G., Srivastava, E.D., Sadlier, M., Swann, P., James, J.Y., & Rhodes, J. (1991).

Stress management for irritable bowel syndrome: A controlled trial. *Digestion,* **50,** 36–42.

Shorter, E. (1994). *From the mind into the body: The cultural origin of psychosomatic symptoms.* New York: Free Press.

Simon, G.E., & Gureje, O. (1999). Stability of somatization disorder and somatization symptoms among primary care patients. *Archives of General Psychiatry,* **56,** 90–99.

Smith, G.R., Rost, K., & Kashner, T.M. (1995). A trial of the effect of a standardized psychiatric consultation on health outcomes and cost in somatizing patients. *Archives of General Psychiatry,* **52,** 238–243.

Speckens, A.E.M., van Hemert, A.M., Spinhoven, P., Hawton, K.E., Bolk, J.H., & Rooijmans, H.G.M. (1995). Cognitive behavioural therapy for medically unexplained physical symptoms: A randomised controlled trial. *British Medical Journal,* **311,** 1328–1332.

Spiegel, D., Bloom, J.R., Kraemer, H.C., & Gottheil, E. (1989). Effect of psychosocial treatment on survival of patients with metastatic breast cancer. *Lancet,* **2,** 288–291.

Spitzer, R.L., Williams, J.B., Kroenke, K., Linzer, M., de Gruy, F.V., III, Hahn, S.R., Brody, D., & Johnson, J.G. (1994). Utility of a new procedure for diagnosing mental disorders in primary care. The PRIME-MD 1000 study. *Journal of the American Medical Association,* **272,** 1749–1756.

Straus, S.E., Dale, J.K., Tobi, M., Lawley, T., Preble, O., Blaese, R.M., Hallahan, C., & Henle, W. (1988). Acyclovir treatment of the chronic fatigue syndrome: Lack of efficacy in a placebo-controlled trial. *New England Journal of Medicine,* **26,** 1692–1698.

Sullivan, M., Clark M., & Katon, W. (1993). Psychiatric and otologic diagnosis in patients complaining of dizziness. *Archives of Internal Medicine,* **153,** 1479–1484.

Svedlund, J., Sjodin, I., Ottosson, J.O., & Dotevall, G. (1983). Controlled study of psychotherapy in irritable bowel syndrome. *Lancet,* **2,** 589–592.

Swartz, M., Landerman, R., George, L., Blazer, D.G., & Escobar, J. (1991). Somatization disorder. In L. Robins & D.A. Regier (Eds.), *Psychiatric disorders in America* (pp. 221–257). New York: Free Press.

Tun, P.A., Nathan, D.M., & Perlmutter, L.C. (1990). Cognitive and affective disorders in elderly diabetics. *Clinics in Geriatric Medicine,* **6,** 731–746.

Van Dulmen, A.M., Fennis, J.F.M., & Bleijenberg, G. (1996). Cognitive-behavioral group therapy for irritable bowel syndrome: Effects and long-term follow-up. *Psychosomatic Medicine,* **58,** 508–514.

Vercoulen, J.H.M.M., Swanink, C.M.A., Zitman, F.G., Vreden, S.G.S., Hoofs, M.P.E., Fennis, J.F.M., Galama, J.M.D., van der Meer, J.W.M., & Bleijenberg, G. (1996). Randomised, double-blind, placebo-controlled study of fluoxetine in chronic fatigue syndrome. *Lancet,* **347,** 858–861.

Vlaeyen, J.W.S., Teeken-Gruben, N.J.G., Goossens, M.E.J.B., Rutten-van Molken, M.P.M.H., Pelt, R.A.G.B., van Eek, H., & Heuts, P.H.T.G. (1996). Cognitive-educational treatment of fibromyalgia: A randomized clinical trial. I. Clinical effects. *Journal of Rheumatology,* **23,** 1237–1245.

Warwick, H.M.C., Clark, D.M., Cobb, A.M., & Salkovskis, P.M. (1996). A controlled trial of cognitive-behavioural treatment of hypochondriasis. *British Journal of Psychiatry,* **169,** 189–195.

Wearden, A.J., Morriss, R.K., Mullis, R., Strickland, P.L., Pearson, D.J., Appleby, L., Campbell, I.T., & Mossi, J.A. (1998). Randomized, double-blind, placebo controlled study of fluoxetine and graded exercise for chronic fatigue syndrome. *British Journal of Psychiatry,* **172,** 485–490.

Whorwell, P.J., Prior, A., & Farragher, E.B. (1984). Controlled trial of hypnotherapy in the treatment of severe refractory irritable bowel syndrome. *Lancet*, **2**, 1232–1234.

Wittchen, H.U., Robins, L.N., Cottler, L., Sartorius, N., Burke, J.D., & Regier, D. (1991). Cross-cultural feasibility, reliability, and sources of variance of the Composite International Diagnostic Interview (CIDI): The Multicenter WHO/ ADAMHA Field Trials. *British Journal of Psychiatry*, **159**, 645–653; correction (1992) **160**, 136.

Wolfe, F., Cathey, M.A., & Hawley, D.J. (1994). A double-blind placebo controlled trial of fluoxetine in fibromyalgia. *Scandinavian Journal of Rheumatology*, **23**, 255–259.

Wolfe, F., Smythe, H.A., Yunus, M.B., Bennett, R.M., Bombardier, C., & Goldenberg, D.L. (1990). The American College of Rheumatology 1990 criteria for the classification of fibromyalgia: Report of the multicenter criteria committee. *Arthritis and Rheumatism*, **33**, 160–172.

Chapter 10

# HYPOCHONDRIASIS AND HEALTH ANXIETY IN THE ELDERLY

*Allison G. Snyder\* and Melinda A. Stanley†*

## INTRODUCTION

In light of the particular physical and psychological issues faced by the elderly, differences in the presentation of psychiatric disorders might be expected in this population when compared with younger adults. In this chapter, aspects of hypochondriasis and health anxiety that are unique to older adults are highlighted. Although only minimal information addressing hypochondriasis in older individuals is available, the literature on other anxiety disorders in older populations provides valuable insight for understanding this disorder and its associated symptoms. Throughout this chapter, the term 'older' is used interchangeably with 'elderly' to reflect individuals who are age 60 years and older. To begin the chapter, the characteristics of hypochondriasis in the elderly are reviewed, as are clinical features of other anxiety disorders as they relate to health anxiety in older adults. A cognitive-behavioral model of health anxiety and hypochondriasis is then discussed in terms of its application to an older population. Next, assessment and treatment issues pertinent to the measurement of hypochondriasis and health anxiety in the elderly are addressed. In these sections, particular emphasis is given to the unique challenges of assessing and treating older individuals. The chapter concludes with future considerations for work in this domain.

\*Katy-West Houston OB/GYN Associates, USA; †University of Texas-Houston Health Science Center, USA

*Health Anxiety*
Edited by G.J.G. Asmundson, S. Taylor & B.J. Cox
© 2001 John Wiley & Sons Ltd.

# EPIDEMIOLOGY AND PHENOMENOLOGY OF HYPOCHONDRIASIS AND RELATED ANXIETY IN THE ELDERLY

## Hypochondriasis

Limited information is available regarding the prevalence of hypochondriasis in the elderly. Available point-prevalence estimates from older community samples range from 3.9% to 33.0% (Palmore, 1970; Stenback, Kumpulainen, & Vauhkenen, 1978). As compared with comparable estimates of 4.2% to 13.8% for hypochondriasis in general medical patients (Barsky, Wyshak, & Klerman, 1990; Noyes et al., 1993), the rates for current cohorts of older individuals are potentially much greater. However, the available prevalence data for later life hypochondriasis are limited by methodological problems. In particular, variability in the definition and diagnostic criteria for hypochondriasis, as well as the tendency to dichotomize the syndrome as either present or absent, rather than viewing symptoms on a continuum, probably contributed to the broad range in estimates reported. Additionally, critical variables such as medical morbidity and depression, important factors associated with aging, were ignored in these studies and may exacerbate further the discrepancies observed. As such, epidemiological studies that account for potential confounding variables are needed to identify the true prevalence of hypochondriasis in the elderly.

Although the relative prevalence of hypochondriasis across different age groups remains unclear, a common impression is that older adults exhibit greater hypochondriacal concerns compared with younger adults. This prevailing stereotype of the elderly being preoccupied with their bodily functioning and fearful of having a disease is consistent with early characterizations of hypochondriasis found in the literature (e.g., Busse, 1976, 1987; Leon, Gillum, Gillum, & Gouze, 1979). One study found that over half of all hypochondriacal patients presenting for care at a specialty clinic were over 60 years of age, with the majority being female (Busse, 1976).

More recent investigations, controlling for potential confounding variables, have indicated that hypochondriacal symptoms are no more common or severe in the elderly compared with other age groups (e.g., Barsky, Frank, Cleary, Wyshak, & Klerman, 1991; Costa & McCrae, 1980; Levkoff, Cleary, & Wetle, 1987). In the only study to examine the association between age and hypochondriasis directly, Barsky et al. (1991) found that hypochondriacal symptoms existed across the lifespan and were unrelated to age. In this study, 60 patients who met the DSM-III-R diagnostic criteria for hypochondriasis and 100 comparison patients from a general medical clinic completed a battery of self-report and clinician-rated measures. The Whiteley Index (Pilowsky, 1967) and Somatic Symptom Inventory (see Barsky et al., 1991 for description of the measure) were used to assess hypochondriacal symptoms. Comparisons revealed that hypochondriacal patients did not differ in age from the non-hypochondriacal comparison group. Moreover, within the hypochondriacal group, patients over 65 years of age did not differ from younger patients in hypochondriacal attitudes, somatization, tendency to amplify bodily sensations, or global assessment of their overall health. In fact, a non-significant trend was observed, with the elderly group endorsing less disease fear and disease conviction. The absence of age differences existed despite greater levels of medical morbidity among the elderly patients as determined by physician rating and medical record audit. Differences by age within the hypochondriacal group did emerge, however, regarding social and functional activity levels, with older patients reporting greater difficulty participating in social events and activities of daily living. This decline in functioning with age was not observed in the comparison group, despite similar medical morbidity, suggesting that older hypochondriacal patients are less functional than younger patients despite similarities in hypochondriacal symptoms. This finding suggests that severe health anxiety may be more debilitating in the elderly even when symptom severity is comparable to younger patients.

Given that this study was cross-sectional, not longitudinal, cohort effects must be considered when drawing conclusions. The unique features or experiences that characterize the various age groups, not age itself, may account for the presence or absence of differences noted. For example, differences in reporting styles and willingness to disclose symptoms, historical events during the cohort's lifetime, and selective attrition may influence findings in a cross-sectional study design. Thus, the potential impact of cohort effects needs to be considered when interpreting the results of all studies that address the relationship between age and hypochondriasis given the absence of longitudinal studies in this area.

In addition to the phenomenology of hypochondriacal fears themselves, the role of personality factors in hypochondriasis also has been examined across the lifespan. This general relationship is described in greater detail in Chapter 4, but two variables, neuroticism and anxiety sensitivity (AS), are addressed briefly here relative to late-life hypochondriasis. First, neuroticism, a stable and enduring personality characteristic across age, has been suggested as an underlying factor for hypochondriacal symptoms in adults of all ages (Costa & McCrae, 1985). Data supporting a positive association between number of medical complaints and neuroticism have been documented with both older and younger males irrespective of diagnosis (i.e., hypochondriasis versus normals; Costa & McCrae, 1980). That is, higher levels of neuroticism are associated with greater numbers of somatic complaints regardless of age. In fact, somatic concern, also a stable trait, appears to be an enduring individual characteristic that is a better predictor of number of somatic complaints than age. As such, these findings provide indirect support for consistency in personality features associated with hypochondriasis across older and younger individuals. Given the exclusive use of males in these studies, however, additional research is needed to assess the role of neuroticism in hypochondriasis among older females.

Due to the heightened attention to bodily sensations characteristic of hypochondriasis as well as aging, AS may be another important personality dimension associated with health anxiety in the elderly. AS is the tendency to believe that anxiety-related bodily symptoms are dangerous or threatening. The relation between AS and hypochondriasis has not been addressed directly in older adults, although data do suggest a positive association between AS and neuroticism (Lilienfeld, 1997). In at least one non-clinical sample of older adults, AS also was identified as a predictor of panic symptoms (Deer & Calamari, 1998). This finding is consistent with the AS literature pertaining to younger adults (Taylor, 1995; Taylor, Koch, & McNally, 1992). The specific role of AS in the development or maintenance of hypochondriacal fears in older adults, however, remains unknown.

In summary, early studies suggest a higher prevalence of hypochondriasis among the elderly, however, the accuracy of these rates is uncertain due to methodological issues. Recent investigations with stronger methodological controls suggest similar manifestations of hypochondriasis between older and younger adults. This constancy in phenomenology persists despite increasing rates of medical problems among older adults. Further support for the stability of hypochondriacal symptoms irrespective of age is reflected in the association between personality dimensions and hypochondriasis. Therefore, although the elderly face different challenges both psychologically and physically, these factors do not appear to result in variability in the prevalence or severity of hypochondriacal fears compared with younger adults. However, some evidence suggests that the impact of severe health anxiety in later years may result in greater functional disability. Longitudinal studies are needed to assess changes in the manifestation of health anxiety symptoms and their effects throughout the aging process.

## Health-Related Fears and Other Anxiety Disorders

Although the true prevalence of hypochondriasis remains unclear, the prevalence and nature of anxiety disorders in older community and primary care samples suggests that health anxiety is a significant clinical concern in later life. Specifically, health-related anxiety is an important factor in generalized anxiety disorder (GAD), phobias, panic disorder (PD), and obsessive-compulsive disorder (OCD) as manifested in the elderly. In addition, factors associated with aging, such as higher rates of medical illness, physical fragility, and a heightened sense of mortality, may contribute to excessive preoccupation with health-related issues. In fact, 10% to 15% of older adults exhibit a marked concern about their health and overestimate their level of physical impairment (Ables, 1997).

Anxiety disorders in later life clearly pose a significant mental health problem for older adults. Epidemiological Catchment Area (ECA) data, for example, indicated 1- and 6-month prevalence rates of 4.6% and 5.5% for anxiety disorders in individuals aged 65 and older (Regier et al., 1988; Weissman et al., 1985). Although these figures are slightly lower than those from younger anxious samples, they nevertheless indicate that late-life anxiety disorders are problematic, with higher prevalence rates even than for depression in older samples (Regier et al., 1988; Weissman et al., 1985). It is important to note that ECA figures may have underestimated the percentage of older adults with significant anxiety problems. First, many older individuals under-report or deny psychological symptoms (Lasoski, 1986; Oxman, Barrett, Barrett, & Gerber, 1987). Second, published ECA figures were derived largely from community-dwelling samples (Weissman et al., 1985), and rates of anxiety disorders appear to be much higher among institutionalized elderly (Cheok, Snowdon, Miller, & Vaughan, 1996; Parmalee, Katz, & Lawton, 1993). Third, initial ECA data omitted consideration of two major anxiety disorders, GAD and post-traumatic stress disorder (PTSD), that are relatively common among older adults (Averill & Beck, 2000; Blazer, George, & Hughes, 1991). Finally, significant late-life anxiety symptoms that do not meet diagnostic criteria for psychiatric disorders have been estimated to occur in up to 20% of community samples (Feinson & Thoits, 1986; Himmelfarb & Murrell, 1983). Thus, available data suggest that anxiety disorders and serious anxiety symptoms occur frequently in older adults.

It appears that phobic-spectrum disorders (i.e., agoraphobia, social phobia, and specific phobia) may be the most common anxiety syndromes among the elderly (Blazer et al., 1991). Although health-related fears are frequently part of the clinical picture for patients with agoraphobia and specific phobias, detailed information regarding the prevalence and nature of specific disease-related fears is absent from the older adult literature. However, specific phobias related to illness, death, or blood and injury may be common. For example, Liddell, Locker, and Burman (1991) reported that older adults endorsed fears that focused on illness, injury, or death of a loved one, thoughts of an untimely death, auto accidents, being in a fight, looking foolish, failing a test, and suffocating. Clearly, many of these concerns reflect aging-related issues and are associated with health and well-being. Thus, given the potentially high prevalence of health-related fears not encompassed within the hypochondriasis diagnosis per se, information regarding the frequency and impact of these types of fears in older adults is important to the understanding of the continuum of health anxiety.

Among the more pervasive anxiety disorders, GAD is the most common (Blazer et al., 1991). GAD is characterized by excessive worry and anxiety accompanied by physical symptoms including muscle tension, disturbed sleep, restlessness, and fatigue. In addition, behavioral avoidance and procrastination arising from the anxiety symptoms often result in impaired functioning and diminished quality of life. The somatic symptoms of GAD are similar to many of the vague, non-specific physical complaints common in primary care settings. In fact, an association has been found between self-reported worry and perceived illness in the elderly (Wisocki, 1988; Wisocki, Handen, & Morse, 1986).

Although worry is present across all ages, predominant worry themes vary by age group. In a descriptive study, Person and Borkovec (1995) categorized the topic of community participants' worries into five content areas: (a) family/interpersonal, (b) illness/health/injury, (c) work/school, (d) finances, and (e) miscellaneous. Older adults (aged 65 and older) reported more frequent worries about health, whereas younger adults (aged 25 to 64) worried more about family and finances. These data suggest that older adults are preoccupied by concerns regarding health and illness, even in the absence of a diagnosis of hypochondriasis or other anxiety disorders.

Other investigations have revealed similar findings regarding the worry themes of older adults despite the fact that current cohorts of these individuals worry less overall compared with younger adults (Powers, Wisocki, & Whitbourne, 1992; Wisocki, 1988). For example, Wisocki (1988) found that the primary, health-related worries of 94 elderly community participants included fear of sensory and motor losses, failing memory, illness or accident involving family member, loss of independence, and depression. No differences by gender, marital status, or socioeconomic status were observed for these themes. Similarly, Skarborn and Nicki (1996) found health-related worries the most prevalent concern among a community sample of Canadian older adults (65 years and older). This pattern was consistent across both mobile and homebound elderly.

Among older adults diagnosed with GAD, health-related fears also are common. For example, Beck, Stanley, and Zebb (1996) compared a sample of older GAD patients with a group of normal controls who were matched for age, gender, and education. Health-related worries, along with social and financial concerns, were greater for the older adults with GAD compared with same-aged controls.

Although the diagnosis of hypochondriasis may not be more common in the elderly, anxiety disorders are prevalent and many of these are characterized by health-related fears and worries. Even among community-dwelling older adults, fears and worries reflect a significant concern regarding their health and well-being. Although the themes of worry appear realistic for elderly individuals, the intensity and excessiveness of the worries can vary greatly, with anxiety disorders falling at the far end of the spectrum. Overall, worries and fears predominated by health-related themes remain a substantial problem that impact overall quality of life for a subset of the elderly population (Skarborn & Nicki, 1996).

## Associated Risk Factors

A number of factors associated with aging, as well as gender and ethnicity, may increase the older individual's vulnerability to severe health anxiety or the emergence of later-life hypochondriacal symptoms. First, the social isolation experienced by many elderly persons may increase the likelihood or intensity of hypochondriacal symptoms (Barsky, 1993; Busse, 1976). Social isolation in later life can be the result of many age-related changes including retirement, death of a spouse, and institutionalization. A second risk factor for older adults is the high prevalence of psychological disorders having somatic concerns as secondary features (Barsky, 1993). Anxiety and depressive disorders, both common in the elderly, are characterized by physiological disturbances, particularly in older adults. And finally, the greater medical morbidity and physical fragility of older individuals may increase their risk for health anxiety (Barsky, 1993). Normal bodily changes associated with aging may serve to heighten attention directed toward, and preoccupation with, health and disease, suggesting a potential vulnerability to subclinical levels of health anxiety. Methodologically sound studies are needed to clarify this relationship.

Higher rates of hypochondriasis have been reported among older women compared with older men (Busse, 1976). However, due to the methodological limitations associated with the prevalence studies described previously, the true nature of gender differences among the elderly diagnosed with hypochondriasis remains unclear. No information regarding ethnic differences in hypochondriasis among the elderly is available in the literature.

Slightly more information is available regarding these demographic factors for anxiety disorders [see Stanley & Beck (2000) for review]. As with younger adults, older women (65 and older) stand a greater chance of experiencing an anxiety disorder, relative to older men, with a documented 2:1 ratio (e.g., Regier et al., 1988; Weissman et al., 1985). Similar findings also exist for self reported anxiety levels. For example, women report higher levels of trait anxiety (Himmelfarb & Murrell, 1983) and fearfulness (Liddell et al., 1991), as well as greater frequency of specific phobias (Fredrikson, Annas, Fischer, & Wik, 1996). Thus, it appears that among the elderly, women are at greater risk for anxiety problems than men. The higher rate of anxiety in women combined with their greater tendency to seek medical care may result in higher rates of health-related anxiety in older women compared with men, although no data have yet addressed this issue.

Although ethnicity may play an important role in anxiety disorders, there is a paucity of data on this topic. The available data indicate lower rates of DSM-III disorders in general among elderly African-Americans relative to elderly Caucasians, except for cognitive impairment (Weissman et al., 1985). An exception is GAD, in which African-American women had the highest prevalence and African-American men the lowest prevalence with rates among non-black women and men falling between these two groups (Blazer et al., 1991). In general, ethnic variables have been overlooked in the literature on anxiety disorders in the elderly. When ethnicity is reported, ethnic minority groups often are under-represented (e.g., Feinson & Thoits, 1986), limiting any conclusions based upon the data. Future investigations hopefully will pay greater attention to this potentially critical variable.

## Comorbidity and Differential Diagnosis

As with many mental health issues, hypochondriasis often coexists with other disorders. For example, hypochondriasis and health-related anxiety may present with other psychiatric disorders including panic disorder (PD), OCD, specific phobias, GAD, depression, and somatization disorder. Information regarding the nature of these disorders and their relation with hypochondriasis further elucidates the manifestation of health anxiety in the elderly.

### Panic Disorder

Extensive study of the association between hypochondriasis and PD in younger adults revealed that panic patients often exhibit hypochondriacal symptoms (Noyes, Reich, Clancy, & O'Gorman, 1986; Otto, Pollack,

Sachs, & Rosenbaum, 1992; Starcevic, Kellner, Uhlenhuth, & Pathak, 1992). Also, evidence that panic attacks may develop in the presence of hypochondriasis (Fava, Grandi, Saviotti, & Conti, 1990), and that hypochondriasis may predispose to the development of PD (Fava & Kellner, 1993) has been documented. Although believed to be rare among the elderly, evidence has emerged suggesting that later-life PD is more common that originally thought (Luchins & Rose, 1989; Raj, Corvea, & Dagon, 1993; Sheikh, King, & Taylor, 1991). Examination of early-onset (age ≤59 years) versus late-onset (age ≥60 years) PD indicates that the phenomenology of PD appears similar across older and younger individuals (Raj et al., 1993). Interestingly, however, the late-onset group was more likely to have medical disorders such as chronic obstructive pulmonary disease (COPD), vertigo, and Parkinson's disease. Given the available information, a similar relationship to that found between hypochondriasis and PD in younger adults may exist in the elderly.

*Obsessive-Compulsive Disorder*

As with PD, OCD has been examined extensively in relation to hypochondriasis with younger adults. Researchers have emphasized the similarities between the preoccupation with illness and reassurance-seeking behaviors of hypochondriasis and the obsessions and rituals of OCD (Savron et al., 1996). Hypochondriasis has also been proposed as an obsessive-compulsive spectrum disorder due to the common feature of preoccupation with bodily sensations or appearance (Hollander et al., 1996; McElroy, Phillips, & Keck, 1994). Although OCD is infrequent among older adults (Regier et al., 1988; Weissman et al., 1985), the severity and phenomenology of clinical features of the disorder appear to be similar across age groups (Kohn, Westlake, Rasmussen, Marsland, & Norman, 1997). Despite higher levels of handwashing and fear of having sinned in older compared with younger patients, few differences in the clinical presentation of OCD were found by age. As such, findings regarding the relation between hypochondriasis and OCD in younger adults likely are reflective of the association in older adults.

*Specific Phobias*

Given the significant diagnostic similarities, a connection between a health-related specific phobia and hypochondriasis has also been considered. The main distinction between the two disorders has been proposed to involve differentiating the fear of getting a particular disease (specific phobia) from the fear of already having a disease (hypochondriasis; American Psychiatric Association, 1994). Specific illness phobias might be more prevalent among the elderly, given both heightened concerns about health and the relatively increased prevalence of phobias among older adults. However, no data have yet addressed the prevalence of disease-focused specific phobias in older adults. Differential diagnosis between these phobias and hypochondriasis may be more difficult for older adults, particularly those with comorbid medical disorders. It is also possible that the diagnostic similarities between illness phobia and hypochondriasis may result in inaccurate diagnosis, leading to the conclusion of the elderly as hypochondriacal when in reality, they are suffering with a specific phobia related to disease.

*Generalized Anxiety Disorder*

As stated above, older patients with GAD report a predominance of health-related worries. This prevalence suggests a possible overlap between GAD and hypochondriasis among the elderly. In fact, Barsky, Wyshak, and Klerman (1992) found GAD to be the most common comorbid condition among all-aged hypochondriacal patients, with a lifetime prevalence of 71.4%. However, despite a high prevalence of illness and health concerns in GAD that suggest the possibility of significant overlap between the two disorders (Craske, Rapee, Jackel, & Barlow, 1989), a recent investigation of younger GAD patients revealed no increased risk for comorbid hypochondriais (Starcevic et al., 1992). In this sample, the worries about illness characteristic of some GAD patients were independent from disease phobias and hypochondriacal beliefs. This distinction is consistent with the DSM-IV criterion for GAD that the related worry is 'not about having a serious illness' (American Psychiatric Association, 1994). As such, when diagnosed accurately, GAD and hypochondriasis appear to be separate and distinct entities for younger adults. Given the phenomenological similarities in GAD for older and younger patients, the same association likely exists in the elderly.

*Depression*

Depression has been examined widely in regard to its association with hypochondriasis. Due to its prevalence in the elderly (Regier et al., 1988; Weissman et al., 1985), depression is an important comorbid factor to consider. Symptoms of hypochondriasis are prevalent among the depressed elderly (Blazer, 1998), with one study documenting hypochondriacal concerns in 60% of elderly inpatients admitted for depression (Kramer-Ginsberg, Greenwald, Aisen, & Brod-Miller, 1989). Such findings are consistent with the concept of 'masked depression', which is characterized by the emphasis of somatic complaints and minimization of dysphoric mood. This emphasis on somatic symptoms may reflect the reluctance of many older adults to acknowledge psychological or emotional difficulties. However, Kramer-Ginsberg et al. (1989) found no differences between hypochondriacal and non-hypochondriacal patients in global depressive symptom severity, regardless of age and severity of medical illness. This study was limited by restrictions in the sample age ($M = 75 \pm 5.78$ years) and range of medical status. In contrast, Lyness, King, Conwell, Cox, and Caine (1993) found that increasing age and depressive symptomatology were predictors of greater somatic concern in depressed inpatients. Again, cohort effects may account for the differences in presentation. For example, elderly individuals may have been raised to believe that physical, not emotional, complaints are acceptable to express. Also, greater somatic concerns might be explained by growing medical problems, rather than increasing age. As such, the nature of the relation between hypochondriasis and depression in older adults remains unclear.

*Somatization Disorder*

Somatization disorder (SD), like hypochondriasis, is classified as a somatoform disorder. However, SD is characterized by the presence of multiple somatic symptoms that are biomedically unexplained, with an onset before age 30. The 1-month prevalence of SD in adults has been documented as less than 1% (Regier et al., 1988). In a cross-sectional study of psychiatric and medical outpatient women (aged 18–86 years), no differences were observed in the prevalence and characteristics of SD in older (55 years and older) compared with younger patients (Pribor, Smith, & Yutzy, 1994). These findings suggest the possibility of a chronic, stable course to SD across the lifespan, a phenomenon that could potentially be an artifact of diagnostic criteria requiring onset before age 30. However, longitudinal studies that include male participants are needed to substantiate this conclusion.

Examination of the diagnostic criteria for SD reflects critical distinctions from hypochondriasis and challenges for accurate diagnosis in the elderly. First, as already noted, a diagnosis of SD requires the presence of somatic symptoms prior to age 30, and this requirement for diagnosis requires the elderly patient to recall symptom onset dating back at least 30 years. No similar age-related criterion exists for hypochondriasis. As such, this diagnostic criterion makes assessment of SD in the elderly especially challenging. A second distinction of SD from hypochondriasis is the requirement of at least eight somatic symptoms (out of 40) that exist across four specific categories of symptom types. Whereas hypochondriasis focuses more specifically on the belief that one has a particular disease, SD encompasses a broader spectrum of bodily complaints. Given the increasing medical morbidity in the elderly, efforts to insure that each somatic complaint does not have a medical explanation is critical.

*Summary*

Overall, the elderly seem to experience hypochondriasis at rates similar to younger adults. This phenomenon may suggest that older adults are more effective in their coping efforts given that prevalence rates remain the same across age groups, despite increasing rates of medical morbidity in older ages. However, as previously mentioned, potential cohort effects must be acknowledged. This finding is contradictory to the inaccurate perception that most elderly individuals are preoccupied with disease and illness. Those older adults who suffer with anxiety disorders are likely to experience fears and worries regarding health, disease, illness, and overall well-being. As such, the presentation of late-life anxiety is likely to be dominated by health-related issues. This assumption is supported by the fact that anxiety often is manifested by an emphasis on somatic symptoms in older adults.

## GENERAL MODEL OF HYPOCHONDRIASIS: APPLICATION TO THE ELDERLY

A number of theories exist to explain hypochondriasis, including psychodynamic conceptualizations (Barsky & Klerman, 1983; Starcevic, 1989), biological approaches (Nemiah, 1977), and cognitive-behavioral perspectives (Warwick & Salkovskis, 1989, 1990). The most widely accepted approach to conceptualizing hypochondriasis is the cognitive-behavioral model. A detailed description of this model is provided in Chapter 4. Only a cursory review of the general theory is presented here in order to highlight the special issues regarding its application to older adults.

### Cognitive-Behavioral Model

The cognitive-behavioral model of hypochondriasis emphasizes the multiplicity of factors likely involved in the etiology of the disorder, including the awareness of family medical history that, in turn, heightens sensitivity to specific symptoms, along with the experience of specific traumatic events related to illness. Dysfunctional attitudes and assumptions related to health and disease are proposed to form during early experiences. These attitudes may result in selective attention to health-related information, specifically attending to cues that are consistent with disease and ignoring evidence indicative of good health. In the cognitive-behavioral model, this 'confirmatory bias' serves to maintain initial dysfunctional assumptions about health. Further contributing to the development of health anxiety and hypochondriasis are critical incidents that serve to activate dysfunctional assumptions. Such incidents include death of a relative, poor medical management, and intense media focus on a disease. The faulty perception of health-related stimuli, however, forms the central focus within the cognitive-behavioral approach to hypochondriasis and extreme health anxiety.

Once anxiety about health has developed, mechanisms also are suggested that maintain the problem, namely physiological arousal, selective attention, and avoidance behaviors. The anxiety about health and illness symptoms often results in physiological arousal, which in turn is often misinterpreted as further evidence of physical disease as the result of selective attention processes. Thus, amplification of normal physiological functions results in increasing anxiety, thus exacerbating illness fears. Concurrent with the biased appraisal of threatening cues is the evaluation of being unable to cope with such a threat. Typical behavioral responses that result from this perceived inability to cope include various actions designed to avoid, check for, or totally exclude physical illnesses. Examples of these responses might include checking of vital signs, calls to the physician, restrictions in physical activity, and monitoring of bodily changes. These behaviors maintain the anxiety through a process of negative reinforcement. Overall, the model provides a framework for understanding the development and maintenance of hypochondriasis and severe health anxiety.

## Application to the Elderly

As evidenced by the growing literature on aging and psychological disorders, the assumption that such disorders are manifested in the same manner across age groups can lead to inaccurate generalizations. Therefore, the cognitive-behavioral model of hypochondriasis and health anxiety outlined above must be assessed regarding its applicability to the elderly. No empirical data yet have addressed this issue, but a number of hypotheses are proposed as follows.

First, many factors associated with aging support the likelihood that older adults experience selective attention for health-related stimuli. For example, the elderly often experience greater somatic changes in addition to the natural decrease in physical agility. Such events might serve to heighten attention to physiological functioning in older individuals. Also, changes in sensory perception frequently associated with aging might facilitate later onset of hypochondriacal fears. Specifically, the faulty perception of health-related stimuli may result from changes in auditory or visual acuity. Additionally, declines in cognitive functioning demonstrated by memory impairment or dementia also might contribute to a preoccupation with health-related cues.

Second, experiences faced during later life may serve as critical incidents in the emergence of hypochondriacal fears. For example, the elderly are likely to experience a greater number of traumatic events related to health including the illness or death of a spouse or close friend, personal experience with disease, and falls or bodily injuries. In addition, by nature of their declining health status, older adults have greater opportunities to interact with medical personnel, increasing their chances for medical mismanagement. As such, older individuals by nature of their experiences are likely exposed to numerous events that may serve as critical incidents leading to severe health anxiety.

Third, the true physiological changes associated with aging may serve to exacerbate difficulties managing health anxiety. The increased physiological arousal that accompanies or is caused by the experience of real somatic changes in the elderly may be misinterpreted as a sign of illness. The fear of possible illness then heightens the existing physiological arousal, resulting in greater attention to bodily responses. This entire cycle may be exacerbated by medication effects in the elderly. Given that older adults experience greater physical fragility and disease irrespective of a diagnosis of hypochondriasis, this bodily dysfunction may only serve to intensify pre-existing health anxiety or decrease perceived ability to function in patients diagnosed with hypochondriasis. These factors may contribute to greater functional impairment in older patients with hypochondriasis, although symptom severity seems to remain consistent across age groups (Barsky et al., 1991).

Finally, the role of perceived inability to cope may have a central role in the etiology and maintenance of hypochondriasis for older adults. In fact, this factor may account for the lack of apparent increase in the prevalence of hypochondriasis among the elderly despite their increasing health problems. Although older adults are faced with increased physical fragility and higher rates of disease, they also have years of life experience fostering opportunities for the development of effective coping strategies. As such, the increasing threat associated with greater vulnerability to disease with age may be offset by the presence of coping strategies refined over time. However, avoidance and checking of symptoms that, at low levels, can be effective coping behaviors are associated with health-related fears in older adults and can negatively reinforce health anxiety. Further research is needed to clarify the nature of effective coping behaviors in the elderly relative to health-related stimuli.

Overall, the cognitive-behavioral model of hypochondriasis does appear to have applicability to elderly patients with hypochondriasis, although direct tests of this hypothesis are needed. Given the numerous factors associated with aging that might serve to facilitate the development of hypochondriacal concerns based on this model, the absence of data supporting increases in the diagnosis of hypochondriasis with age is notable. As stated previously, the majority of research in this domain has employed cross-sectional designs that are vulnerable to cohort effects, and the impact of these needs to be examined in longitudinal studies. In addition, potential confounding variables, such as mortality and protective factors, need to be examined in the context of the relationship between age and hypochondriasis.

## ASSESSMENT OF HYPOCHONDRIASIS AND HEALTH ANXIETY IN THE ELDERLY

Although comprehensive overviews of the assessment of hypochondriasis and health anxiety are provided in Chapters 5 and 6, some unique issues need to be considered when working with elderly patients. This section outlines some of the critical variables that require consideration when assessing health anxiety in older adults.

### General Considerations

As detailed in Chapter 6, patients diagnosed with hypochondriasis often exhibit comorbid disorders and symptoms that add to the complexity of the diagnostic assessment. Particularly when assessing health anxiety in older adults, differential diagnosis often is complicated by the coexistence of both psychological and medical symptoms. Recognizing health anxiety in older medical patients may be even more difficult given tendencies among older cohorts to present with somatic rather than psychological symptoms and to attribute anxiety-related symptoms to physical illness, thereby denying or under-reporting psychological difficulties (Blazer, 1998; Gurian & Miner, 1991).

In order to assess for health anxiety in the elderly, both medical and psychological evaluations are needed. Given the increased rates of medical morbidity, it is critical to attend to possible biomedical diseases in the older patient with health anxiety. As such, a basic medical examination is essential. The recommended examination for older adults (65 and older) involves a thorough history, physical, and laboratory evaluation that includes routine labs, an electrocardiograph (ECG), and a thyroid study (Barbee & McLaulin, 1990). When elderly patients present with a recent onset of somatic complaints, organic causes need to be ruled out immediately. Although these initial medical steps are usually completed for patients with health anxiety, careful consideration of potential medical problems possibly overlooked or undetected is critical when assessing older patients.

Once biomedical factors have been assessed, examination of psychological factors can proceed. As stated previously, anxiety disorders are the most prevalent mental health issue faced by older adults. As such, when conducting an assessment for hypochondriasis and health anxiety, other anxiety disorders such as specific phobias, panic disorder, and GAD must be considered. This differential diagnosis can be complicated by the overlap in symptoms between hypochondriasis and other anxiety disorders (see Chapter 6). Depressive disorders also need to be assessed in light of their prevalence in the elderly and their common coexistence with anxiety disorders and hypochondriasis (Hyer, Gouveia, Harrison, Warsaw, & Coutsouridis, 1987). Therefore, the differential diagnosis with older adults can be challenging.

In addition to issues surrounding differential diagnosis of medical and psychological disorders, other more general factors need to be considered when assessing hypochondriasis in the elderly. First, the instruments used for assessment need to be sensitive to age-related changes in cognitive and sensory functioning (Hersen & VanHasselt, 1992). For example, the physical presentation of the self-report measures can impact their utility. Font style and size of characters used must be selected to increase clarity and minimize the impact of possible visual impairments. These slight adjustments to the forms can facilitate administration and increase the accuracy of data obtained. Second, when conducting clinical interviews, the volume, pace, and clarity of the interviewer's speech is important. Many older adults have hearing deficits, and some are too embarrassed to acknowledge their difficulties. It is essential to speak loud enough to be heard and to avoid the use of psychological jargon.

Third, assessment with older adult requires more active participation on the part of the assessor in order to structure the process. The interviewer might offer initiatives that invite the patient to discuss the problems rather than relying on the patient to raise important issues (Barbee & McLaulin, 1990). To reduce apprehension in the elderly patient, the interviewer might also inquire first about current life circumstances and then follow with questions regarding affective functioning. Since older adults have more life experiences to recall, the interviewer can facilitate the collection of background information by helping to keep historical accounts organized (Pfieffer, 1979). Fourth, given the tendency for diagnostic assessments to be lengthy, frequent breaks are essential for older patients. Planning breaks to use the restroom or get some water make the assessment experience more tolerable to the elderly patient, in turn enhancing the likelihood of accurate data collection (Akkerman et al., in press).

Finally, in addition to minimization or denial of psychological symptoms, older adults often engage in a pattern of social desirability responding (Salzman, 1979). For older adults, it is often the case that somatic complaints are acceptable and psychological disturbances are not. As such, when assessing older individuals, sensitivity to these cohort effects is important, especially when dealing with individuals who experience health anxiety.

*Measures*

A number of self-report measures of hypochondriasis and health anxiety are used in the field. These are reviewed in some detail in Chapter 6 and will not be discussed here. Instead, attention will be given to those measures with some demonstrated utility among older adults.

Despite special issues relative to assessment of the elderly, only one assessment tool, the Hypochondriasis Scale for Institutional Geriatric Use (HSIG; Brink et al., 1978), has been developed specifically for measuring symptoms of health anxiety in older adult patients. The HSIG is a 6-item scale with a yes/no format (0 to 6) that measures underlying attitudes about health, not the actual level of somatic complaints. Scores of 3 or more are considered indicative of hypochondriacal attitude. Developed initially for use with the long-term care aged, similar norms have been noted for community elders, younger adults, and college and high school students (Brink, 1984), suggesting utility across many settings. The similarities across age groups on this measure are additional support for the notion that the elderly are no more susceptible to hypochondriasis than younger adults. A strength of the HSIG is that scores are not influenced by situational variables such as retirement, bereavement, or physical disability, all stresses pertinent when assessing older adults (Brink, Janakes, & Martinez, 1981). Given the strong sensitivity of the measure in identifying hypochondriasis, along with its ease of administration, the HSIG might be a useful screening tool in primary care settings where older adults tend to present for care.

The Whiteley Index (Pilowsky, 1967) and the Somatic Symptom Inventory (Barsky et al., 1991) also have demonstrated good psychometric properties when used to assess hypochondriasis in a broad-aged sample that included elderly patients (Barsky et al., 1991). However, specific psychometric data for these measures exclusively with older adults was not reported. The Whiteley Index, a 13-item measure of hypochondriacal beliefs and attitudes, yields three factors, including bodily preoccupation, disease phobia, and disease conviction with non-response to reassurance. The Somatic Symptom Inventory is composed of 26 items selected from the MMPI hypochondriasis subscale and the Hopkins Symptom Checklist somatization subscale (Derogatis, 1983; Derogatis, Lipman, Rickels, Uhlenhuth, & Covi, 1974; Lipman, Covi, & Shapiro, 1977). This inventory has demonstrated strong intercorrelations with the Whiteley Index and together the two measures accurately identify hypochondriacal patients in medical settings (Barsky et al., 1986).

Although not a measure of hypochondriasis, the Worry Scale (WS; Wisocki, 1988), a 35-item instrument designed to assess worries specifically in older adults, may be useful in the accurate assessment of health anxiety symptoms. WS items, rated on a 1 to 5 scale, comprise three subscales addressing specific concerns about health, finances, and social situations. Specific items contained in the WS–Health subscale include worries about becoming incapacitated, declining eyesight and hearing, losing control of bladder and kidney functions, along with having a serious illness or accident. Total WS scores correlate highly with general measures of anxiety, as well as self-ratings of poorer health and more chronic illness (Wisocki, 1988). Excellent internal consistency for all WS subscales was demonstrated for a sample of older adults with well-diagnosed GAD (alphas = 0.85–0.95; Stanley, Beck, & Glassco, 1996a; Stanley, Novy, Bourland, Beck, & Averill, 2001). Given the predominance of health-related worries in older GAD patients and the frequent coexistence of GAD in hypochondriacal patients, the WS may serve as a valuable measure in facilitating differentiation between health worries and disease fears although the scale has yet to be used for this purpose.

Another relevant measure when assessing health anxiety is the Anxiety Sensitivity Index (ASI; Reiss, Peterson, Gursky, & McNally, 1986). The ASI reflects somatic fears, specifically fear of one's own anxiety symptoms. Although the psychometric properties of the ASI have yet to be assessed for older adults, the information obtained may be useful in clarifying the clinical presentation of older hypochondriacal patients. Other anxiety measures also may be useful in characterizing the clinical picture for older hypochondriacal patients. Recent investigations have documented the psychometric properties of traditional anxiety measures for use with older adults (Stanley, Beck, & Zebb, 1996b). In addition to the WS, the State–Trait Anxiety Inventory (Spielberger, Gorsuch, & Lushene, 1970), the Beck Anxiety Inventory (Beck & Steer, 1993), the Padua Inventory (Sanavio, 1988), and the Fear Questionnaire (Marks & Mathews, 1979) appear to have some utility in assessing anxiety among older adults (Morin et al., 1999; Stanley et al., 1996b; Stanley et al., 2001; Wetherall &

Arean, 1997). Further investigations are needed to determine the utility of these measures with older adults in distinguishing hypochondriasis from anxiety, OCD, and phobias.

In addition to anxiety measures, measures of depression have been examined for their utility with older adults and these may be useful in providing a comprehensive evaluation of older adults with health anxiety. The Geriatric Depression Scale (GDS; Yesavage et al., 1983), designed specifically for the elderly, may be a particularly useful tool for assessing depressive symptoms in hypochondriacal patients given its deletion of somatic items. Strong psychometric properties for the GDS have been documented in older adults with depression (Sheikh & Yesavage, 1986), as well as older adults with GAD (Snyder, Stanley, Novy, Averill, & Beck, 2000).

In sum, the assessment of hypochondriasis and health anxiety in the elderly requires special considerations. Along with sensitivity to their increased medical problems, the cognitive and perceptual changes characteristic of older adults must be acknowledged in the manner assessments are conducted. Although many measures of hypochondriacal symptoms are available, few have been examined for their utility with older individuals. Some data exist regarding the utility of scales for the assessment of anxiety and depressive symptoms in the elderly. These measures can be used to clarify the clinical picture of hypochondriasis and health anxiety in older adults.


## TREATMENT ISSUES RELEVANT TO THE ELDERLY

Despite the prevalence and importance of health anxiety, effective treatment approaches are only in the relatively early stages of development, especially compared to those targeting anxiety disorders such as panic disorder, GAD, and phobias. Limits in this area are due, in part, to the fact that patients with hypochondriasis often resist psychological intervention and present almost solely in medical settings. Although prognosis for hypochondriasis is generally poor, there is promising evidence for a cognitive-behavioral treatment (CBT) approach (Salkovskis & Warwick, 1986; Warwick & Marks, 1988). Comprehensive reviews of current treatment options for hypochondriasis are provided in Chapters 3, 7, 8, and 9. Absent from the literature are data regarding the effectiveness of treatment interventions for health anxiety in the elderly. Accordingly, treatment recommendations for working with the elderly rely upon available information for treatment of younger adults along with the evidence pertaining to treatment of other anxiety disorders in the elderly.

## Psychosocial Interventions

*Hypochondriasis*

The most promising treatment approach for severe health anxiety is based upon the cognitive-behavioral formulation of hypochondriasis. This approach involves the modification of etiological and maintaining factors through cognitive restructuring and reattribution, exposure therapy, and response prevention. Although evaluated solely with adults younger than 60 years of age (Warwick, Clark, Cobb, & Salkovskis, 1996), this treatment approach seems appropriate for elderly patients with hypochondriasis and health anxiety given the stability of symptoms across the lifespan. And, unlike popular perception, the elderly are capable of benefiting from psychotherapy (Lasoski, 1986). However, a few caveats may need to be considered to enhance the effectiveness of psychological treatment with older adults (see Stanley & Averill [1999], for review).

For example, the cognitive-behavioral approach to hypochondriasis involves reframing health-related assumptions and attributions. This reframing process may be especially difficult for older adults who do have a greater number of medical and physical problems, as well as increased risk for various diseases. Also, with elderly patients who may be experiencing some cognitive decline, this process may require simplification by the therapist. In order to facilitate patient understanding, abbreviated sessions focused on concrete tasks might enhance outcome. Therefore, treatment may take a greater number of sessions compared with younger adults. Limitations imposed by managed care organizations regarding the number of sessions authorized could be problematic, especially if younger patients demonstrate improvement in few sessions. To facilitate comprehension, terms such as 'cognitions' can be replaced with 'thoughts', removing possible communication barriers between therapist and the older patient. Additionally, repetition of therapeutic elements in treatment provides the opportunity for clarification of key elements. Given the prevalence of memory problems in the elderly, this repetition seems especially important. Written materials summarizing the information covered during treatment sessions might also be useful as a reference for between-session review.

Although the majority of patients receiving treatment for health anxiety will be apprehensive about psychological interventions, this is especially true for the elderly who are often reluctant to seek assistance for mental health issues (Lasoski, 1986). This reluctance has been attributed to the fact that some older adults associate psychological difficulties with 'being crazy' or a sign of weakness (Small, 1997). This fear is often reinforced by feedback that their problems are 'all in [his/her] head', a common response in the medical field to patients for whom no biomedical cause for reported symptoms can be documented. Accordingly, the therapeutic alliance is especially important when treating older patients with health anxiety. Their inherent distrust for mental health professionals and likely frustration at being referred by their physicians can be reversed through the development of a strong therapeutic alliance. Also helpful with older adults is the use of group interventions. During group treatment, elderly patients have an opportunity to develop social supports, an important variable often missing in their lives. The group setting also serves to normalize their experiences, thus reducing the stigma associated with psychological treatment. Data indicate that CBT for hypochondriasis is feasible in a group setting (Stern & Fernandez, 1991).

A number of professional issues also exist that might effect the use of CBT for hypochondriasis with older adults. For instance, primary care physicians are less likely to refer older than younger patients for psychological treatment and there has been an over-reliance on drug treatment for late-life mental health issues (Ford & Sbordone, 1980). Also, primary care physicians may be hesitant to refer older patients who have coexistent mental and physical illnesses. When primary care physicians do refer elderly patients, often few psychologists specializing in geriatric care are available. These issues need to be addressed in order to insure effective care for the hypochondriacal elderly patient.

Preliminary studies of this cognitive-behavioral approach to the treatment of severe health anxiety in younger adults indicate its utility in managing a challenging issue faced by physicians and psychologists alike. Larger clinical trials, however, are needed before any conclusions are drawn, and evaluation of CBT by age groups is necessary in order to ensure its utility in the elderly.

*Anxiety Disorders*

Although the efficacy of treatment for health anxiety has yet to be examined in an elderly sample, investigations of CBT have been initiated for other well-diagnosed anxiety disorders in later life. In particular, initial trials studying the effectiveness of CBT of GAD in the elderly have been undertaken. These treatment studies are relevant to the treatment of health anxiety in the elderly for at least two reasons. First, the treatment components for GAD share many similarities with the CBT of hypochondriasis, in particular cognitive restructuring and exposure therapy. Second, GAD is the most prevalent of the pervasive anxiety disorders among older individuals and is often accompanied by a preponderance of health-related worries. As such, treatment outcome studies of GAD in the elderly may provide information regarding the utility of similar interventions in the health anxiety domain.

In one such study, the efficacy of CBT was evaluated relative to nondirective supportive psychotherapy for 48 older adults with a principal diagnosis of GAD (Stanley et al., 1996b). CBT included progressive deep muscle relaxation, cognitive therapy, and graduated exposure practice in worry-producing situations. Supportive psychotherapy involved nondirective discussions of anxiety symptoms and experiences. After 14 weeks of group sessions, posttreatment evaluations revealed significant decreases in both treatment conditions on self-report and clinician-rated measures of worry, anxiety, and depression. Overall, the data suggested the potential utility of psychosocial interventions in the treatment of late-life GAD. However, the absence of a no-treatment or waitlist control condition seriously restricted the conclusions that could be drawn from the data.

Two other clinical trials are currently underway to assess the utility of CBT for the treatment of GAD in later life. In one study, the efficacy of 15 weeks of CBT is being compared to a minimal contact control condition in a sample of adults age 60 and older with a principal diagnosis of GAD (Stanley et al., 1999). As with the previous study, CBT involves relaxation training, cognitive therapy, and graduated exposure to anxiety-producing stimuli. Preliminary results suggest meaningful decreases in worry, anxiety, and depression, along with increases in overall quality of life following CBT, with no such changes following minimal contact control. In another study, the effect of CBT for late-life GAD is being investigated in a sample of patients taking benzodiazepines on a regular basis (Gorenstein, Papp, & Kleber, 1999). Patients are randomly assigned to CBT plus medical management, the goal of which is to reduce benzodiazepine use, or medical management alone. Preliminary results suggest potentially greater decreases in various measures of worry and anxiety following CBT plus medical management compared with medical management alone.

In summary, available data suggest the potential utility of CBT for the treatment of late-life anxiety. Specifically, data regarding the utility of CBT with late-life GAD suggest a positive outcome for CBT among elderly health anxiety patients. However, firm conclusions await completion of ongoing and subsequent clinical trials designed to evaluate outcome in well-diagnosed patient groups including older adults with severe health anxiety.

## Pharmacological Interventions

To date, only one controlled trial of drug treatment for hypochondriasis has been reported in the literature (see Chapter 8). Case reports suggest treatment success using selective serotonin reuptake inhibitors (SSRIs) (see Fallon et al., 1996). The evidence regarding the pharmacological treatment of hypochondriasis is covered in Chapter 8 and will not be discossed in detail here. However, several issues relevant to the use of medications with elderly patients will be addressed.

As mentioned above, primary care physicians rely heavily on medications to treat later-life mental health issues. In fact, benzodiazepines, a common choice for treating anxiety, were found to be the most frequently prescribed psychotropic medication to adults aged 60 to 69 years in an assessment of physicians' prescribing practices (Holm, 1988). But when using medications to treat anxiety in older adults, treatment decisions must be guided by a comprehensive understanding of changes in pharmacokinetics and drug responses as they pertain to the elderly (Barbee & McLaulin, 1990). Such changes include alterations in absorption, metabolism, distribution, and excretion of drugs and their metabolites (see Jenike, 1985, for review). Ignorance of such factors could lead to drug toxicity, often exhibited by changes in cognition. Specifically, the toxic effects of medications are observed as psychomotor slowing and anterograde amnesia in the elderly.

In addition to understanding the pharmacological effects of medication in the elderly, possible interaction effects of a medication with the other drugs often prescribed to older adults also require attention. Unlike many younger adults, the majority of older individuals are taking multiple prescriptions with the average elderly (65+) person filling 13 prescriptions annually (Blazer, 1998). A thorough assessment of all medications and their relational effects is essential when initiating pharmacotherapy with an elderly patient.

Finally, practical issues can influence the effectiveness of pharmacological interventions with older patients diagnosed with health anxiety. Adherence to the medication regimen requires a clear understanding of the rationale for treatment, the dosage instructions, and the possible side-effects of the medication. Failure to address any of these components might result in poor adherence and, in turn, decreased effectiveness.

## General Treatment Issues

Although patients suffering with severe health anxiety are unlikely to seek mental health services, this issue is exacerbated when that patient is an older adult. Overall, older adults are less likely to receive formal treatment for mental health issues compared to their younger counterparts. In fact, older adults represent only 2% to 3% of the patients seen in private practice and hospital outpatient clinics (Butler & Lewis, 1982), and only 4% to 5% at community mental health centers are 65 or older (Redick & Taube, 1980). This underutilization is probably even greater for older patients who focus on somatic symptoms.

Practical issues that can interfere with obtaining psychological services also must be recognized when treating older patients (Stanley & Averill, 1999). For example, arranging transportation to treatment settings may be difficult when older patients rely on family members or public transportation for assistance. Also, many older individuals prefer not to drive during peak traffic times or on high-volume roads, thereby limiting their access to clinical services. Payment for psychological services also might interfere with the elderly seeking care. Fixed incomes paired with increasing medical costs can be prohibitive for some older adults. Additionally, when older adults do seek assistance, few mental health treatment providers have expertise in working with the elderly. In sum, although many issues are comparable to treatment with younger patients, a number of critical issues are unique to working with older adults. These issues may impact the effectiveness of treatment with older patients with health anxiety.

## FUTURE CONSIDERATIONS

Overall, the domain of hypochondriasis and health anxiety in the elderly needs further investigation regarding phenomenology, assessment, and treatment. However, information obtained from studies of younger hypochondriacal patients and older patients with anxiety disorders provides direction for future endeavors. Longitudinal studies that assess hypochondriacal symptom severity and its impact on functioning into later-life are needed to more fully understand the nature of hypochondriasis in the elderly. Additional studies examining the psychometric properties of assessment tools with the elderly, along with treatment outcome studies with older adults, will be important next steps in this domain.

## REFERENCES

Ables, N. (1997). *What practitioners should know about working with older adults.* Washington, DC: American Psychological Association.
Akkerman, R., Stanley, M., Beck, J.G., Novy, D., Averill, P., Snyder, A., & Diefenbach, G. (in press). Recruiting old adults with generalized anxiety. *Journal of Mental Health and Aging.*

American Psychiatric Association (1994). *Diagnostic and statistical manual of mental disorders* (4th edn.). Washington, DC: Author.

Averill, P., & Beck, J.G. (2000). Posttraumatic stress disorder in older adults: A conceptual review. *Journal of Anxiety Disorders*, **14**, 133–156.

Barbee, J., & McLaulin, J. (1990). Anxiety disorders: Diagnosis and pharmacotherapy in the elderly. *Psychiatric Annals*, **20**, 439–445.

Barsky, A. (1993). The diagnosis and management of hypochondriacal concerns in the elderly. *Journal of Geriatric Psychiatry*, **26**, 129–141.

Barsky, A.J., & Klerman, G. (1983). Overview: Hypochondriasis, bodily complaints and somatic styles. *American Journal of Psychiatry*, **140**, 273–283.

Barsky, A.J., Frank, C.B., Cleary, P.D., Wyshak, G., & Klerman, G.L. (1991). The relation between hypochondriasis and age. *American Journal of Psychiatry*, **148**, 923–928.

Barsky, A.J., Wyshak, G., & Klerman, G.L. (1986). Hypochondriasis: An evaluation of the DSM-III criteria in medical outpatients. *Archives of General Psychiatry*, **43**, 493–500.

Barsky, A.J., Wyshak, G., & Klerman, G. (1990). The prevalence of hypochondriasis in medical outpatients. *Social Psychiatry and Psychiatric Epidemiology*, **25**, 89–94.

Barsky, A.J., Wyshak, G., & Klerman, G. (1992). Psychiatric comorbidity in DSM-III hypochondriasis. *Archives of General Psychiatry*, **49**, 101–108.

Beck, A., & Steer, R. (1993). *Beck Anxiety Inventory manual* (2nd edn.). San Antonio, TX: Psychological Corporation.

Beck, J.G., Stanley, M., & Zebb, B. (1996). Characteristics of generalized anxiety disorder in older adults: A descriptive study. *Behaviour Research and Therapy*, **34**, 225–234.

Blazer, D. (1998). *Emotional problems in later life: Investigative strategies for professional caregivers*. New York: Springer Publishing Company.

Blazer, D., George, L., & Hughes, D. (1991). The epidemiology of anxiety disorders: An age comparison. In C. Salzman & B. Lebowitz (Eds.), *Anxiety in the elderly: Treatment and research* (pp. 17–30). New York: Springer Publishing Company.

Brink, T. (1984). Use and limitations of the HSIG. *Clinical Gerontologist*, **3**, 68–70.

Brink, T., Belanger, J., Bryant, J., Capri, D., Janakes, C., Jasculca, S., & Oliveira, C. (1978). Hypochondriasis in an institutional geriatric population: Construction of a scale (HSIG). *Journal of the American Geriatric Society*, **26**, 557–559.

Brink, T., Janakes, C., & Martinez, N. (1981). Geriatric hypochondriasis: Situational factors. *Journal of the American Geriatric Society*, **29**, 37–39.

Busse, E.W. (1976). Hypochondriasis in the elderly: A reaction to social stress. *Journal of the American Geriatrics Society*, **24**, 145–149.

Busse, E.W. (1987). Hypochondriasis in the elderly. *Comprehensive Therapy*, **13**, 37–42.

Butler, R., & Lewis, M. (1982). *Aging and mental health* (3rd edn.). St. Louis, MO: C.V. Mosby.

Cheok, A., Snowdon, J., Miller, R., & Vaughan, R. (1996). The prevalence of anxiety disorders in nursing homes. *International Journal of Geriatric Psychiatry*, **11**, 405–410.

Costa, P.T., & McCrae, R.R. (1980). Somatic complaints in males as a function of age and neuroticism: A longitudinal analysis. *Journal of Behavioral Medicine*, **3**, 245–257.

Costa, P.T., & McCrae, R.R. (1985). Hypochondriasis, neuroticism, and aging. *American Psychologist*, **40**, 19–28.

Craske, M., Rapee, R., Jackel, L., & Barlow, D. (1989). Qualitative dimensions of worry in DSM-III-R generalized anxiety disorder subjects and non-anxious controls. *Behaviour Research and Therapy, 27,* 397–402.

Deer, T.M., & Calamari, J.E. (1998). Panic symptomatology and anxiety sensitivity in older adults. *Journal of Behavior Therapy and Experimental Psychiatry, 29,* 303–316.

Derogatis, L. (1983). *SCL-90-R: Administration, scoring, and procedures manual II.* Towson, MD: Clinical Psychometric Research.

Derogatis, L., Lipman, R., Rickels, K., Uhlenhuth, E.H., & Covi, L. (1974). The Hopkins Symptom Checklist (HSCL): A self-report symptom inventory. *Behavior Science, 19,* 1–15.

Fallon, B., Schneier, F., Marshall, R., Campeas, R., Vermes, D., Goetz, D., & Liebowitz, M. (1996). The pharmacotherapy of hypochondriasis. *Psychopharmacology Bulletin, 32,* 607–611.

Fava, G., Grandi, S., Saviotti, F., & Conti, S. (1990). Hypochondriasis with panic attacks. *Psychosomatics, 31,* 351–353.

Fava, G., & Kellner, R. (1993). Staging: A neglected dimension in psychiatric classification. *Acta Psychiatrica Scandinavica, 87,* 225–230.

Feinson, M., & Thoits, P. (1986). The distribution of distress among elders. *Journal of Gerontology, 41,* 225–233.

Ford, C., & Sbordone, R. (1980). Attitudes of psychiatrists toward elderly patients. *American Journal of Psychiatry, 137,* 571–575.

Fredrikson, M., Annas, P., Fischer, H., & Wik, G. (1996). Gender and age differences in the prevalence of specific fears and phobias. *Behaviour Research and Therapy, 34,* 33–39.

Gorenstein, E., Papp, L., & Kleber, M. (1999, November). Cognitive-behavioral therapy for anxiety and anxiolytic drug dependence in later life: Interim report. In M. Stanley (Chair), *Assessment and treatment of anxiety in late life.* Symposium conducted at the meeting of the Association for Advancement of Behavior Therapy, Toronto, Canada.

Gurian, B., & Miner, J. (1991). Clinical presentation of anxiety in the elderly. In C. Salzman & B. Lebowitz (Eds.), *Anxiety in the elderly: Treatment and research* (pp. 31–44). New York: Springer Publishing Company.

Hersen, M., & VanHasselt, V. (1992). Behavioral assessment and treatment of anxiety in the elderly. *Clinical Psychology Review, 12,* 619–640.

Himmelfarb, S., & Murrell, S. (1983). Reliability and validity of five mental health scales in older persons. *Journal of Gerontology, 116,* 159–167.

Hollander, E., Kwon, J., Stein, D., Broatch, J., Rowland, C., & Himelein, C. (1996). Obsessive-compulsive and spectrum disorders: Overview and quality of life issues. *Journal of Clinical Psychiatry, 57* (suppl. 8), 3–6.

Holm, M. (1988). Prescription of benzodiazepines in the county of Arhus, Denmark. *Danish Medical Journal, 35,* 495–500.

Hyer, L., Gouveia, I., Harrison, W., Warsaw, J., & Coutsouridis, D. (1987). Depression, anxiety, paranoid reactions, hypochondriasis, and cognitive decline of later-life inpatients. *Journal of Gerontology, 42,* 92–94.

Jenike, M. (1985). *Handbook of geriatric psychopharmacology.* Littleton, MA: PSG Publishing Company.

Kohn, R., Westlake, R., Rasmussen, S., Marsland, R., & Norman, W. (1997). Clinical features of obsessive-compulsive disorder in elderly patients. *American Journal of Geriatric Psychiatry, 5,* 211–215.

Kramer-Ginsberg, E., Greenwald, B., Aisen, P., & Brod-Miller, C. (1989). Hypochondriasis in the elderly depressed. *Journal of the American Geriatric Society, 37,* 507–510.

Lasoski, M. (1986). Reasons for low utilization of mental health services by the elderly. In T.L. Brink (Ed.), *Clinical gerontology: A guide to assessment and intervention* (pp. 1–18). New York: The Haworth Press.

Leon, G., Gillum, B., Gillum, R., & Gouze, K.R. (1979). Personality stability and change over a 30-year period-middle age to old age. *Journal of Consulting and Clinical Psychology, 47*, 517–524.

Levkoff, S., Cleary, P., & Wetle, T. (1987). Differences in the appraisal of health between aged and middle-aged adults. *Journal of Gerontology, 42*, 114–120.

Liddell, A., Locker, D., & Burman, D. (1991). Self-reported fears (FSS-II) of subjects aged 50 years and older. *Behaviour Research and Therapy, 29*, 105–112.

Lilienfeld, S.O. (1997). The relation of anxiety sensitivity to higher and lower order personality dimensions: Implications for the etiology of panic attacks. *Journal of Abnormal Psychology, 106*, 539–544.

Lipman, R., Covi, L., & Shapiro, A. (1977). The Hopkins Symptom Checklist (HSCL): Factors derived from the HSCL-90. *Psychopharmacology Bulletin, 13*, 43–45.

Luchins, D., & Rose, R. (1989). Late-life onset of panic disorder with agoraphobia in three patients. *American Journal of Psychiatry, 146*, 920–921.

Lyness, J., King, D., Conwell, Y., Cox, C., & Caine, E. (1993). Somatic worry and medical illness in depressed inpatients. *The American Journal of Geriatric Psychiatry, 1*, 288–295.

Marks, I., & Mathews, A. (1979). Brief standardized self-rating for phobic patients. *Behaviour Research and Therapy, 17*, 263–267.

McElroy, S., Phillips, K., & Keck, P. (1994). Obsessive compulsive spectrum disorder. *Journal of Clinical Psychiatry, 55* (suppl. 10), 33–51.

Morin, C., Landreville, P., Colecchi, C., McDonald, K., Stone, J., & Ling, W. (1999). The Beck Anxiety Inventory: Psychometric properties with older adults. *Journal of Clinical Geropsychology, 5*, 19–29.

Nemiah, J. (1977). Alexithymia. *Psychotherapy and Psychosomatics, 28*, 199–206.

Noyes, R., Kathol, R.G., Fisher, M.M., Phillips, B.M., Suelzer, M.T., & Holt, C.S. (1993). The validity of DSM-III-R hypochondriasis. *Archives of General Psychiatry, 50*, 961–970.

Noyes, R., Reich, J., Clancy, J., & O'Gorman, T. (1986). Reduction in hypochondriasis with treatment of panic disorder. *British Journal of Psychiatry, 149*, 631–635.

Otto, M., Pollack, M., Sachs, G., & Rosenbaum, J. (1992). Hypochondriacal concerns, anxiety sensitivity, and panic disorder. *Journal of Anxiety Disorders, 6*, 93–104.

Oxman, T., Barrett, J.E., Barrett, J., & Gerber, P. (1987). Psychiatric symptoms in the elderly in a primary care practice. *General Hospital Psychiatry, 9*, 167–173.

Palmore, E. (1970). *Normal aging.* Durham, NC: Duke University Press.

Parmalee, P., Katz, I., & Lawton, M. (1993). Anxiety and its association with depression among institutionalized elderly. *American Journal of Geriatric Psychiatry, 1*, 46–58.

Person, D., & Borkovec, T. (1995, August). *Anxiety disorders among the elderly: Patterns and issues.* Paper presented at the 103rd annual meeting of the American Psychological Association, New York, NY.

Pfieffer, E. (1979). Interviewing the anxious older patient. In *Diagnosis and Treatment in the Aged Symposium, Tuscon 1977,* (pp. 13–15). Nutley, NJ: Hoffman-LaRoche, Inc.

Pilowsky, I. (1967). Dimensions of hypochondriasis. *British Journal of Psychiatry, 113*, 39–43.

Powers, C.B., Wisocki, P.A., & Whitbourne, S.K. (1992). Age differences and correlates of worrying in young and elderly adults. *The Gerontologist*, **32**, 82–88.

Pribor, E., Smith, D., & Yutzy, S. (1994). Somatization disorder in elderly patients. *American Journal of Geriatric Psychiatry*, **2**, 109–117.

Raj, B.A., Corvea, M.H., & Dagon, E.M. (1993). The clinical characteristics of panic disorder in the elderly: A retrospective study. *Journal of Clinical Psychiatry*, **54**, 150–155.

Redick, R.W., & Taube, C.A. (1980). Demography and mental health care of the aged. In J.E. Birren & R.B. Sloane (Eds.), *Handbook of mental health and aging* (pp. 57–71). Englewood Cliffs, NJ: Prentice-Hall, Inc.

Regier, D., Boyd, J., Burke, J., Rae, D., Myers, J., Kramer, M., Robins, L., George, L., Karno, M., & Locke, B. (1988). One-month prevalence of mental disorders in the United States: Based on five epidemiologic catchment area sites. *Archives of General Psychiatry*, **45**, 977–986.

Reiss, S., Peterson, R.A., Gursky, D.M., & McNally, R.J. (1986). Anxiety sensitivity, anxiety frequency, and the prediction of fearfulness. *Behaviour Research and Therapy*, **24**, 1–8.

Salkovskis, P., & Warwick, H. (1986). Morbid preoccupations, health anxiety and reassurance: A cognitive behavioural approach to hypochondriasis. *Behaviour Research and Therapy*, **24**, 597–602.

Salzman, C. (1979). Diagnosis and treatment of anxiety in the aged. In *Diagnosis and Treatment in the Aged Symposium, Tuscon 1977* (pp. 13–15). Nutley, NJ: Hoffman-LaRoche, Inc.

Sanavio, E. (1988). Obsessions and compulsions: The Padua Inventory. *Behaviour Research and Therapy*, **26**, 169–177.

Savron, G., Fava, G., Grandi, S., Rafanelli, C., Raffi, A., & Belluardo, P. (1996). Hypochondriacal fears and beliefs in obsessive-compulsive disorder. *Acta Psychiatrica Scandinavica*, **93**, 345–348.

Sheikh, J., King, R., & Taylor, C. (1991). Comparative phenomenology of early-onset versus late-onset panic attacks: A pilot survey. *American Journal of Psychiatry*, **148**, 1231–1233.

Sheikh, J., & Yesavage, J. (1986). Geriatric Depression Scale: recent evidence and development of a shorter version. In T.L. Brink (Ed.), *Clinical gerontology: A guide to assessment and intervention* (pp. 165–173). New York: The Hawthorn Press.

Skarborn, M., & Nicki, R. (1996). Worry among Canadian seniors. *International Journal of Aging and Human Development*, **43**, 169–178.

Small, G. (1997). Recognizing and treating anxiety in the elderly. *Journal of Clinical Psychiatry*, **58**, 41–47.

Snyder, A., Stanley, M., Novy, D., Averill, P., & Beck, J.G. (in press). Measures of depression in older adults with generalized anxiety disorder: A psychometric evaluation. *Depression and Anxiety*.

Spielberger, C., Gorsuch, R., & Lushene, R. (1970). *Manual for the State–Trait Anxiety Inventory*. Palo Alto, CA: Consulting Psychologists Press.

Stanley, M., & Averill, P. (1999). Strategies for treating generalized anxiety in the elderly. In M. Duffy (Ed.), *Handbook of counseling and psychotherapy with older adults*. New York: John Wiley & Sons, Inc.

Stanley, M., & Beck, J.G. (2000). Anxiety disorders. *Clinical Psychology Review*, **20**, 731–754.

Stanley, M., Beck, J.G., & Glassco, J. (1996a). Treatment of generalized anxiety disorder in older adults: A preliminary comparison of cognitive-behavioral and supportive approaches. *Behavior Therapy*, **27**, 565–581.

Stanley, M., Beck, J.G., & Zebb, B. (1996b). Psychometric properties of four anxiety measures in older adults. *Behaviour Research and Therapy*, **34**, 827–838.

Stanley, M., Beck, J.G., Novy, D., Averill, P., Swann, A., Snyder, A., & Bourland, S. (1999, November). Cognitive behavioral treatment of GAD in older adults. In M. Stanley (Chair), *Assessment and treatment of anxiety in late life*. Symposium conducted at the meeting of the Association for Advancement of Behavior Therapy, Toronto, Canada.

Stanley, M., Novy, D., Bourland, S., Beck, J.G., & Averill, P. (2001). Assessing older adults with generalized anxiety: A replication and extension. *Behaviour Research and Therapy*, **39**, 221–235.

Starcevic, V. (1989). Contrasting patterns in the relationship between hypochon- driasis and narcissism. *British Journal of Medical Psychology*, **62**, 311–323.

Starcevic, V., Fallon, S., Uhlenhuth, E.H., & Pathak, D. (1994). Generalized anxiety disorder, worries about illness, and hypochondriacal fears and beliefs. *Psychotherapy and Psychosomatics*, **61**, 93–99.

Starcevic, V., Kellner, R., Uhlenhuth, E.H., & Pathak, D. (1992). Panic disorder and hypochondriacal fears and beliefs in agoraphobia. *Journal of Affective Disorders*, **24**, 73–85.

Stenback, A., Kumpulainen, M., & Vauhkenen, M. (1978). Illness and health in sep- tuagenarians. *Journal of Gerontology*, **33**, 57–61.

Stern, R., & Fernandez, M. (1991). Group cognitive and behavioural treatment for hypochondriasis. *British Medical Journal*, **303**, 1229–1230.

Taylor, S. (1995). Issues in the conceptualization and measurement of anxiety sen- sitivity. *Journal of Anxiety Disorders*, **9**, 163–174.

Taylor, S., Koch, W., & McNally, R. (1992). How does anxiety sensitivity vary across the anxiety disorders? *Journal of Anxiety Disorders*, **6**, 249–259.

Warwick, H., Clark, D., Cobb, A., & Salkovskis, P. (1996). A controlled trial of cognitive-behavioural treatment of hypochondriasis. *British Journal of Psychiatry*, **169**, 189–195.

Warwick, H., & Marks, I. (1988). Behavioural treatment of illness phobia. *British Journal of Psychiatry*, **152**, 239–241.

Warwick, H., & Salkovskis, P. (1989). Hypochondriasis. In J. Scott, J.M.G. Williams, & A.T. Beck (Eds.), *Cognitive therapy in clinical practice. An illustrative casebook* (pp. 78–102). London, UK: Routledge.

Warwick, H., & Salkovskis, P. (1990). Hypochondriasis. *Behaviour Research and Therapy*, **28**, 105–117.

Weissman, M., Myers, J., Tischler, C., Holzer, C., Leaf, P., Orvaschel, H., & Brody, J. (1985). Psychiatric disorders (DSM-III) and cognitive impairment among the elderly in a US urban community. *Acta Psychiatrica Scandinavica*, **71**, 366–379.

Wetherall, J., & Arean, P. (1997). Psychometric evaluation of the Beck Anxiety Inventory with older medical patients. *Psychological Assessment*, **9**, 136–144.

Wisocki, P.A. (1988). Worry as a phenomenon relevant to the elderly. *Behavior Therapy*, **19**, 369–379.

Wisocki, P., Handen, B., & Morse, C. (1986). The Worry Scale as a measure of anxiety among homebound and community active elderly. *The Behavior Thera- pist*, **5**, 91–95.

Yesavage, J., Brink, T., Rose, T., Lum, O., Huang, V., Adey, M., & Leirer, V. (1983). Development and validation of a geriatric depression screening scale: A pre- liminary report. *Journal of Psychiatric Research*, **17**, 37–49.

Part III

# RELATED CONDITIONS

Chapter 11

# HEART-FOCUSED ANXIETY IN MEDICAL AND ANXIETY-RELATED PSYCHOLOGICAL CONDITIONS

*Georg H. Eifert\*, Michael J. Zvolensky[†], and Carl W. Lejuez[††]*

## INTRODUCTION

Each year up to 100,000 persons in the United States suffer from some form of chest pain in the presence of angiographically normal coronary arteries and no significant heart disease (Beitman et al., 1989). Although many of these patients will be satisfied with negative medical examination results, others will anxiously ruminate about the possibility of suffering from a yet undiagnosed physical disease. These persons are upset and worried about chest pain or other heart-related sensations because of their potential negative consequences (e.g., pain, death), and continue to seek help for these symptoms (Bass, Wade, Hand, & Jackson, 1983; Ockene, Shay, Alpert, Weiner, & Dalen, 1980). Not surprisingly, the cost of such cardiac-related behavioral response patterns to the health care system over both the short and long term is immense (e.g., Aikens, Wagner, Setzer, & Smith, 1997).

It is increasingly apparent that individuals with all types of cardiac-related concerns present with different combinations and degrees of chest pain, panic, illness fear, and safety-seeking behavior. Some of these persons may be suffering from panic disorder, hypochondriasis, or both. Yet, even if a person meets criteria for one of these psychiatric disorders,

\*University of Hawaii, USA; [†]University of Vermant, USA; [††]University of Maryland, USA

*Health Anxiety*
Edited by G.J.G. Asmundson, S. Taylor & B.J. Cox
© 2001 John Wiley & Sons Ltd.

an exclusive focus on that condition may miss other important aspects of a person's problem (Eifert & Lau, 2001). In this chapter, we suggest that the explicit recognition of heart-focused anxiety will permit a better understanding of the psychological and behavioral functioning involved with cardiac-related problems, and may facilitate the application of appropriate treatments for these conditions (Eifert, 1992; Eifert, Hodson, Tracey, Seville, & Gunawardane, 1996).

Toward this end, we review the concept of heart-focused anxiety, defined as a fear of heart malfunctioning or disease based on the belief that it may produce harmful consequences. Our first aim is to critically examine the relation between chest pain, panic, and heart-focused anxiety both in persons with and without heart disease. Based on this analysis, we identify heart-focused anxiety as an important psychological variable in the production of elevated anxious and fearful responding. We then discuss heart-focused anxiety in relation to other clinically relevant variables in anxiety-related problems such as hypochondriacal concerns, including physical symptoms, disease fear, disease conviction, and safety-seeking behavior (Fleet & Beitman, 1998; Mendels, Chernoff, & Blatt, 1986). Finally, we briefly discuss the clinical importance of heart-focused anxiety in the assessment and treatment of certain anxiety and cardiac-related problems.


# CHEST PAIN

## Significance of Chest Pain

Chest pain involves a wide variety of cardiorespiratory symptoms including sensations of chest tightening, heart palpitations, pain in limbs/extremities, dyspnea, choking/suffocation sensations, sweating, and numbness (Bass, 1990). These recurrent symptoms typically occur in an abrupt and intense manner, and frequently in response to stressful life events (Brown & Harris, 1989). Because these physical symptoms mimic cardiac problems, many individuals believe that they are experiencing an angina or heart attack. Physical sensations also may be accompanied by fears and thoughts of dying as well as other catastrophic thoughts (Eifert, 1992). The prevalence of chest pain in community samples of healthy persons has been estimated to range from 15% to 18% (Kennedy & Schwab, 1997). Additionally, of those individuals who seek help in an emergency room (ER), approximately 7% to 10% present with a primary complaint of chest pain (American College of Emergency Physicians, 1995; Katon, 1996; Richards, 1992).

*Cardiac Chest Pain*

Chest pain is the most frequently reported symptom of individuals suffering from Ischemic Heart Disease (Gotto, 1992), which is a general label for a number of syndromes that are a function of *ischemia*—an imbalance between supply/demand of the heart for oxygenated blood. Given that most instances of myocardial ischemia are caused by coronary artery obstruction due to arteriosclerosis, myocardial ischemia is frequently referred to as coronary artery disease. Depending on the rate and severity at which arterial narrowing occurs, a variety of distinct cardiac syndromes may develop (e.g., angina pectoris, chronic coronary artery disease, myocardial infarction, and sudden cardiac death). Even when obstruction of the main coronary arteries can be ruled out as a cause of chest pain, such pain may be accounted for by other cardiac problems (e.g., Prinzmetals angina and microvascular angina) that can be difficult to diagnose (Hegel, Abel, Etscheidt, Cohen-Cole, & Wilmer, 1989). Although there is a unique type of pathogenesis for each of these conditions, all are characterized, to a greater or lesser extent, by chest pain or discomfort (Gotto, 1992). It should be noted that chest pain can also be caused by non-cardiac medical problems, most commonly esophageal reflux (Skorton & Ryan, 1992).

*Non-cardiac Chest Pain*

Traditionally, Non-cardiac Chest Pain (NCCP), also referred to as Atypical Chest Pain, Non-organic Chest Pain, or Syndrome X, is defined as chest pain or discomfort in the absence of coronary artery disease or other medical conditions such as esophageal reflux (Aikens, Wagner, Lickerman, Chin, & Smith, 1998). Research indicates that 20–35% of patients presenting to ERs with chest pain are ultimately found to have no detectable organic basis for their cardiac concerns (Beitman et al., 1989; Chambers & Bass, 1990; Eifert & Hickey, 1990; Gibler et al., 1995). Typically, these patients are offered no other treatment beyond feedback that there is nothing physically wrong with them; this is true even when psychiatric conditions are present (Wulsin, Hillard, Geier, Hissa, & Rouan, 1988). As a result, these individuals remain 'active' in the health care system over long periods of time (Ockene et al., 1980).

NCCP is associated with various types of cardiovascular, respiratory problems (Lumley, Torosian, Ketterer, & Pickard, 1997), as well as psychological disorders (Beck, Berisford, Taegtmeyer, & Bennett, 1990). For this reason, NCCP often is studied in relation to other types of medical and psychological problems (e.g., Carter, Servan-Schreiber, & Perlstein, 1997). Importantly, NCCP patients demonstrate similar levels of medical utilization, functional (life) impairment, and fear of pain and autonomic sensations as coronary artery disease patients (Eifert et al., 1996). Yet, the incidence of death as a function of myocardial infarction or another cardiac problem in this population (approximately 1–3%) is not higher than in the general population (Fleet & Beitman, 1998). NCCP typically has a chronic and intermittent course, with particular elevations of cardiac-related distress and pain during times of stress (Ketterer et al., 1996).

*Non-cardiac vs. Cardiac Chest Pain*

Several studies (Wulsin et al., 1988) have attempted to identify criteria to differentiate cardiac from non-cardiac chest pain (e.g., description, location, responsiveness to treatment). Cardiac chest pain typically is described by patients in straightforward terms as a tight, gripping, central substernal chest pain that often occurs during or soon after exercise and is rapidly relieved by rest or nitroglycerine. Patients with NCCP, by contrast, often describe pain in complex metaphorical terms as occurring spontaneously, usually away from the midline of the chest. It is typically felt unilaterally in the vicinity of the cardiac apex, and is associated with local or diffuse tenderness over the anterior chest wall. NCCP can last for several hours, rarely occurs with physical exertion, and is not relieved by rest or nitroglycerine. Medically, diagnostic differentiation between these conditions is best determined with angiography analysis (Richards, 1992).

It is becoming increasingly apparent that individuals with NCCP differ from patients with cardiac chest pain and normal controls at the psychological level of analysis. First, persons with NCCP report a greater hypersensitivity to cardiac-related stimuli, disease conviction, and cardioprotective behavior relative to coronary artery disease patients (Eifert et al., 1996). Second, NCCP patients report significantly elevated levels of cardiac-related distress, including pain and anxiety, relative to nonclinical controls during biological challenge (Bass, 1990; Beck, Berisford, & Taegtmeyer, 1991). Third, NCCP patients report significantly greater levels of catastrophic thinking and emotional distress focused on cardiac cues relative to persons with a cardiac problem as well as nonclinical controls (Eifert et al., 1996). Fourth, compared to normal controls and coronary disease patients, NCCP patients report significantly more and greater levels of depression in structured interviews and tests (e.g., Beitman et al., 1987b; Elias, Robbins, Blow, Rice, & Edgecomb, 1982). Finally, NCCP patients tend to display low pain thresholds for cardiac-related stress tests (e.g., esophageal balloon distention) that do not generalize to other types of pain stressors such as mechanical finger pressure (Bradley, Richter, Scarinci, Haile, & Schan, 1992).

Taken together, these findings suggest that NCCP patients may have a history that promotes a hypervigilance and anxiety-related response bias for cardiac sensations and events. This psychological process often is apparent in psychopathological conditions such as panic disorder. To address this issue, we now provide a brief overview of the nature and prevalence of panic disorder and related anxiety conditions in medical settings, and then turn to a discussion of the relation between NCCP and the importance of heart-focused anxiety in this arena.

## PANIC DISORDER AND RELATED ANXIETY CONDITIONS IN MEDICAL SETTINGS

### Panic Disorder

Panic disorder is characterized by recurrent panic attacks and anxiety about the possibility of experiencing such attacks in future circumstances (American Psychiatric Association, 1994; Barlow, 1988). Because panic attacks involve a variety of escalating bodily symptoms, including cardiorespiratory distress, researchers have studied panic disorder in relation to specific medical conditions. In a representative study, Katon, Hall, and Russo (1988) investigated 74 persons with chest pain and no history of coronary artery disease referred for angiography. In this investigation, approximately 40% of the patients with negative angiography results met criteria for panic disorder and approximately 7% of persons with positive angiograms met criteria for panic disorder. Similar findings have been obtained by other researchers across a wide variety of settings (Beitman et al., 1987a, 1989; Fleet et al., 1998, 1996; Wulsin, Arnold, & Hillard, 1991). Thus, despite methodological differences between studies, panic disorder occurs in at least 25–30% of persons presenting with chest pain with no or minimal coronary artery disease. Moreover, at least 5–15% of persons presenting with chest pain meet criteria for both panic disorder and coronary artery disease. As Fleet, Dupois, Marchand, Burelle, and Beitman (1997) have noted, such prevalence data are markedly higher when compared to the prevalence of panic disorder in the general population (approximately 3%) or primary care medical populations (approximately 7%).

### Non-fearful Panic Disorder

Panic-related problems are also observed in medical settings. Within this area, Kushner and Beitman (1990), among others, have led efforts to define and study what is referred to as *non-fearful panic disorder*. Essentially, these individuals meet criteria for the definition of panic disorder but do not experience any cognitive symptoms (i.e., fear of losing control or going crazy, fear of dying). The occurrence of non-fearful panic disorder in medical settings ranges from 15% to 40% (Kushner & Beitman, 1990). In patients undergoing cardiac or other medical evaluations (e.g., neurological examinations), studies have found that approximately 20% to 40% of persons experience panic attacks without cognitive distress (Beitman et al., 1987a). Wilson, Sandler, and Asmundson (1993) suggested that these individuals may be particularly likely to seek medical rather than psychological consultation for their problem because of the lack of an affective component.

Taken together, several studies have shown that there is a high prevalence of panic disorder of all types in cardiology and ER settings. Some of these individuals may also experience, or be at risk for developing, hypochondriacal beliefs and concerns (Bass, 1990; Eifert, Lejuez, & Bouman, 1998). As the fear of these individuals is focused on the heart and its functioning, we now turn to a discussion of what has been traditionally termed Non-cardiac Chest Pain (NCCP).

## Non-cardiac Chest Pain

Research discussed in previous sections indicates that NCCP can be reliably distinguished from other medical and psychological conditions, most notably by its focus on painful chest sensations that are perceived as dangerous. Thus, although chest pain may be the most prominent presenting symptom, its use as the central diagnostic and defining feature obscures the strong involvement of anxiety and general negative affect in what appears to be a significant subset of patients (Beitman, 1992; Eifert et al., 1996). It is unclear from previous studies what precise proportion of patients with NCCP also have clinically significant levels of anxiety. Apart from the 25–40% of NCCP patients who meet criteria for panic disorder, there appears to be a subset of NCCP patients who have excessive heart-focused anxiety and illness fears with or without panic disorder. In other words, the condition of these persons is not adequately conceptualized as recurrent chest pain with some overlay of panic or depression. In addressing this issue, we have provided a multidimensional analysis of this condition, referring to it as heart-focused anxiety (Eifert, 1992; Eifert & Lau, 2001). We view heart-focused anxiety as a more comprehensive, accurate, and psychologically meaningful term than NCCP, with its exclusive focus on one physical symptom (e.g., Bass, 1990; Nutzinger, Pfersmann, Welan, & Zapotoczky, 1987; Richter & Beckmann, 1973).

At this stage, we know little about why some patients with NCCP simply have chest pain but few or no psychological problems, and why other patients with NCCP have a variety of anxiety-related problems. There is, however, an increasing amount of research indicating that *within* the NCCP group, anxiety and depressive symptoms are uniquely predictive of continued chest pain and life disruption (Potts & Bass, 1993). In an important line of programmatic research, Aikens, Michael, Levin, and Lowry (1999a), and Aikens et al. (1999b) found that young age, NCCP chronicity, the presence of cardiac and panic symptoms, as well as historical exposure to cardiac-related concerns all are associated with elevated reports of cardiac distress and ER utilization (see also Eifert & Forsyth, 1996). Thus, a closer examination of heart-focused anxiety could help to refine our understanding of psychological problems in NCCP populations.

## CONCEPTUAL BASIS AND RELEVANCE OF HEART-FOCUSED ANXIETY

### Anxiety Sensitivity and Heart-Focused Anxiety

*Anxiety Sensitivity*

Anxiety sensitivity refers to the fear of anxiety-related symptoms that is based on beliefs that such sensations have negative somatic, social, or psychological consequences (Reiss & McNally, 1985). For example, if a person perceives bodily sensations associated with autonomic arousal as a sign of imminent harm, this 'high anxiety sensitive' individual will probably experience elevated levels of anxiety. Research indicates heightened anxiety sensitivity levels, as measured by the Anxiety Sensitivity Index (ASI; Reiss, Peterson, Gursky, & McNally, 1986), predict (longitudinally) unexpected panic attacks in the natural environment (Schmidt, Lerew, & Jackson, 1997) and elevated anxious responding in the laboratory (Holloway & McNally, 1987). Other research indicates that heightened ASI levels may serve as a *general* amplification factor for a wide variety of interoceptive events and sensations, including panic, hypochondriacal, and pain-related responding (Asmundson, Norton, & Norton, 1999; Asmundson & Taylor, 1996; Otto, Demopulos, McLean, Pollack, & Fava, 1998; Taylor, Koch, & McNally, 1992).

Contemporary research indicates that anxiety sensitivity is a multidimensional concept. For instance, the 16-item ASI (Reiss et al., 1986) has a hierarchical factor structure, being comprised of three lower-order dimensions that all load on a single higher-order factor (see Zinbarg, Mohlman, & Hong, 1999, for a review). Across a wide variety of populations the three first-order factors appear to measure fears of adverse physical outcomes (Physical Concerns), cognitive concerns (Psychological Concerns), and fears of the public display of anxiety symptoms (Social Concerns; e.g., Stewart, Taylor, & Baker, 1997; Zinbarg, Brown, & Barlow, 1997; Zvolensky, McNeil, Porter, & Stewart, 2001). Furthermore, these first-order anxiety sensitivity factors differentially predict anxious and fearful responding across populations with different types of interoceptive concerns (Schmidt, 1999) and, therefore, may represent different psychological mechanisms for certain types of psychopathology (Cox, 1996). For example, researchers have found that the Physical Concerns dimension of the ASI best predicts fear and panic responding in both laboratory and naturalistic contexts relative to other ASI first-order factors (Aikens, Zvolensky, & Eifert, 2000; Schmidt, 1999; Zvolensky, Goodie, McNeil, Sperry, & Sorrell, 2001). These findings, in conjunction with related research, suggest that predictions of anxious and fearful responding improve with higher levels of correspondence between the particular anxiety sensitivity domain and events that closely match that fear.

*Differentiation Between Heart-Focused Anxiety and Anxiety Sensitivity*

Heart-focused anxiety is related to, but more specific than other psychological factors that have been linked to the development and maintenance of anxiety problems, including anxiety sensitivity and trait anxiety (Taylor & Cox, 1998). For example, whereas trait anxiety is indicative of anxiety-based negative affect *in general*, heart-focused anxiety pertains specifically to the fear of heart-related events, sensations, and functioning. In a similar way, heart-focused anxiety differs from other types of health-related anxiety in that it is specific to the heart rather than to the more diverse and frequently generalized health concerns of individuals with hypochondriasis (Bass, 1990; Eifert et al., 1998). For example, a fear of dying of a heart attack is elicited and becomes salient only during episodes of acute chest pain or heart palpitations. In this way, heart-focused anxiety represents a distinct concern that is different from fears about other anxiety-related sensations and events (e.g., social events).

At this juncture, one might reasonably argue that heart-focused anxiety could be considered a subdimension (i.e., lower-order factor) of the global anxiety sensitivity construct (Reiss, 1991; Taylor & Cox, 1998). At the same time, available research shows that the relation between the ASI (global and lower-order factors) and the Cardiac Anxiety Questionnaire share only moderate zero-order correlations (Eifert et al., 2000). Additionally, the Cardiac Anxiety Questionnaire (see below) correlates moderately with the specific subscales of related indices such as the Illness Attitudes

Scale that tap worry about illness. In this way, the Cardiac Anxiety Questionnaire can be thought to be a distinct and perhaps more comprehensive index of the heart-focused anxiety construct. For instance, the Cardiac Anxiety Questionnaire specifically addresses theoretically relevant dimensions of heart-focused anxiety (i.e., fear, avoidance, attention) not indexed by the ASI (see Eifert et al., 2000, for a further discussion of this issue). With the advent of recently developed standardized measures that can assess multiple dimensions of anxiety sensitivity (Eifert et al., 2000; Taylor & Cox, 1998), researchers will be in a better position to study the nature of heart-focused anxiety in relation to other constructs (i.e., incremental predictive validity relative to anxiety sensitivity and trait anxiety), and how it relates to the onset and maintenance of various psychopathological conditions (see also disease fear section).

## Assessment of Heart-Focused Anxiety

To assess crucial aspects of heart-focused anxiety, we recently developed the Cardiac Anxiety Questionnaire (Eifert et al., 2000) using a large clinical sample. We found the Cardiac Anxiety Questionnaire to comprise three factors pertaining to heart-related fear, avoidance, and attention. Specifically, Factor I ('fear') appears to tap fear and worry about chest and heart sensations and heart functioning. Factor II ('avoidance') appears to pertain to the avoidance of activities believed to elicit cardiac symptoms. Factor III ('attention') primarily taps heart-focused attention and monitoring of cardiac activity. Furthermore, significant intercorrelations between these three subscales support the notion that heart-focused anxiety is a multidimensional construct. We note that the Cardiac Anxiety Questionnaire has also been found useful as a screening measure in clinical research examining heart-focused anxiety in medical populations (e.g., Aikens, Wagner, & Saelinger, 1999c; Van Etten, Abelson, Lowell, Schwartz, & Briggs, 1999). In addition, the questionnaire has been used as an outcome measure in cognitive-behavioral interventions for such individuals (e.g., Eifert & Lau, 2001; Esler et al., 1999; Van Etten, Abelson, Lowell, Schwartz, & Briggs, 1999).

## Response Domains Associated with Heart-Focused Anxiety

Heart-focused anxiety can cut across a number of DSM categories including hypochondriasis, panic disorder, specific phobia, and pain disorder.

There are four response features commonly associated with heart-focused anxiety in these syndromes: (a) physical symptoms, (b) presence of organic disease or disease conviction, (c) disease fear, and (d) safety-seeking behavior. Our discussion of these features is aimed at further delineating how heart-focused anxiety frequently cuts across diagnostic categories, and specifically occurs prominently in NCCP where individuals may not meet any DSM-IV criteria at all. Accordingly, researchers and clinicians may find these response features associated with heart-focused anxiety to be important dimensions for assessment and treatment purposes.

### Physical Symptoms (e.g., Chest Pain, Heart Palpitations)

These are neither essential nor unique components of heart-focused anxiety, but they are often precursors of the 'somatic uncertainty' which plays an important role in the development and exacerbation of heart-related worries (Eifert, 1992). Indeed, heightened somatic activity is a characteristic of all anxiety disorders (Barlow, 1988) ranging from intense and rapidly rising somatic arousal as in panic attacks to less intense generally heightened arousal frequently observed in individuals with generalized anxiety disorder (Westra & Stewart, 1998). The same range of intensity of physical arousal and symptoms can also be found in persons with illness phobias, certain other specific phobias, and somatization-related disorders (see Eifert et al., 1998).

### Disease Conviction

This involves the knowledge, suspicion, or conviction of having heart disease, which may or may not be based in reality (i.e., substantiated by organic disease). In cases of patients without heart disease, concerns and ruminations often focus on the inability of health care providers to detect an organic problem. As a result, patients 'convince' themselves that they are ill, despite evidence and reassurance to the contrary. In contrast, a patient with actual heart disease may ruminate about organic disease that has been demonstrated to be present. Further, a patient may be convinced that the extent of his or her disease process is more extensive than what was diagnosed. Although different medical precautions and procedures must be followed depending upon the presence or absence of organic pathology, the way patients behave in regard to their symptoms is likely to be similar regardless of whether these symptoms are a function of real or perceived disease. That is, the individual may ruminate over symptoms, whether the heart disease is acknowledged or unacknowledged, because in both cases they are convinced of its existence.

## Disease Fear

Disease fear—or its extreme form, disease phobia—is a persistent unfounded fear of suffering from or contracting a disease (Bianchi, 1971; Eifert, 1992) that may occur in the presence *or* absence of a conviction or suspicion of having a disease. Similar to hypochondriasis (see Chapter 1), heart-focused anxiety also requires a distinction between disease fear and disease conviction (Pilowsky, 1967). For example, one individual may be afraid of having a heart attack without being convinced or suspicious of having heart disease. Another individual may be afraid of having a heart attack *and* be convinced of having heart disease despite medical tests to the contrary. Disease fear also may involve a phobic-like response to the possibility of having a current existing heart-related disease deteriorate. For instance, Fava and Grandi (1991) provided examples of patients who were reassured of current good health by negative medical results but, nonetheless, continued to fear future emergence of disease. Similarly, an individual with minimal heart disease may accept that the current level of disease is not a problem, but still worry excessively that in future the condition may progress and worsen.

## Safety/Reassurance-Seeking Behavior

This involves repeated requests for medical examinations and tests, bodily checking, verbal complaints, and seeking reassurance. The function of such behavior is to reduce worry and anxiety over heart-focused physical illness (Eifert, 1992; Salkovskis, 1996; Warwick & Salkovskis, 1990). Safety seeking typically provides only temporary benefits as the patient begins to doubt the veracity of the test or worry that further disease progress has occurred since the last examination. Again, excessive safety-seeking behavior may occur in the presence or absence of physical disease, but the standards for what is considered excessive may differ depending on the presence or absence of coronary artery disease. Although safety-seeking behavior involves obsessive-compulsive features, the content of heart-focused obsessions differ from obsessional intrusions in that the person's illness beliefs are consistent with the experiences of the individual and are largely regarded as sensible (Rachman, 1974). Finally, individuals with excessive heart-focused anxiety do escape or avoid situations where symptoms occur, albeit to a lesser extent than individuals with panic disorder with agoraphobia (Beck, Berisford, Taegtmeyer, & Bennett, 1990). Hence, individuals with heart-focused anxiety try to avoid their physical symptoms and pain by avoiding activities that they believe bring on the dreaded physical symptoms. At the same time, they also engage in a number of other behaviors that are designed to protect their heart (Aikens, Michael, Levin, & Lowry, 1999a; Ockene et al., 1980).

## CLINICAL IMPLICATIONS OF HEART-FOCUSED ANXIETY

### Potential Etiological Processes of Heart-Focused Anxiety

Research discussed in this chapter suggests that responding in an anxious manner to cardiac-related events may contribute to greater levels of perceived pain, disability, disease fear, disease conviction, cardioprotective behavior (e.g., avoidance), and future episodes of elevated anxiety or panic. In this section, we identify three (theoretical) possibilities by which elevated or exaggerated heart-focused anxiety may set the occasion for greater levels of chest pain, anxiety symptoms, and illness behavior associated with disability. In view of the scarcity of data related to etiological processes, we offer these suggestions to help guide much needed future research in this area.

First, persons who fear the consequences of anxiety-related sensations, including cardiac events and symptoms, are significantly more likely to avoid activities that produce such interoceptive activity (e.g., exercise, caffeine intake; Aikens et al., 1999a; Lethem, Slade, Troup, & Bentley, 1983). For example, a person who fears having a heart attack when experiencing even slight changes in cardiac activity is more likely to avoid activities that produce such sensations. In addition to loss of physical capabilities and vigor, this person may actually increase the chance of experiencing anxiety and chest pain through the principles of negative reinforcement. Cardioprotective behavior results in the temporary, but immediate, postponement (i.e., avoidance) or reduction (escape) of pain and distress. Over time, reduced levels of cardiac-related activity, particularly physical exercise, is likely to result in a further loss of physical endurance and strength. As an extension, when heart-focused anxiety contributes to avoidance, a healthy person may fail to learn that cardiac activity due to physical exertion does not indicate danger, thereby perpetuating a vicious cycle of emotional distress (Asmundson et al., 1999).

A second way in which elevated heart-focused anxiety may lead to increased levels of anxiety and pain is through the presence of negative affect. Persons with elevated heart-focused anxiety are more emotionally distressed (Eifert, Zvolensky, Sorrell, Hopko, & Lejuez, 1999). This association between heart-focused anxiety and negative affect—including subjective pain, anxiety, and perhaps, over time, depression—may contribute to response competition. That is, exaggerated negative emotional responding related to heart functioning may compete with healthy or otherwise effective behavior. For example, if an individual with elevated heart-focused anxiety experiences increased levels of anxiety in response to perceived or real cardiac sensations, this person is likely to allocate attention to this potentially threatening interoceptive input. Although such responding may be adaptive over the short term (e.g., rapid detection of threat can allow one to avert harm), it may lead to problems over time. Indeed, a low threshold for experiencing assumed heart-related bodily changes as threatening may increase the chances of elevated state anxiety and cardioprotective behavior (e.g., avoidance) occurring (Mathews & MacLeod, 1994).

A third way heart-focused anxiety may lead to greater cardiac impairment involves heightened levels of somatic activity. In cases where a person with cardiac-related psychological concerns confronts feared stimuli, research suggests that they are likely to experience emotional distress. One of the key factors of such distress is bodily arousal, particularly for panic disorder and closely related conditions (Eifert et al., 1996). Such somatic activity often is difficult or impossible to reduce once it has started (Gotto, 1992). That is, once the initial surge of activation of the autonomic nervous system has occurred, it is very difficult to control the termination of this response in the immediate context. Over time, repeated occurrences of such responding may increase the probability of emotional distress, interoceptive awareness and conditioning, and perhaps the exacerbation or occurrence of medical problems such as injury or, in cases of persons with coronary artery disease, angina attacks (Fleet & Beitman, 1998; Flor, Birbaumer, & Turk, 1990; Mendels et al., 1986).

## Treatment Implications for Heart-Focused Anxiety

There are a few controlled outcome studies (e.g., Clark et al., 1998; Klimes Manyou, Pearce, Coles, & Fagg, 1990; Warwick, Clark, Cobb, & Salkovskis, 1996) and several case studies (e.g., Salkovskis & Warwick, 1986; Visser & Bouman, 1992) that have evaluated the efficacy of behavioral treatments for excessive health anxiety. Although empirically supported treatments exist for panic disorder, specific phobia, and hypochondriasis, unique aspects of heart-focused anxiety are likely to limit patient responsivity to these interventions when used without modification. To illustrate this point, we briefly present a case study of a patient with extreme levels of heart-focused anxiety (Eifert & Lau, 2001).

## Case Study

The patient was a 20-year-old female ('Kate') who met DSM-IV criteria for hypochondriasis and panic disorder. She reported severe anxiety-provoking daily chest pain, several panic attacks per month, and firmly believed she was suffering from coronary artery disease. She was convinced that her chest pain indicated that she had serious coronary artery disease and that she was going to die from it one day. Negative results from numerous physical exams, laboratory tests, x-rays, and EKGs failed to reassure her that her heart was healthy. Hospital records revealed she had visited the emergency rooms approximately five times each week for 8 months. She also called her family physician on a daily basis. As a consequence of her frequent ER visits and hospitalizations, she was in debt for several thousand dollars.

In the first phase of treatment, we targeted Kate's excessive reassurance-seeking behavior, disease conviction, and cardioprotective avoidance behavior. Treatment consisted of (a) preventing reassurance-seeking behavior, (b) chest-focused relaxation training, (c) providing her with more accurate explanations for her chest pain, (d) conducting mini-experiments to support these alternative explanations, (e) developing self-reassurance strategies, and (f) exposure to heart-related interoceptive cues and previously avoided situations. Accordingly, in the first 13 sessions, treatment focused on reducing cardiophobic avoidance behavior by exposure to previously avoided strenuous activities as well as cardiac disease-related stimuli and situations. Behavioral experiments were used to develop alternative symptom explanations and to teach Kate to reassure herself.

After a patient-initiated treatment suspension, a partial relapse occurred with symptoms shifting from predominant disease fear to panic. The initially successful treatment of one problem (hypochondriasis) had not much improved the other. Thus, additional treatment focused on (a) exposure to $CO_2$-enriched air to specifically address the fear of choking, (b) renewed exposure to avoided situations and exercise, (c) continued chest muscle relaxation training and breathing retraining, and (d) self-reassurance techniques. Interoceptive exposure was tailored to Kate's most prominent fear, that of suffocation, by exposing her to a series of 15-second inhalations of 20% $CO_2$-enriched air using a methodology that we employed in several anxiety-related lab experiments (e.g., Eifert, Zvolensky, Lejuez, & Forsyth, 2001). Kate exhibited intense arousal and fear, but after some initial high subjective units of distress ratings, her fear ratings went down significantly, whereas physical responses remained intense. We also repeated exposure to a coronary care unit to address remaining illness-related fears. After the additional 13 sessions, focusing on reducing panic, measures of heart-focused anxiety, and illness behavior were in the normal or near-normal range. Emergency room visits, doctor phone calls, and conviction of suffering from coronary artery disease were down to zero. Occasional panic attacks and chest pain no longer worried Kate. Positive changes were maintained at 8- and 14-month follow-up.

This case vignette illustrates that persons with heart-focused anxiety may present with different combinations of physical symptoms, hypochondriacal concerns (disease fear, disease conviction), and safety-seeking behavior. Moreover, the relative strength, intensity, frequency, and combination of physical symptoms and anxiety-related behaviors may change over time and during the course of treatment. Apart from any topographical similarities, these behaviors may also have different origins in different people, and they may serve quite different functions. It would therefore be inappropriate and inadequate to treat such persons simply with a manual for panic disorder, hypochondriasis, or OCD. What is required is an individualized theory-driven approach that helps to organize and relate the various aspects of the problem and then targets the relevant maintaining dysfunctional processes. For instance, similar to other patients with illness concerns, patients with excessive heart-focused anxiety may become easily dissatisfied with, and tend to walk away from, any psychological treatment that does not acknowledge and focus on these illness concerns (Salkovskis, 1996). Focusing on the major components of heart-focused anxiety is likely to increase treatment motivation, hope for help, and compliance, as well as prevent premature treatment termination and relapse.

## CONCLUSION

Overall, heart-focused anxiety is a common psychological phenomenon in patients presenting with chest pain in cardiology and other medical settings. When such anxiety becomes persistent and interferes with a person's life functioning, it is frequently and easily confused with other psychological and medical disorders. Rather than continuing to consider this process to be primarily and simply a problem of chest pain, we conceptualize this problem as a function of elevated heart-focused anxiety and corresponding illness-focused behavior. There are some direct clinical implications that emerge from our conceptualization of heart-focused anxiety that highlight the advantages of this construct over and above traditional conceptualizations of anxiety sensitivity.

A greater level of attention to heart-focused anxiety will help raise awareness of this specific and common psychological concern that is apparent across various clinical populations. This is important because research suggests that elevated heart-focused anxiety increases the probability that individuals, regardless of their specific condition, will become upset and worried about chest pain or other heart-related sensations (e.g., heart palpitations). As a result, individuals tend to anxiously monitor their heart and pulse, avoid activities believed to bring on symptoms, and in an attempt to reduce anxiety, repeatedly seek reassurance from health care professionals. Thus, in patients without physical disease, heart-focused anxiety frequently results in costly cycles of reassurance-seeking (e.g., unnecessary doctor visits, medical examinations) followed by renewed anxiety and worry (Aikens et al., 1999c). In patients with coronary artery disease, heart-focused anxiety can provoke and exacerbate the severity and frequency of angina attacks and increase the probability of cardiovascular death (Fleet & Beitman, 1998).

For these reasons, the explicit recognition of heart-focused anxiety would be useful in tailoring clinical assessments in high volume medical settings such as emergency departments and primary care clinics. Indeed, it would be desirable to use brief self-report measures such as the Cardiac Anxiety Questionnaire to help identify patients with high levels of heart-focused anxiety. It is likely that such early recognition could facilitate appropriate referrals and treatment of such patients, regardless of their medical status. For instance, a more accurate and timely assessment and treatment of heart-focused anxiety could decrease patients' levels of functional impairment, increase their quality of life, and reduce health care costs. Thus, identifying heart-focused anxiety in patients *with* coronary artery disease may help in their rehabilitation and minimize their functional impairment just as it helps heart-anxious persons *without* heart disease to break the cycle of heart-focused anxiety, increased attention and worry, reassurance-seeking, and renewed anxiety.

In regard to anxiety pathology, it is likely that the explicit recognition of heart-focused anxiety as a clinically relevant psychological variable will offer new insight into how individuals develop certain anxiety-related problems. Indeed, the heart-focused anxiety concept encompasses psychological elements common to various disorders such as hypochondriasis and panic. Yet unlike existing concepts such as anxiety sensitivity, heart-focused anxiety specifically pertains to fear and worry about heart sensations, cardioprotective avoidance of activities that could bring on symptoms, and heart-focused attention and monitoring of cardiac-related stimuli (Eifert et al., 2000). The recognition of these response domains will likely help clinicians take into account the frequently intricate relation between core psychological processes and focus treatment on identified relevant response domains.

Although it will be the task of future research to address these assessment and treatment issues, it is critical to examine and address the specified dimensions of heart-focused anxiety in such work. We believe that advances in the recognition, assessment, and treatment of heart-focused anxiety will be significantly affected by our ability to advance the understanding of the processes involved in heart-related anxiety concerns. For this reason, such psychopathological research is vital and should not be neglected because of the more immediate pressing clinical need to develop effective screening and treatment procedures for persons with excessive heart-focused anxiety.

**Authors' Note:** Please address correspondence to Georg H. Eifert, Department of Psychology, University of Hawaii, 3950 Kalai Waa St, #T101, Hawaii 96753, USA; E-mail: geifert@aol.com.

## REFERENCES

Aikens, J.E., Michael, E., Levin, T., & Lowry, E. (1999a). The role of cardioprotective avoidance beliefs in noncardiac chest pain and associated emergency department utilization. *Journal of Clinical Psychology in Medical Settings*, **6**, 317–332.

Aikens, J.E., Michael, E., Levin, T., Myers, T.M., Lowry, E., & McCracken, L.M. (1999b). Cardiac exposure history as a determinant of symptoms and emergency department utilization in noncardiac chest pain patients. *Journal of Behavioral Medicine*, **22**, 605–617.

Aikens, J.E., Wagner, L.I., Lickerman, A.J., Chin, M.H., & Smith, A. (1998). Primary care physician responses to a panic disorder vignette: Diagnostic suspicion levels and pharmacological management strategies. *International Journal of Psychiatry in Medicine*, **28**, 179–188.

Aikens, J.E., Wagner, L.I., Setzer, N.S., & Smith, A. (1997). Panic disorder recognition and management by primary care physicians. *Annals of Behavioral Medicine*, **19**, S172.

Aikens, J.E., Wagner, L.I., & Saelinger, L.J. (1999c). Reduced medical utilization and costs in anxious and depressed primary care patients receiving behavioral intervention. *Advances in Medical Psychotherapy and Psychodiagnostics*, **10**, 169–178.

Aikens, J.E., Zvolensky, M.J., & Eifert, G.H. (2001). *Fear of cardiopulmonary sensations in emergency room noncardiac chest pain patients. Journal of Behavioral Medicine*, **24**, 155–167.

American College of Emergency Physcians (1995). Clinical policy for the initial approach to adults presenting with a chief complaint of chest pain, with no history of trauma. *Annals of Emergency Medicine*, **25**, 274–299.

American Psychiatric Association (1994). *Diagnostic and statistical manual of mental disorders* (4th edn.). Washington, DC: Author.

Asmundson, G.J.G., Norton, P.J., & Norton, G.R. (1999). Beyond pain: The role of fear and avoidance in chronicity. *Clinical Psychology Review*, **19**, 97–119.

Asmundson, G.J.G., & Taylor, S. (1996). Role of anxiety sensitivity in pain-related fear and avoidance. *Journal of Behavioral Medicine*, **19**, 573–582.

Barlow, D.H. (1988). *Anxiety and its disorders*. New York: Guilford.

Bass, C.M. (1990). Functional and cardiorespiratory symptoms. In C.M. Bass (Ed.), *Somatization: Physiological and psychological illness* (pp. 171–206). London: Blackwell.

Bass, C.M., Wade, C., Hand, D., & Jackson, G. (1983). Patients with angina with normal and near normal coronary arteries: Clinical and psychosocial state 12 months after angiography. *British Medical Journal*, **287**, 1505–1507.

Beck, J.G., Berisford, M.A., & Taegtmeyer, H. (1991). The effects of voluntary hyperventilation on patients with chest pain without coronary artery disease. *Behaviour Research and Therapy*, **29**, 611–621.

Beck, J.G., Berisford, M.A., Taegtmeyer, H., & Bennett, A. (1990). Panic symptoms in chest pain without coronary artery disease: A comparison with panic disorder. *Behavior Therapy*, **21**, 241–252.

Beitman, B.D. (1992). Panic disorder in patients with angiographically normal coronary arteries. *American Journal of Medicine*, **92**, 33–40.

Beitman, B.D., Basha, I., Flaker, G., DeRosear, L., Mukerji, V., & Lamberti, J. (1987a). Non-fearful panic disorder: Panic attacks without fear. *Behaviour Research and Therapy*, **25**, 487–492.

Beitman, B.D., Basha, I., Flaker, G., DeRosear, L., Mukerji, V., & Lamberti, J. (1987b). Major depression in cardiology patients without coronary artery disease and with panic disorder. *Journal of Affective Disorders*, **13**, 51–59.

Beitman, B.D., Mukerji, V., Lamberti, J.W., Schmid, L., DeRosear, L., Kushner, M., Flaker, G., & Basha, I. (1989). Panic disorder in patients with chest pain and angiographically normal coronary arteries. *American Journal of Cardiology*, **63**, 1399–1403.

Bianchi, G.N. (1971). Origins of disease phobia. *Australian and New Zealand Journal of Psychiatry*, **5**, 241–257.

Bradley, L.A., Richter, J.E., Scarinci, I.C., Haile, J.M., & Schan, C.A. (1992). Psychosocial and psychophysical assessments of patients with unexplained chest pain. *American Journal of Medicine*, **27**, 65–73.

Brown, G.W., & Harris, T.O. (Eds.) (1989). *Life events and illness*. New York: Guilford.

Carter, C.S., Servan-Schreiber, D., & Perlstein, W.M. (1997). Anxiety disorders and the syndrome of chest pain with normal coronary arteries: Prevalence and pathophysiology. *Journal of Clinical Psychiatry*, **58**, 70–75.

Chambers, J.B., & Bass, C. (1990). Chest pain with normal coronary anatomy: A review of natural history and possible aetiological factors. *Progress in Cardiovascular Diseases*, **33**, 161–184.

Clark, D.M., Salkouskis, P.M., Hackmann, A., Wells, A., Fennell M., Ludgate, J., Ahmad, S., Richards, H.C., & Gelder, M. (1998). Two psychological treatments for hypochondriasis: A randomised controlled trial. *British Journal of Psychiatry*, **173**, 218–225.

Cox, B.J. (1996). The nature and assessment of catastrophic thoughts in panic disorder. *Behaviour Research and Therapy*, **34**, 363–374.

Eifert, G.H. (1992). Heart-focused anxiety: A paradigmatic behavioral model of heart-focused anxiety and non-anginal chest pain. *Behaviour Research and Therapy*, **30**, 3299–345.

Eifert, G.H., & Forsyth, J.F. (1996). Heart-focused and general illness fears in relation to parental medical history and separation experiences. *Behaviour Research and Therapy*, **34**, 735–739.

Eifert, G.H., & Hickey, A.R. (1990). *Incidence rates of atypical chest pain at the accident and emergency department of the Townsville General Hospital*. Unpublished manuscript, James Cook University, Townsville, Australia.

Eifert, G.H., Hodson, S.E., Tracey, D.R., Seville, J.L., & Gunawardane, K. (1996). Cardiac anxiety, illness beliefs, psychological impairment: Comparing healthy heart-anxious patients with cardiac and surgical patients. *Journal of Behavioral Medicine*, **19**, 385–399.

Eifert, G.H., & Lau, A.W. (2001). Using behavioral experiments in the treatment of cardiophobia: A case study. *Cognitive and Behavioral Practice*, **8**, 305–317.

Eifert, G.H., Lejuez, C.W., & Bouman, T.K. (1998). Somatoform disorders. In A.S. Bellack & M. Hersen (Eds.), *Comprehensive clinical psychology* (Vol. 6, pp. 543–565). Oxford: Pergamon.

Eifert, G.H., Thompson, R.N., Zvolensky, M.J., Edwards, K., Haddad, J.H., Frazer, N.L., & Davig, J. (2000). The Cardiac Anxiety Questionnaire: Development and preliminary validity. *Behaviour Research and Therapy*, **38**, 1039–1053.

Eifert, G.H., Zvolensky, M.J., Lejuez, C.W., & Forsyth, J.F. (2001). Assessing the perceived predictability of anxiety-related events: A report on the perceived predictability Index. *Journal of Behavior Therapy and Experimental Psychiatry*, **31**, 201–218.

Eifert, G.H., Zvolensky, M.J., Sorrell, J.T., Hopko, D.R., & Lejuez, C.W. (1999). Predictors of self-reported anxiety and panic symptoms: An evaluation of anxiety sensitivity, suffocation fear, heart-focused anxiety, and breath-holding duration. *Journal of Psychopathology and Behavioral Assessment*, **21**, 293–305.

Elias, M.F., Robbins, M.A., Blow, F.C., Rice, A.P., & Edgecomb, J.L. (1982). Symptom reporting, anxiety and depression in arteriographically classified middle-aged chest pain patients. *Experimental Aging Research*, **8**, 45–51.

Esler, J.L., Barlow, D.H., Spiegel, D.A., Posner, D., Wooland, R., & Blanchard, E.B. (1999, November). *A brief cognitive behavioral intervention for patients with noncardiac chest pain.* Poster session presented at the 33rd Convention of the Association for Advancement of Behavior Therapy, Toronto, Ontario.

Fava, G., & Grandi, S. (1991). Differential diagnosis of hypochondriacal fears and beliefs. *Psychotherapy and Psychosomatics*, **55**, 114–119.

Fleet, R.P., & Beitman, B.D. (1998). Cardiovascular death from panic disorder and panic-like anxiety: A critical review of the literature. *Journal of Psychosomatic Research*, **44**, 71–80.

Fleet, R.P., Dupuis, G., Marchand, A., Burelle, D., Arsenault, A., & Beitman, B.D. (1996). Panic disorder in emergency department chest pain patients: Prevalence, comorbidity, suicidal ideation, and physician recognition. *American Journal of Medicine*, **101**, 371–380.

Fleet, R.P., Dupuis, G., Marchand, A., Burelle, D., & Beitman, B.D. (1997). Detecting panic disorder in emergency department chest pain patients: A validated model to improve recognition. *Annals of Behavioral Medicine*, **19**, 124–131.

Fleet, R.P., Dupuis, G., Marchand, A., Kaczorowski, J., Burelle, D., Arsenault, A., & Beitman, B.D. (1998). Panic disorder in coronary artery disease patients with noncardiac chest pain. *Journal of Psychosomatic Research*, **44**, 81–90.

Flor, H., Birbaumer, N., & Turk, D.C. (1990). The psychobiology of pain. *Advances in Behaviour Research and Therapy*, **12**, 47–84.

Gibler, W.B., Runyon, J.P., Levy, R.C., Sayre, M.R., Kacich, R., Hattemer, C.R., Hamilton, C., Gerlach, J.W., & Walsh, R.W. (1995). A rapid diagnostic and treatment center for patients with chest pain in the emergency department. *Annals of Emergency Medicine*, **25**, 1–8.

Gotto, A.M. (1992). Risk factors for atherosclerosis. In A. Gotto (Ed.), *Atherosclerosis* (pp. 33–50). Kalamazoo, MI: Upjohn.

Hegel, M.T., Abel, G.G., Etscheidt, M., Cohen-Cole, S., & Wilmer, C.T. (1989). Behavioral treatment of angina-like chest pain in patients with hyperventilation syndrome. *Journal of Behavior Therapy and Experimental Psychiatry*, **20**, 31–39.

Holloway, W., & McNally, R.J. (1987). Effects of anxiety sensitivity on the response to hyperventilation. *Journal of Abnormal Psychology*, **96**, 330–334.

Katon, W. (1996). Panic disorder: Relationship to high medical utilization, enexplained physical symptoms, and medical costs. *Journal of Clinical Psychiatry*, **57**, 11–22.

Katon, W., Hall, M.L., & Russo, J. (1988). Chest pain: Relationship of psychiatric illness to coronary angiographic results. *American Journal of Medicine*, **84**, 1–9.

Kennedy, B.L., & Schwab, J.J. (1997). Utilization of medical specialists by anxiety disorder patients. *Psychosomatics*, **38**, 109–112.

Ketterer, M.W., Brymer, J., Rhoads, K., Kraft, P., Kenyon, L., Foley, B., Lovallo, W.R., & Voight, C.J. (1996). Emotional distress among males with syndrome X. *Journal of Behavioral Medicine*, **19**, 455–466.

Klimes, I., Mayou, R.A., Pearce, M.J., Coles, L., & Fagg, J.R. (1990). Psychological treatment for atypical non-cardiac chest pain: A controlled evaluation. *Psychological Medicine*, **20**, 605–611.

Kushner, M.G., & Beitman, B.D. (1990). Panic attacks without fear: An overview. *Behaviour Research and Therapy*, **28**, 469–479.

Lethem, J., Slade, P.D., Troup, J.D.G., & Bentley, G. (1983). Outline of a fear-avoidance model of exaggerated pain perception-I. *Behaviour Research and Therapy*, **21**, 401–408.

Lumley, M.A., Torosian, T., Ketterer, M.W., & Pickard, S.D. (1997). Psychosocial factors related to noncardiac chest pain during treadmill exercise. *Psychosomatics*, **38**, 230–238.

Mathews, A., & MacLeod, C. (1994). Cognitive approaches to emotion and emotional disorders. *Annual Review of Psychology*, **45**, 25–50.

Mendels, J., Chernoff, R.W., & Blatt, M. (1986). Alprazolam as an adjunct to propranolol in anxious outpatients with stable angina pectoris. *Journal of Clinical Psychiatry*, **47**, 8–11.

Nutzinger, D.O., Pfersmann, D., Welan, T., & Zapotoczky, H. (1987). *Herzphobie: Klassifikation, diagnostik und therapie* [Heart-focused anxiety: Classification, diagnosis, and therapy]. Stuttgart, Germany: Ferdinand Enke.

Ockene, J.S., Shay, M.J., Alpert, J.S., Weiner, B.H., & Dalen, J.E. (1980). Unexplained chest pain in patients with normal coronary artery arteriograms. A follow up study of functional status. *New England Journal of Medicine*, **303**, 1249–1252.

Otto, M.W., Demopulos, C.M., McLean, N.E., Pollack, M.H., & Fava, M. (1998). Additional findings on the association between anxiety sensitivity and hypochondriacal concerns: Examination of patients with major depression. *Journal of Anxiety Disorders*, **12**, 225–232.

Pilowsky, I. (1967). Dimensions of hypochondriasis. *British Journal of Medical Psychology*, **113**, 89–93.

Potts, S.G., & Bass, C.M. (1993). Psychosocial outcome and use of medical resources in patients with chest pain and normal or near-normal coronary arteries: A long-time follow-up study. *Quarterly Journal of Medicine*, **86**, 583–593.

Rachman, S. (1974). Some similarities and differences between obsessional ruminations and morbid pre-occupations. *Canadian Psychiatric Association Journal*, **18**, 71–73.

Reiss, S. (1991). Expectancy theory of fear, anxiety, and panic. *Clinical Psychology Review*, **11**, 141–153.

Reiss, S., & McNally, R.J. (1985). Expectancy model of fear. In S. Reiss & R.R. Bootzin (Eds.), *Theoretical issues in behavior therapy* (pp. 107–121). San Diego: Academic Press.

Reiss, S., Peterson, R.A., Gursky, D.M., & McNally, R.J. (1986). Anxiety, sensitivity, anxiety frequency, and the prediction of fearfulness. *Behaviour Research and Therapy*, **24**, 1–8.

Richards, S.D. (1992). Atypical chest pain: Differentiation from coronary artery disease. *Postgraduate Medicine*, **91**, 257–258.

Richter, H.E., & Beckmann, D. (1973). *Herzneurose* [Cardiac neurosis]. Stuttgart, Germany: Georg Thieme Verlag.

Salkovskis, P.M. (1996). The cognitive approach to anxiety: Threat beliefs, safety seeking behavior, and the special case of health anxiety and obsessions. In P.M. Salkovskis (Ed.), *Frontiers of cognitive therapy* (pp. 49–74). New York: Guilford.

Salkovskis, P.M., & Warwick, H.M.C. (1986). Morbid preoccupations, health anxiety and reassurance: A cognitive-behavioural approach to hypochondriasis. *Behaviour Research and Therapy*, **24**, 597–602.

Schmidt, N.B. (1999). Examination of differential anxiety sensitivities in panic disorder: A test of anxiety sensitivity predicting fearful responding to a 35% $CO_2$ challenge. *Cognitive Therapy and Research*, **23**, 3–19.

Schmidt, N.B., Lerew, D.R., & Jackson, R.J. (1997). The role of anxiety sensitivity in the pathogenesis of panic: Prospective evaluation of spontaneous panic attacks during acute stress. *Journal of Abnormal Psychology*, **106**, 355–364.

Skorton, D.J., & Ryan, T.J. (1992). Diagnosis of coronary artery disease. In A. Gotto (Ed.), *Atherosclerosis* (pp. 89–127), Kalamazoo, MI: Upjohn.

Stewart, S.H., Taylor, S., & Baker, J.M. (1997). Gender differences in dimensions of anxiety sensitivity. *Journal of Anxiety Disorders*, **11**, 179–200.

Taylor, S., & Cox, B.J. (1998). An expanded anxiety sensitivity index: Evidence for a hierarchic structure in a clinical sample. *Journal of Anxiety Disorders*, **5**, 463–483.

Taylor, S., Koch, W.J., & McNally, R.J. (1992). How does anxiety sensitivity vary across the anxiety disorders? *Journal of Anxiety Disorders*, **6**, 249–259.

Van Etten, M., Abelson, J., Lowell, M., Schwartz, S., & Briggs, H. (1999, November). *Finding behavior therapy candidates in a noncardiac chest pain population*. Poster session presented at the 33rd Convention of the Association for Advancement of Behavior Therapy, Toronto, Ontario.

Visser, S., & Bouman, T.K. (1992). Cognitive-behavioural approaches in the treatment of hypochondriasis: Six single case cross-over studies. *Behaviour Research and Therapy*, **30**, 301–306.

Warwick, H.M.C., Clark, D.M., Cobb, A.M., & Salkovskis, P.M. (1996). A controlled trial of cognitive-behavioural treatment of hypochondriasis. *British Journal of Psychiatry*, **169**, 189–195.

Warwick, H.M.C., & Salkovskis, P.M. (1990). Hypochondriasis. *Behaviour Research and Therapy*, **28**, 105–117.

Westra, H.A., & Stewart, S.H. (1998). Cognitive-behavioural therapy and pharmocotherapy: Complementary or contradictory approaches to the treatment of anxiety? *Clinical Psychology Review*, **18**, 307–340.

Wilson, K.G., Sandler, L.S., & Asmundson, G.J.G. (1993). Fearful and non-fearful panic attacks in a student population. *Behaviour Research and Therapy*, **31**, 407–411.

Wulsin, L.R., Arnold, L.M., & Hillard, J.R. (1991). Axis I disorders in ER patients with atypical chest pain. *International Journal of Psychiatry in Medicine*, **21**, 37–46.

Wulsin, L.R., Hillard, R.J., Geier, P., Hissa, D., & Rouan, G.W. (1988). Screening emergency room patients with atypical chest pain for depression and panic disorder. *International Journal of Psychiatry in Medicine*, **18**, 315–323.

Zinbarg, R.E., Brown, T.A., & Barlow, D.H. (1997). Hierarchical structure and general factor structure saturation of the Anxiety Sensitivity Index: Evidence and implications. *Psychological Assessment*, **9**, 277–284.

Zinbarg, R.E., Mohlman, J., & Hong, N.N. (1999). Dimensions of anxiety sensitivity. In S. Taylor (Ed.), *Anxiety sensitivity: Theory, research, and treatment of the fear of anxiety* (pp. 83–114). Mahwah, NJ: Erlbaum.

Zvolensky, M.J., Goodie, J.L., McNeil, D.W., Sperry, J.A., & Sorrell, J.T. (2001). Anxiety sensitivity in the prediction of pain-related fear and anxiety in a heterogeneous chronic pain population. *Behaviour Research and Therapy*, **39**, 683–696.

Zvolensky, M.J., McNeil, D.W., Porter, C.A., & Stewart, S.H. (2001). Assessment of anxiety sensitivity in young American Indians and Alaska Natives. *Behaviour Research and Therapy*, **39**, 477–493.

Chapter 12

# HYPOCHONDRIASIS AND HEALTH ANXIETY AMONG PAIN PATIENTS

*Heather D. Hadjistavropoulos\*, Katherine M.B. Owens\*, Thomas Hadjistavropoulos\*, and Gordon J.G. Asmundson\**

## INTRODUCTION

Pain has been described as a complex multidimensional construct involving both sensory and emotional components (Merskey & Bogduk, 1994). The dominant theory of pain, namely the gate control theory, views pain as a state that can be modified by both ascending and descending activities in the central nervous system (Melzack & Wall, 1988). Psychological variables are acknowledged, in some instances, to play a causal role in the experience of pain (Linton & Skevington, 1999). In other cases, psychological variables are considered to be a consequence of pain, or serve to buffer or maintain pain. Given the role of psychological factors in pain, comprehensive psychological evaluations are advocated for use with pain patients (Turk & Melzack, 1992). Among the factors recommended for consideration when examining individuals in pain is hypochondriasis or, in its non-clinical form, health anxiety (Lautenbacher & Rollman, 1999).

This chapter examines the relationship of hypochondriasis and health anxiety with pain. Pain is a symptom common to numerous conditions such as soft tissue injury, cancer, diabetes, and vascular disease (Crombie & Davies, 1999). Among these, however, back pain is the most prevalent problem. Indeed, its 6-month prevalence is estimated to be 41%, and its incidence by age 70 is estimated to be 85% (Von Korff, Dworkin, Le

---

\*Clinical Research and Development Program, Regina Health District, and Department of Psychology, University of Regina, Regina, Saskatchewan, Canada

*Health Anxiety*
Edited by G.J.G. Asmundson, S. Taylor & B.J. Cox
© 2001 John Wiley & Sons Ltd.

Resche, & Kruger, 1988). Most research that examines the relationship of pain with hypochondriasis and health anxiety inevitably focuses on back pain, or on mixed pain samples wherein back pain is the most frequent complaint. Most research in this area also focuses on chronic pain, defined by the International Association for the Study of Pain (IASP) as pain that persists or recurs for 3 months or more (Merskey & Bogduk, 1994). Chronic pain is also common, with a 12-month prevalence of 22% in primary care patients (Gureje, Von Korff, Simon, & Gater, 1998). We high-light, where possible, information regarding other prevalent pain con-ditions (e.g., headaches, gastrointestinal pain) as well as acute pain (i.e., clinical and experimentally induced), however, our main focus will be on chronic back pain.

To begin, we present research regarding the relationship of pain and hypochondriasis. Our attention then turns to research concerning health anxiety and pain and we discuss other variables that may account for the relationship found between the two variables. Finally, implications of the research for the assessment and treatment of pain patients are discussed and we propose future directions for research.

## HYPOCHONDRIASIS AND PAIN

Despite the recognition that hypochondriasis is important to consider in pain patients, little attention has been given to determining the prevalence of a DSM diagnosis of hypochondriasis in this population. Table 12.1 sum-marizes the studies that have examined the prevalence of psychiatric disturbance, including hypochondriasis, among primarily chronic back pain patients. The early studies in this area (Fishbain, Goldberg, Meagher, Steele, & Rosomoff, 1986; Katon, Egan, & Miller, 1985; Reich, Tupin, & Abramowitz, 1983) suffered from one or more limitations, such as low sample size, selective samples, lack of assessment of the reliability of diag-nostic categories assigned, and poor reporting of data. The degree of confidence that can be placed in the estimated prevalence of hypochon-driasis in pain patients based on these studies is compromised by these limitations.

Three recent studies, that are methodologically stronger, estimated the lifetime prevalence of a DSM-III-R diagnosis of hypochondriasis to be between 0 and 1% among chronic low back pain patients (Gatchel, Polatin, Mayer, & Garcy, 1994; Kinney, Gatchel, Polatin, Fogarty, & Mayer, 1993; Polatin, Kinney, Gatchel, Lillo, & Mayer, 1993). Interestingly, in all three studies, the vast majority of chronic pain patients were diagnosed with somatoform pain disorder. The dominant clinical feature of this disorder, as described in the DSM-III-R, is a preoccupation with pain in the absence

**Table 12.1** Summary of concurrent DSM psychiatric diagnoses among pain patients

| DSM | Somatoform disorders | Other concurrent Axis I disorders | Limitations |
|---|---|---|---|
| Reich et al. (1983). Sample: 43 chronic pain patients who did not respond to conventional treatment and were referred to a multidisciplinary pain program; 65% female | | | |
| III | Overall 53.0% <br> Conversion Disorder 2.0% <br> Hypochondriasis 7.0% <br> Somatization Disorder 12.0% <br> Psychogenic Pain Disorder 32.0% | Mood Disorders 29.0% <br> Anxiety Disorders 7.0% <br> Substance Use Disorder 28.0% <br> Adjustment Disorder 14.0% <br> Schizophrenia-type Psychoses 0.0% <br> Organic Mental Disorder 2.0% | • Reliability of DSM-III diagnoses not assessed <br> • Select sample <br> • Small sample |
| Katon et al. (1985). Sample: 37 chronic pain patients (91% back pain, 9% headache) admitted to a three-week inpatient treatment pain program with no medically treatable problem; 54.1% female | | | |
| III | Overall 16.2% <br> Conversion Disorder 0.0% <br> Hypochondriasis 0.0% <br> Somatization Disorder 16.2% <br> Psychogenic Pain Disorder 0.0% | Mood Disorders 32.4% <br> Anxiety Disorders Unclear <br> Substance Use Disorder Unclear <br> Adjustment Disorder 0.0% <br> Schizophrenia-type Psychoses 0.0% <br> Organic Mental Disorder 0.0% | • Small sample <br> • Select sample <br> • Poor reporting of data |
| Fishbain et al. (1986). Sample: 283 chronic pain patients (73% back) in a comprehensive pain program with previous poor response to conventional treatment; 85% diagnosed with myofascial pain syndrome; 44% female | | | |
| III | Overall 42.7% <br> Conversion Disorder 37.8% <br> Hypochondriasis <1% <br> Somatization Disorder 3.9% <br> Psychogenic Pain Disorder <1% | Mood Disorders 56.2% <br> Anxiety Disorders 62.5% <br> Substance Use Disorder 14.9% <br> Adjustment Disorder 13.0% <br> Schizophrenia-type Psychoses 0.0% <br> Organic Mental Disorder 8.2% | • Reliability of DSM-III not assessed <br> • Limited understanding of myofascial pain may have increased diagnosis of conversion disorder |

Polatin et al. (1993). Sample: 200 low back pain patients in a functional restoration program; 33.1% female

| III-R | | | |
|---|---|---|---|
| Overall | 99.0% | Mood Disorders | 49.0% |
| Conversion Disorder | 0.0% | Anxiety Disorders | 17.0% |
| Hypochondriasis | 1.0% | Substance Use Disorder | 19.0% |
| Somatization Disorder | 1.0% | Adjustment Disorder | 0.0% |
| Somatoform Pain Disorder | 97.0% | Schizophrenia-type Psychoses | 3.0% |
| | | Organic Mental Disorder | 0.0% |

Gatchel et al. (1994). Sample: 152 chronic low back pain patients attending three-week functional restoration program; 39% female; patients diagnosed with degenerative disc disease, lumbar radicular syndrome, post-operative epidural fibrosis, segmental instability, and non-specific low back pain

| III-R | | | |
|---|---|---|---|
| Overall | 92.0% | Affective Disorders | ~46% |
| Conversion Disorder | 0.0% | Anxiety Disorders | ~5% |
| Hypochondriasis | 0.0% | Substance Use Disorder | 3.0% |
| Somatization Disorder | 0.0% | Adjustment Disorder | 0.0% |
| Somatoform Pain Disorder | 92.0% | Schizophrenia-type Psychoses | 0.0% |
| | | Organic Mental Disorder | 0.0% |

Kinney et al. (1993). Sample: 90 consecutive chronic low back pain patients (14.9 month pain duration) who presented for functional restoration treatment.

| IV | | | |
|---|---|---|---|
| Overall | ns | Affective Disorders | 50.0% |
| Conversion Disorder | ns | Anxiety Disorders | 25.0% |
| Hypochondriasis | 1.0% | Substance Use Disorder | 11.0% |
| Somatization Disorder | 1.0% | Adjustment Disorder | ns |
| Pain Disorder | 99.0% | Schizophrenia-type Psychoses | ns |
| | | Organic Mental Disorder | ns |

Aigner & Bach (1999). Sample: 90 consecutive chronic pain patients (6 year pain duration) with a broad spectrum of pain problems attending a multidisciplinary pain treatment center.

| IV | | | |
|---|---|---|---|
| Overall | 92.0% | Affective Disorders | 18.9% |
| Conversion Disorder | 0.0% | Anxiety Disorders | ns |
| Hypochondriasis | 5.6% | Substance Use Disorder | ns |
| Somatization Disorder | 4.4% | Adjustment Disorder | ns |
| Pain Disorder | 65.6% | Schizophrenia-type Psychoses | ns |
| | | Organic Mental Disorder | ns |

*Note:* ns = not specified.

of adequate physical findings that might account for the pain or its intensity. In contrast, in hypochondriasis, the dominant clinical feature is the preoccupation with, or fear of having, a serious disease based on misinterpretation of bodily symptoms. This preoccupation or fear also occurs in the absence of adequate physical findings. In the DSM-III-R there were no clear rules regarding whether somatoform pain disorder could be diagnosed along with hypochondriasis. It would appear, however, that when somatoform pain disorder was diagnosed, hypochondriasis was largely ruled out. This would account for the lower prevalence of hypochondriasis observed in these studies relative to estimates of prevalence reported in primary care settings (Escobar et al., 1998; Kirmayer & Robbins, 1991) and general medical clinics (Barsky, Wyshak, Klerman, & Latham, 1990; see Chapter 1).

Since the introduction of the DMS-IV, only one study has examined the prevalence of hypochondriasis among chronic pain patients (Aigner & Bach, 1999). In this study, the point prevalence of hypochondriasis was determined to be 5.6%, which is consistent with estimates of the prevalence of hypochondriasis in other settings (see Chapter 1) but higher than estimates in the chronic pain samples reported above. It is quite possible that changes in the DSM-IV resulted in a *higher* likelihood of diagnosing hypochondriasis among chronic pain patients. In particular, the criteria for somatoform pain disorder were changed and this condition was relabeled as pain disorder. According to DSM-IV, in pain disorder, pain is the focus of presentation and is severe enough to warrant clinical attention and to cause clinically significant distress or impairment. Furthermore, psychological factors are judged to have an important role in the onset, severity, exacerbation, or maintenance of the pain. Symptoms are not intentionally produced or feigned and pain is not accounted for by a mood, anxiety, or psychotic disorder. It is possible that elimination of the need for preoccupation with pain to occur in the absence of adequate physical findings increased the likelihood that hypochondriasis would be diagnosed among pain patients, particularly those with chronic musculoskeletal complaints that persist long after identifiable physical pathology has healed.

Clearly, there is a current need for further examination of the prevalence of hypochondriasis among pain patients. On the surface it would seem that other changes in the DSM-IV, namely hierarchical rules, could serve to artificially *reduce* the likelihood of diagnosing hypochondriasis among pain patients. In the DSM-IV, for instance, it is now stated that hypochondriasis should only be diagnosed when the preoccupation or fear is not better accounted for by another somatoform disorder. It is possible that some clinicians would regard symptoms of hypochondriasis (e.g., worry about health, preoccupation with pain, reassurance seeking, misinterpretation of symptoms, and failure to respond to reassurance) as psychological factors that play a role in the pain condition. Essentially, the pain disorder category is so broad that it has the potential to subsume a diagnosis of hypochondriasis in many patients with chronic pain complaints. At this point, we contend that future consideration needs to be given to whether grouping all pain patients together, regardless of the nature of psychological factors that contribute to the pain condition, provides a loss of information that is important, if not critical, to the assessment and treatment of pain. This observation is consistent with that made by Turk and colleagues (Turk, Okifuji, Sinclair, & Starz, 1996), who have suggested that there is a need to identify subgroups of pain patients who differ with respect to their perception of and response to symptoms, social support, and ability to cope. Treating pain patients as a uniform group impedes understanding of the condition and compromises the development of cost-effective efficient treatment strategies that are tailored to specific patients' needs.

One further factor that may contribute to a tendency to underdiagnose hypochondriasis among chronic pain patients concerns the presence of a medical condition. Specifically, health care practitioners may automatically rule out hypochondriasis if an underlying medical condition is present. The DSM acknowledges, however, that a coexisting general medical condition may be present in hypochondriasis, if, based on our present knowledge, the health-related fear is beyond what is known organically to underlie the condition (Fishbain & Rosomoff, 1987). Lack of awareness that physical illness and hypochondriasis may coexist might result in low estimates of the prevalence of hypochondriasis, especially among those pain patients who have some underlying organic pathology. Likewise, lack of confidence in medical and diagnostic tests to rule out underlying pathology probably results in a reluctance to diagnose this condition among pain patients.

It is generally difficult to make any definitive statements about the prevalence of hypochondriasis among pain patients. The early studies that examined the presence of hypochondriasis in chronic pain patients suffered from a number of methodological limitations. In later studies that used the DSM-III-R, it appears that a diagnosis of somatoform pain disorder may have overruled a diagnosis of hypochondriasis. Finally, there has only been one study of hypochondriasis in pain patients since the introduction of DSM-IV. This study suggests that approximately 5–6% of pain patients meet diagnostic criteria for hypochondriasis. Future studies that examine the prevalence of hypochondriasis among pain patients based on current diagnostic criteria are warranted.

To the best of our knowledge there have been no studies that have compared whether pain patients who have a diagnosis of hypochondriasis differ in any tangible or discernible way from those who do not. The studies that are available are focused more on the construct of health anxiety than on hypochondriasis. This construct is described below along with findings concerning the relationship between pain and health anxiety.

## HEALTH ANXIETY AND PAIN

Issues regarding the conceptualization of health anxiety are discussed in detail in Chapter 1. It is, however, important to reiterate a few of these points here. Health anxiety, unlike hypochondriasis, refers to a dimensional rather than a psychiatric or categorical construct (Hitchcock & Mathews, 1992; Warwick & Salkovskis, 1990). Anxiety about health is represented along a continuum, with mild to no concern about bodily sensations at one end and preoccupation with, and fear of, bodily symptoms and conviction in disease at the other (Salkovskis & Warwick, 1986). The term *health anxiety* is preferred over others (e.g., hypochondriacal beliefs) since the construct is typically measured independent of assessment of medical problems and it is recognized that there can be substantial health anxiety even in those who have serious medical conditions (Warwick & Salkovskis, 1990). In other words, medical background is often ignored and the focus is instead on questionnaires tapping patients' attitudes, beliefs, and concerns about health, such as fear of illness, illness worries, or conviction in disease.

## Evidence for Elevated Health Anxiety Among Pain Patients

A number of instruments are commonly used for the assessment of health anxiety among pain patients, including the Illness Attitudes Scale (IAS; Kellner, Abbott, Winslow, & Pathak, 1987), the Illness Behaviour Questionnaire (IBQ; Pilowsky & Spence, 1983), and Scale 1 (Hypochondriasis) of the Minnesota Multiphasic Personality Inventory I and II (MMPI I and II; Hathaway & McKinley, 1983, 1989). These measures are described in detail in Chapter 5. As is noted in Chapter 5, it is important to keep in mind that elevated scores on these measures in the absence of other information simply imply anxiety, preoccupation, and distress about health; that is, the elevations should not necessarily be regarded as being out of proportion to underlying medical findings. Use of the MMPI Scale 1 probably presents the greatest difficulties when measuring health anxiety among pain patients since this measure focuses more on somatic symptoms than on health anxiety (Hathaway & McKinley, 1989). In the case of the IAS, results may be diluted somewhat when the total score is used without omission of health habits items since these items are not typically regarded as being related to health anxiety (Hadjistavropoulos, Frombach, & Asmundson, 1999). It is also possible that new IAS factor-analytically derived subscales may be more informative than the total measure (Hadjistavropoulos & Asmundson, 1998). Finally, when using the IBQ to understand the relationship between health anxiety and pain, attention needs to be focused primarily on Hypochondriasis and Disease Conviction subscales since the other subscales (e.g., Psychological versus Somatic Focus, Affective Inhibition, Affective Disturbance, Denial, Irritability) tap other aspects of illness behavior beyond health anxiety.

There is clear evidence of increased health anxiety among pain samples as compared to controls. This holds whether the IAS, IBQ Hypochondriasis and Disease Conviction subscales, or MMPI Scale 1 are examined. Re-examination of data obtained from a study by Hadjistavropoulos, Hadjistavropoulos, and Quine (2000) showed that among 81 chronic pain patients who were attending a multidisciplinary pain program for the treatment of musculoskeletal injury, the average total IAS score was 35.2 ($SD$ = 10.5). Other data collected by Hadjistavropoulos and Asmundson (2000) show that, among patients attending a primary pain clinic for physiotherapy, the average total IAS score was 32.6 ($SD$ = 13.1). Among controls, the average IAS total score has been found to be 26.2 ($SD$ = 7.9; Hadjistavropoulos, 1995). In other words, IAS scores among pain patients in both chronic pain and primary pain clinic samples are almost one standard deviation higher than those found among controls. It is important to note, however, that while the total IAS score for pain patients is elevated, it is not as high as scores reported for patients with a DSM-IV diagnosis of hypochondriasis ($M$ = 50.2, $SD$ = 13.7; Bouman & Visser, 1998). Indeed, examination of our data (Hadjistavropoulos et al., 2000) indicates that only 15% of pain patients score in the range that is reported for patients diagnosed with hypochondriasis.

The MMPI Scale 1 score has also been shown to be consistently elevated among pain samples (T score above 70) compared to both normal controls and acute pain patients (for review see Watson, 1982). Although exact scores are not readily available, IBQ Hypochondriasis and Disease Conviction scores have been reported to be elevated among chronic pain patients seeking treatment at a pain center compared to private practice patients who reported problems with persistent pain (Chapman, Sola, & Bonica, 1979). Kellner, Wiggins, and Pathak (1986) found that the IBQ Hypochondriasis subscale among law students was 0.9 ($SD$ = 1.1), and the IBQ Disease Conviction subscale was 0.8 ($SD$ = 0.9). A mixed group of patients with intractable pain scored 1.4 ($SD$ = 2.0) on the Hypochondriasis subscale, and 3.3 ($SD$ = 1.7) on the Disease Conviction subscale

(Demjen & Bakal, 1981; Pilowsky & Spence, 1975). Based on these two data sets, it would appear that pain patients, compared to controls, obtain higher scores on the Disease Conviction subscale and, to a lesser extent, the Hypochondriasis subscale of the IBQ. Overall, available data seem to suggest that health anxiety, regardless of the measure used, is elevated among pain patients when compared to healthy controls.

## The Role of Pain in the Development of Health Anxiety

Pain may play a role in the development of health anxiety. In particular, one's experiences with pain may influence the development of beliefs about symptoms, disease, and health. Alternatively, pain may serve as a trigger of pre-existing beliefs about health that, in turn, lead to health anxiety. We have speculated that the greater one's pain severity or the more chronic the condition, the greater the likelihood that elevated health anxiety will be observed. To explore the role of pain in the development of health anxiety, health beliefs should ideally be examined before and after the development of pain. A control group not experiencing pain should also be studied. This design is, however, rarely feasible. A viable alternative is to investigate the development of health anxiety using a longitudinal approach examining health beliefs as the pain state progresses. If health anxiety develops and increases because of experience with pain, one would expect that more entrenched dysfunctional beliefs and attitudes would develop among those who have greater difficulties with pain.

We recently examined the interrelationship of health anxiety and pain, and, in particular, the role that pain may play in the development of health anxiety using a longitudinal approach (Hadjistavropoulos & Asmundson, 2000). Two hundred and twenty-seven musculoskeletal patients were asked at the time of their first visit to a physiotherapy clinic to respond to a questionnaire package. Approximately three months after completing the first questionnaire package, patients were asked to respond to questionnaires again. Over 50% ($n = 117$) responded at follow-up. The average pain duration was 24.2 months ($SD = 63.3$). There was, however, substantial variability in pain duration with 48% of the sample suffering from acute pain (pain less than three months in duration) at the time of entry into the study. Health anxiety was measured using the total IAS after omitting health habits items. The data suggested that, after controlling for initial levels of health anxiety, pain severity, somatic symptoms, disability, or pain duration measured at the time of entry into the study did not predict health anxiety at follow-up. In fact, it was not possible to predict increased health anxiety from baseline with any of the variables assessed in the study (e.g., avoidance, reassurance-seeking, pain beliefs, negative affect, and anxiety sensitivity).

Our findings do not support a role for pain in the exacerbation of health anxiety over time (Hadjistavropoulos & Asmundson, 2000). There is other evidence, however, to suggest that health anxiety waxes and wanes with pain, and, thus, that pain may be a trigger for initial experiences of health anxiety. Elevations in health anxiety have been found, for instance, to decrease to normal levels in response to a positive treatment outcome with pain using both the MMPI Scale 1 (Barnes, Gatchel, Mayer, & Barnett, 1990; Moore, Berk, & Nypaver, 1984) and the IBQ Disease Conviction scores (Schnurr, Brooke, & Rollman, 1990; Waddell, Pilowsky, & Bond, 1989).

The aforementioned research seems to suggest that pain is a trigger for health anxiety, but not necessarily a factor that determines the severity of health anxiety over time. Still, the role of pain in the development of health anxiety needs to be examined further. As noted above, it would be ideal to explore health anxiety before and subsequent to the development of pain. Do first-time pain patients, compared to controls, have an increased probability of first onset of severe health anxiety? It seems from the above data that no single pain-related variable (e.g., pain severity, somatic symptoms, pain duration) is predictive of increased health anxiety. More sophisticated models, however, may reveal that pain severity, or pain duration, interact with other variables, such as the propensity to be fearful, in the development of health anxiety. Structural equation modeling geared toward the examination of the potential moderating role of pain in the development of health anxiety is warranted and may serve to shed light on this complex issue.

## Does Health Anxiety Influence Response to Pain?

The evidence to suggest that pain may play a role in the development of health anxiety is far from compelling. There is, however, more convincing evidence to suggest that health anxiety affects a patient's physical, behavioral, and cognitive response to pain.

*Physical Response to Pain*

Health anxiety, as assessed by the IBQ factor analytically derived Hypochondriasis/Affective Disturbance subscale, has been associated with greater somatic awareness among chronic pain patients (Main & Waddell, 1987). Furthermore, pain intensity scores are found to be greater among those scoring higher on the Disease Conviction subscale of the IBQ (Dworkin, Cooper, & Siegfried, 1996) and those scoring higher on the MMPI Scale 1 (Lichtenberg, Skehan, & Swensen, 1984; McCreary, Turner, & Dawson, 1979). More compelling evidence for the role of health anxiety in affecting pain comes from our recent work in this area (Hadjistavropoulos & Asmundson, 2000). We found that health anxiety measured by the IAS (omitting health habits items) at the time of pain assessment related significantly to increased pain severity and somatic sensations at 3-month follow-up. These findings remained even after controlling for initial pain severity and somatic sensations.

Evidence suggesting that health anxiety affects response to pain is not limited to chronic pain, but is also apparent when studying acute pain. Gramling, Clawson, and McDonald (1996) investigated acute experimental pain perception and physiological responsivity to a cold pressor task in female students varying in degree of health anxiety (that was carefully assessed using multiple measures). They found that the higher the level of health anxiety the lower the baseline heart rate. Furthermore, those who were more health anxious exhibited a significant increase in heart rate during the cold pressor task and a significant drop in hand temperature relative to controls. Hand temperature remained lower among the health anxious subjects after the cold pressor task was terminated. Other researchers have observed that cardiac deceleration is related to anticipation and detection of information. On the other hand, cardiac acceleration appears to be related to the processing of information once it is detected (Jennings, 1986). When the findings from Gramling and colleagues (1996) are interpreted in this context it appears likely that health anxious participants were anxiously anticipating the cold pressor task and thus the drop in heart rate. Once they began the cold pressor task they appeared to have been more focused on the task and thus the increase in heart rate. Interestingly, these physiological differences between health anxious and non-health anxious individuals did not result in differences in the pain severity reported by participants. Pain unpleasantness, on the other hand, did differ between health anxious and non-health anxious individuals.

*Behavioral Response to Pain*

Health anxiety has also been found to be associated with distinct behavioral responses to pain, including reassurance-seeking and avoidance. Research with irritable bowel patients suggests that health anxiety is related to reassurance-seeking behavior. Specifically, greater reported fear about the possible serious nature of irritable bowel symptoms (i.e., abdominal pain and altered bowel patterns with no known underlying organic condition) is associated with a tendency to seek out or consult with a physician (Kettell, Jones, & Lydeard, 1992). Patients who perceive their symptoms to be normal or trivial are much less likely to consult a physician, whereas patients who worry about the possibility of cancer are much more likely to do so (Kettell et al., 1992).

Other research supports the association of health anxiety with avoidance among pain patients. Health anxiety measured at the time of initial treatment has been found to predict increased disability, palliative coping, and avoidance of pain at 3-month follow-up, even after controlling for baseline behavior (Hadjistavropoulos & Asmundson, 2000). Health anxiety as assessed by the Hypochondriasis/Affective Disturbance subscale of the IBQ has been found to be related to greater disability among chronic pain patients (Main & Waddell, 1987). Furthermore, the IBQ Disease Conviction subscale has been found to be related to increased overt guarding behavior (Keefe, Crisson, Maltbie, Bradley, & Gil, 1986) and interference of pain with daily activities (Dworkin et al., 1996) among chronic pain patients, as well as increased health care utilization among general practice patients (Pilowsky, Smith, & Katsikitis, 1987).

Similar results, suggesting greater avoidance behavior among health anxious pain patients, have been obtained using the MMPI Scale 1. Turner, Calsyn, Fordyce, and Ready (1982) found that patients with elevated MMPI Scale 1 scores used a combination of narcotic and sedative medications more frequently and also reported greater physical disability. McCreary and Colman (1984) similarly found that, among chronic low back pain patients, Scale 1 of the MMPI was associated with use of more narcotics combined with other medication. Moreover, Scale 1 of the MMPI has been found to be predictive of the number of sick days following physiotherapy for back pain (Hellzén Ingemarsson, Nordholm, & Sivik, 1997). Finally, Scale 1 of the MMPI has been found to be related to a greater likelihood of receiving full disability pension 6 to 12 years after initial assessment (Åkerlind, Hörnquist, & Bjurulf, 1992).

Health anxiety also appears to play a role in behavioral responsivity to acute experimental pain. High health anxious individuals, compared to those with lower health anxiety, have been found to terminate a cold pressor task more frequently and leave their feet in the cold water bath for a significantly shorter period (Gramling et al., 1996). These behaviors can be interpreted as signs of avoidance.

Although high health anxiety is associated with avoidance and reassurance-seeking, it is not entirely clear how differences extend to the behavioral overt expression of pain. Health anxious individuals, identified by the IAS, who are exposed to a cold pressor task have been found to be more expressive of cold pressor pain and discomfort, especially as pain progresses over time (Hadjistavropoulos, 1995). Chronic pain patients scoring higher on the Disease Conviction subscale of the IBQ have also been found to show more pain behavior (e.g., rubbing, guarding, grimacing; Keefe et al., 1986). On the other hand, health anxious pain patients, assessed by the IAS, observed during occupational therapy have not been found to be more verbally or non-verbally expressive of pain (Hadjistavropoulos, Asmundson, Quine, & LaChapelle, in press). Differences between studies may be the result of varying task demands and levels of induced pain and, as such, indicate a need for further investigation.

*Cognitive Response to Pain*

A number of findings have emerged regarding the impact of health anxiety on cognitive response to pain. Patients with high initial levels of health anxiety, three months later report both increased anxiety about pain and greater emotional preoccupation, even after controlling for initial levels of these variables (Hadjistavropoulos & Asmundson, 2000). Also, during physiotherapy, health anxious pain patients have been found to worry more about their health and injury, and to attend to and cata-strophically misinterpret sensations more frequently than those scoring lower on health anxiety (Hadjistavropoulos et al., 2000). Furthermore, it has been found that, among health anxious patients, attending to sensations results in lower anxiety and pain than engaging in distraction. In contrast, patients who score lower on health anxiety experience greater worry about health if they attend to sensations than if they engage in dis-traction (Hadjistavropoulos et al., 2000). It appears, then, that the use of coping strategies such as attention to sensations and distraction differen-tially affect patients depending on their level of health anxiety. For health anxious patients, use of attention appears to result in short-term anxiety reduction.

Health anxious pain patients (whether measured by the IBQ Hypochon-driasis/Affective Disturbance subscale or the MMPI Scale 1) demonstrate and report more inappropriate signs and symptoms, which do not coin-cide with underlying anatomy and physiology (Main & Waddell, 1987; Waddell et al., 1989; Novy et al., 1998). Those patients scoring high on Scale 1 of the MMPI have also been found to be more likely to report pain on injection of a non-disrupted disc, a procedure expected to be non-painful (Block, Vanharanta, Ohnmeiss, & Guyer, 1996). One potential explanation for these findings is that the health anxious patients are mis-interpreting normal benign sensations as indicative of disease and, thus, report pain.

Varied cognitive responses among health anxious individuals in response to acute pain have also been found. In the context of experimental acute pain, health anxious individuals interpret the cold pressor task as significantly more unpleasant (although not more intense) relative to those who score lower on health anxiety (Gramling et al., 1996). Health anxious individuals, when confronted with a painful cold pressor task, engage in negative somatic monitoring (i.e., focused on the negative and emotional features of physical sensations) and catastrophic thinking. Those who experience lower levels of health anxiety, on the other hand, have been found to utilize an objective monitoring style (i.e., a focus on the objective, concrete, and non-emotional aspects of the symptoms as manifested in cognitions such as 'It is a tingling sensation'; Hadjistavropoulos, Craig, & Hadjistavropoulos, 1998). Finally, health anxious individuals also have a difficult time performing an attention concentration task when they expect a painful stimulus (Pauli, Schwenzer, Brody, Rau, & Birbaumer, 1993). Individuals lower in health anxiety, in comparison, do not have the same difficulties with the task. These results collectively suggest that health anxious individuals have an attentional bias or preoccupation with painful sensations; however, application of modified cognitive psychology paradigms (e.g., emotional Stroop color-naming) common to investigations of attentional biases in the anxiety disorders remain forthcoming with health anxious individuals and hypochondriacal patients.

## Health Anxiety and Treatment Outcome

Taken as a whole, although pain does not appear to result in increased health anxiety over time, health anxiety does appear to place patients at risk for poor adjustment to pain. In particular, health anxiety is related to increased pain, somatic sensations, avoidance, reassurance seeking, as well as more attention to symptoms and dysfunctional cognitions regarding pain. There do not appear to be any major discrepancies in the impact of health anxiety on acute clinical or experimental pain or chronic pain, although less attention has been given to acute pain.

The significance of the results becomes particularly salient when considered in the context of treatment outcome. Health anxious patients (primarily as measured by Scale 1 of the MMPI) have been found to have a negative prognosis after surgery and conservative treatment (see Love and Peck, 1987, for review). The literature in this area is quite extensive and comprehensive review is beyond the scope of this chapter; however, some specific examples will be given for illustrative purposes. Wiltse and Rocchio (1975) studied patients admitted to hospital for chemonucleolysis. They found that pretreatment MMPI Scale 1 scores predicted physician's ratings of the patient's recovery one year after the procedure. Similarly, Turner, Herron, and Weiner (1986) found that Scale 1 of the MMPI, measured prior to surgery, predicted outcome following lumber laminectomy and discectomy. MMPI Scale 1 scores (T scores greater than 70) correctly predicted outcome (good vs. poor outcome one year after surgery rated by orthopedic surgeon who was blind to the MMPI results) of 83% of patients, and work status (working vs. not working) of 81% of patients. A number of other studies also suggest that Scale 1 of the MMPI is predictive of successful outcome for back pain patients (Dzioba & Doxey, 1984; Herron & Pheasant, 1982; Herron, Turner, & Weiner, 1986; McCreary et al., 1979; Turner, Robinson, & McCreary, 1983). Caution, however, should be exercised when interpreting the results of studies using Scale 1 of the MMPI. As noted earlier, this measure taps somatic focus more than health anxiety per se. Nonetheless, the results do not appear to be limited to the MMPI Scale 1. Patients who score high on Disease Conviction of the IBQ also show poor outcome in response to back surgery after controlling for differences in physical pathology and psychological distress (Waddell et al., 1989). Furthermore, chronic pain patients (66% back pain) with no clear underlying physiological problem, who had higher scores on the Disease Conviction and Hypochondriasis subscales of the IBQ at baseline, reported lower well-being following 12 weeks of short-term dynamic psychotherapy (Pilowsky & Barrow, 1990). Overall, the results can be taken to suggest that health anxiety impacts substantially upon treatment outcome. Nonetheless, further research using other measures of health anxiety (e.g., the IAS or available diagnostic interviews described in Chapter 5) would be desirable.

## What is the Critical Aspect of Health Anxiety?

A pressing question regarding the relationship between health anxiety and pain concerns whether findings regarding the relationship can be better accounted for by other factors, such as attention or negative affectivity. Arntz and his colleagues (Arntz, Dreessen, & Merckelbach, 1991; Arntz & De Jong, 1993; Arntz, Dreessen, & De Jong, 1994), for instance, suggested that attention is more important than anxiety per se in impacting pain. They found that attention towards pain increases the pain experience, whereas distraction reduces it. Furthermore, they found that anxiety, once controlling for attention, has little impact on response to pain. In other words, their results suggest that pain-related anxiety motivates individuals to attend to pain, but that the critical pain-increasing factor is attention rather than anxiety. Arntz and colleagues specifically focused on artificially induced pain of relatively short duration and, consequently, more work needs to be done on acute and chronic clinical pain. Also, their work has not included hypochondriacal or health anxious patients. Nonetheless, the work raises an important question that needs to be addressed regarding the importance of attention in the health anxiety–pain relationship.

Other researchers have examined whether findings concerning health anxiety and pain can be accounted for solely by other constructs, such as trait negative affectivity. Trait negative affectivity, also referred to as neuroticism, trait anxiety, and general maladjustment (Watson & Clark, 1984), has been defined as 'a broad dimension of individual differences in the tendency to experience negative, distressing emotions . . .' (Costa & McCrae, 1987, p. 301). Though moderately high correlations (e.g., 0.45–0.49) have been found between measures of health anxiety and measures of negative affectivity (e.g., Hitchcock & Mathews, 1992), the evidence suggests that the constructs are distinguishable. Hitchcock and Mathews (1992), for instance, found that even when negative affectivity is controlled for, health anxiety is still related to a tendency to catastrophize about illness. Watson and Pennebaker (1989) found that, unlike individuals scoring high on health anxiety, those who are high on negative affectivity do not have an increased likelihood of seeking reassurance or medical attention. Most recently, our group found that, while the two constructs are correlated at levels similar to those reported by Hitchcock and Mathews (1992) (i.e., $r = 0.45$), health anxiety as measured by the IAS continues to predict physical (i.e., somatic symptoms, pain severity), cognitive (i.e., emotional preoccupation, beliefs about the stability of pain), and behavioral (i.e., palliative behavior, disability) aspects of pain over and above trait negative affectivity (Hadjistavropoulos & Asmundson, 2000).

A related area of investigation in the study of chronic pain is concerned with specific fears or anxiety about pain rather than health anxiety per se. The Pain Anxiety Symptom Scale (PASS), for example, has been developed to measure pain-related anxiety, including fearful interpretations, avoidance and escape, physiological responses, and symptoms of cognitive interference (McCracken, Zayfert, & Gross, 1992). Asmundson and Larsen (2000) recently reviewed the measure and reported that fear and anxiety about pain are associated with greater pain, depression, higher dysfunction, and disability. Pain-related anxiety is also associated with more days of work loss (Waddell, Newton, Henderson, Somerville, & Main, 1993). Previous research has shown that anxiety about pain provides better information about pain, disability, and avoidance than more generalized anxiety (e.g., State–Trait Anxiety Inventory; McCracken, Gross, Aikens, & Carnrike, 1996). Our group recently examined the relation of pain-related anxiety and health anxiety, finding that the IAS (excluding health habit items) correlated significantly with the PASS total score ($r = 0.55$). Despite the high correlation, the IAS continues to explain variance in adjustment to pain even after controlling for scores on the pain-related anxiety. Specifically, we found that the IAS, measured at the time of intake to a primary physiotherapy clinic, is predictive of somatic symptoms, disability, and emotional preoccupation experienced at 3-month follow-up even after controlling for scores on the PASS.

A final related construct that is gaining increasing attention in the area of pain is anxiety sensitivity. Anxiety sensitivity is the fear of anxiety-related bodily sensations, which is thought to result from beliefs that these sensations will result in harmful somatic, social, or psychological consequences (Reiss & McNally, 1985). Patients with high anxiety sensitivity scores respond with fear and avoidance to a number of stimuli, including pain (Asmundson & Taylor, 1996) and appear to be at risk of increased pain behavior (Asmundson & Norton, 1995; Asmundson, Norton, & Veloso, 1999). Noting that anxiety sensitivity and health anxiety are correlated ($r = 0.55$), we explored whether anxiety sensitivity could explain relationships that have been found between health anxiety (measured by the IAS) and pain adjustment (Hadjistavropoulos & Asmundson, 2000). Even after controlling for anxiety sensitivity, however, health anxiety continued to predict numerous aspects of pain adjustment at 3-month follow-up (e.g., pain severity, somatic symptom reporting, disability, palliative coping strategies, negative affect, emotional preoccupation, beliefs that pain is stable). The preliminary data strongly suggest that the constructs are distinguishable.

Overall, it appears that health anxiety, at least as measured by the IAS, is distinguishable from other constructs. That is, the IAS continues to explain variance in adjustment to pain even when controlling for variables such as trait negative affectivity, pain-related anxiety, or anxiety sensitivity. Further research could address whether this finding holds true if other measures of health anxiety are used.

## CLINICAL IMPLICATIONS

It is beyond the scope of this chapter to provide a comprehensive summary of assessment and treatment of health anxious pain patients. There are, however, some noteworthy clinical implications that stem from our review, as well as from recent work on the assessment and treatment of health anxious individuals (Barsky, Geringer, & Wool, 1988; Bouman & Visser, 1998; Salkovskis, 1989; Salkovskis & Warwick, 1986; Warwick, 1995). The implications, however, primarily rest with chronic as compared to acute pain patients. Assessment and treatment of acute pain patients is typically carried out in busy medical practices. Within this context, health anxiety is not likely to be noticed, unless it is extreme, the patient's condition becomes chronic, or both. Lack of attention to health anxiety in the acute pain stage is unfortunate since it is probable that health anxiety places patients at risk for chronic pain. Early attention to health-related fears and beliefs might also serve to prevent future problems by reducing avoidance, reassurance seeking, and catastrophic interpretations of sensations.

In contrast to acute pain, detailed assessments of psychological status are often undertaken with chronic pain patients, especially with those who have musculoskeletal conditions. Such assessments are often multimodal and focus on physical, social, behavioral, cognitive, and affective components of pain (Turk & Rudy, 1990). Such assessments also commonly include both interviews and psychological tests (Turk & Melzack, 1992). The current review points to the need for clinicians to screen for the level of health anxiety among chronic pain patients within the context of the multimodal assessment. The measurement of health anxiety is likely to provide clinicians with information on probable cognitive, behavioral, and physical responses to chronic pain and may also suggest an increased risk for poorer treatment outcomes. Furthermore, information on health anxiety may provide specific direction on how to tailor treatment for pain patients.

Although there has been considerable research on effective treatment for chronic pain patients (see Flor, Fydrich, & Turk, 1992) and there is a growing body of research on effective treatment for health anxiety (e.g., Bouman & Visser, 1998; Clark et al., 1998; Warwick, Clark, Cobb, & Salkovskis, 1996), no controlled research has examined specific treatment strategies for health anxious pain patients. As such, our treatment recommendations are tentative and require systematic investigation. Psychological treatment for pain is typically within the context of a multidisciplinary programme (Barkin et al., 1996). Cognitive-behavioral treatment has become a standard component of this (Grant & Haverkamp, 1995; Pearce, 1983) and involves the provision of information, training in specific coping skills (e.g., relaxation training), problem solving, as well as a more general focus on altering dysfunctional cognitive and behavioral patterns (Barkin et al., 1996). Our review suggests that health anxious individuals may require this general treatment program tailored specifically to their needs and that further attention may need to be given to therapeutic alliance, attention diversion, cognitive reframing, avoidance, and reassurance seeking for treatment to be effective.

Treatment for health anxiety is discussed in detail in other chapters (see Chapters 3, 7, 8, and 9). Nonetheless, there are some aspects of treatment of health anxious pain patients that we would like to elaborate. In particular, the treatment of these patients may require a greater emphasis on the role of attention in their pain and fear experiences. Psychological treatment for the pain patient routinely involves assisting patients in developing and employing techniques to divert their attention away from pain. Training in various forms of relaxation (e.g., progressive muscle relaxation, stretching relaxation, breathing retraining, imagery) is not uncommon (Barkin et al., 1996) and has been found to be effective in reducing pain, depression, and disability (Turner, 1982). Distraction (e.g., through imagery, reading, listening to music, watching movies, counting) is also a common component of treatment and has been found to be effective in many instances (Fernandez & Turk, 1989). We expect that training in attention diversion would also be beneficial for health anxious pain patients. It is clear that such patients are more focused on their pain, for instance, than pain patients with low health anxiety. Attention to pain for health anxious patients appears to reduce anxiety, at least in the short term (Hadjistavropoulos et al., in press). Given the strong need to attend to sensations, it is likely that attentional diversion will be more difficult for health anxious pain patients and considerably more training in these techniques may be needed. Given evidence collected by Arntz and colleagues (Arntz et al., 1991, 1994; Arntz & De Jong, 1993) that anxiety likely influences pain via attention to pain, training in attention diversion becomes even more critical. During therapy, it is likely that clinicians will need to focus on helping patients understand how attention to sensations may be exacerbating anxiety and pain in the long term.

We (Hadjistavropoulos et al., 2000) have found that when health anxious pain patients are asked to use distraction during physiotherapy they actually experience greater pain and distress compared to when they are asked to attend to sensations. It may be that some allowance for attentional focus in a controlled way may be necessary. Barsky et al. (1988) recommend that health anxious individuals be encouraged to focus upon relaxation and to notice benign perceptions. In doing so, the patients are turning their greatest difficulty (selective attention) into an asset. That is, they learn to use somatic monitoring and amplification to enhance their relaxation. In general, it may be the case that more individualized sessions that take into account the patient's concerns and rate of learning are needed with health anxious pain patients.

A further area of treatment that may be somewhat unique for the chronic pain patient concerns avoidance behavior. In the cognitive-behavioral treatment of pain, it is typical for treatment to involve activity pacing, specifically encouraging patients to reduce excessive guarding and avoidance (Nicholas & Sharp, 1997). Patients are taught that extensive avoidance of activities initially results because they have learned that certain activities are painful. Avoidance, however, in the long term, can result in loss of function and reduced conditioning (Asmundson, Norton, &

Norton, 1999). The more patients avoid, the more difficult it is for them to know when they no longer need to avoid or that the activity no longer produces pain. Health anxious pain patients may be avoiding for yet another reason—as a method of reducing health anxiety itself. That is, they may be avoiding in order to evade physical sensations that result in anxiety about their health (also see Asmundson & Taylor, 1996). This possibility needs to be carefully considered by the clinician. Health anxious pain patients need to be provided with education on how anxiety can be maintained by a wide variety of avoidance behaviors. Often, it may be prudent to develop a hierarchy of activities, situations, or events that are being avoided unnecessarily, and work on graduated exposure to these cues. By exposing themselves to the sensations and refraining from excessive avoidance, it is predicted that patients will habituate to the stimuli (Bouman & Visser, 1998).

We have observed several health anxious patients to avoid movements that provoke pain (e.g., picking up children, exercising during physical therapy, walking). Upon detailed questioning, it became clear that they were avoiding these activities not simply because they provoked pain, but because of the symptoms produced by the activity and the subsequent anxiety about their health. Indeed, numerous patients reported experiencing extreme anxiety during rehabilitation (e.g., physiotherapy, occupational therapy, exercise therapy) and, therefore, would avoid or not fully participate in it.

Interestingly, recent research (Hadjistavropoulos, et al., in press) suggests that patients who exhibit lower levels of health anxiety benefit immediately during occupational therapy by reducing pain behavior. Following instructions to inhibit pain behavior, patients who are less health anxious are more likely to report reductions in anxiety and somatic sensations during therapy. They also report fewer passive coping statements. Patients who are health anxious, on the other hand, do not experience the same reductions in anxiety, somatic sensations, and passive coping statements. This is despite evidence that they change their overt behavior to the same extent as control patients. This research suggests that it is not enough to provide health anxious patients with instructions to inhibit pain behavior. Instead, more education surrounding pain behavior and practice may be needed for benefits to be observed.

## FUTURE DIRECTIONS

There are numerous possible directions for research when considering hypochondriasis and health anxiety in the context of pain. First, there is considerable need for a further look at the prevalence of hypochondriasis among pain patients, and the distinction between hypochondriasis and pain disorder. Research is also needed on how pain patients diagnosed with hypochondriasis respond to pain. There is abundant research on how individuals varying on measures of health anxiety differ in response to pain, but there is a paucity of research on hypochondriasis and pain. Do findings regarding health anxiety and pain extend to patients with comorbid hypochondriasis and pain?

In general, studies have focused on health anxiety and primarily musculoskeletal pain. More research is needed to explore the extent to which findings generalize to other pain conditions as well as acute pain. Further investigation is also required to understand what accounts for the onset, risk, and nature of health anxiety as well as the development of health anxiety over time. It is apparent that various aspects of pain (e.g., pain duration, severity) do not result in increased health anxiety over time. Models tested to date, however, have been simplistic, and the interaction of multiple factors in the development of health anxiety should be studied. It is likely that the models examined to date fail to recognize the complexity of the relationship between pain and health anxiety. With respect to the impact of health anxiety on pain, further research needs to more closely consider whether attention is the key component of this relationship. Are other aspects of health anxiety such as catastrophic misinterpretations, avoidance, and reassurance seeking also important?

Finally, research is needed in the area of treatment strategy and outcome. Are there benefits to tailoring treatment for pain patients to meet the needs of the health anxious individual? What is the relative importance of cognitive versus behavioral aspects of treatment for health anxious pain patients? What factors are predictive of positive treatment outcome versus failures? If health anxiety resolves, what factors predict relapse? Will reinjury or relapse of health problems predict a relapse of health anxiety? Overall, despite wide recognition that health anxiety is important in pain, many important questions still remain to be answered.

**Authors' Note:** The assistance of James Cresswell, Diane LaChapelle, and Linda Picot with compilation of articles and manuscript preparation was greatly appreciated. The comments of the editors were also invaluable. Correspondence concerning this chapter should be addressed to Heather D. Hadjistavropoulos, Associate Professor, University of Regina, Regina, Saskatchewan, S4S 0A2. Tel: (306) 585-5133; Fax: (306) 585-4827; E-mail: hadjista@uregina.ca

# REFERENCES

Aigner, M., & Bach, M. (1999). Clinical utility of DSM-IV Pain Disorder. *Comprehensive Psychiatry*, **40**, 353–357.

Åkerlind, I., Hörnquist, J.O., & Bjurulf, P. (1992). Psychological factors in the long-term prognosis of chronic low back pain patients. *Journal of Clinical Psychology*, **48**, 596–605.

Arntz, A., & De Jong, P. (1993). Anxiety, attention and pain. *Journal of Psychosomatic Research*, **37**, 423–432.

Arntz, A., Dreessen, L., & De Jong, P. (1994). The influence of anxiety on pain: Attentional and attributional mediators. *Pain*, **56**, 307–314.

Arntz, A., Dreessen, L., & Merckelbach, H. (1991). Attention, not anxiety, influences pain. *Behaviour Research and Therapy*, **29**, 41–50.

Asmundson, G.J.G., & Larsen, D.K. (2000). Pain Anxiety Symptoms Scale. In J. Maltby, C.A. Lewis, & A. Hill (Eds.), Commissioned reviews of 250 psychological test (pp. 607–612). Wales, UK: Edwin Mellen Press.

Asmundson, G.J.G., & Norton, G.R. (1995). Anxiety sensitivity in patients with physically unexplained chronic back pain: A preliminary report. *Behaviour Research and Therapy*, **33**, 771–777.

Asmundson, G.J.G., Norton, P.J., & Norton, G.R. (1999). Beyond pain: The role of fear and avoidance in chronicity. *Clinical Psychology Review*, **19**, 97–119.

Asmundson, G.J.G., Norton, P.J., & Veloso, F. (1999). Anxiety sensitivity and fear of pain in patients with recurring headaches. *Behaviour Research and Therapy*, **37**, 703–713.

Asmundson, G.J.G., & Taylor, S. (1996). Role of anxiety sensitivity in pain-related fear and avoidance. *Journal of Behavioral Medicine*, **19**, 573–582.

Barkin, R.L., Lubenow, T.R., Bruehl, S., Husfeld, B., Ivankovich, O., & Barkin, S.J. (1996). Management of chronic pain. Part II. *Disease-a-Month*, **42**, 457–508.

Barnes, D., Gatchel, R.J., Mayer, T.G., & Barnett, J. (1990). Changes in MMPI profile levels of chronic low back pain patients following successful treatment. *Journal of Spinal Disorders*, **3**, 353–355.

Barsky, A.J., Geringer, E., & Wool, C.A. (1988). A cognitive-educational treatment for hypochondriasis. *General Hospital Psychiatry*, **10**, 322–327.

Barsky, A.J., Wyshak, G., Klerman, G.L., & Latham, K.S. (1990). The prevalence of hypochondriasis in medical outpatients. *Social Psychiatry and Psychiatric Epidemiology*, **25**, 89–94.

Block, A.R., Vanharanta, H., Ohnmeiss, D.D., & Guyer, R.D. (1996). Discographic pain report: Influence of psychological factors. *Spine*, **21**, 334–338.

Bouman, T.K., & Visser, S. (1998). Cognitive and behavioural treatment of hypochondriasis. *Psychotherapy and Psychosomatics*, **67**, 214–221.

Chapman, C.R., Sola, A.E., & Bonica, J.J. (1979). Illness behaviour and depression compared in pain center and private practice patients. *Pain*, **6**, 1–7.

Clark, D.M., Salkovskis, P.M., Hackmann, A., Wells, A., Fennell, M., Ludgate, J., Ahmad, S., Richards, H.C., & Gelder, M. (1998). Two psychological treatments for hypochondriasis. A randomised controlled trial. *British Journal of Psychiatry*, **173**, 218–225.

Costa, P.T., Jr., & McCrae, R.R. (1987). Neuroticism, somatic complaints, and disease: Is the bark worse than the bite? *Journal of Personality*, **55**, 299–316.

Crombie, I.K., & Davies, H.T.O. (1999). Requirements for epidemiological studies.

In I.K. Crombie, P.R. Croft, S.J. Linton, L. LeResche, & M. Von Korff (Eds.), *Epidemiology of pain* (pp. 17–24). Seattle: IASP Press.

Demjen, S., & Bakal, D. (1981). Illness behaviour and chronic headache. *Pain,* **10,** 221–229.

Dworkin, R.H., Cooper, E.M., & Siegfried, R.N. (1996). Chronic pain and disease conviction. *The Clinical Journal of Pain,* **12,** 111–117.

Dzioba, R.B., & Doxey, N.C. (1984). A prospective investigation into the orthopaedic and psychological predictors of outcome of first lumbar surgery following industrial injury. *Spine,* **9,** 614–623.

Escobar, J.I., Gara, M., Waitzkin, H., Silver, R.C., Holman, A., & Compton, W. (1998). DSM-IV hypochondriasis in primary care. *General Hospital Psychiatry,* **20,** 155–159.

Fernandez, E., & Turk, D.C. (1989). The utility of cognitive coping strategies for altering pain perception: A meta-analysis. *Pain,* **38,** 123–135.

Fishbain, D.A., Goldberg, M., Meagher, B.R., Steele, R., & Rosomoff, H. (1986). Male and female chronic pain patients categorized by DSM-III psychiatric diagnostic criteria. *Pain,* **26,** 181–197.

Fishbain, D.A., & Rosomoff, H.L. (1987). Reply to letter from Drs. Jaeger and Skoorsky [Letter to the editor]. *Pain,* **29,** 265–266.

Flor, H., Fydrich, T., & Turk, D.C. (1992). Efficacy of multidisciplinary pain treatment centers: A meta-analytic review. *Pain,* **49,** 221–230.

Gatchel, R.J., Polatin, P.B., Mayer, T.G., & Garcy, P.D. (1994). Psychopathology and the rehabilitation of patients with chronic low back pain disability. *Archives of Physical Medicine and Rehabilitation,* **75,** 666–670.

Gramling, S.E., Clawson, E.P., & McDonald, M.K. (1996). Perceptual and cognitive abnormality model of hypochondriasis: Amplification and physiological reactivity in women. *Psychosomatic Medicine,* **58,** 423–431.

Grant, L.D., & Haverkamp, B.E. (1995). A cognitive-behavioural approach to chronic pain management. *Journal of Counseling and Development,* **74,** 25–31.

Gureje, O., Von Korff, M., Simon, G.E., & Gater, R. (1998). Persistent pain and well-being: A World Health Organization study in primary care. *Journal of the American Medical Association,* **280,** 147–151.

Hadjistavropoulos, H.D. (1995). *Cognitive and behavioural responses to illness information in health anxiety.* Unpublished doctoral dissertation, University of British Columbia, Vancouver, British Columbia.

Hadjistavropoulos, H.D., & Asmundson, G.J.G. (1998). Factor analytic investigation of the Illness Attitudes Scale in a chronic pain sample. *Behaviour Research and Therapy,* **36,** 1185–1195.

Hadjistavropoulos, H.D., & Asmundson, G.J.G. (2000). *A longitudinal investigation of health anxiety and pain.* Manuscript in preparation.

Hadjistavropoulos, H.D., Asmundson, G.J.G., Quine, A., & LaChapelle, D.L. (in press). *The role of patient health anxiety among chronic pain patients in determining response to therapy.* Pain Research and Management.

Hadjistavropoulos, H.D., Craig, K.D., & Hadjistavropoulos, T. (1998). Cognitive and behavioural responses to illness information: The role of health anxiety. *Behaviour Research and Therapy,* **36,** 149–164.

Hadjistavropoulos, H.D., Frombach, I.K., & Asmundson, G.J.G. (1999). Exploratory and confirmatory factor analytic investigations of the Illness Attitudes Scale in a nonclinical sample. *Behaviour Research and Therapy,* **37,** 671–684.

Hadjistavropoulos, H.D., Hadjistavropoulos, T., & Quine, A. (2000). Health anxiety moderates the effects of distraction versus attention to pain. *Behaviour Research and Therapy,* **38,** 425–438.

Hathaway, S.R., & McKinley, J.C. (1983). *Minnesota Multiphasic Personality Inventory manual.* New York: Psychological Corporation.

Hathaway, S.R., & McKinley, J.C. (1989). *Minnesota Multiphasic Personality Inventory II manual.* New York: Psychological Corporation.

Hellzén Ingemarsson, A., Nordholm, L., & Sivik, T. (1997). Risk of long-term disability among patients with back pain. *Scandinavian Journal of Rehabilitation Medicine,* **29**, 205–212.

Herron, L.D., & Pheasant, H.C. (1982). Changes in MMPI profiles after low-back surgery. *Spine,* **7**, 591–597.

Herron, L., Turner, J., & Weiner, P. (1986). A comparison of the Millon Clinical Multiaxial Inventory and the Minnesota Multiphasic Personality Inventory as predictors of successful treatment by lumbar laminectomy. *Clinical Orthopaedics and Related Research,* **203**, 232–238.

Hitchcock, P.B., & Mathews, A. (1992). Interpretation of bodily symptoms in hypochondriasis. *Behaviour Research and Therapy,* **30**, 223–234.

Jennings, J.R. (1986). Bodily changes during attending. In M. Coles, E. Donchin, & S.W. Porges (Eds.), *Psychophysiology: Systems, processes, and applications.* New York: Guilford Press.

Katon, W., Egan, K., & Miller, D. (1985). Chronic pain: Lifetime psychiatric diagnoses and family history. *American Journal of Psychiatry,* **142**, 1156–1160.

Keefe, F.J., Crisson, J.E., Maltbie, A., Bradley, L., & Gil, K.M. (1986). Illness behavior as a predictor of pain and overt behavior patterns in chronic low back pain patients. *Journal of Psychosomatic Research,* **30**, 543–551.

Kellner, R., Abbott, P., Winslow, W.W., & Pathak, D. (1987). Fears, beliefs, and attitudes in DSM-III hypochondriasis. *The Journal of Nervous and Mental Disease,* **175**, 20–25.

Kellner, R., Wiggins, R.G., & Pathak, D. (1986). Hypochondriacal fears and beliefs in medical and law students. *Archives of General Psychiatry,* **43**, 487–489.

Kettell, J., Jones, R., & Lydeard, S. (1992). Reasons for consultation in irritable bowel syndrome: Symptoms and patient characteristics. *British Journal of General Practice,* **42**, 459–461.

Kinney, R.K., Gatchel, R.J., Polatin, P.B., Fogarty, W.T., & Mayer, T.G. (1993). Prevalence of psychopathology in acute and chronic low back pain patients. *Journal of Occupational Rehabilitation,* **3**, 95–103.

Kirmayer, J.L., & Robbins, J.M. (1991). Three forms of somatization in primary care: Prevalence, co-occurrence, and sociodemographic characteristics. *Psychotherapy and Psychosomatics,* **179**, 647–655.

Lautenbacher, S., & Rollman, G.B. (1999). Somatization, hypochondriasis, and related conditions. In A.R. Block, E.F. Kremer, & E. Fernandez (Eds.), *Handbook of pain syndromes: Biopsychosocial perspectives* (pp. 613–632). New Jersey: Lawrence Erlbaum Associates.

Lichtenberg, P.A., Skehan, M.W., & Swensen, C.H. (1984). The role of personality, recent life stress and arthritic severity in predicting pain. *Journal for Psychosomatic Research,* **28**, 231–236.

Linton, S.J., & Skevington, S.M. (1999). Psychological factors. In I.K. Crombie, P.R. Croft, S.J. Linton, L. LeResche, & M. Von Korff (Eds.), *Epidemiology of pain* (pp. 25–42). Seattle: IASP Press.

Love, A.W., & Peck, C.L. (1987). The MMPI and psychological factors in chronic low back pain: A review. *Pain,* **28**, 1–12.

Main, C.J., & Waddell, G. (1987). Psychometric construction and validity of the Pilowsky Illness Behaviour Questionnaire in British patients with chronic low back pain. *Pain,* **28**, 13–25.

McCracken, L.M., Gross, R.T., Aikens, J., & Carnrike, C.L.M., Jr. (1996). The assessment of anxiety and fear in persons with chronic pain: A comparison of instruments. *Behaviour Research and Therapy*, **34**, 927–933.

McCracken, L.M., Zayfert, C., & Gross, R.T. (1992). The Pain Anxiety Symptoms Scale: Development and validation of a scale to measure fear of pain. *Pain*, **50**, 67–73.

McCreary, C., & Colman, A. (1984). Medication usage, emotional disturbance and pain behaviour in chronic low back pain patients. *Journal of Clinical Psychology*, **40**, 15–19.

McCreary, C., Turner, J., & Dawson, E. (1979). The MMPI as a predictor of response to conservative treatment for low back pain. *Journal of Clinical Psychology*, **35**, 278–284.

Melzack, R., & Wall, P.D. (1988). *The challenge of pain* (rev. edn.). Markham, ON: Penguin Books.

Merskey, H., & Bogduk, N. (Eds.) (1994). *Classification of chronic pain: Descriptions of chronic pain syndromes and definitions of pain terms* (2nd edn.). Seattle: IASP Press.

Moore, M.E., Berk, S.N., & Nypaver, A. (1984). Chronic pain: Inpatient treatment with small group effects. *Archives of Physical Medicine and Rehabilitation*, **65**, 356–361.

Nicholas, M., & Sharp, T.J. (1997). Cognitive-behavioural programs: Theory and application. In A.R. Molloy & I. Power (Eds.), *International Anesthesiology Clinics: Vol. 35. Acute and chronic pain* (pp. 155–170). Philadelphia: Lippincott-Raven Publishers.

Novy, D.M., Collins, H.S., Nelson, D.V., Thomas, A.G., Wiggins, M., Martinez, A., & Irving, G.A. (1998). Waddell signs: Distributional properties and correlates. *Archives of Physical Medicine and Rehabilitation*, **79**, 820–822.

Pauli, P., Schwenzer, M., Brody, S., Rau, H., & Birbaumer, N. (1993). Hypochondriacal attitudes, pain sensitivity, and attentional bias. *Journal of Psychosomatic Research*, **37**, 745–752.

Pearce, S. (1983). A review of cognitive-behavioural methods for the treatment of chronic pain. *Journal of Psychosomatic Research*, **27**, 431–440.

Pilowsky, I., & Barrow, C.G. (1990). A controlled study of psychotherapy and amitriptyline used individually and in combination in the treatment of chronic intractable, 'psychogenic' pain. *Pain*, **40**, 3–19.

Pilowsky, I., Smith, Q.P., & Katsikitis, M. (1987). Illness behaviour and general practice utilisation: A prospective study. *Journal of Psychosomatic Research*, **31**, 177–183.

Pilowsky, I., & Spence, N.D. (1975). Pain and illness behaviour: A comparative study. *Journal of Psychosomatic Research*, **20**, 131–134.

Pilowsky, I., & Spence, N.D. (1983). *Manual for the Illness Behaviour Questionnaire (IBQ)*. Adelaide, Australia: University of Adelaide.

Polatin, P.B., Kinney, R.K., Gatchel, R.J., Lillo, E., & Mayer, T.G. (1993). Psychiatric illness and chronic low-back pain: The mind and the spine—Which goes first? *Spine*, **18**, 66–71.

Reich, J., Tupin, J.P., & Abramowitz, S.I. (1983). Psychiatric diagnosis of chronic pain patients. *American Journal of Psychiatry*, **140**, 1495–1498.

Reiss, S., & McNally, R.J. (1985). Expectancy model of fear. In S. Reiss & R.R. Bootzin (Eds.), *Theoretical issues in behavior therapy* (pp. 107–121). San Diego, CA: Academic Press.

Salkovskis, P.M. (1989). Somatic problems. In K. Hawton, P.M. Salkovskis, J.W. Kirk, & D.M. Clark (Eds.), *Cognitive behaviour therapy for psychiatric problems: A practical guide* (pp. 235–276). Oxford, UK: Oxford University Press.

Salkovskis, P.M., & Warwick, H.M.C. (1986). Morbid preoccupation, health anxiety and reassurance: A cognitive-behavioural approach to hypochondriasis. *Behaviour Research and Therapy*, **24**, 597–602.

Schnurr, R.F., Brooke, R.I., & Rollman, G.B. (1990). Psychosocial correlates of temporomandibular joint pain and dysfunction. *Pain*, **42**, 153–165.

Turk, D.C., & Melzack, R. (Eds.) (1992). *Handbook of pain assessment*. New York: The Guilford Press.

Turk, D.C., Okifuji, A., Sinclair, J.D., & Starz, T.W. (1996). Pain, disability, and physical functioning in subgroups of fibromyalgia patients. *Journal of Rheumatology*, **23**, 1255–1262.

Turk, D.C., & Rudy, T.E. (1990). Neglected factors in chronic pain treatment outcome studies referral patterns, failure to enter treatment, and attrition. *Pain*, **43**, 7–25.

Turner, J.A. (1982). Comparison of group progressive-relaxation training and cognitive-behavioural group therapy for chronic low back pain. *Journal of Consulting Clinical Psychology*, **50**, 757–765.

Turner, J.A., Calsyn, D.A., Fordyce, W.E., & Ready, L.B. (1982). Drug utilization patterns in chronic pain patients. *Pain*, **12**, 357–363.

Turner, J.A., Herron, L., & Weiner, P. (1986). Utility of the MMPI Pain Assessment Index in predicting outcome after lumbar surgery. *Journal of Clinical Psychology*, **42**, 764–769.

Turner, J.A., Robinson, J., & McCreary, C.P. (1983). Chronic low back pain: Predicting response to nonsurgical treatment. *Archives of Physical Medicine and Rehabilitation*, **64**, 560–563.

Von Korff, M., Dworkin, S., Le Resche, L., & Kruger, A. (1988). An epidemiologic comparison of pain complaints. *Pain*, **32**, 173–183.

Waddell, G., Newton, M., Henderson, I., Somerville, D., & Main, C.J. (1993). A Fear-Avoidance Beliefs Questionnaire (FABQ) and the role of fear-avoidance beliefs in chronic low back pain and disability. *Pain*, **52**, 157–168.

Waddell, G., Pilowsky, I., & Bond, M.R. (1989). Clinical assessment and interpretation of abnormal illness behaviour in low back pain. *Pain*, **39**, 41–53.

Warwick, H.M.C. (1995). Assessment of hypochondriasis. *Behaviour Research and Therapy*, **33**, 845–853.

Warwick, H.M.C., Clark, D.M., Cobb, A.M., & Salkovskis, P.M. (1996). A controlled trial of cognitive-behavioural treatment of hypochondriasis. *British Journal of Psychiatry*, **169**, 189–195.

Warwick, H.M.C., & Salkovskis, P. (1990). Hypochondriasis. *Behaviour Research and Therapy*, **28**, 105–117.

Watson, D. (1982). Neurotic tendencies among chronic pain paints: An MMPI item analysis. *Pain*, **14**, 365–385.

Watson, D., & Clark, L.A. (1984). Negative affectivity: The disposition to experience aversive emotional states. *Psychological Bulletin*, **96**, 465–490.

Watson, D., & Pennebaker, J.W. (1989). Health complaints, stress, and distress: Exploring the central role of negative affectivity. *Psychological Review*, **96**, 234–254.

Wiltse, L.L., & Rocchio, P.D. (1975). Preoperative psychological tests as predictors of success of chemonucleolysis in the treatment of low-back syndrome. *The Journal of Bone and Joint Surgery*, **57-A**, 478–483.

Chapter 13

# PSYCHOTIC DISORDERS WITH HYPOCHONDRIACAL FEATURES: DELUSIONS OF THE SOMA

*David Kingdon\*, Shanaya Rathod†, and Douglas Turkington‡*

## INTRODUCTION

Hypochondriacal beliefs can be held with sufficient conviction that they effectively meet criteria for delusions. In such circumstances they might be described as a *monosymptomatic hypochondriacal psychosis*, an illness characterised by a single, sustained hypochondriacal delusion over a considerable length of time. The DSM-IV (American Psychiatric Association, 1994) formalizes the diagnosis as Delusional Disorder, Somatic Type. Hypochondriacal beliefs may also present as part of psychotic disorders, including schizophrenia or depressive psychosis. The purpose of this chapter is to highlight characteristics of, and explain management strategies for, psychotic disorders with hypochondriacal features.

## DEFINING DELUSIONS

Over the years, many clinicians and researchers have attempted to define delusions. In general, they can be viewed as erroneous beliefs that usually involve a misinterpretation of perceptions or experiences. The original concept can be attributed to the work of Jaspers (1913/1963) who defined

*Professor of Mental Health Care Delivery, University of Southampton, Royal South Hants Hospital, Brintons Terrace, Southampton; †Specialist Registrar, Royal South Hants Hospital, Brintons Terrace, Southampton; ‡Senior Lecturer, Department of Psychiatry, Royal Victoria Infirmary, Queen Victoria Road, Newcastle upon Tyne

*Health Anxiety*
Edited by G.J.G. Asmundson, S. Taylor & B.J. Cox
© 2001 John Wiley & Sons Ltd.

the following criteria for a delusion: (a) that the belief is held with extra-ordinary conviction and with profound subjective certainty, (b) that it is maintained against the effect of other experiences and of convincing counter argument, and (c) that it is impossible with regard to its content. This definition is now under challenge as the dichotomous nature (e.g., impossible or not impossible, amenable to reason or not) does not fit with evidence that continua exist. Indeed, recent work on delusions highlights that they are not rigidly fixed. Rather, they appear to be complex, multi-dimensional phenomena (Kendler, Glazer, & Morgenstein, 1983) that seem to fluctuate in intensity over time, even without treatment (Alloy, 1988), and which can be, under certain conditions, modified through rea-soning (Kingdon, Turkington, & John, 1994). Moreover, they need not be bizarre in nature (i.e., they can be culturally syntonic and well structured; Munro, 1992).

Delusions can be considered primary or secondary. They have been described as primary (i.e., autochthonous) when arising suddenly from unaccountable origins and where they seem to have no relationship to mood states and, essentially, no meaning. Secondary delusions, on the other hand, are described as being more understandable in relation to the prevailing affective state and cultural climate (Sims, 1995).

It is increasingly believed (Kingdon & Turkington, 1994) that maintenance of individual delusions depends upon the strength of the belief which, in turn, may depend upon the time period over which the belief has been present and the psychological and social consequences of relinquishing the belief. These latter two factors are more important if a person has acted on a delusion for a long time and faced repeated confrontation, in which circumstances entrenchment (i.e., strengthening of the belief) is likely. Also important to maintenance of the delusion are the opportunity to dis-cover alternative explanations, the manner in which these alternative explanations are presented (i.e., the degree of collaborative information gathering as opposed to didactic statements of fact), and the quality of the relationship with the therapist, including parameters such as trust, empathy, honesty, and personal disclosure.

## MONOSYMPTOMATIC HYPOCHONDRIACAL PSYCHOSIS

Is there a clear demarcating line between hypochondriasis and mono-symptomatic hypochondriacal psychosis? It seems more likely that a continuum exists (see Strauss, 1969), ranging from normal health con-cerns, to exaggerated concerns, to hypochondriasis and, in some cases, culminating in hypochondriacal delusions. Below we review the history, clinical presentation, and etiology of this condition.

## History

Kraeplin (1921/1976) described three subtypes of delusional content, including erotomania, paranoid jealousy, and megalomania. He also noted that

> a hypochondriacal form is frequently described as another kind of paranoid delusion with depressive colouring. It is certain that hypochondriacal delusions are frequently expressed by paranoiacs. Nevertheless, I have not found it possible in careful sifting of my experiences to find an indubitable case of paranoia characterised only, or at least predominantly, by this kind of delusion. I think therefore that I would meantime abstain from the delimitation of a hypochondriacal paranoia.

Similarly, Cameron (1959) described '. . . a rare condition in which a delusional system develops logically out of some misinterpretation of an actual event [and] does not interfere with the rest of the individual's thinking or general personality' (p. 52).

Despite these early descriptions, we now know that these symptoms are not so rare. They have, in fact, been known to non-psychiatric specialists, such as dermatologists and general physicians, by many different names (e.g., le delire dermatozoaire, dermatozoenwahn, dermatophobia, parasitoses delirantes) and for many years. For example, Perrin (1896) coined the term *parasitophobic neurodermatitis* to explain an intense fear of having parasites living under the skin. He also felt that pruritis and other skin conditions played a role initially, and hence, the delusion was viewed as an elaboration of the primary pathological experience. MacNamara (1928) reported five cases of primary tactile hallucinations (all females complaining of black things, insects, or microbes, living under their skin) and suggested that they suffered from little or no mental disorder (i.e., they showed normal affections, proper orientation, good powers of judgment).

Similarly, Ekbom (1938) described *delusional parasitosis* (or Ekbom's Syndrome), a persistent condition in which the patient, primarily females over the age of 50, believes that small animals such as insects, lice, vermin, or maggots are living and thriving on or within the skin. These patients are typically hallucinating or are deluded that they are victims of attacks of these small animals and are prepared to undertake extreme measures, such as use of caustic fluids on furnishings and even on themselves, to rid themselves of the perceived infestation. Wilson and Miller (1946; cited in Berrios, 1985) and, more recently, Skott (1978) have described other cases of delusional parasitosis. Today this condition often presents to environmental health and housing departments of the government in the form of repeated requests by the sufferer to have their premises investigated despite negative findings (Edwards, 1977; cited in Munro, 1980).

## Clinical Presentation

Somatic delusions can occur in several forms. The most common include false convictions that there is:

- emission of a foul odour from the skin, mouth, rectum, or vagina;
- an infestation of insects on or in the skin;
- an internal parasite;
- certain parts of the body that are definitely (contrary to evidence) misshapen or ugly; and
- part of the body not functioning.

The patient presents as preoccupied, without convincing justification, with somatic beliefs. Symptoms cause persistent distress or interference in daily living and lead the person to seek medical treatment or investigations. There is also persistent refusal to accept medical reassurance that there is no physical disease or disorder causing the symptoms or physical abnormality. Ekbom (1938) noted a unique characteristic, that being the energy and persistence with which the person seeks out innumerable medical consultations and opinions. Often the person is very insistent in demanding that the doctor confirm the diagnosis that they have already made for themselves, and expresses anger and disclaim if this is not accepted. The same story can be told repeatedly without adding details, demands become increasingly idiosyncratic and irrational, and paranoid and very circumstantial complaints about the incompetence of medical advisers are common. There may be accompanying anxiety. The skin may appear normal or there may be signs of scratching. Skott (1978) found, in her series of patients with infestation delusions, that a significant number had borderline intellectual handicap. Considerable tact is needed to enlist the person's grudging cooperation (Gould & Gragg, 1976) and in some cases this is never obtained.

The prevalence of monosymptomatic hypochondriacal psychosis is unknown. Psychiatrists are rarely referred these patients although most will know some who meet this diagnosis. Munro (1980) stated that the incidence is equal in both sexes. This is in contrast with the reports of Ekbom (1938) and Skott (1978), who indicated greater incidence in women. The age of onset of monosymptomatic hypochondriacal psychosis has also been debated. Ekbom (1938) stated that his patients were over 50 years of age, although Yamada, Nakajima and Noguchi (1998) stated a younger age of onset for the condition. Onset may be insidious or acute.

## Models of Etiology

Delusions, in general, are complex phenomena and a number of factors have been implicated in their causation. Psychoanalytic, neuroanatomic, and various multifactor models have been proposed. These models are briefly outlined below.

### Psychoanalytic Models

In one of the earliest psychoanalytic models, Freud (1896/1962) proposed that the paranoia was due to failure to maintain homosexual wishes under repression. Other psychoanalytical models state that delusions reflect memories, affects, and fantasies that the individual had prior to the onset of psychosis (Freeman, 1981; Garety, 1990; Nelki, 1988).

### Neuroanatomic Models

Cumming (1988) suggested that the parietal lobes of the cerebrum play an important role in determining normal body schema (i.e., an individual's awareness of the spatial characteristics of his or her own body). There may also be some input from the thalamus and somatoesthetic systems. Cumming denotes body experience to schema plus associated psychological, situational, emotional, and intentional factors. Connolly (1978; cited in Munro, 1980) noted that there seems to be a correlation between olfactory hallucinations and one's view of one's sexuality (i.e., gender doubt), suggesting some functional interrelationship between these two modalities at the limbic structures.

### Multi-factor Models

The vulnerability–stress model posits that the interaction between biological, psychological, and social factors are important in the formation of delusions. This model also holds that normal experience and psychosis are on two ends of a continuum. Vulnerability may occur at a biological level due to genetic predisposition or due to other factors, such as head injury. Ciompi (1988) and Perris (1989) argued that the vulnerability–stress model also needs to take into account the psychological processes involved in an individual's learning and adaptation. Hence, the interaction between the biological factors and dysfunctional cognitive or

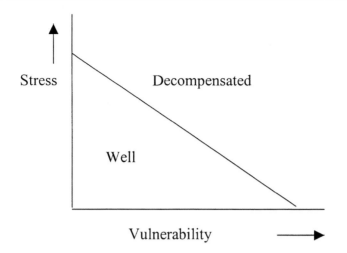

**Figure 13.1**   Vulnerability–stress model (adapted from Zubin & Spring, 1977).

emotional schemata is important. Personality (Jaspers, 1913/1963) and negative affect may contribute to vulnerability to stresses. Cameron (1959) suggested that predelusional patients are often anxious, fearful, socially withdrawn, and distrustful individuals who are reluctant to confide in others. As illustrated in Figure 13.1, exposure to stress (e.g., significant life event, social isolation, interpersonal incompetence) may lead to formation of psychotic (i.e., decompensated) symptoms. The more vulnerable an individual is, the less stress is required to precipitate a psychotic condition.

Hemsley and Garety (1986) present a similar multifactor model in which they discuss the relationship between delusional beliefs and failures in specific stages of belief formation. They state that in some, personality, affect, self-esteem and motivation play a part in the formation of delusions whereas for others, abnormality of perception and judgment are important. This model, illustrated in Figure 13.2, posits that expectations arising prior to receipt and processing of information can influence belief formation which, in turn, may be modified by both how the information is processed, by arousal levels, and by any reinforcement or disconfirmation to the belief. Not only does the model emphasize the concept of continuum between normal experiences and delusions through intermediate stages, but also highlights and incorporates components of the vulnerability–stress model.

The importance of the multifactor models lies in the way in which they can be applied in therapy and with families to reduce stigmatization and

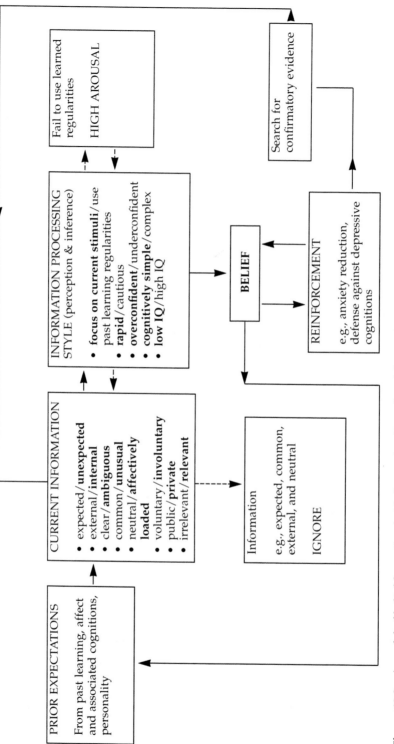

**Figure 13.2** A model of belief formation (with factors implicated in delusion formation in bold). From *Delusions: Investigations into the Psychology of Delusional Reasoning*, by P.A. Garety and D. Hemsley (1994). Reprinted by permission of Psychology Press Limited, Hove, UK.

increase understanding. However, it is important to remember that, as in all cases of hypochondriasis, there always remains the possibility that the hypochondriacal symptoms will relate to an underlying yet unidentified physical disorder. This information needs to be given due attention if and when it emerges.

*Application to Monsymptomatic Hypochondriacal Psychosis*

How does this model apply to delusions that are part of monosymptomatic hypochondriacal psychosis? Several theorists have proposed that some delusional beliefs are founded in an attempt to explain anomalous experiences (Maher, 1974) and, in the case of delusions of the soma, appear to be extreme interpretations of unusual bodily or somatic experiences (Southard, 1912). Fleck (1955; cited in Hopkinson, 1970) has suggested that three stages occur in the development of delusions of infestation, including (a) abnormal cutaneous sensation, (b) illusion, and (c) delusion.

Along these lines, fashion, media, and cultural trends tend to influence the way in which individuals become preoccupied with their health, diet, clothes, and weight and in the form of delusions and hallucinations. The psychotic symptoms may begin with an interest in any one or more of the above, which develops out of proportion to the circumstances in relation to particular life events, and the individual may become anxious about his or her body and its function. Such somatic preoccupation may lead to increased focus and checking on physical sensations (e.g., breathing, heart-rate, bowel function) which can alter these functions (e.g., hyperventilation, racing heart, diarrhea) leading to increasing concern in a positive upward spiral mediated by anxiety. This may, in some, become an obsession with constant fear of physical symptoms and over-awareness of physiological signs. At this stage, the individual may retain some insight and may also be temporarily convinced that they are not physically ill; but, in some, such insight is not achievable at any time.

# HYPOCHONDRIASIS IN DEPRESSIVE PSYCHOSIS AND SCHIZOPHRENIA

It has long been recognized that patients with depressive psychosis can develop hypochondriacal beliefs, including delusions of bodily change. These classically include beliefs that they have no internal organs or that specific organs (e.g., the stomach) have rotted away (Cotard, 1882). In schizophrenia, delusional ideas of a hypochondriacal nature may include beliefs that objects have been inserted into one's body (e.g., silicon chips, microphones) so that others can control or spy on them, or that specific bodily parts are being targeted for persecution or have impossible functions (Ziese, 1967; cited in Hopkinson, 1970). Sometimes, people with schizophrenia develop complex delusional systems to explain their sensations. Sensory (e.g., tactile) sensations can give rise to delusional systems. These are frequently misinterpreted anxiety symptoms. To illustrate, paresthesiae are often misinterpreted as being touched, numbness as nerve loss, blurred vision as interference with sight, and these may be attributed to external forces such as police, government, and neighbors or, alternatively, to internal causes as a serious illness.

Organic conditions, such as temporal lobe epilepsy and drug intoxication, may produce tactile hallucinations. The cocaine bug (formication) is a typical example, as sometimes it may present as a circumscribed hypochondriasis. Liebaldt and Klages (1961; cited in Berrios, 1985) consider that this may occur in manic depressive psychosis, toxic states, cerebrovascular disease in the elderly, organic cerebral disease, and even as an induced delusion in relatives of pest control officers.

## TREATMENT

The treatment of hypochondriasis when part of psychotic disorders is, initially, that of the underlying disorder. The first line treatment of depressive psychosis is medication, often supplemented by electroconvulsive therapy. This is generally successful, at least for that episode (McGuffin, 1997). Treatment of schizophrenia involves antipsychotic medication, and monosymptomatic hypochondriacal disorders have been noted to particularly respond to pimozide (Munro & Chmara, 1982; also see Chapter 8). However, these interventions can be limited, or even absent in effect, and certainly need to be administered as part of a broad comprehensive package of care addressing social needs and issues to do with relationships.

Many patients presenting with hypochondriacal disorders are isolated and may require support in developing social networks; but, they may be very resistant to doing so. Cognitive-behavioral techniques used for reducing hypochondriacal beliefs (as described in Chapters 3 and 7), including delusional beliefs, may be appropriate. Even when used to treat bizarre and entrenched symptoms, cognitive-behavioral treatments involve a structured, collaborative approach. This approach has been used successfully to treat similar psychotic conditions, such as schizophrenia (Chadwick, Birchwood, & Trower, 1996; Kingdon & Turkington, 1994; Sensky et al., 2000).

Patients with monosymptomatic hypochondriacal psychosis are notoriously difficult to engage in treatment. They react vehemently if the suggestion is made, or they interpret it as being made, that they are imagining their somatic symptoms. Suggestions that the symptoms may be stress-related are likewise dismissed. So, a method of intervention that provides minimal prompts is indicated, even though it may seem slow. Many patients will resist attending clinics to see psychiatrists or psychologists, but often can be persuaded to be seen in community settings or in their own homes. Introduction by an intermediary (e.g., the family doctor, practice nurse) may also assist in the introduction of the psychiatrist or psychologist. A Socratic approach, which involves gentle questioning and exploration to draw on the patient's own beliefs and ideas about his or her problems without preconceptions, can be effective. In this circumstance, saying something like the following may be useful: 'I've just come because your doctor asked me to. It may be a complete waste of both our time, but if you can just explain what the problem is, I can go and talk with him about it.'

Therapy focuses on understanding the patient's specific concerns (e.g., of infestation or bodily change) and, by a process of guided discovery, examines the development of these concerns, the circumstances in which they are nested, relevant life stresses, and, particularly, the specific sensations that have been interpreted as being caused by the perceived infestation or bodily change. Alternative explanations are developed, ideally through suggestions by the patient themselves, and specific reasons for such sensations, especially as symptoms of anxiety, are explored. Direct debate, and certainly confrontation, rarely changes the beliefs. Gentle exploration may lead to engagement in treatment and strengthening of the therapeutic relationship, which, in turn, enables other important areas to be explored. As illustrated below in the case example, sometimes agreeing on tasks to explore and test the reality of the beliefs can further be effective.

It may be that the techniques used successfully in treatment-resistant delusions (Turkington & Siddle, 1998) can be beneficial; although, they have not been subject to clinical trials in this area. Following exploration and engagement, these techniques involve inference chaining the beliefs to understand them better. For example, one might begin with questions such as 'I accept that you find these symptoms particularly distressing. Which part of your problem is affecting you most?'. This may then be supplemented, if necessary, by questions such as 'Is it the pain or discomfort? Is it that you are ashamed of what's happening? Is it that it makes you isolated?'. It may then be that these individual issues can be dealt with directly. If discomfort is a factor, the therapist might suggest 'Although we don't seem to be able to get rid of your discomfort, could we look at ways of helping you cope better with it?'. Dealing with isolation would involve supported reintroduction to social networks. By initially focusing on the delusional idea and working through it, patients are sometimes more prepared to accept compromise solutions. The aim needs to be to reduce distress and disability caused by the symptoms rather than removal of the belief. The latter may follow after the focus is taken off it and underlying needs are dealt with first.

The following case illustrates some of the treatment and management strategies described above, as applied in a patient with delusional disorder. Similar approaches, supplemented with pharmaceutical intervention, may be most appropriate in cases involving schizophrenia and depressive psychosis.

## Case Study

Lorraine is a 19-year-old single woman with a 10-year history of believing that she emits a foul odor. At the onset of menstruation she developed the belief that she smelled strongly of a mixture of menstrual blood, urine, and feces. Classmates had teased her about her early onset of puberty and she became increasingly socially anxious and isolated 'because of the smell'. Over the years since leaving school she lived the life of a hermit, venturing into social situations only when it was absolutely necessary. She chose to go shopping at the quietest time of day and would immediately leave the shop if there was a queue. She never had a boyfriend and managed to opt out of so many activities that she no longer had any friends. Lorraine eventually presented for psychiatric help because she was becoming increasingly depressed due to her isolation. The last activity, which she had given up, was a weekly aerobics class at a local gym. At assessment there was no evidence of a depressive illness, but she remained very fixed in her belief about the foul smell coming from her body. The degree of conviction expressed, as measured on the Maudsley Assessment of Delusions Schedule (Gunn, Robertson, & Sharrock, 1990), was high, with maximal scores on negative behaviors (e.g., avoidance) linked to the delusion, complete lack of insight regarding her delusional beliefs, and an elevated score on idiosyncrasy (i.e., the extent to which the belief is shared by others).

Following full psychiatric assessment, Lorraine was asked to carefully attend to the characteristics of the smell and to cues that made her think that it had worsened. An experiment was devised which included Lorraine charting other people's reactions to her presence (e.g., facial expressions, sneezes, twitching, people running away in disgust). She agreed to return to the gym and actively look for other people's typical reactions to a foul smell while she was exercising. She was surprised to report that there had been no such reactions, but she rationalized this by adding that there were a lot of smells in the gym anyway. The next test was to use a relaxation tape and breathing exercises and to attempt to spend 10 minutes in a local shop browsing. She did not manage the full time, but again found no reactions in others except for one shop assistant who clearly had the flu.

Lorraine had numerous automatic thoughts concerning potential disapproval from others, along with underlying beliefs about her own unlovability. As Lorraine began to understand how her symptoms had developed she became more active in carrying out homework exercises. It seemed important to formulate the case in a cohesive manner. Lorraine revealed that she believed that her father had never liked her. She also thought that she was an unwanted child. To compensate for this she had tried very hard to be approved of by authority figures and peers. It seemed that the sexual pressures of puberty and the repeated teasing by her friends markedly traumatized her approval drive, leading to the emergence of the delusion in question.

The delusion was most shifted by one particular experiment where she took a bag of fish and chips on to the subway. Despite the fact that there was a smell for which she was responsible, there was little reaction from other passengers except for one young man who asked her for a chip. By this time (Session 6) her conviction in the delusion had dropped by 25% and she was engaging in more social activities. She was desensitized to disapproval by making a video of a session during which she coped with the videoing process and some feigned therapist disapproval with minimal anxiety. Through a discussion of the dysfunctionality of always needing approval, she came to attempt to hold a less demanding belief (i.e., 'It is nice when people like you, but they don't have to and if they don't that's just life').

At the end of 10 sessions there had been a 70% reduction in belief severity (i.e., strength of conviction). Lorraine still thought she smelled, but only at times, and even then she didn't let it interfere with her social life. Lorraine received no medication. She eventually visited her father and was surprised to find that he had been worried about her and was very pleased to see her again. He later admitted that when Lorraine was young the demands of his job allowed him very little time to spend with his children. At one year follow-up, Lorraine remained in a greatly improved state of mental health.

## CONCLUSION

Monosymptomatic hypochondriacal psychosis has been known to non-psychiatric specialists by numerous names for many years. More recently, this condition has come to the attention of mental health professionals and, with greater frequency, has fallen within their treatment purview. It can be difficult to treat, perhaps because of numerous influencing factors. While conclusive evidence is lacking, pharmacological and psychological management can be beneficial. Likewise, cognitive-behaviour therapy has considerable potential for hypochondriacal beliefs occurring in the context of conditions such as schizophrenia and depressive psychosis. As we come to better understand delusions of the soma, our approaches to managing them may become more effective.

## REFERENCES

Alloy, L.B. (1988). Expectations and situational information as co-contributers to covariation assessment: A reply to Goddard & Allen. *Psychological Review*, **95**, 299–301.

American Psychiatric Association (1994). *Diagnostic and statistical manual of mental disorders* (4th edn.). Washington, DC: Author.

Berrios, G.E. (1985). Delusional parasitosis and physical disease. *Comprehensive Psychiatry*, **26**, 395–403.

Cameron, N.A. (1959). The paranoid pseudocommunity revisited. *American Journal of Sociology*, **65**, 52–58.

Chadwick, P., Birchwood, M., & Trower, P. (1996). *Cognitive therapy for delusions, voices and paranoia*. Chichester, UK: Wiley.

Ciompi, L. (1988). *The psyche and schizophrenia: The bond between affect and logic*. Cambridge, MA: Harvard University Press.

Cotard, J. (1882). Du delire des negations. In M. Shepard & S. Hirsch (Eds.), *Themes and variations in European psychiatry*. Bristol: John Wright.

Cumming, W.J.K. (1988). The neurobiology of the body schema. *British Journal of Psychiatry*, **153**, 11–17.

Ekbom, K.A. (1938). Der presenile dermatozoenwahn. *Acta Psychiatrica et Neurologica Scandinavica*, **13**, 227–259.

Freeman, T. (1981). On the psychopathology of persecutory delusions. *British Journal of Psychiatry*, **139**, 529–532.

Freud, S. (1962). *The aetiology of hysteria* (J. Strachey, Trans.). London: Hogarth Press. (Original work published 1896.)

Garety, P.A. (1990). *Reasoning, rationality and delusions: Studies in the concepts, characteristics and rationality of delusions*. Unpublished doctoral dissertation, University of London.

Garety, P.A., & Hemsley, D.R. (1994). *Delusions: Investigations into the psychology of delusional reasoning*. Oxford: Oxford University Press.

Gould, W.M., & Gragg, T.M. (1976). Delusions of parasitosis. *Archives of Dermatology*, **112**, 1745–1748.

Gunn, J., Robertson, G., & Sharrock, R. (1990). *Maudsley Assessment of Delusions Schedule*. Report to the Macarthur Foundation.

Hemsley, D.R., & Garety, P.A. (1986). Formation and maintenance of delusions: A Bayesian analysis. *British Journal of Psychiatry*, **149**, 51–56.

Hopkinson, G. (1970). Delusions of infestation. *Acta Psychiatrica Scandinavica*, **46**, 111–119.

Jaspers, K. (1963). *General psychopathology* (J. Hoening & M. Hamilton, Trans.). Manchester: University of Manchester Press. (Original work published 1913.)

Kendler, K.S., Glazer, W.M., & Morgenstein, H. (1983). Dimensions of delusional experience. *American Journal of Psychiatry*, **140**, 466–469.

Kingdon, D.G., & Turkington, D. (1994). *Cognitive-behavioral therapy of schizophrenia*. New York: Guilford.

Kingdon, D.G., Turkington, D., & John, C. (1994). Cognitive behavior therapy of schizophrenia. *British Journal of Psychiatry*, **164**, 581–587.

Kraeplin, E. (1976). Manic-depressve insanity and paranoia (R.M. Barclay, Trans.). New York: Asno. (Original work published 1921.)

MacNamara, E.D. (1928). A note on cutaneous and visual hallucinations in the chronic hallucinatory psychosis. *Lancet*, **1**, 807–808.

Maher, B.A. (1974). Delusional thinking and cognitive disorder. In H. London & R.E. Nisbett (Eds.), *Thought and feeling: Cognitive alteration of feeling states*. Chicago: Aldine.

McGuffin, P. (1997). Affective disorders. In R. Murray, P. Hill, & P. McGuffin (Eds.), *The essentials of postgraduate psychiatry*. Cambridge: Cambridge University Press.

Munro, A. (1980). Monosymptomatic hypochondriacal psychosis. *British Journal of Hospital Medicine*, **23**, 34–38.

Munro, A. (1992). Psychiatric disorders characterized by delusions: Treatment in relation to specific types. *Psychiatric Annals*, **22**, 232–240.

Munro, A., & Chmara, J. (1982). Monosymptomatic hypochondriacal psychosis: A diagnostic checklist based on 50 cases of the disorder. *Canadian Journal of Psychiatry*, **27**, 374–376.

Nelki, J. (1988). Making sense of a delusion of smell: A psychotherapeutic approach. *British Journal of Medical Psychology*, **61**, 267–275.

Perrin, L. (1896). Des nervodernies parasitophobiques. *Annakes de Dermatologie et Syphilograpie*, **7**, 129–138.

Perris, C. (1989). *Cognitive therapy for patients with schizophrenia*. New York: Cassel.

Sensky, T., Turkington, D., Kingdon, D., Scott, L.J., Scott J., Siddle, R., Carroll, M., & Barnes, T. (2000). A randomized controlled trial of cognitive-behavioural therapy for persistent symptoms in schizophrenia resistant to medication. *Archives of General Psychiatry*, **57**, 165–172.

Sims, A. (1995). *Symptoms in the mind: An introduction to descriptive psychopathology*. London: W.B. Saunders Co. Ltd.

Skott, A. (1978). *Delusions of infestation*. Sweden: Gotab Kungalu.

Southard, E.E. (1912). On the somatic sources of somatic delusions. *Journal of Abnormal Psychology*, **7**, 326–339.

Strauss, J.S. (1969). Hallucinations and delusions as points on a continua function. *Archives of General Psychiatry*, **21**, 581–586.

Turkington, D., & Siddle, R. (1998). Cognitive therapy for treatment of delusions. *Advances in Psychiatric Treatment*, **4**, 235–242.

Yamada, N., Nakajima, S., & Noguchi, T. (1998). Age at onset of delusional disorder is dependent on the delusional theme. *Acta Psychiatrica Scandinavica*, **97**, 122–124.

Zubin, J., & Spring, B. (1977). Vulnerability—a new view on schizophrenia. *Journal of Abnormal Psychology*, **86**, 103–126.

Chapter 14

# DEATH ANXIETY

*Robert J. Kastenbaum**


## INTRODUCTION

Is death anxiety bad for our health? How can death anxiety be recognized and what, if anything, should we do about it? But wait—is there really a distinctive organismic state that answers to the name of death anxiety, or are we perpetuating a flawed and misleading construct? These are among the questions that will be explored here. Where are the answers? After offering a few basic distinctions and guidelines, we will begin with two classical, rival theories of death anxiety, which are based on opposing views of human nature. Next, we will describe and examine the harvest of empirical data from half a century of academic research. We will then explore death anxiety both in clinical situations and everyday life, drawing upon a newer generation of theoretical approaches, as well as observations made by a variety of field researchers and care providers.


## HOW TO APPROACH DEATH ANXIETY IN HEALTH AND ILLNESS?

Death anxiety is not only a potential factor in illness and treatment, but also part of everyday life. Health care professionals recognize that there is a constantly shifting balance between well-being and illness or dysfunction. We would not want to underestimate the continuity of lifestyle patterns through health and illness. Furthermore, we would not want to assume a perfect correlation between objective and subjective jeopardy. Some people choose occupations or recreations that place them at an ele-

*Arizona State University, USA

*Health Anxiety*
Edited by G.J.G. Asmundson, S. Taylor & B.J. Cox

vated risk for injury and death. Others lead careful, routinized lives. Nevertheless, many risk-takers feel a rush of excitement—an 'action high'—rather than a crippling sense or terror. They feel something out of the ordinary, but do not characterize it as anxiety, certainly not *death* anxiety. By contrast, there are 'safe' people who are haunted by a sense of lurking danger. For them, when the sky is the bluest and all is going right, there may be a disabling apprehension of impending doom.

Similarly, some people fear for their lives during a minor illness or after slight injury, while others display serenity when they are experiencing life-threatening illness or injury. I remember, for example, a resident in a geriatric facility who had periodic episodes of panic in which she was certain she would die at any moment although, in fact, there was no detectable imminent threat. When she did enter the end-phase of her life, she was remarkably serene. 'It's just my time,' she observed. Somehow the alarm response had become deactivated when she was in the presence of the real thing. Other residents, though, brought their characteristic responses to stress and threat with them to their last days. My colleagues and I learned to appreciate the individuality and complexity of death-related anxiety both in relatively safe and perilous situations.

The first pair of suggested guidelines, then, are as follows:

1. It is useful to explore connections between anxiety in life-threatening situations and a person's characteristic orientation toward jeopardy throughout life. However, we would not assume this connection to be simple and direct.
2. Subjective appraisal of the situation should be determined by observation and inquiry, not assumed on the basis of the objective circumstances (noting also that the actual risk cannot always be estimated objectively).

The following additional guidelines will become applicable as we move further into the subject:

3. Anxiety should not automatically be regarded as simply a property of the individual, although this has been the emphasis of most death anxiety research. Individuals interact with situations that have their own levels and expressions of death anxiety as well as their own coping strategies (often of systematic avoidance).
4. Death anxiety is not invariably the most accurate and useful way of classifying a person's response in a death-related situation. Understanding the specific stressors and the possible functional value of the response can provide a more adequate guide to effective care.
5. A *non-anxious* response to a life-threatening situation deserves open-minded study on the part of care providers and researchers. Too often,

such responses are interpreted according to the observer's conceptual frame rather than taken as a starting point for inquiry. Particular attention might be given to the tendency to conclude hastily that the lack of an anxious response is proof of denial.

We are now ready to consider a pair of rival death anxiety theories that have occupied center ring with little competition until recently.

## TWO CLASSICAL THEORIES OF DEATH ANXIETY

Theories are not created in vacuums. The first theory under consideration here arose during the heady years of early psychoanalytic discovery and speculation. It was among the first crop of psychodynamic formulations, but also under the influence of both a long tradition of grand philosophical formulations, and the rapidly emerging field of neuroscience. The second theory takes its pedigree from unsettling nineteenth-century thinkers who rejected conventional assurances about the human condition, society, and the universe, and by their successors whose minds had been seared by the Second World War and an apparent failure of social institutions and values.

### Whatever We Fear, It's Not Death

'Anxiety is the reaction to danger.' This was Freud's (1926/1959, p. 76) pithy conclusion about the function of anxiety. Anxiety is part of our survival kit, a signal-function. Often anxiety is the mark of a competent person coping with dangerous situations. Anxiety may be considered neurotic if it is persistent and out of proportion to the actual dangers, thereby interfering with normal functioning.

Freud's thinking about anxiety also took more provocative and controversial forms, however. He suggested that the birth process flooded the neonate with intensely painful stimulation that it could not control or moderate. The 'birth trauma' would, therefore, become the benchmark for profound helplessness and catastrophic anxiety. A subsequent anxiety-arousing experience could plunge the individual into the hellish experience of birth. This theory might explain why an apparently trivial event could evoke a panic attack. There is a modicum of indirect support in the fact that the accelerated heart rate, breathing difficulties, and other neurophysiological events that occur in a panic attack seem to have their parallels in the flooding of the neonate nervous system with sensory excitement and its urgent need for motoric discharge and the onset of independent breathing.

Overall, however, there was little empirical support for the birth trauma explanation and it failed to flourish. Freud himself took umbrage when Rank (1936/1945) built a more elaborate theory upon the birth trauma edifice. Although the birth trauma theory has not won many converts in recent years, we will see that it might not be entirely irrelevant to our present interest in death anxiety.

Within psychoanalytic circles, most of the controversy swirled around the relationship between repression and anxiety: Does repression cause anxiety or is it the other way around? At first Freud was convinced that anxiety was produced by the repression of libidinal drives. The bottled-up tensions had to find other modalities of discharge, such as somatic symptoms or overt anxiety. He later discarded this theory, though novelists and dramatists have continued to exploit the theme of repressed emotions going berserk. 'Letting it all hang out' (roughly, abreaction) was thought to be the cure for the mental and physical ills associated with sexual repression. Subsequent clinical experience and research has not been especially kind to this proposition.

Freud's second theory—that we use repression and a host of other defenses to protect ourselves from anxiety—turned things around. Freud proposed a developmental sequence in which the infant/child attempts to cope with anxiety in various stage-marked ways. Anxiety itself is not toxic, but, rather, a signal that one might be in danger of losing something very important (e.g., a valued relationship). This can be a realistic assessment, or it can be a neurotic manifestation in which one experiences 'the illusion of a contentless anxiety state' (Josephs, 1994, p. 19) because the actual reason for one's disturbance has been kept out of awareness. It is this revised theory of anxiety that contributed most to the clinician's tactic of analyzing defenses and the inner conflicts they are intended to control. In an ideal case, one would become more aware of conflicts and become more skillful in coping with them. There would result both a reduction in the anxiety generated by unresolved conflicts and a more effective and less burdensome set of defenses.

What, then, of death anxiety? Is it subject to understanding and treatment just like other forms of anxiety? Or, is it a special case that requires a special theoretical model and treatment approach? Neither. Freud dismissed death anxiety as a vital and primary concern.

How did he do that? First, he universalized upon his personal introspections:

> Our own death is indeed quite unimaginable, and whenever we make the attempt to imagine it we can perceive that we really survive as spectators. Hence the psychoanalytic school could venture on the assertion that at the

bottom nobody believes in his own death, or to put the same thing in a different way, in the unconscious every one of us is convinced of his own immortality. (Freud, 1926/1959, pp. 304–305)

Next, he attempted to ground the inability to comprehend our personal mortality in the very nature of unconscious processes:

What we call our 'unconscious' (the deepest strata of our minds, made up of instinctual impulses) knows nothing whatever of negatives or of denials—contradictions coincide in it—and so it knows nothing whatever of our own death, for to that we can give only a negative purport. It follows that no instinct we possess is ready for a belief in death. (Freud, 1926/1959, p. 305)

Freud characterized the 'unconscious system' as functioning independent of time, causality, and traditional logic. There are rule-governed processes, but these do not answer to the patterns of reasoning that are more attuned to external events and interpersonal discourse. Therefore, 'Sigmund is mortal' can make no impression in the unconscious system because it has no interest in hypothetical-deductive logic.

Freud hammered what he considered to be the final nail in the death anxiety coffin with a simple observation—the fact that we are alive means that we have not experienced death. How, then, can we fear death? It must be that when we experience apparent death anxiety, we really are afraid of something else, something frightening we have already encountered in our lives. This formulation accorded well with Freud's overall approach to neurosis and treatment. The presenting symptom—and the cover story that goes along with it—is at some remove from the real problem and its origin in earlier experiences. Death anxiety was then deftly replaced with *thanatophobia*. A person in mortal terror may be anxious enough, but it is not for the stated reason. Death has become a symbol or image that represents at the same time that it conceals the actual basis for anxiety. Castration anxiety is perhaps the most (in)famous example offered by Freud. The fear of being cut off in the prime of life is a coded way of expressing unresolved castration anxiety. (Obviously, this formulation is even less convincing when applied to women.)

Leaving aside the dubious case of displaced castration anxiety, Freud would have the clinician treat overt death anxiety as an invitation to discover some conflict or vulnerability that is based upon previous life experiences rather than take the complaint at face value. The implicit message was not only clear, but received a warm welcome from most psychoanalytically oriented practitioners—we don't have to worry about death because even people who are worrying about death aren't worrying about death.

We are entitled to wonder both why Freud was so quick to dismiss death anxiety and why the great majority of psychoanalysts were so docile in agreeing with this proposition. In retrospect, it appears that Freud and his followers were not yet ready to face personal mortality with the same zeal they devoted to sexuality. Furthermore, Freud managed to avoid dealing with the implicit connection between death anxiety and his dramatic theory of birth trauma. We may not have experienced death, but if Freud's assertion is correct, we have experienced a toxic state of terror and vulnerability as we came into this world. This would not have been a bad model for death anxiety. At the least it would have suggested that there are actual experiences that might arouse later death-related fears. Once embarked along this path, we might identify other experiences that could be interpreted as offering a foretaste of death, such as separation from a loved one or psychic numbing. Seen in this light, death anxiety might be taken seriously as death anxiety, not hastily dismissed as a mere proxy for the 'real' anxiety.

## We Fear Nothing but Death

The psychoanalytic downgrading of death anxiety was still the dominant attitude at the time that Becker (1973) offered a forceful alternative. Becker nearly matches Freud in audacity. He offers a radical analysis of society that is no less unsettling than Freud's dissection of the individual psyche. What is society? Pretty much a lie writ large. Pretty much a desperate attempt to deny the core of reality—that every birth will have its death. Becker acknowledges that others had already made this point. For example, William James stated in *The Varieties of Religious Experience*:

> Let sanguine healthy-mindedness do its best with its strange power of living in the moment and ignoring and forgetting, still the evil background is really there to be thought of, and the skull will grin in at the banquet. (1902/1958, p. 281)

'Sanguine healthy-mindedness' is an attitude promoted by a society that is just trying to do its job of protecting us from terror. Social institutions have many functions, of course. But here, Becker competes with Freud in discovering deeper strata. At bottom, social beliefs and practices serve to disguise and distract us from acute awareness of mortality. Religion is a major player in this process—even in societies that substitute materialistic or chauvinistic ideologies for religious faith per se as Rank (1936/1945) and others have asserted. Mass media now provide additional opportunities to deny, cover up, neutralize, and trivialize death. As societies become more versatile in their control of influence operations, so they also become more proficient in helping us to live the lie.

Schizophrenia receives particular attention from this perspective. Becker agrees with Searles' (1961) position that the person who has the most unfiltered awareness of mortality is the person we label as schizophrenic. For this person, society's massive defenses against death anxiety have failed or become inaccessible, while personal defenses have also proved inadequate. Schizophrenia is a desperate attempt to live with terror. According to Becker, the schizophrenic 'lacks the secure instinctive programming of lower organisms, and he lacks the secure cultural programming of average men. No wonder he appears to average men as "crazy..."' (1973, pp. 63–64). The schizophrenic is every person standing naked in a terrifying universe, shorn of consensual illusions, disguises, and distractions.

The avoidance of death terror accounts for much of our behavior as individuals and as a society, again, according to Becker. We desperately need our collective belief systems, routines, and illusions in order to dodge what some have called the ontological confrontation—the direct, unfiltered awareness of mortality. Pervasive social pressure operates against admitting openly to death anxiety. Instead, when we experience a mortal twinge, we are apt to cling even more urgently to the props of sociocultural belief and practice, or, this failing, transform the nascent terror into a more socially acceptable phobia.

Becker's formulation is both similar and contrary to Freud's. For Becker the fears that bubble up on the surface of our lives have arisen from roiling depths of despair. The specifics are diametrically opposed to Freud's thanatophobia in which expressed fears of death are insubstantial in themselves, but useful cues to unresolved developmental conflicts. By contrast, for Becker, the surface fears have no apparent relationship to death, yet death it is that underlies these manifestations. Becker adopts Freud's approach to sleuthing cleverly through scattered clues to their remote solutions. Although he offers relentless criticisms both of Freud and his theories, he nevertheless proves adept in using Freudian concepts and methods while so doing. Despite their fundamental differences, Becker and Freud agree that surface expressions of fear and anxiety provide neither a complete nor an authentic account of what it is that truly ails us. It is not surprising, then, that both medical and mental health practitioners often find it difficult to assess the role of death-related anxiety in their patients' presenting symptoms and behaviors.

## What Lessons from Freud and Becker?

There are several lessons one might draw from these rival theories.

First, we might become more aware of the basic paradigm each of us brings to our work. Freud's downgrading of death anxiety is couched within the framework of early evolutionary psychobiology. The human is a complex organism that begins life in helplessness and remains dependent for a long time. Themes and conflicts develop from the interplay between instinctive needs and their drives to satisfaction on the one hand, and the priorities and strictures of society on the other. Few come through psychosexual development without psychic scars, unresolved conflicts, and a repertoire of defenses that often add to the burden. Freud recognizes, indeed revels, in our predilection for symbolic manipulations and quirky fantasies, but also that we are nevertheless firmly entrenched within the animal kingdom, though more talented in making ourselves and each other more miserable than are our fellow creatures. Furthermore, no logic or evidence can persuade us that we really and truly will die.

Becker offers an alternative paradigm from his existential perspective.

> Man has a symbolic identity that brings him sharply out of nature. He is a symbolic self, a creature with a name, a life history. He is a creator with a mind that boards out to speculate about atoms and infinity, who can place himself imaginatively at a point in space and contemplate bemusedly his own planet. This immense expansion, this dexterity, this ethereality, this self-consciousness gives to man literally the status of a small god in nature, as the Renaissance thinker knew. Yet, at the same time, as the Eastern sages also knew, man is a worm and food for worms. (1973, p. 27)

Becker's paradigm does not allow us to pretend that death is merely a rumor. The 'mind that soars out' is also self-conscious and inclined to reflect on its position in (and out) of the world. When we act dumb about death, this is just pretty good acting. When we have to try too hard to act dumb, there is something seriously amiss in society's protective veil, our own coping resources, or both.

The implicit lesson here is that we might all too easily preinterpret our patient's, client's, or student's anxieties on the basis of our operating paradigms rather than apply ourselves to discovering their particular truths. A Freudian traditionalist might encounter many cases manifesting thanatophobia, but never a client experiencing authentic death terror. Similarly, an existentialist might assume the deathhead behind every word and gesture without considering alternative possibilities.

Second, we notice that both theories concern themselves with death anxiety within everyday life with no imminent threat other than what the mind might conceive. Neither give much attention to the person who is (a) sitting anxiously in the doctor's office, awaiting test results and prognosis; (b) detecting bodily changes possibly indicative of the type of cancer that killed a parent and grandparent; (c) encountering unexpected turbulence 30,000 feet over nowhere; or even (d) afraid to turn out the lights because of that horror movie on late night television. What does happen in the presence of stress, threat, and emergency? Freud would ask 'Is there no accident or illness that can truly persuade us of our mortality?' while Becker would query 'Are there no circumstances that can truly persuade us that death is a relief, a release, a preferred alternative to continued life, or even a consummation greatly to be desired?'. There is a broad spectrum of attitudes toward death and a broad spectrum of situations in which the prospect of death becomes salient. Freud and Becker have assumed a universality of personal response and situational contingency that neglects the specifics that patients and their care providers confront in practice.

Finally, Freud and Becker agree on the wisdom of improving self-knowledge and reducing our investment in defensive works. The better we know—and accept—ourselves, the more freedom we can experience in everyday life. Freud speaks in terms of energy now made available rather than employed in controlling instinctual conflicts. Becker speaks of a society more open, honest, and realistic, less weighted down with institutional repression and denial of death awareness. Whether we prefer the surface thanatophobia or the death terror model, we might work toward improved self-knowledge and acceptance along with more effective but less cumbersome defenses.

## EMPIRICAL STUDIES OF DEATH ANXIETY

Most studies have used samples of the general non-hospitalized population, predominantly undergraduates, along with a sprinkling of health care professionals and a scattering of other groups. Racial composition of the samples is not always reported, but Caucasians appear to be over-represented. A more thorough discussion of results, methodologies, and findings has been offered elsewhere (Kastenbaum, 2000).

The typical study uses a self-report psychometric instrument with fixed choices, either true–false or Likert. Earlier studies most often relied on a total score for death anxiety. There is now, however, a trend toward providing more specific scores (e.g., distinguishing between fear of death and fear of dying). Several other characteristics of the typical study are worth keeping in mind to guide our interpretation of the findings:

1. The studies are cross-sectional; therefore, we do not learn how death anxiety might change with age and experience within the individual.
2. Few studies examine the relationship between self-reported anxiety levels and the respondent's actual behavior in death-related situations; therefore, we cannot conclude that high scores predict disturbed and disorganized response to actual situations, or that very low scores

signify denial (as often assumed). A less speculative interpretation would be that low scores simply represent a low level of death anxiety. The most frequently used measures do not provide a basis for choosing between the denial versus low anxiety interpretations.

3. The range of death-related cognitions, feelings, and situations is constricted by the item selections and allows no opportunities for respondents to identify their own particular concerns and their relative intensity. In the most popular measure, the Death Anxiety Scale (Templer, 1970), for example, all items receive equal weighting. In posttesting discussion, I have often found marked differences between respondents with the same scale score because different items were salient for them. Furthermore, respondents with relatively low scores have told me they feel extremely anxious about a particular aspect of dying or death.

4. Many published studies neglect to report the actual level of death anxiety for their samples. Instead, attention is focused on correlations with other measures, or tests of significance for group comparisons. The anxiety level database, therefore, has not been expanded and updated nearly as much as might have been expected. The quest for correlations with other variables and possible group differences has attracted much more attention than the examination of death anxiety itself.

5. The paucity of experimental studies has made it difficult to identify process, let alone establish causality. We have not learned as much as we should have about precisely how death-related anxiety operates in real-life situations.

6. For the most part, these studies are driven neither by urgent practical concerns nor by articulate theory. Many studies merely report group comparisons or correlations. When added to the fact that the respondents' own thoughts are not expressed in their own words, this approach has been severely self-limiting.

Fortunately, there are also a number of more innovative and resourceful studies to draw upon. The major findings summarized below represent the harvest from studies of special quality as well as findings that have been reported with reasonable consistency in the mainstream research.

## WHAT HAVE WE LEARNED ABOUT DEATH ANXIETY?

Ask people directly and they usually report having a low-to-moderate concern about death as they go through their everyday lives. This has been the pervasive finding from mainstream studies over the past three decades, and is not a psychometric artifact. The rival theories of Freud and Becker both take a hit, or so it would seem. Most people do admit to death-related fears, yet the level of concern falls well short of thanatophobia. It would take a complex sequence of speculations to square this finding with Freud's propositions. Similarly, the view that we are into heavy denial of our underlying death terror also lacks support. A set of studies with a different methodology has also found that most respondents report relatively benign imagery about death. When asked either to offer their own personifications of death or to select from a research-derived list, it was *The Gentle Comforter* (usually an elderly male figure) who was the most often chosen (Kastenbaum, 2000). There were, though, people who saw death as a terrifying figure (*The Macabre*). One could devise interpretations from either the Freudian or Beckerian perspective based on the intense anxiety-laden images offered by some respondents. Perhaps these are Freud's thanatophobes who are 'really' suffering from repressed conflicts that have nothing really to do with death. Perhaps these are schizophrenic-equivalents who are not protected from the universal and intrinsic death terror because either their own ego defenses or society's denial mechanisms have proven inadequate. Neither of these 'perhapses' can be readily dismissed from consideration. It would be troubling, however, if theories should remain insulated from empirical findings that are not supportive of their propositions.

If we accept self-reports at face value, the parsimonious conclusion is that most people are neither afflicted with disabling anxiety nor burdened with massive defenses against death. If we second-guess or reject self-reports without adequate empirical basis, then why do we ask people in the first place? As discussed below, when research becomes more enterprising we do learn something beyond the obvious.

Another common finding is that women tend to report higher levels of death anxiety. This gender-related difference is not anticipated in either the Freudian or Beckerian approach, both of which assert universal responses (i.e., nobody/everybody is anxious about death). This finding does not readily lend itself to a self-stress interpretation since the mortality rate for males is higher at all age levels while their self-reported death anxiety tends to be lower. Furthermore, one might expect that with their higher self-reported death anxiety, women would be more likely to avoid death-related situations. Again, the data suggest otherwise. Women more frequently provide services to terminally ill people and are much more likely to enroll in death education courses. This pattern has been observed for many years. We might have expected that a higher level of death anxiety would be associated with more avoidance of death-related situations, but the opposite is true with respect to gender. At the least, the gender-related findings suggest that the relationship between death anxiety and behavior is not so very simple.

The relationship between age and death anxiety also runs counter to the most common hypotheses, being that:

1. People become *more* anxious with advanced age because of the decreased distance from death, and
2. People become *less* anxious because death does not threaten as many goals and values and, through a continuing developmental process, we come to terms with personal mortality.

Neither of these plausible hypotheses has been firmly supported. Instead the lesson seems to be that chronological age is *not* the most important variable in shaping a person's orientation toward death, as gerontologists have already discovered in many other realms of functioning. Lifestyle, experience, maturation, and current life situation—especially significant relationships—seem to have more influence than age per se. In general, older people do not report higher levels of death anxiety. There is little support for the proposition that most elderly adults live with a heightened dread of death. In-depth studies, such as Munnich's (1966) pioneering research in The Netherlands, indicate that most elders develop fairly effective strategies for coping with the prospect of death. A combination of accepting and ignoring death seemed to work well for most people in Munnich's study, as it did for patients in a Massachusetts geriatric hospital (Weisman & Kastenbaum, 1968). Few were disturbed by death-related anxiety in their everyday lives, although preservation of health and independent functioning was a common concern. Studies have suggested that an effective perspective on personal mortality may require a preliminary period of life review. The 'young–old' in their transition to a new status may indeed experience an upsurge of general anxiety, including a heightened awareness of death. It may be that death anxiety comes under control again as people transitioning into the later adult years come to terms with their new situation. As noted, the available studies are cross-sectional, so we still know very little about the changes that might occur within the same individual over time.

There is reason to believe that the *type* of death concern may differ with life situation and cultural tradition. Strichertz and Cunnington (1981–1982) found, for example, that young adults express most concern about the possible loss of loved ones, death as punishment, and the finality of death. Working adults, though, appear most concerned about fear of pain in dying as well as the possibility of premature death. Older adults were most fearful not of death, but of becoming dependent and being kept alive in an undignified vegetative state. A quick death was preferable to prolonged dependency and helplessness. The older adults also showed more concern for the impact of their dying and death on their loved ones. Like most people who have provided services to elderly men and women, I have repeatedly heard the impassioned statements, 'I don't want to be kept alive like *that!*' and 'I don't want to be a burden'. Understanding the individual's most salient death-related concern is obviously a useful beginning to effective care.

Kalish and Reynolds (1977) explored death attitudes among younger and older adults from four ethnic/racial backgrounds, including African-American, Japanese-American, Mexican-American, and Anglo. It was the younger echelon in all groups who most often reported having 'the unexplainable feeling that they were going to die [soon]'. This sense of foreboding and imminent death without specifiable cause is perhaps the most direct characterization of death anxiety that has emerged from any study. The oldest respondents in all groups were more likely to report thinking of death as a peaceful ending that they were prepared to accept. There were cultural differences in the prayers, practices, and rituals that respondents associated with dying and death, but considerable agreement among people of a like age in all the samples.

Particularly interesting is a study conducted in Hong Kong that supplemented a death anxiety scale with behavioral observation of cancer patients. Ho and Shiu (1995) noted that the local Chinese culture had an extremely high level of anxiety about cancer. Nevertheless, the death anxiety scores of cancer patients were no higher than a comparison group of patients with hand injuries and no higher than the norms for a general population. What had happened to all that anxiety? The researchers observed patterns of communication about dying and death and found that those patients who did have high anxiety scores more often engaged in passive aggressive behavior. Ho and Shiu (1995, p. 64) explained that:

> The Chinese seldom express their anger openly and tend to avoid direct confrontation in dealing with conflicts. Rather they would use . . . indirect language, middlemen, face-saving ploys, and so on to resolve conflicts. This is especially so in dealing with mystical things like death. Hence it is likely that Chinese cancer patients with very strong fear toward death tend to use an indirect way to express their anxiety and anger.

It is easy to misread responses to the stress of dying or the threat of death for people who differ from us with respect to age, personality, socialization, and cultural heritage. Furthermore, what is often characterized as denial of death is actually often something quite different, such as selective attention, selective response, compartmentalization, deception, or resistance (Kastenbaum, 2001). Denial is a desperate attempt to avoid catastrophic anxiety by blanking out a significant aspect of reality. It is not unusual to experience a brief episode of denial during overwhelming situations; but, during a prolonged period of stress, uncertainty, and jeopardy, most people use less extreme strategies. The findings of Ho and Shiu (1995) are a useful reminder that a person may be dealing with death anxiety in a subtle and complex manner that represents neither denial nor an absence of fear, but, rather, an attempt to manage a difficult situation with whatever means they have at their disposal within their personal resources and their situational configuration.

Attempts have been made to identify those who are most likely to experience high death anxiety in their everyday lives. Religious affiliation, belief, and experience have thus far proven too complex to demonstrate an overall relationship with death anxiety. A frequent clinical observation is that people who are secure in a religious faith are not highly anxious about death per se. However, belief in an afterlife does not necessarily protect people from anxieties related to terminal illness, dependency, and loss of function. Moreover, the prospect of dying too soon can arouse intense anxiety even though one might feel that death itself is nothing to fear.

There are, nevertheless, some fairly clear trends from empirical research. The following factors are associated with higher levels of self-reported death anxiety in everyday life:

1. Lower socioeconomic circumstances
2. Lower educational level
3. Growing up in a broken or dysfunctional home
4. Lack of effective interpersonal support

Do these differences occur also in death-related situations? There is insufficient evidence on this point. Furthermore, the differences in everyday life, though consistent, are not overwhelming. People with the benefits of affluence, education, intact home background, and current interpersonal support seem to have a useful cushion, but are still vulnerable to death anxiety.

Personality characteristics have also been linked to death anxiety. Lefcourt and Shepherd (1995), for example, found that people with humorless authoritarian personalities were more likely to avoid dealing with the question of organ donation. The researchers took this avoidance as a clue to a resistance to facing their mortality in many other situations as well. However, it appears probable that the 'humorless authoritarian personalities' would not have revealed their suspected higher death anxiety on a self-report measure. Other studies have shown that people with relatively high death anxiety tend to be more open, sensitive, and vulnerable, as well as less focused on achievement and material success. These traits resonate with the gender-related findings, although there is substantial crossover.

People who express a clear sense of purpose in their lives and confidence in their coping abilities appear to be less subject to death anxiety. Would this connection hold up for health care providers as well? Viswanatham (1996) found that physicians who reported a strong sense of purpose and control in their lives also expressed a lower level of death anxiety. Furthermore, physicians with high death anxiety expressed a preference for telephone rather than face-to-face contact with their terminally ill patients. As Kasper (1959) observed, in a landmark paper, the still influential medical tradition that one should not become personally involved with patients continues to serve as justification for reducing contact with terminally ill patients who would otherwise arouse the physician's own anxiety.

As might be expected, people with other sources of disturbance in their lives are more likely to demonstrate a higher level of death-related anxiety, even to the point of panic and terror. Feeling out of control and helpless, a person may express the sense of impending catastrophe through the metaphor of death. Correspondingly, a surge in death anxiety often can be quelled through a reduction in life stress and threat. Within a geriatric hospital, for example, we found that fear of abandonment by family frequently was the trigger for an episode of death anxiety, while assurances of family devotion or the provision of a meaningful substitute relationship frequently was effective in dissolving both general and death-related anxiety (Weisman & Kastenbaum, 1968). Mental illness and situational stress tend to be associated with a higher level of death anxiety. Reducing stress and rebuilding the individual's sense of competence and security does not banish death anxiety, but allows it to subside to a less disruptive level.

'Anxiety' and 'stress' seem to inhabit the same zone of discomfort and peril, but little attempt has been made to connect research and theory from both realms. Reviewing the literature, Lazarus (2000), in *Stress and Emotion*, builds the case for health effects. Social stress, for example, has been shown to increase vulnerability to infectious diseases, while positive mood seems to serve as insulation. Would prolonged, intense, or often repeated episodes of death anxiety actually contribute to illness and death? Would a rejecting or indifferent social environment and low self-esteem serve both to heighten death anxiety and reduce the ability or inclination to fight for survival? Intense emotional activation has been linked to sudden death in people whose physical health has already been compromised (Leventhal, Patrick-Miller, Leventhal, & Burns, 1997). Do panic attacks qualify as intense emotional activation and, if so, is

it possible that acute fear of death can result in death? It may be premature to indulge in hypotheses about possible connections among death
anxiety, stress, and health, but certainly there is a wealth of data that
could be consulted to develop an integrated approach among these areas
of concern.

## BACK TO THEORY

One more set of findings deserves our attention before we focus on death
anxiety in health care situations. We have already seen that self-reported
death anxiety is relatively low in the general population. However, it has
also been noted that at least some people who present themselves as
not concerned about death engage in patterns of avoidance that suggest
intense underlying anxiety. Meanwhile, breakdowns in psychological
defense and intense situational stress can result in a surge of death anxiety
even if there is no imminent objective threat of death. Nevertheless,
behavior in battlefield and other emergency situations has often suggested that people can respond boldly and bravely to actual danger. Here,
then, are (a) people working hard to avoid indirect confrontations with
dying and death, (b) people unnerved by fear of death without objective
threat, and (c) people putting their lives into imminent jeopardy. What's
going on?

A few well-crafted studies over the years have offered a possible explanation for one facet of this pattern. Young men participating in a pioneering study (Alexander & Adlerstein, 1959) self-reported very little
concern about dying and death. Nevertheless, almost all showed a distinct and fearful attitude toward death on a semantic differential measure.
And *all* showed spikes in electrical skin response when a death-related
word was flashed during a word association test. There was a clear
disconnection between controlled verbal response and uncontrolled
psychophysiological response to a death stimulus (with the semantic
differential response in-between). Other studies by this research team
came up with similar findings. A follow-up study by Feifel and
Branscomb (1973) again asked the question, 'Who is afraid of death?' and
supported the earlier findings. The results suggested that *everybody*
is afraid of death on the basic organismic level, tapped through
psychophysiological measures, whether or not the person is willing and
able to verbally admit this anxiety.

We may now be in a position to integrate sets of observations into a useful
perspective on death anxiety. Freud's concept of thanatophobia as a coded
or symbolic expression of other fears has its place, although not to the
exclusion of other phenomena. An underlying death terror that influences

social institutions, as well as individual behavior, also has its place although, again, not to the all-dominant extent asserted by Becker. But at least two other elements must be added that have been neglected by the rival classic theories. First, we should acknowledge that anxiety is not the only deep response to the prospect of death. People construct death in a variety of ways, including but not limited to numbed resignation, trusting acceptance, and active seeking. Anxiety is certainly a significant component of our outlook on death, but does not tell the whole story. Second, the *survival function* of death anxiety deserves more attention than it has received.

The perspective suggested here might be summarized as follows:

1. We alert ourselves to possible danger with a momentary flash of signal anxiety. Between such episodes a 'pilot light' vigilance function is maintained.
2. When we perceive ourselves as safe, we are not likely to report a high level of death anxiety. The typical low to moderate death anxiety score is an accurate representation of current status. It is not a form of denial because at the moment there is nothing to deny. Observe the same person in a threat situation and we may see quite a different picture.
3. Death anxiety can be understood as the phenomenological side of a complex organismic reaction to danger, to feeling ourselves at the edge of what is known, familiar, and safe. It can be a response either to palpable or symbolically mediated threat. Indeed, we know some of the most potent risk factors only through cognitive and symbolic processes, as when a physician interprets a laboratory report or a pilot reads the gauges. Susceptibility to edge anxiety (i.e., anxiety in response to being on the brink of the unknown) is part of our survival equipment and often draws upon the lessons of our experience.
4. Edge anxiety is not only or mainly a state of alarm. It is also the first step in preparation for actions intended to increase our chances of survival. The person who alarms at false positives may appear jumpy or neurotic. There is indeed a syndrome in which people are too vulnerable to being 'set off' (Simons, 1996). However, a dulled sense of risk itself poses a heightened risk. Public service messages in Arizona insistently advise adults to keep a close eye on children in or near water. Nevertheless, every week there are reports of drownings and near-drownings because the moderate base-line alertness function is not equipped for the challenge of constant vigilance in everyday surroundings. There is also a phenomenon that might be described as *paradoxical inattention*—the more probable and imminent the risk, the less attention is given to monitoring the situation and the less weight given to signs of incipient jeopardy. This phenomenon is vividly illus-

trated in *The Perfect Storm* (Junger, 1997), as experienced sailors consistently ignore risk and actions that would increase their chances of survival.

On this view, a robust response to danger signals improves the survival odds for the individual and for those who depend on that individual for guidance and protection. A constant or recurring state of anxiety, however, undermines general functioning and reduces the ability to respond effectively to the most serious threats. Terror may be conceived as a catastrophic state of being that rises even beyond painful and disruptive anxiety. Fear of annihilation undercuts other considerations and disables the more adaptive coping strategies. Even the prospect of terror can itself be terrifying. People may, therefore, live in a state of *anticipatory terror* that has multiple stress effects on physical as well as psychological functioning.

A theoretical approach derived from Becker (1973) is now stimulating research into the reduction of vulnerability to disabling forms of death anxiety. *Terror management theory* (Tomer, 1994) draws the inference that whatever raises and strengthens self-esteem might protect against death anxiety. This is also known as the *anxiety-buffer hypothesis*. A resourceful set of experiments by Harmon-Jones et al. (1997) supported this hypothesis, albeit within the limits of academic rather than field research. One does not have to accept Becker's (1973) proposition that all anxiety is at root death anxiety in order to find heuristic value in the buffering effects of both personal self-esteem and a positive and effective worldview to which the individual can subscribe.

## WHAT INFLUENCES DEATH ANXIETY IN CLINICAL SITUATIONS?

We turn now to a more direct consideration of death anxiety in health care situations. There is a core of survival concern that is especially salient in death anxiety; yet, this is best regarded as neither a unitary concept nor a domain apart from the phenomena and conditions of general anxiety.

Several conditions frequently encountered in clinical situations are likely to arouse and intensify the patient's anxiety. These same conditions also arouse anxiety when they occur in other situations, but here the cumulative effect is more likely to be transfigured by the prospect of death. The conditions identified below have long been familiar to observers of interactions in health care situations. What has perhaps not received particular attention is the implication of these conditions for death anxiety. The basic scenario emerging from theory and research can help us to view these factors within a coherent framework. That is, death-related anxiety shifts from its normal signal-function to a dysphoric and disabling state when we perceive ourselves to be at the edge of annihilation without confidence in our coping abilities and intrinsic worth and without support from a source of power greater than ourselves (e.g., society, religious faith). Here, then, is a sampling of events and processes in the clinical situation that can contribute to disturbing levels of death anxiety.

*1. Whatever Induces Alienation Also is Likely to Increase Death-Related Anxiety*

The health care system is often criticized for its impersonal treatment of patients (staff, too, for that matter). This assembly-line approach may have some benefits with respect to efficiency, but it reveals a cold, blank face of society just when the patient most needs affirmation of membership in a caring community. The more alienation experienced in clinical situations, the more individuals are likely to doubt their own coping abilities and fall prey to a sense of helplessness.

*2. Whatever Deprives the Person of Significant Roles Also is Likely to Increase Death-Related Anxiety*

Analyses of 'the sick role' (Kassebaum & Bagman, 1972; Parsons, 1972) and of 'the dying role' (Parker-Oliver, 2000) have been illuminating. Nevertheless, little has actually been revealed of any positive role for people who have become patients. This is often a blow to the already shaken sense of personal competence as well as another invitation to dwell upon doubts and fears in the absence of any opportunity to demonstrate continued competence. Terminally ill hospice patients have expressed the wish to maintain some kind of useful role until the very end of their lives (Kastenbaum, 2001). Feeling capable of being useful in some way is a valuable hedge against death anxiety, but one that is often shorn away during the process of 'patientification'.

*3. Whatever Weakens Interpersonal Support Also is Likely to Increase Death-Related Anxiety*

The palliative care and hospice literature has consistently emphasized the critical importance of supportive relationships (Saunders, 1997). Every parent who has comforted a child who feels scared in the middle of the night also appreciates the sustaining value of caring relationships. Hospital practices have too often deprived patients of adequate and flexible visitation privileges and confronted them with a bewildering array of strangers instead of reassuring faces seen every day. Lacking dependable meaningful companionship, patients are more likely to experience themselves not only as at the edge, but at the edge, alone.

### 4. Whatever Fractures a Coherent Worldview Also is Likely to Increase Death-Related Anxiety

Patients struggle to maintain their overall worldview while at the same time trying to decipher and trust the hospital microcosm. Anxiety spikes are probable when they are confronted with sudden, rushed, and insufficiently explained procedures, as well as when medications and other expected events do not occur as scheduled. Patients often report increased tension and anxiety as they observe conflict and disorganization within the system that is supposed to safeguard their lives. I have seen patients in almost speechless terror and despair when they perceive serious faultlines in the structure of the medical system.

### 5. Whatever Forces Patients to Wait 'Too Long' Also is Likely to Increase Death-Related Anxiety

Tension often builds during a period of enforced waiting, especially when there are no adequate outlets for activity and diversion. Once the tension system has been aroused, it tends to continue and to feed on itself, especially for people who have a predisposition to anxiety or a limited physical ability to tolerate tension. 'Too long' is essentially a subjective matter. A wait or delay that seems merely routine to health care personnel, can be slow torture to the patient and recruit death-related fears as the apprehension continues to build.

### 6. Whatever Increases Test or Performance Anxiety is Also Likely to Increase Death-Related Anxiety

Test anxiety (a common example of performance anxiety) can produce psychophysiological effects similar to those experienced by people facing medical procedures (Lazarus, 2000). In many subtle and idiosyncratic ways patients may feel themselves to be under scrutiny and evaluation and, therefore, to feel apprehensive about 'failing the test'. The pressures to perform can include physical functions not really under their control (e.g., the young athlete hospitalized after an accident who felt like a sorry loser because he had not provided as much urinary output as the nurse had demanded). Often the performance anxiety centers around interactive situations. 'What a relief!' said one dying woman after her visitor left. 'Now I can get back to—you know—and not have to look good for anybody!' People who have been well socialized into our competitive way of life with multiple assessments of performance from preschool onward may take their concerns about failing expectations into the medical situation and interpret perceived failures as evidence that death is near.

*7. Whatever Produces Adverse Physical and Mental Effects Without Sufficient Preparation and Response Also is Likely to Increase Death-Related Anxiety*

Patients who have previously coped well with the stress of illness and treatment may be shaken when an unexpected or insufficiently explained or understood adverse reaction occurs. An episode of bleeding or oozing fluids. A first experience with incontinence or aspiration. Nausea, dizziness, unstable ambulation. A moment of mental confusion and disorientation. Such adverse effects may result from the condition, the treatment, both, or neither. A sudden flash of death terror is possible if the patient's experience encourages the interpretation that the adverse effect is a harbinger of imminent demise.

*8. Whatever Induces Severe Doubts About the 'Rightness' of One's Life Also is Likely to Increase Death-Related Anxiety*

This is a vulnerability that many people bring with them into the situation. It differs from the problems previously identified in its more direct association with the prospect of death. People may perceive, correctly or incorrectly, that the time is arriving for a final reckoning. Not everybody engages in a thorough-going life review. However, a few concerns from the past may now grip the person (e.g., that unresolved conflict with a family member). There is a whole class of potential concerns that may be considered as anxieties aroused *in prospect* of death, though not intense anxiety about death per se.

*9. Whatever Produces Inadequate and Distorted Communication is Also Likely to Increase Death-Related Anxiety*

There is no lack of evidence about the inadequacy and distortion of patient–staff communication in medical care situations. One of the more impressive and dramatic set of examples is provided by a large-scale descriptive and intervention study of physician interactions with life-threatened patients (SUPPORT, 1995). Among other things, inadequate communication was found to increase the likelihood for ineffective and inappropriate responses, and, therefore, to further undermine the patient's coping responses. Many patients in the SUPPORT study had excellent reason for death-related anxiety; they were made to feel alienated and powerless, condemned to continued suffering, and shown the faceless face of a society shorn of traditional religious and humanistic values.

## CONCLUSION

There is such a phenomenon as pure terror in the face of death. This, however, is not what we usually find in health care situations. Rather, we encounter people who are trying to cope with their peril realistically and find some way to get through with their basic sense of values intact. To 'get through' can apply either 'to renewed health' or 'to an acceptable or blessed death'. The prospect of death usually becomes more salient because of the condition that has brought the person into treatment. Many facets of the clinical situation, especially in the hospital, are likely to arouse anxieties that resonate with the fear of death. There may be terrifying flashes of intense death anxiety if belief in one's own competence and worth is undermined by unnerving events and processes. It may be such an emotionally catastrophic experience that the only alternative seems to be a retreat into the depths of depression.

It doesn't have to be this way, of course. Most nursing and medical personnel are motivated to provide not only effective, but also comforting, coherent, and compassionate care. Circumstances all too often limit their opportunities to do so. The 'System' cannot be blamed for everything. Nevertheless, there is much room for improvement in the existing structure of health care, especially when relating to the human element.

There is another challenge that I would like to propose to educators and researchers. Have we not underestimated the skill and judgment required in dealing with a potentially life-threatening situation, whether real or perceived? Ideally, we would respond immediately to a danger cue (i.e., to signal-anxiety). But almost as quickly we would dismiss this surge of anxiety once it has prodded us into effective action. This means we must, in short order, both seize upon and then inhibit the anxiety surge. A difficult order, this, because there is a strong impulse toward zapping the alarm. It disturbs our peace (precisely its function). Somehow, then, we must overcome the impulse to disable the alarm so effectively that we return to our peaceable if perhaps hazardous situation. There is also, however, the characteristic of an arousal system to stay aroused beyond its optimal point of signal function. We may become captivated by the anxiety surge which can also recruit other latent apprehensions and, therefore, isolate us from the actual threat while we stew in the juices of mixed acute and chronic anxieties.

It is by no means a sure thing that we will develop an effective way of using rather than being consumed by anxiety. And, in its first microburst, all signal anxieties may be regarded as previews of a more fully developed death anxiety. Every anxiety signal bespeaks a potential threat, and every potential threat delivers us to the edge of non-being. Educators and researchers are invited to examine these dynamics with care and precision and to devise ways of helping people to develop anxiety management skills that will be especially helpful during the stress of both real and perceived serious illness.

## REFERENCES

Alexander, I., & Adlerstein, A. (1959). Death and religion. In H. Feifel (Ed.), *The meaning of death* (pp. 271–283). New York: McGraw-Hill.

Becker, E. (1973). *The denial of death*. New York: Free Press.

Butler, R.N. (1963). The life review. An interview of reminiscence in the Aged. *Psychiatry*, **26**, 69–70.

Feifel, H., & Branscomb, A.B. (1973). Who's afraid of death? *Journal of Abnormal Psychology*, **8**, 282–288.

Freud, S. (1926/1959). *Inhibitions, symptoms, and anxiety*. New York: W. W. Norton.

Harmon-Jones, E., Simon, L., Greenberg, J., Pyszczynski, T., Solomon, S., & McGregor, H. (1997). Terror management theory and self-esteem: Evidence that increased self-esteem reduces mortality salience effects. *Journal of Personality and Social Psychology*, **72**, 24–36.

Ho, S.M.Y., & Shiu, W.C.T. (1995). Death anxiety and coping mechanisms of Chinese cancer patients. *Omega, Journal of Death and Dying*, **31**, 59–66.

James, W. (1902/1958). *Varieties of Religious Experience: A Study in Human Nature*. New York: Mentor.

Josephs, L. (1994). Psychoanalytic and related interpretations. In B.B. Wolman & G. Stricker (Eds.), *Anxiety and related disorders. A handbook* (pp. 11–29). New York: Wiley Interscience.

Junger, S. (1997). *The perfect storm*. New York: HarperCollins.

Kalish, R.A., & Reynolds, D. (1977). *Death and ethnicity: A psychocultural study*. Los Angeles: University of Southern California Press.

Kasper, A.M. (1959). The doctor and death. In H. Feifel (Ed.), *The meaning of death* (pp. 259–270). New York: McGraw-Hill.

Kassebaum, G., & Bagman, R. (1972). Dimensions of the sick role in chronic illness. In E.G. Jaco (Ed.), *Patients, physicians, and illness* (pp. 130–144). New York: The Free Press.

Kastenbaum, R. (2000). *The psychology of death* (3rd edn.). New York: Springer Publishing Co.

Kastenbaum, R. (2001). *Death, society, and human experience* (7th edn.). Boston: Allyn & Bacon.

Lazarus, R.S. (2000). *Stress and emotion*. New York: Springer.

Lefcourt, H.M., & Shepherd, R.S. (1995). Organ donation, authoritarianism, and perspective-taking humor. *Journal of Research in Personality*, **29**, 121–138.

Leventhal, H., Patrick-Miller, L., Leventhal, E.A., & Burns, E.A. (1997). Does stress-emotion cause illness in elderly people? In K.W. Schaie & M.P. Lawton (Eds.),

*Annual review of gerontology and geriatrics* (Vol. 17, pp. 138–184). New York: Springer Publishing Co.

Munnichs, J.M.A. (1966). Old age and finitide: A contribution to psychogerontology. Basel: S. Korger.

Parsons, T. (1972). Definitions of health and illness in the light of American values and social structure. In E.G. Jaco (Ed.), *Patients, physicians, and illnesses* (pp. 97–117). New York: The Free Press.

Parker-Oliver, D. (2000). The social construction of the 'dying role' and the hospice drama. *Omega, Journal of Death and Dying*, **40**, 29–38.

Rank, O. (1936/1945). *Will therapy and truth and reality*. New York: Knopf.

Saunders, C. (1997). Hospices worldwide: A mission statement. In C. Saunders & R. Kastenbaum (Eds.), *Hospice care on the international scene* (pp. 3–12). New York: Springer.

Searles, H.F. (1961). Schizophrenia and the inevitability of death. *Psychiatric Quarterly*, **35**, 631–641.

Simons, R.C. (1996). *Boo! Culture, experience, and the startle reflex*. New York: Oxford University Press.

Strichertz, M., & Cunnington, L. (1981–1982). Death concerns of students, employed persons, and retired persons. *Omega, Journal of Death and Dying*, **12**, 373–380.

SUPPORT (1995). A controlled trial to improve care for seriously ill hospitalized patients. *Journal of the American Medical Association*, **274**, 1591–1599.

Templer, D. (1970). The construction and validation of a Death Anxiety Scale. *Journal of General Psychology*, **72**, 165–166.

Tomer, A. (1994). Death anxiety in adult life—Theoretical perspectives. In R.A. Neimeyer (Ed.), *Death anxiety handbook* (pp. 31–44). Washington, DC: Taylor & Francis.

Viswanatham, R. (1996). Death anxiety, locus of control, and purpose in life of physicians. *Psychosomatics*, **37**, 339–345.

Weisman, A.D., & Kastenbaum, R. (1968). *The psychological autopsy: A study of the terminal phase of life*. New York: Behavioral Publications.

Part IV

# CONCLUSIONS AND FUTURE DIRECTIONS

Chapter 15

# FUTURE DIRECTIONS AND CHALLENGES FOR THEORY, ASSESSMENT, AND TREATMENT

*Gordon J.G. Asmundson\*, Steven Taylor†, Kristi D. Wright‡, and Brian J. Cox§*

## INTRODUCTION

The contributors to this volume have examined important issues and developments in understanding, assessing, and treating health anxiety. Although health anxiety is ubiquitous, it is, for some, an experience that can be extreme, distressing, and debilitating. Intense health anxiety, particularly hypochondriasis, has been of continuing interest to theorists, researchers, and clinicians. This has led to considerable progress in understanding factors that mediate and moderate the health anxiety, and to increased efficiency and efficacy in the areas of assessment and treatment. Each of the preceding chapters has discussed important considerations for future investigations of severe health anxiety. The following is a summary of some of the most important issues that remain to be addressed:

- What are the causal relationships among health anxiety and important psychopathologic variables? Is severe health anxiety a result of some general vulnerability, such as elevated neuroticism?
- How is health anxiety best conceptualized? If health anxiety exists on a continuum of severity, then how are severe cases best classified within existing diagnostic frameworks? When should severe health anxiety be considered primary versus secondary to other clinical problems? Can

\* Regina Health District and Universities of Regina and Saskatchewan; † University of British Columbia; ‡ University of Regina and Regina Health District; § University of Manitoba

*Health Anxiety*
Edited by G.J.G. Asmundson, S. Taylor & B.J. Cox
© 2001 John Wiley & Sons Ltd.

subtypes of hypochondriasis be identified that differ in phenomenology, mechanisms, or response to treatment?

- What is the natural (untreated) course of health anxiety? Does it tend to become severe at a particular age? How do developmental processes and events, such as aging-related deterioration in physical health, influence health anxiety?
- What are the environmental (e.g., social learning) and genetic influences on health anxiety? Which are most important? Does culture and media influence symptom severity and expression?
- What biological mechanisms are involved in severe health anxiety? Will functional brain imaging studies reveal abnormalities in patients with hypochondriasis that have been identified in other disorders (e.g., obsessive-compulsive disorder)?
- What combination of assessment tools provides the most reliable, valid, and efficient way of assessing health anxiety? How is treatment outcome best measured? Which treatment approaches are most efficient and effective? Which factors are associated with positive treatment outcome and which factors predict relapse?
- Which treatments or combinations of treatment are most effective in treating severe health anxiety?

In this chapter we discuss and expand on some of these questions, and outline directions and challenges for future research. It is our hope that this discussion will help to guide and shape efforts to extend our understanding of severe presentations of health anxiety so that these might be prevented or, at minimum, successfully treated.

## NEGATIVE EMOTIONALITY AND COMORBIDITY

### The General Neurotic Syndrome

What causes severe health anxiety to co-occur with other clinical phenomena? Health anxiety is correlated with the personality dimension known as neuroticism or negative emotionality (Chapter 4). Specifically, the more severe the person's general tendency to experience unpleasant emotions—such as anxiety, dysphoria, and irritability—the greater the tendency to be anxious about one's health. Also, severe health anxiety (i.e., hypochondriasis) is commonly comorbid with many other disorders, such as anxiety disorders and mood disorders (Chapter 6). Comorbidity may be concurrent (two or more disorders present at the same time) or lifetime (disorders may or may not overlap at a given time). Thus, a person with hypochondriasis may go on to develop another disorder once hypochondriasis remits. Conversely, a person might go into remission for a given disorder (e.g., major depression) and then go on to develop hypochondriasis or some other disorder. Such patterns have long been observed (Kendell, 1974; Tyrer, 1989), yet their theoretical and clinical significance has been largely overlooked until recently.

A 'common diathesis' model may account for much of the comorbidity between hypochondriasis and other disorders. That is, the disorders may arise from a common cause, such as negative emotionality (neuroticism). In one of the most detailed common diathesis models, Tyrer (1985) argued that the frequent comorbidity among mood disorders, anxiety disorders, and other conditions indicates the presence of a unitary syndrome, called the *general neurotic syndrome*. Episodes of depression, anxiety, and so forth can be expressions of this syndrome. Tyrer (1985, 1989; Tyrer, Seivewright, Ferguson, & Tyrer, 1992) defined the syndrome by the presence of three or more of the following:

- Two or more of panic disorder, agoraphobia, social phobia, non-psychotic depression, generalized anxiety disorder, and hypochondriasis are present together, either currently or at times in the past.
- At least one disorder developed, at some point, in the absence of major stress.
- Features of dependent or obsessive-compulsive personality disorders are present. Features of avoidant personality disorder also may be present.
- There is a history of a similar syndrome in first-degree relatives.

Tyrer (1985) proposed that the general neurotic syndrome has a fluctuating course, with frequent changes in symptoms and disorders. Generalized anxiety and depressive symptoms tend to be chronic whereas symptoms of other disorders (e.g., hypochondriasis) may develop in response to adverse life events (e.g., a severe physical illness). Tyrer acknowledged that some people could have specific disorders without the general neurotic syndrome. For example, a person might have a pure syndrome of hypochondriasis occurring in the absence of current or past emotional disorders. Research suggests that the general neurotic syndrome occurs in over a third of patients presenting for treatment of anxiety or depression (Tyrer et al., 1992).

## Specific and Non-specific Factors in Hypochondriasis

The concept of the general neurotic syndrome is important in helping us understand the possible causes of severe health anxiety and associated problems. Yet, the concept is insufficient by itself. Given two people with the general neurotic syndrome, why does one develop hypochondriasis while the other does not? Why do some people develop pure hypochondriasis, in the absence of other emotional disorders? The concept of the general neurotic syndrome does not provide specific insight into these questions; however, it does remind us that hypochondriasis often occurs in a context of other clinical problems, and that severe health anxiety may be caused by mechanisms common to many forms of psychopathology. That said, we should not ignore the possibility that hypochondriasis may also arise, in part, from specific mechanisms not shared by other disorders.

## Hierarchic Structure of Psychopathology

Recent findings show that psychopathology is hierarchically structured, with numerous lower-order factors loading on a small number of general or higher-order factors (Arrindell, 1993; Taylor, 1998; Zinbarg & Barlow, 1996). Some of the lower-order factors include agoraphobic fears, worry proneness, and fear of arousal-related bodily sensations (i.e., anxiety sensitivity). Health anxiety is also likely to be a lower-order factor (Cox, Borger, Asmundson, & Taylor, 2000). Higher-order factors include negative emotionality. If one assumes that each factor corresponds to a discrete set of mechanisms (Cattell, 1978), then these findings suggest that hypochondriasis and other emotional disorders comprise a mix of general and specific mechanisms (Taylor, 2000). The general mechanisms may be those underlying Tyrer's general neurotic syndrome. The specific mechanisms may determine whether or not the person develops specific problems such as severe health anxiety. There also may be mechanisms that lie in the midrange of the hierarchy, between specific and general, that contribute to several clinical problems. For example, anxiety sensitivity might contribute to both hypochondriasis and panic disorder.

## Cognitive Mechanisms

Growing evidence suggests that cognitive factors play an important role in the etiology and maintenance of hypochondriasis and other emotional disorders (Chapter 3). If hypochondriasis arises from a combination of specific and non-specific factors, then the question arises as to whether there are specific and non-specific *cognitive* mechanisms in this disorder.

The specific cognitive mechanisms that set one disorder apart from another are described in Beck's (1976) *cognitive specificity hypothesis*.

Specific sorts of beliefs are said to be associated with specific disorders. Depression, for example, is associated with beliefs about loss, failure, and self-denigration. Social phobia is associated with beliefs in the necessity of gaining the approval of others. Strong beliefs in the dangerousness of bodily sensations is a moderately specific factor, implicated in hypochondriasis (Chapter 6), chronic pain (Asmundson, Kuperos, & Norton, 1997; Chapter 12), and panic disorder (Taylor, 2000).

With regard to more general cognitive mechanisms, Martin (1985) proposed that individual differences in cognitive processing underlie individual differences in negative emotionality. People with intense negative emotionality, compared to people with milder forms of this trait, are said to have faster and better recall of unpleasant memories (especially memories about the self), along with slower and poorer recall of pleasant experiences. They may also selectively attend to cues in the environment that have close association to their negative emotion. Biased memory and attentional processes are associated with various maladaptive beliefs about oneself, the world, and one's future. These non-specific factors may contribute to hypochondriasis and other disorders.

Future research is needed to further investigate the specific and non-specific cognitive mechanisms in health anxiety, and to explore their implications for treating hypochondriasis. Presumably, treatments will need to target all mechanisms implicated in the disorder, specific and non-specific, in order to produce enduring reductions in hypochondriacal symptoms.

## Other Mechanisms

Other mechanisms, including psychobiological factors involved in sensation and perception, also may cause or contribute to hypochondriasis. The greater the intensity with which a person experiences benign bodily sensations, the greater the opportunities for catastrophically misinterpreting the sensations (cf. Chapter 3). Accordingly, people who experience abnormally intense sensations are at risk for developing hypochondriasis or other disorders. This is vividly illustrated in the tragic case of James V.

> For reasons no one understood, Mr. V. felt as if a million bugs crawled over him. To quiet his torment, he scratched himself so tenaciously that he ripped open his skin, even though he fell within the range of what is considered average intelligence and was aware of the damage he was inflicting. . . . Heavily scarred from his assaults, . . . [he] had a high tolerance for pain and would break his bones and tear off his fingernails as well as scratch himself. (*Globe & Mail Newspaper*, Saturday, October 30, 1999, p. A21)

Mr. V. eventually died at age 25 from infections of the blood and spine.

Further research into factors influencing the intensity of body sensations may provide helpful in understanding and treating hypochondriasis and other disorders. Research into interoceptive acuity and somatic amplification (e.g., Chapter 5) is an important step in this direction.

## CONCEPTUALIZATION AND CLASSIFICATION

The questions of whether severe health anxiety, particularly hypochondriasis, should be considered primary or secondary to other diagnoses has been an issue of long-standing debate. This stems from early observations that hypochondriasis was most often part of another emotional disorder (Kenyon, 1964; Ladee, 1966) and extends to more recent conceptualizations (for example, see Kellner, 1992). It is now recognized that hypochondriasis can occur in the absence of other past or current emotional disorders (e.g., Barsky, Wysak, & Klerman, 1986). However, observations of overlap and comorbidity with other conditions, particularly other somatoform disorders and several of the anxiety disorders, have prompted similar debate (Chapter 6). Most recently, this debate has focused not so much on whether hypochondriasis is, or is not, a primary condition but, rather, on where it belongs in current diagnostic classification systems.

The following points summarize questions regarding classification that have been raised in several of the chapters of this book:

- Should hypochondriasis be reclassified as an Axis II (personality) disorder? Are observations of its chronic course and pervasive impact on cognition and behaviour sufficient to warrant such a change?
- Should hypochondriasis be reclassified as an anxiety disorder? Are its phenomenological similarities and extensive comorbidity with several of the anxiety disorders sufficient to warrant such a change?
- Is there sufficient evidence to support reclassification as either an Axis II or anxiety disorder?

The answers to these questions are by no means simple. The choice of the most appropriate classificatory category, and, indeed, the general importance of the issue, is largely dependent on the type of classification system utilized. If one uses a phenomenologically based classification system, such as the DSM-IV or ICD-10, then location is determined by criteria such as symptom similarity and patterns of comorbidity with other disorders. If, on the other hand, one uses an etiologically based classification system, then location will be determined by criteria such as similarity of underlying biological or cognitive mechanisms. Currently, hypochondriasis is grouped with the other somatoform disorders (i.e., somatization disorder, undifferentiated somatoform disorder, conversion disorder, pain disorder, body dysmorphic disorder) on 'the basis of clinical utility . . . rather than on assumptions regarding shared etiology or mechanism' (American Psychiatric Association, 1994, p. 445).

## Symptom Similarity and Patterns of Comorbidity

In addition to other somatoform disorders, hypochondriasis shares features with personality disorders (Chapter 4) and anxiety disorders (Chapter 6). So, the issue might be construed as one of determining which group of disorders has the greatest phenomenologic similarity to hypochondriasis.

The argument that hypochondriasis belongs with the personality disorders is not persuasive for several reasons. First, the most common age of onset of hypochondriasis is in adulthood and sometimes in late adulthood, whereas personality disorders usually arise earlier in life (American Psychiatric Association, 1994). Second, unlike personality disorders, hypochondriasis can be transient (Chapter 10). Third, a number of Axis I disorders have an early onset (e.g., generalized anxiety disorder, obsessive-compulsive disorder, posttraumatic stress disorder, dysthymia, anorexia nervosa, bulimia nervosa). If hypochondriasis is moved to Axis II, then most of the neuroses also should go there. This, in effect, would negate the heuristic value of distinguishing between Axis I and Axis II. Fourth, the hypochondriacal personality profile is not overly specific, being defined primarily by the rigidity (i.e., enduring nature) of the symptoms (Schmidt, 1994). Does this mean that an enduring fear of spiders or of having blood draw constitutes a personality disorder? Probably not. So, based on these points of contention, it does not appear to be appropriate to consider hypochondriasis as a personality disorder.

Should hypochondriasis remain classified as a somatoform disorder? Like each of the other somatoform disorders, the focus is on the body, in particular 'the presence of physical symptoms that suggest a general medical condition . . . and are not fully explained by a general medical condition' (American Psychiatric Association, 1994, p. 445). However, on this basis, panic disorder might also be classified as a somatoform disorder; during panic attacks panic patients feel like they are dying from a catastrophic physical event (e.g., heart attack, stroke).

Like the anxiety disorders, most notably obsessive-compulsive disorder and panic disorder, the central features of hypochondriasis include fears and morbid preoccupations. If hypochondriasis is reclassified as an anxiety disorder, then should body dysmorphic disorder also be reclassified? Hypochondriasis is similar to body dysmorphic disorder in that there is an excessive preoccupation with a perceived physical anomaly. Consequently, if one disorder is moved, then it seems fitting for the other to be moved as well.

With regard to patterns of comorbidity, hypochondriasis is commonly comorbid with anxiety and mood disorders. It is currently unclear whether hypochondriasis is more commonly associated with these disorders than with somatoform disorders. If hypochondriasis is found to be most commonly comorbid with anxiety disorders, then this might add weight to the argument for moving it into the domain of the anxiety disorders.

## Mechanism Similarity

If one uses an etiologically based classificatory system, disorders with similar mechanisms would be grouped together. According to cognitive approaches to health anxiety (Chapter 3), the mechanisms of hypochondriasis are very similar to those of the anxiety disorders, particularly panic disorder. This notion supports the argument for moving hypochondriasis to the anxiety disorders. But, on the other hand, the small body of family and twin research, despite its many limitations, suggests that hypochondriasis per se may not be heritable and that the relatives of hypochondriacal patients are most likely to have somatization disorder (Chapter 6). The former finding stands in contrast to the anxiety disorders, which are heritable (e.g., Kendler, Neale, Kessler, Heath, & Eaves, 1992). The latter finding raises the possibility that hypochondriasis and somatization disorder share some sort of vulnerability factor, perhaps genetic. This notion could be used to support the argument that hypochondriasis belongs among the somatoform disorders. So, with blurred distinctions such as these, the current state of research on causal mechanisms does not enable us to specify the 'correct' classification site for hypochondriasis.

## Reclassify or Not?

How important is the issue of where hypochondriasis is placed within diagnostic classification systems? Is this simply an exercise in nosological nit-picking? Fallon (1999) suggests that nosological refinements aid in drawing legitimate distinctions between disorders, improve our understanding of the disorders, and, thereby, allow us to apply more appropriate treatment regimens. Schmidt (1994) argued that placement within the classification system has implications for the perceptions that physicians and allied health professional hold regarding the hypochondriacal patient—as a 'whiner and complainer' when placed within the somatoform disorders versus one in need of overcoming debilitating fear if conceptualized as an anxiety disorder.

As noted above, the answer to these questions also depends, to some degree, on the nature of the classification system one employs. In the context of an etiologically based system, where it is presumed that similar mechanisms underlie similar conditions and similar responses to specific treatments, the issue is of considerable importance to both theory and treatment. Phenomenologically based systems, on the other hand, have few implications for theory or treatment. Indeed, cognitive-behavior therapy and selective serotonin reuptake inhibitors are effective for many different kinds of disorders regardless of where they fall in the DSM-IV.

Given the current state of knowledge, it appears that reclassification of hypochondriasis as an Axis II disorder is not warranted. The data and arguments are also inconclusive about whether hypochondriasis should be reclassified as an anxiety disorder. The most conservative solution at present, and the one least likely to confuse users of the DSM-IV, is to leave hypochondriasis with the somatoform disorders. Future research may yield more definite data on which to base decisions regarding this issue.

## ENVIRONMENTAL AND GENETIC FACTORS

Studies so far have failed to find evidence of genetic factors in hypochondriasis (Noyes, Happel, & Yagla, 1999; Noyes, Holt, Happel, Kathol, & Yagla, 1997; Torgersen, 1986). Larger, more powerful studies, using more sophisticated methodology (e.g., structural equation modeling: Wade, Bulik, Neale, & Kendler, 2000), may reveal general and specific genetic influences on health anxiety. Health anxiety, like other emotional phenomena, is probably caused by a mix of environmental and genetic factors. Cognitive mechanisms involved in hypochondriasis also are probably shaped by a mix of environmental factors (e.g., learning experiences) and genetic factors (cf. Rowe, 1994). A general genetic factor—involved in health anxiety and other affective phenomena—may be the genetic substrate of the proneness to experience negative emotions.

Little is known about the environmental factors that non-specifically influence health anxiety and other affective phenomena. Animal research suggests that chronic exposure to unpredictable and uncontrollable environments during childhood may increase the propensity for acquiring emotional disorders (Mineka & Hendersen, 1985). Community studies suggest that stressful life events in childhood also increase the risk for emotional problems (e.g., Brown, Harris, & Eales, 1993). Each of these factors may influence health anxiety.

Consistent with these conjectures, hypochondriacal patients, compared to people without hypochondriasis, are more likely to have had suffered traumatic sexual experiences, physical violence, and major parental upheaval during childhood and adolescence (Barsky, Wool, Barnett, & Cleary, 1994). Early physical and sexual abuse has been implicated in many disorders (e.g., Ford, 1995; Taylor, 2000), so these stressful events may represent non-specific factors. Other stressors may be more specific in shaping health anxiety, such as the sudden onset of a serious illness, recovering from a serious illness, or the loss of a loved one (Barsky & Klerman, 1983; Bianchi, 1971; Noyes, Wesner, & Fisher, 1992). Longitudinal studies are needed to help build a more complete understanding of the relationships among health anxiety and environmental events.

With regard to more subtle influences on health anxiety, Martin and colleagues (Chapter 2) suggest that culture and media may impact symptom severity and expression. Somatization is more common in non-industrialized countries than in Western countries (Angel & Guarnaccia, 1989; Katon, Kleinman, & Rosen, 1982; Kirmayer, 1984). To understand the reasons for these differences it may be important to examine how countries differ in terms of cultural factors and in terms of the impact of the media in shaping people's beliefs about health and illness.

In Western nations the availability of health-related information to the general public has greatly increased in the past few decades. This is especially apparent when one considers that there are over 15,000 easily accessible health-related sites on the Internet today. The availability of such information has the potential to be empowering for health anxious patients. On the other hand, Martin and colleagues suggest that the surplus of such information may cultivate misinterpretation of physical symptoms and thereby escalate the seeking of unnecessary medical attention. An individual might seek information from an Internet site in an attempt to alleviate concerns that a recently developed rash is not actually skin cancer. They may, however, find information that erroneously supports their belief that the rash is a symptom of skin cancer which, in turn, fuels fear about their health. Because there is little research in this area, further evaluation of the impact that media has on health anxiety is necessary. The findings of such studies may have important implications for treating hypochondriasis.

# CLINICAL IMPLICATIONS

Research on assessment and treatment of severe health anxiety has been receiving increased attention over the past few years. Much of this research is described in various chapters of this book, particularly those presented in Part II, along with specific practical recommendations. In this section we summarize some of the primary practical recommendations.

## Assessment

Comprehensive assessment is a necessity when seeking to accurately identify severe health anxiety (Chapter 5). This involves, first, excluding the presence of an organic pathology (e.g., through review of the patient's medical history and consultation with any medical professionals involved in current treatment) and, second, a detailed examination of the presenting health anxiety symptoms. The latter may involve a combination of structured interview (for the purpose of confirming a diagnosis of hypochondriasis where applicable) and self-report measures. Through application of the self-report method, the clinician can gather considerable information on core symptoms (e.g., illness fears, illness beliefs, safety behaviours, disruptive effects) and associated features (e.g., bodily sensations, anxiety, depression, neuroticism, death anxiety) of health anxiety. This information may be very useful in treatment planning and outcome evaluation. In the case of outcome evaluation, consideration should also be given to indices of functional ability and health care utilization.

Despite the utility of these assessment recommendations, a number of related questions warrant careful consideration. For example, with regard to the structured interviews for hypochondriasis (as reviewed in Chapter 5) there are no empirical data available to suggest that diagnostic reliability and validity of one is better that another. A challenge for investigators seeking to resolve this issue is the identification of a *gold standard* against which to make their comparisons. Likewise, the combination of self-report measures that provides maximal symptom information with minimal overlap remains to be determined. Is this goal attained by assembling a battery of measures for assessing core symptoms and associated features? Is there a need to develop new measures that more accurately and efficiently capture requisite symptom information? What utility is gained by assessing associated features? These questions have been empirically addressed by researchers interested in chronic pain (for example, see Mikail, DuBreuil, & D'Eon, 1993) and warrant attention in the arena of severe health anxiety.

When dealing with special populations, such as the elderly or those from other cultures, there are a number of factors that warrant consideration. Snyder and Stanley (Chapter 10) indicate that assessment of health anxiety in the elderly requires that measures be constructed in an age-sensitive manner (e.g., large font to accommodate possible visual difficulties) and that interviewers be cognizant of, and adjust to, factors such as hearing difficulty, fatigue, and potential cohort effects (e.g., older individuals often respond in a socially desirable manner). Likewise, Escobar and colleagues (Chapter 9) suggest that cultural and language factors can impede assessment if not acknowledged. Difficulties can be avoided if the measures utilized have been translated and if terminology is simplified or a translator is available. Validation of translated versions of many of the self-report measures of health anxiety remains an avenue of future investigation.

Severe health anxiety is thought to most often have onset in early adulthood. Little else is known about onset. Clearly absent from the chapters of this book is consideration of severe health anxiety in children and adolescents. Is it common for symptoms to present at an early age? Are there special concerns for assessment? Will researchers identify predisposing factors that are operative at an early age? It will be of considerable interest to gain a better understanding of the factors that predispose one to become overly anxious about one's health. Such knowledge would allow for possible prevention of conditions such as hypochondriasis through early screening and intervention. Whether screening is undertaken in children or adults, considerable caution is warranted so that those who screen positive are not stigmatized because of their elevated concern about their health (Taylor, Rabian, & Fedoroff, 1999).

## Treatment

More work is needed to better understand how to best treat severe health anxiety. Psychosocial treatments such as cognitive-behavior therapy (Chapters 3 and 7) and enhanced medical care (Chapter 9) are considered to have potential efficacy for hypochondriasis as well as associated problems (Chapters 11 to 14). Of these, cognitive-behavior treatment has received the most empirical attention and appears to be a most promising approach in both individual and group formats. While most studies to date have focused on adults younger than 60 years of age (Warwick, Clark, Cobb, & Salkovskis, 1996), Snyder and Stanley (Chapter 10) suggest that the cognitive-behavioral approach is appropriate for use with the elderly. Additionally, positive outcomes for cognitive-behavior therapy have been noted in Latino populations (Chapter 9) and, when combined with appropriate medication, in patients with psychosis (Chapter 13). These observations are encouraging, although there remains a need for controlled trials of cognitive-behavior therapy in special populations.

Enhanced medical care is an interesting approach in which the primary objective is to improve care by having patients meet with their physician on a regular basis to discuss their symptoms whether present or not. This treatment approach has been shown to be effective for somatizing patients in primary care settings (Rost, Kashner, & Smith, 1994; Smith, Rost, & Kashner, 1995). However, as with cognitive-behavior therapy, many questions remain. Can the average physician implement and maintain this approach? Is it equally effective for all forms of severe health anxiety (e.g., hypochondriasis, illness phobia)? Is it effective for clinical conditions for which elevated health anxiety may be a component but not necessarily the primary concern (e.g., chronic musculoskeletal pain, irritable bowel syndrome, heart-focused anxiety)?

Pharmacological interventions also appear effective (Chapter 8). Preliminary evidence, based on case studies and a few controlled trials, suggests that selective serotonin reuptake inhibitors can alleviate hypochondriasis, and that pimozide can reduce delusional forms of this disorder (Fallon et al., 1996; Haman & Avnstorp, 1982; Munro, 1978a, 1978b; Munro & Chmara, 1982; Ungvari & Vladar, 1986).

Which treatment approach is best? This is a question for which the available empirical literature does not provide a definitive conclusion. It is also a question that, while simple on the surface, is multifaceted and complicated by numerous practical issues. While cognitive-behavior therapy appears most promising, it is an approach that is not easily accessible to all. Indeed, therapists with specific training in cognitive-behavioral therapy typically reside in large urban centers, making access to those living in remote rural areas difficult and costly. Even where access is not a limiting factor, the time commitment and effort required in application of the approach may be excessive, thus making it unappealing. In these cases, enhanced medical care and pharmacotherapy, being readily available in most geographic locations and unhindered by time and effort requirements, may be most practical.

It is apparent that further investigation of efficacy of the aforementioned treatment approaches is required. Enns and colleagues (Chapter 8) assert that this should include comparative studies of different pharmacological and non-pharmacological alternatives, longer-term maintenance treatment studies, as well as studies of the efficacy of treatment combinations. Furer and colleagues (Chapter 7) note that combined treatment approaches have not proven beneficial with the anxiety disorders (also see Taylor, 2000). However, this finding may not generalize to hypochondriasis. Other possible approaches that warrant consideration include briefer cognitive-behavioral treatment programs, self-help programs, and community-based psycho-education programs. Development of the former will be dependent on understanding the effective components of cognitive-behavior treatment (Salkovskis & Bass, 1997). Self-help and community-based psycho-education programs have been shown effective for a number of conditions, including chronic pain (LeFort, Gray-Donald, Rowat, & Jeans, 1998) and social phobia (Walker, Cox, Frankel, & Torgrud, 1999), and may prove to be viable options for those with severe health anxiety who live in remote locations.

## FUTURE RESEARCH DIRECTIONS

The above discussion suggests many avenues for future research. Below we summarize these as several focal categories that, in our opinion, will prove most fruitful in contributing to our current understanding of severe health anxiety.

- Large-scale behavioral-genetic studies using structural equation modeling are needed to examine the environmental and genetic factors in severe health anxiety, and to determine whether these factors are specific to hypochondriasis, or whether they are shared with other disorders (e.g., other somatoform disorders, anxiety disorders).
- Longitudinal and cross-sectional comorbidity studies are needed to determine whether people who develop hypochondriasis (at some point in their lives) are more likely to also develop comorbid anxiety versus somatoform disorders.
- Longitudinal studies are also needed to evaluate the importance of factors—such as somatic amplification, interoceptive acuity, absorption, and alexithymia—that putatively influence severe health anxiety. The important question in the context of these studies would be whether these factors are causes, consequences, or co-occurences.
- Basic mechanism research is needed to better understand dysfunctional biologic and cognitive systems involved in hypochondriasis, and to determine whether these are more similar to those observed in the in anxiety disorders versus those in the other somatoform disorders.
- Investigation of the merits of splitting hypochondriasis into subtypes (e.g., those with greater fear of having an illness vs. those with greater illness conviction; those with cardiac-focused anxiety vs. those worried about musculoskeletal pain) is warranted. Such splitting would be of considerable value if it shed light on etiology or treatment.
- Treatment research is needed to better understand the treatments that, alone or in combination, are most effective. Researchers also

need to tease apart the effective components of cognitive-behavioral approaches, so that these can be made as time-efficient as possible and adapted to serve those living in remote locations.

## CONCLUSION

This book has served to provide a comprehensive review of current knowledge, important issues and developments, and future research directions pertaining to health anxiety. Significant in-roads have been made with regard to the understanding of basic mechanisms, assessment, and treatment. These advances are encouraging, but many important questions await resolution. This book, we hope, will guide and shape the work of researchers and clinicians as they strive toward better understanding and effectively treating the suffering and debility that accompanies severe health anxiety in all its forms.

## REFERENCES

American Psychiatric Association (1994). *Diagnostic and statistical manual of mental disorders* (4th edn.). Washington, DC: Author.

Angel, R., & Guarnaccia, P.J. (1989). Mind, body, and culture: Somatization among Hispanics. *Social Science and Medicine*, **28**, 1229–1238.

Arrindell, W.A. (1993). The fear of fear concept: Stability, retest artifact and predictive power. *Behaviour Research and Therapy*, **31**, 139–148.

Asmundson, G.J.G., Kuperos, J.L., & Norton, G.R. (1997). Do patients with chronic pain selectively attend to pain related information? Preliminary evidence for the mediating role of fear. *Pain*, **72**, 478–488.

Barsky, A.J., & Klerman, G.L. (1983). Overview: Hypochondriasis, bodily complaints and somatic styles. *American Journal of Psychiatry*, **140**, 273–283.

Barsky, A.J., Wool, C., Barnett, M.C., & Cleary, P.D. (1994). Histories of childhood trauma in adult hypochondriacal patients. *American Journal of Psychiatry*, **151**, 397–401.

Barsky, A.J., Wysak, G., & Klerman, G.L. (1986). Hypochondriasis: An evaluation of the DSM-III criteria in medical outpatients. *Archives of General Psychiatry*, **43**, 493–500.

Beck, A.T. (1976). *Cognitive therapy and the emotional disorders.* New York: International Universities Press.

Bianchi, G.N. (1971). Origins of disease phobia. *Australia and New Zealand Journal of Psychiatry*, **5**, 241–257.

Brown, G.W., Harris, T.O., & Eales, M.J. (1993). Aetiology of anxiety and depressive disorders in an inner-city population. 2. Comorbidity and adversity. *Psychological Medicine*, **23**, 155–165.

Cattell, R.B. (1978). *The scientific use of factor analysis in the behavioral and life sciences.* New York: Graywind.

Cox, B.J., Borger, S.C., Asmundson, G.J.G., & Taylor, S. (2000). Dimensions of hypochondriasis and the five-factor model of personality. *Personality and Individual Differences*, **29**, 99–108.

Fallon, B. (1999). Hypochondriasis vs. anxiety disorders: Why should we care? *General Hospital Psychiatry*, **21**, 5–7.

Fallon, B.A., Schneirer, F.R., Marshall, R., Campeas, R. Vermes, D. Goetz, D., & Liebowitz, M.R. (1996). The pharmacotherapy of hypochondriasis. *Psychopharmacology Bulletin*, **32**, 607–611.

Ford, C.V. (1995). Dimensions of somatization of hypochondriasis. *Neurologic Clinics*, **13**, 241–253.

Haman, K., & Avnstorp, C. (1982). Delusions of infestation treated by pimozide: A double-blind crossover clinical study. *Acta Dermato-Venereologica*, **62**, 55–58.

Katon, W., Kleinman, A., & Rosen, G. (1982). Depression and somatization: A review, Part I. *American Journal of Medicine*, **72**, 127–135.

Kellner, R. (1992). Diagnosis and treatment of hypochondriacal syndromes. *Psychosomatics*, **33**, 278–289.

Kendell, R.E. (1974). The stability of psychiatric diagnoses. *British Journal of Psychiatry*, **124**, 352–356.

Kendler, K.S., Neale, M.C., Kessler, R.C., Heath, A.C., & Eaves, L.J. (1992). The genetic epidemiology of phobias in women: The interrelationship of agoraphobia, social phobia, situational phobia, and simple phobia. *Archives of General Psychiatry*, **49**, 273–281.

Kenyon, F.E. (1964). Hypochondriasis: A clinical study. *British Journal of Psychiatry*, **110**, 478–488.

Kirmayer, L.J. (1984). Culture, affect, and somatization, Part I. *Transcultural Psychiatric Research Review*, **21**, 159–188.

Ladee, G.A. (1966). *Hypochondriacal syndromes*. New York: Elsevier.

LeFort, S.M., Gray-Donald, K., Rowat, K.M., & Jeans, M. (1998). Randomized controlled trial of a community-based psychoeducation program for the self-management of chronic pain. *Pain*, **72**, 27–32.

Martin, M. (1985). Neuroticism as predisposition toward depression: A cognitive mechanism. *Personality and Individual Differences*, **6**, 353–365.

Mikail, S.F., DuBreuil, S.C., & D'Eon, J.L. (1993). A comparative analysis of measures used in the assessment of chronic pain patients. *Psychological Assessment*, **5**, 117–120.

Mineka, S., & Hendersen, R.W. (1985). Controllability and predictability in acquired motivation. *Annual Review of Psychology*, **36**, 495–529.

Munro, A. (1978a). Monosymptomatic hypochondriacal psychosis. A diagnostic entity which may respond to pimozide. *Canadian Psychiatric Association Journal*, **23**, 497–500.

Munro, A. (1978b). Two cases of delusions of worm infestation. *American Journal of Psychiatry*, **135**, 234–235.

Munro, A., & Chmara, J. (1982). Monosymptomatic hypochondriacal psychosis: A diagnostic checklist based on 50 cases of the disorder. *Canadian Journal of Psychiatry*, **27**, 374–376.

Noyes, R., Jr., Happel, R.L., & Yagla, S.J. (1999). Correlates of hypochondriasis in a nonclinical population. *Psychosomatics*, **40**, 461–469.

Noyes, R., Holt, C.M., Happel, R.L., Kathol, R.G., & Yagla, S.J. (1997). A family study of hypochondriasis. *Journal of Nervous and Mental Disease*, **185**, 223–232.

Noyes, R. Wesner, R.B., & Fisher, M.M. (1992). A comparison of patients with illness phobia and panic disorder. *Psychosomatics*, **23**, 92–99.

Rost, K., Kashner, T.M., & Smith, G.R. (1994). Effectiveness of psychiatric intervention with somatization disorder patients: Improved outcomes at reduced costs. *General Hospital Psychiatry*, **16**, 381–387.

Rowe, D.C. (1994). *The limits of family influence: Genes, experience, and behavior*. New York: Guilford.

Salkovskis, P.M., & Bass, C. (1997). Hypochondriasis. In D.M. Clark & C.G. Fairburn (Eds.), *Science and practice of cognitive behaviour therapy*. Oxford: Oxford University Press.

Schmidt, A.J.M. (1994). Bottlenecks in the diagnosis of hypochondriasis. *Comprehensive Psychiatry*, **35**, 306–315.

Smith, G.R., Rost, K., & Kashner, T.M. (1995). A trial of the effect of a standardized psychiatric consultation on health outcomes and cost in somatizing patients. *Archives of General Psychiatry*, **52**, 238–243.

Taylor, S. (1998). The hierarchic structure of fears. *Behaviour Research and Therapy*, **36**, 205–214.

Taylor, S. (2000). *Understanding and treating panic disorder: Cognitive-behavioural approaches*. New York: Wiley.

Taylor, S., Rabian, B., & Fedoroff, I.C. (1999). Anxiety sensitivity: Progress, prospects, and challenges. In S. Taylor (Ed.), *Anxiety sensitivity: Theory, research, and treatment of the fear of anxiety* (pp. 339–353). Mahwah, NJ: Lawrence Erlbaum Associates.

Torgersen, S. (1986). Genetics of somatoform disorders. *Archives of General Psychiatry*, **43**, 502–505.

Tyrer, P. (1985). Neurosis divisible? *Lancet*, **1**, 685–688.

Tyrer, P. (1989). *Classification of neurosis*. Chichester, UK: Wiley.

Tyrer, P., Seivewright, N., Ferguson, B., & Tyrer, J. (1992). The general neurotic syndrome: A coaxial diagnosis of anxiety, depression and personality disorder. *Acta Psychiatrica Scandinavica*, **85**, 201–206.

Ungvari, G., & Vladar, K. (1986). Pimozide treatment for delusion of infestation. *Activitas Nervosa Superior*, **28**, 103–107.

Wade, T.D., Bulik, C.M., Neale, M., & Kendler, K.S. (2000). Anorexia nervosa and major depression: Shared genetic and environmental risk factors. *American Journal of Psychiatry*, **157**, 469–471.

Walker, J.R., Cox, B.J., Frankel, S., & Torgrud, L. (1999, March). *Evaluating two cognitive-behavioral self-help approaches for generalized social phobia*. Poster session presentation at the Anxiety Disorders Association of America's 19th National Conference, San Diego, CA.

Warwick, H.M.C., Clark, D.M., Cobb, A.M., & Salkovskis, P.M. (1996). A controlled trial of cognitive-behavioural treatment of hypochondriasis. *British Journal of Psychiatry*, **169**, 189–195.

Zinbarg, R.E., & Barlow, D.H. (1996). The structure of anxiety and the anxiety disorders: A hierarchical model. *Journal of Abnormal Psychology*, **105**, 181–193.

# AUTHOR INDEX

# SUBJECT INDEX